JOHN WANNA is Professor of Politics and Public Policy at Griffith University. He is the co-author of *Public Policy in Australia* and *Public Sector Management in Australia*, and co-editor of the *Australian Journal of Public Admininstration.*

JOANNE KELLY is a principal research officer in Canada's Treasury Board Secretariat and a research associate of the Centre for Australian Public Sector Management (CAPSM).

JOHN FORSTER is a Senior Lecturer in Economics at Griffith University. He is a founding member of CAPSM and co-editor with John Wanna of *Budgetary Management and Control.*

Managing Public Expenditure in Australia

John Wanna
Joanne Kelly
John Forster

LONDON AND NEW YORK

First published 2000 by Allen & Unwin

Published 2020 by Routledge
2 Park Square, Milton Park, Abingdon, Oxon OX14 4RN
605 Third Avenue, New York, NY 10017

Routledge is an imprint of the Taylor & Francis Group, an informa business

National Library of Australia
Cataloguing-in-Publication entry:

Wanna, John.
Managing public expenditure in Australia.

Bibliography.
Includes index.
ISBN 1 86448 713 5.

1. Finance, Public – Australia – History. 2. Expenditures, Public.
I. Forster, John, 1946– . II. Kelly, Joanne, 1965– . III. title.

352.40994

Set in 10.5/12 pt Bembo by DOCUPRO, Sydney

ISBN-13: 9781864487138 (pbk)

Contents

Acknowledgments

When we commenced a series of projects on budgetary management in 1996 we initially intended to produce a comparative study of budgetary reform in Canada and Australia, analysing the effectiveness of different reform initiatives since the 1970s. It quickly became clear during research in 1996–97 that, while Canada had a rich literature on government budgeting and public finance going back thirty or forty years, Australia had very little apart from a few articles and the occasional edited book. In the only substantial source on Australian public finance by Peter Groenewegen (1990) government budgeting was a relatively minor component. With the major changes of the late 1980s and 1990s, a full-length study of expenditure management at the Commonwealth level was well overdue. We began a large project of mapping the contours of Australian expenditure practices. This book is the end result. A comparative assessment of Canadian and Australian budgetary practice will follow.

We are indebted to the Australian Research Council for an initial two-year grant to support this research—some of which has already appeared in European, American and Canadian publications. Australia is *now* developing a larger scholarly community engaged in budgeting, resource management and accounting—and it is in no small part due to the Australian Research Council's encouragement.

The Department of Finance (later the Department of Finance and Administration) cooperated and generously assisted with the research. A number of senior officials were particularly helpful in granting our requests for access, giving freely of their time, and allowing us to interview other staff. Among them are Steve

Sedgwick, Peter Boxall, Steve Bartos, Len Early, Mike Hutchinson, Grant Hehir and Stein Helgeby—some of whom are no longer with the department.

Other organisations assisted the research at different times, including the Commonwealth Parliament, the Australian National Archives, the National Library of Australia, the Australian National Audit Office, the Treasury Board Secretariat (Canada), the Queensland Parliamentary Library, and Griffith University. The Australian Political Science Association, the Financial Management Institute of Canada, the Association of Budgeting and Financial Management and the International Public Management Network of the United States each allowed us the opportunity to present and test various arguments along the way.

Many people were generous with their time in commenting on drafts. John Nethercote gave the entire draft his close editorial eye, correcting errors and debating some of the interpretations of events. Steve Bartos was also particularly helpful in reading the complete manuscript and drawing our attention to some factual inaccuracies. Others who read parts of the manuscript and provided comment or suggestion were: Pat Barrett, Ian Castles, Sir William Cole, John Dawkins, Malcolm Fraser, Margaret Guilfoyle, Stein Helgeby, Michael Keating, Cyril Monaghan, John Taylor, Ed Visbord, Partick Weller and Lionel Woodward. Their input was important in improving the text even where they disagreed with our assessments. Others who helped at various stages of the project include: Gwen Andrews, Peter Aucoin, Pat Barrett, Valda Blundell, George Carter, Don Craik, Glyn Davis, Michael di Francesco, Peter de Vries, Dom English, Roger Fisher, Paul Goodman, John Harp, John Holmes, Maurice Kennedy, Larry Jones, Mike Joyce, Kath Martin, Dave Miller, Jim Quinn, Rod Rhodes, Bob Shead, John Taylor, Fred Thompson, John Uhr, Peter Walsh, Maurice Wright and Lisa Yolander. A complete list of those formally interviewed in undertaking this research is included in the references. We are grateful to them all for not only providing their insights but for the generous provision of their time and hospitality.

The study was enriched by the contributions of a number of research assistants at various stages—Tracey Arklay, Charles Broughton; Ashley Lavelle, Alexander Gash and Terry Wood. In the Department of Finance and Administration Dom English and Lesa Whitehead expedited administrative requests. Charles Broughton assisted considerably in the completion of the manuscript and in the final stages of production. Alexander Gash proof read the final manuscript and assisted with the index. Olwen Schubert helped finalise the manuscript. Geoff Pryor of the *Canberra Times* generously allowed us to reproduce a selection of his cartoons and gave us access to his back catalogues. The *Age* also granted permission to reprint a cartoon by Ron Tandberg.

When we approached John Iremonger at Allen & Unwin with the idea of undertaking this study, he was quick to commission the project and offer his support—and for the past three years has been a source of encouragement. Karen Penning at Allen & Unwin was always helpful with our queries.

We would also like to thank our colleagues at Griffith University in both the School of Politics and Public Policy, and the School of Economics for their continued support and patience for listening to 'yet more about budgeting'. Thanks also to Wendy Craik and Grant Hawley for their companionship in Canberra. Finally, we would like to thank our respective families for their assistance and forbearance over the years, especially while we were away from home—Jenni Craik, Erinn, Aidan and Sean Wanna, Wendy Tyson and Colin Forster, David and Pauline Kelly.

JW, JK, JF
June 2000

Abbreviations and Acronyms

ABC	Australian Broadcasting Corporation
ABS	Australian Bureau of Statistics
AGPS	Australian Government Printing Service
AIDC	Australian Industry Development Corporation
AIDS	Acquired Immune Deficiency Syndrome
ALP	Australian Labor Party
ANAO	Australian National Audit Office
ANU	Australian National University
APS	Australian Public Service
APS Reformed	*The Australian Public Service Reformed*–Rogers Report (MAB/MIAC)
ASIO	Australian Security Intelligence Organisation
ATO	Australian Taxation Office
ATSIC	Aboriginal and Torres Strait Islander Commission
CSIRO	Commonwealth Scientific and Industry Research Organisation
CTC	Competitive Tendering and Contracting
DEA	Department of Economic Affairs [UK]
DEET	Department of Employment, Education and Training
DEIR	Department of Employment and Industrial Relations
Defence	Department of Defence
DFO	Departmental Finance Officers
DINDEC	Department of Industry and Economy
DoF	Department of Finance
DoFA	Department of Finance and Administration

DFAT	Department of Foreign Affairs and Trade
DIR	Department of Industrial Relations
DPIE	Department of Primary Industries and Energy
DURD	Department of Urban and Regional Development
ED	Efficiency Dividend [on administrative budgets]
EDS	Executive Development Scheme [of the PSC]
ERC	Expenditure Review Committee of cabinet
FAGS	Financial Assistance Grants to the States
FAS	First Assistant Secretary
Finance	DoF 1976–97 / DoFA 1997-present
FMA Act	*Financial Management and Accountability Act 1997*
FMIP	Financial Management Improvement Program
FMIP/SC	Steering Committee of the Financial Management Improvement Program
GAO	General Accounting Office [USA]
GBE	Government Business Enterprise
GDP	Gross Domestic Product
GFEP	General Financial and Economic Policy [Division of Treasury]
GFS	Government Financial Statistics
GST	Goods and Services Tax
HECS	Higher Education Contribution Scheme
HHCS	Health, Housing and Community Services [Department of]
HRSCE	House of Representatives Standing Committee on Expenditure
HRSCFPA	House of Representatives Standing Committee on Finance and Public Administration
IADC (FMIP)	Interdepartmental Advisory Development Committee (for the FMIP)
IDC	Inter-Departmental Committee
IMF	International Monetary Fund
IT	Information Technology
JCPAA	Joint Committee on Public Accounts and Audit
LQG	*Labor and Quality of Government* (1983 ALP policy document)
MIAC	Management Improvement Advisory Council
MAB	Management Advisory Board
MYEFO	Mid-Year Economic and Fiscal Outlook
NCA	National Commission of Audit

NSW	New South Wales
NT	Northern Territory
OECD	Organisation for Economic Cooperation and Development
OER	Overseas Economic Relations [Division of Treasury]
OPEC	Organisation of Petroleum Exporting Countries
OPSB	Office of the Public Service Board
PM&C	Department of Prime Minister and Cabinet
PMB	Program Management and Budgeting
PPBS	Planning, Programming and Budgeting Systems
PSB	Public Service Board
PSC	Public Service Commission (now PSMPC)
PSMPC	Public Service and Merit Protection Commission
R&D	Research and Development
RCAGA	Royal Commission on Australian Government Administration (Coombs Commission)
RCA	Review of Commonwealth Administration (Reid Review)
RCAs	Running Costs Arrangements
RCF	Review of Commonwealth Functions (Razor Gang Review)
RLI	Revenue, Loans and Investment [Division of Treasury]
SA	South Australia
SES	Senior Executive Service
SMR	Senior Ministers' Review
SSD	Social Security Division [of Treasury]
TFEP	Task Force on Economic Policy to the Coombs Commission
Treasury	Department of the Treasury
Vertigan Review	*Review of Budget Estimates Production Arrangements* (1999)
UK	United Kingdom
WA	Western Australia

1 Budgets and public expenditure in democratic society

BUDGETS ARE INDISPENSABLE to executive government; and accountable budgetary processes are a key mechanism of stable, democratic societies. Budgets provide the means through which ideas, decisions and initiatives of governments become meaningful actions. Policy-making helps establish the direction and goals of government, and fulfilment may depend upon political will, but budgets and budgetary processes provide the resources necessary for implementation. Budgetary mechanisms provide the means of achieving goals without recourse to arbitrary or even capricious appropriation of resources by executive government. Budgets help to capture both the roles and responsibilities of government to the community, while simultaneously demonstrating the power of the state to appropriate resources from that community.

The community, nevertheless, expects funds in the government's care will be treated with respect. While these funds become government property, the community retains ownership of them in democratic societies, particularly if it is assumed they are intended to provide benefits to the public. Nevertheless, once those funds are in government hands the public has little influence on how they are used, or the care with which they are managed. In effect, citizens give tacit consent to governments using public dollars for any legal purpose. The voluntariness with which communities allow governments to appropriate funds and the care governments afford them within budgetary frameworks is at the heart of public finance in civil societies.

Although budgeting takes on a variety of forms at different times and in different countries, budgets are a universal phenomenon of modern societies. Some budget systems are simple and customary, others are far more complex and involve intricate, institutionalised practices. Some are highly regulated and rigid while others are continually re-engineered and reshaped to adjust to new contingencies. Many budgets operate on an annual cash-only basis, whereas others operate across multiple years and may include allocations for assets and liabilities in addition to cash disbursements. In short, despite the wishes and efforts of international agencies such as the European Union or the Organisation for Economic Cooperation and Development (OECD) there is no single internationally dominant system of budgeting or set of techniques. Each society devises and evolves its own *modus operandi* and practices. There is no universal combination of institutions or structures, strategies or cultures that characterise budgeting *per se*.

If the art of budgeting varies between jurisdictions and over time, we can still identify many shared requirements, structures and processes. For example, the underlying financial structures of budgets are common across jurisdictions. There are sources of revenues, some means of appropriating revenues, and a means of allocating financial resources to their intended purposes and converting them into activities and outputs. There must be means of quantifying and accounting for amounts raised and disbursed, of storing those financial resources not immediately required and making provision for long-term liabilities. Many governments will often express concern to balance budgets by equalising their expenditures and revenues.

Budgets are not merely financial; they are also about power. They enable governments to resource themselves to perform certain roles or activities within or through the state. At the same time budgets are influenced by the wider power structures in society, and so are of vital interest to all members of society affected by them, regardless of any real ability to take part in the determining process. If politics can be regarded as the process of determining who gets what, when and how, then budgeting provides the means of accomplishing this.

Budgets always have an impact upon the state of the economy, whether the government wishes them to or not.[1] Consequently,

---

1 Within the context of the size of the government sector in the economy it is appropriate to mention a range of debates relating to the significance of public expenditure. One argument is that the size of the government/public domain is too large and plays a role in stifling both effectiveness and efficiency in the private domain. A related idea in economics is the 'crowding-out hypothesis'

budgets represent both the desire and power of governments to influence the direction of the economy, although usually with less control than often claimed. And ideas and practice change. Over recent decades, in Australia as elsewhere, levels of government expenditure have formed an integral part of fiscal policy in order to maintain the economy at high levels of economic activity. Unfortunately, using the major budget statement to do this suffered from two major defects. First, the annual nature of the major budget meant that its timing was not always appropriate for economic policy; and second, the longer term planning of the budget could be seriously distorted for the sake of the immediacy required by short-run macro-economic policy. This macro-economic policy aspect of budgeting has receded in recent years in Australia but remains a potential course of action for governments.

Although budgets and the power to budget are necessary means of matching intent to outcomes and controlling expenditures in democratic societies, governments have long complained that budgets are largely beyond their control, at best only influenced to a marginal degree from year to year. This all points to a contradiction in modern budgeting: budgets *make* governments powerful, yet budgets exert enormous power *over* governments. The instrument that should be a tool of government instead becomes its organising principle and its focus. Governments ostensibly use budgets both to achieve their aims and to control their own activities. But, if most expenditures are 'locked-in' by previous budgetary decisions, then in the immediate term it is budgets that limit or even predetermine what governments can or cannot do. The budget tail wags the government dog. Much of the process of formulating budgets involves making provision for non-discretionary spending items such as pensions, income support, unemployment benefits, payments to sub-national governments, block grants or multi-year funding arrangements and interest payments on existing debt (previous spending). Such non-discretionary items can consume over three-quarters of a proposed budget, so in practical terms governments have little say in its allocation. Moreover, if certain expenditure items 'blow out' due to changing national economic fortunes such as rising unemployment, the government is liable for

---

that suggests that increased government spending *inter alia* increases interest rates and so deters investment in the private sector. Alternatively, other writers have argued that high public expenditure is beneficial and part of the process of building economic and social capacities in mature economies.

the increased expenditure to the detriment of other priorities. The tension between the demands of fiscal policy and the other demands upon government expenditure is a factor in both perceived and real loss of control.

Perhaps because, or in spite of, this lack of control, the process of budgeting in politically adversarial, Westminster-derived systems is highly secretive. Budgets have the potential to do governments enormous electoral harm. So their formulation remains 'behind-closed-doors', with limited numbers of insiders privy to classified information until the formal budget is released. And even then, much of the inside information, knowledge and assumptions are withheld from public and opposition scrutiny. It has become conventional that budgets are constructed piecemeal with a high degree confidentiality with proposals collated by an inner sanctum of trusted officials. Covert operations are run between departments, clandestine meetings are held, confidential files are locked in departmental safes, special cabinet sub-committees make decisions and review political commitments and government officials and printers are sworn to secrecy. It is frequently the case that even cabinet ministers know only parts of a budget. Few inside government know the entire contents of a budget before its delivery. Governments not only control the processes of putting budgets together; they also control and restrict access to information, including the use of deliberate leaks, until they decide 'the Budget' can be released.

The importance, power and secrecy of budgetary processes all conspire to excite media interest which performs a monitoring, investigative and analytical role in opening up budgeting to public view. The media thus play an essential role in budgeting in democracies that is not catered for in the formal budget framework. Frequently, the media have to adopt an almost adversarial role, along with a spectrum of interest groups, as they try to prise information loose, both before and after the presentation of 'the Budget'. Yet, the public purse retains little sustained interest even for the 'serious' media. Resource issues are the day-to-day fare of the bureaucracy, but external interest is sporadic and often opportunistic. Such interest as occurs is generally only brought about by some unfavourable event, such as massive cost over-runs, as with the Collins-class submarines or some actual or implied abuse of spending, subsidies or welfare payments. Then, the government's perceived failures of probity and accountability are widely publicised, frequently in sensationalist terms. In such cases government is often portrayed as financially irresponsible and lacking in management skills by the media and the opposition. Here the inherent secrecy of budgeting works to the media's advantage, allowing it to portray government as having something to hide in the way they manage the public's money.

Every year, the presentation of 'the Budget' to Parliament is greeted with specialist scrutiny and commentary. But the interest is hugely unbalanced. Two components of budgets and budgetary processes receive the lion's share of this attention. These are:

(i) changes in the levels and forms of government revenues or taxes, user charges and other levies, and
(ii) changes in the levels and forms of government spending as transfers, subsidies, purchases and other expenditures.

Taxation affects everyone's hip pocket, and receives substantial attention because of its immediacy and direct personal impacts. This is particularly true in terms of the overall level of taxation and its differential impacts on diverse societal groups. Similarly, we hear much fanfare over the new spending initiatives announced in 'the Budget'. There is intense media speculation about the winners and losers before any budget; and there is immediate analysis of who pays and who benefits after the budget is handed down, but longer term trends are hardly mentioned and analysis is rarely sustained.

Despite such attention to the annual budget and the centrality of budgets to executive government, the economy and society, it is noticeable that a major element of government budgeting—*public expenditure management*—is almost totally ignored. Given its intrinsic importance, expenditure management remains the least known and least understood of the elements of government budgeting and financial management. But why is this the case? What causes such a vital element of government budgeting, and of efficient government especially, to be almost entirely ignored in both public and academic circles?

Some elements of public *spending* do attract deeper interest. In the 1990s government deficits emerged as a significant factor in federal politics, increasingly being treated as signs of an inability to manage public expenditure. A legitimate tool of macro-economic management, Australia's deficits have not been large by international standards. Nevertheless, around the federal election of 1996 the opposition parties made powerful use of an implied and largely symbolic 'black hole' between government revenues and expenditure (see Chapters 10 and 11). There was certainly a deficit, of around $8 billion, and this was treated as public expenditure mis-management writ large. The action of the government in keeping secret the bureaucracy's deficit estimates only fuelled appearances of expenditure over-runs. Increased attention to the deficit is consistent with another ideological concern over public expenditure—the overall size of government and its impact on the private sector. There is widespread community suspicion that governments waste money and that inherent profligacy makes them unable to balance the books.

Governments have fallen for a perceived lack of probity in their budget management. Poor fiscal managers tend to be swept aside in the hope that the opposition can prove to be better guardians of the public purse. New governments have to cut their coats to fit the cloth; if they inherit a substantial deficit, or a deteriorating financial position, or even major expenditure commitments, then attention to budgetary pressures may consume an entire term of office or even more. Many democratic governments around the world have imposed a few years of tough budgetary pain only to relax at some pressure point like a recession or an election, and thereafter faced escalating deficits or debt levels. The 'expanding state' in the long post-war boom years increased spending across the board. Since the end of the post-war long boom in the 1970s governments have come to realise responsible fiscal management is hard to maintain, easy to lose, and very painful to recover. They control budgets and their budgets control them.

Yet, behind the scenes there exists a very different story. Australian Commonwealth governments have generally run tight fiscal policies; the public sector is small by international standards with most expenditure targeted to widely perceived needs. Australian governments have low levels of both deficit and debt, and our systems of expenditure management often receive international acclaim. It is the intention of this study to explain why.

PUBLIC EXPENDITURE MANAGEMENT

Why is it important to examine and explain expenditure management in Australia? In one sense this book as a whole provides an answer to that question, but two answers can immediately be offered.

The first is that a better understanding of expenditure management is vital to transparent and accountable public governance, as well as contributing to a more efficient and effective public management. Expenditure management is a crucial component of government accountability for public funds, including the allocation of resources, their deployment and uses, as well as the efficacy and evaluation of outcomes. Australia is an internationally acknowledged leader in the development of new structures and processes of public expenditure management (Posner and Gordon 1999; OECD 1997). Along with New Zealand, Australian budgeting systems are intensely studied by other governments and international financial organisations such as the OECD, IMF and World Bank. Still, there remains a need to make public expenditure in Australia more open and accountable. An educated and sophisticated electorate is demanding more transparency and accountability from politicians and more knowledge about government intentions with respect to public funds. The electoral defeat of the Kennett government in Victoria (1992–1999) was in part due to the perception that the Premier was taking active steps to avoid public scrutiny and destroy openness. This was especially true of the attempts to diminish the role of the Auditor-General, who is specifically designated to ensure transparency, accountability and efficiency. Large public demonstrations in favour of the Victorian Auditor-General are perhaps unique in the world and symbolise the strength of a kindled community sentiment.[2] Governments disregard such messages at their peril. Accordingly this study aims to increase transparency and accountability by creating an increased understanding of the processes and structures of expenditure management, their successes and failures, and their creation, evolution and possible futures.

The second reason, intimately related to the first, is the enormous significance of public expenditure itself. Government spending represents a very large proportion of the Australian economy. For at least two decades the share of GDP represented by the government sector (Commonwealth, state and local) has fluctuated in a narrow band between 32–36 per cent of GDP.[3] In other words, one third of all economic activity in the economy can be regarded in some way as subject to public expenditure management processes. This does not necessarily mean this economic

2 In 1997 two large street demonstrations saw around 90,000 Victorians protest against the diminution of the Auditor-General's role and perceived political attacks on his office.

3 See Commonwealth Budget Paper No 1, 1997–98:7.22, 7.26.

activity takes place *in* the public sector but that the financing occurs through government. Transfers are appropriated and their provision is subject to public accountability and expenditure management systems as funds move through the public domain and into the private.

Yet, if a succession of governments have defined their public expenditure management as the judicious use of scarce resources and reducing public sector size, then they have been conspicuously unsuccessful given the public sector's constant size in Australia relative to GDP. There are at least three views that can be taken with respect to this finding. The first is the view that budgeting *has been successful* in controlling expenditure, and that the public sector would have been larger were it not for sound expenditure management. A second view suggests that it is not the primary function of public expenditure management mechanisms to reduce the size of the public sector but to *manage funds already in the system.* Part of the reason is that expenditure management systems are not designed to determine the purposes and sizes of budgets. In this view, size reductions (or expansions) represent political issues and are decisions of government rather than functions of management techniques. A third view lies somewhere between these two, suggesting that a *whole arsenal of methods are needed to control the public purse* and that expenditure management is only one weapon in this arsenal: ineffective on its own but potentially powerful when combined with other weapons. What is interesting, and still requires explanation, is that a failure to reduce the size of government is not unique to Australia—rather it appears to be a near universal phenomenon of the past few decades in democratic societies.

These three views of public expenditure management illustrate a real problem in examining many social phenomena—important practical and theoretical questions may have no unambiguous answers. Such is the case with the nature of public expenditure management and the responsibilities of government. Rather than absolving us from the responsibility of examining public expenditure management, this makes such examinations and attempts to understand it even more important.

THE REALM OF EXPENDITURE MANAGEMENT WITHIN GOVERNMENT BUDGETS

To understand public expenditure management better we need to say more about what it is, as well as where it is located in the

Figure 1.1 Financial Flows through the Public Domain

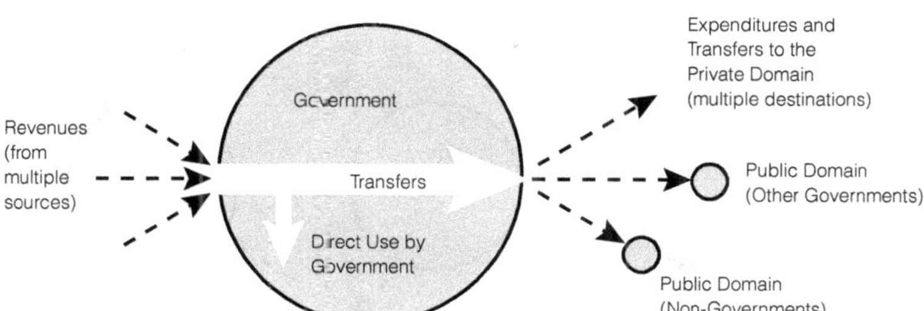

budgetary system. To help achieve this a concise definition is offered. Throughout the text this definition and its various meanings, nuances and shortcomings will be discussed and amplified. This definition is: *Public Expenditure Management is concerned with the planning, management, control and accountability of public financial resources from the point at which those resources enter the public domain, up to the point at which they leave.*

While the meaning of this definition is clear, in practice public expenditure management becomes very complex, and its precise realm is difficult to tie down. This can be seen in relation to Figure 1.1. The arrows in the diagram represent various flows of financial resources over which government has some control. These flows are:

(i) from the private to the public domain (revenues and incomes);
(ii) out of the public domain back into the private (transfers, subsidies and purchases); and
(iii) within and through the public domain (intra-public transfers, program payments, grants and purchases—indicated particularly in Figure 1.2).

Government is shown as the public domain. It receives taxation and other revenues and incomes from citizens and the private sector (shown as the incoming dotted lines). It can then transfer to private organisations and individuals some monies, such as unemployment benefits, pensions and subsidies intended for their private use (shown as the dotted outgoing arrows from the public domain). Such expenditures are usually not part of the expenditure management system once they enter private hands. In addition, government makes payments to organisations that upon receipt may be

Figure 1.2 Public Financial Flows and Australia's Three Tiers of Government

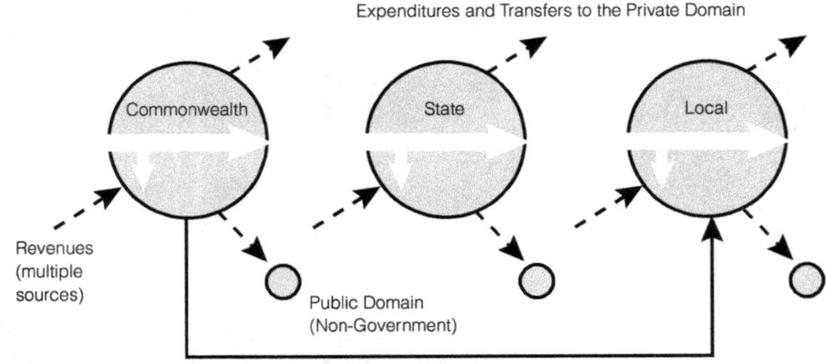

treated as part of the public domain (the solid outgoing arrows from the public domain). In these cases, the organisation itself, the funds or the uses of the funds are regarded as remaining accountable to government.

In Figure 1.1 the public domain includes all levels of government and government bodies, including public service departments and agencies, government business enterprises and all other institutions and agencies given control of public finances.[4] The latter organisations are shown as the non-government sector of the public domain. The manner in which they allocate and manage their expenditures, derived from public funds, remains accountable to government and to parliament. In Figure 1.2 the government sector in the public domain operates across devolved levels and a pattern of intergovernmental transfers or revenue sharing is indicated. Each level of government taken separately functions largely according to the relations shown in Figure 1.1 (except that the Commonwealth operates at the beginning of the chain and local government at the end, and typically local governments do not transfer substantial funds to another jurisdiction—but may impose levies on behalf of other jurisdictions). While the Commonwealth transfers funds to the states (and both do to local government) the accountability for

4 This would also include organisations such as universities, private firms, organisations such as charities and other not-for-profit bodies and even private individuals when they have public finances in their care to be used for public as opposed to private purposes.

the use of those funds rests essentially with state parliaments and local councils.

Accordingly, we use a rather different meaning for the 'public domain' from conventional notion of the public sector. Here the term public domain is constituted by the realm over which governments have at least some formal financial control. This means they can institute expenditure management systems over this realm, even though final recipients or operating agencies may remain private. The public sector is much more defined in terms of direct control but has a very large area of overlap with the public domain. In this study we focus on the Commonwealth level of government.

Crucially our definition of expenditure management excludes the ongoing management of resources and assets once purchased with these financial resources. This is as it should be. Such resources are in the care of and managed by specialists. An example would be the purchase of new aircraft. Up to the point where the aircraft are purchased, including the contractual negotiations, the funds remain in public hands and are subject to public financial management rules. Once the aircraft have been purchased, however, their management is in the hands of engineers, air-frame mechanics and avionics and logistics specialists and outside our frame of analysis. This distinction is vital to understanding the realm of public financial control and helps define the limits of public expenditure management. It also indicates the significance of financial resources for government operations. Financial resources on their own do not do a great deal, but they are efficient instruments for planning and management. They give immense flexibility. They can be measured or consigned to be spent in orderly ways and so allow and promote planning. In addition, they are easily saved in the sense that monies that are not spent immediately can be preserved (after allowing for inflation) for use at some unspecified later date.

ARGUMENTS AND ANALYTICAL APPROACH

This book makes a number of important arguments. While the role of annual budget statements to parliament may have diminished, *budgeting* and *budgetary management* have increased in significance relative to the nature and responsibilities of government. Budgets and the attendant processes have emerged as the main internal organising mechanism of the modern state. Indeed, budgets and financial accounting now represent the unsung discourse of modern governance. Budgets have long quantified the possibilities open to government (or lack thereof), but they are increasingly being used to assess capacity and performance within government. This constitutes a fundamental shift in the role of budgeting from a basic allocative system involving outlay options to an evaluative methodology for assessing the net worth of government activity and costs of provision. It is an accountancy mindset underlying contemporary budgeting that is increasingly being used to answer questions about the appropriate responsibilities of government. Public finance, therefore, remains a core central agency activity of the Commonwealth government. It occupies enormous time and effort behind the scenes, mainly because executive government continually needs to monitor the operationalisation of resource allocations (approvals to spend under appropriations).

This empirical study of budgeting and public finance in the Commonwealth of Australia suggests that government is *not* getting smaller, nor is expenditure less in proportion to GDP. Despite successive governments committing themselves to smaller government and periodically expressing preferences for major cuts to outlays, actual expenditure levels remain robust and many areas of public policy enjoy greater resources now than ever before. Two reasons are suggested for this; first, government responsibilities are not shrinking and governments are still called upon to support community and economic endeavours (even if this is increasingly through arm's length bodies and contractual relationships). Second, much budgetary decision-making within government remains insular and compartmentalised (for instance, between 'revenue', 'savings', 'expenditure outlays' and 'new spending proposals') making it harder for governments to control aggregate spending systematically. Yet, although governments have struggled to contain the growth of total public expenditure as a proportion of GDP, they have increasingly focussed on budgetary reform and resource management. There are some important reasons for this increasing focus.

One after another, Australian governments have been dissatisfied with their budgetary systems and processes. Indeed, dissatisfaction seems a perennial malady. But while governments are often clear about what is wrong with inherited arrangements they are less clear about with what to replace them. They know what they dislike but not what they want. The stop-start pattern of budgetary reform indicates governments are often searching in the dark to discover 'better' practices. They may win agreement or even tacit consent over problems identified with budgetary systems but rarely find agreement about how to rectify them.

Thus evolution led by pragmatic experimentation becomes the norm in budget reform. Budget processes are not framed in the abstract but in reaction to what the key actors considered to have worked or not worked in previous periods or in other jurisdictions. This means expenditure management structures and processes cannot be solely understood as rationally designed or optimised systems. Tempting though it may be to assume, there is no perfect system. If expenditure management systems in Australia have improved, it is as much by evolution, through trial and error, as it is by rational design. As society and the economy changes and the requirements upon government change, so too does the appropriateness or otherwise of (even good) specific expenditure management practices.

Moreover, from the evidence of this study, we would suggest that the Australian record indicates that reforms to the budget process have been driven far more by technocratic concerns than by political ideology or economic rationalism. Governments may make the noise, raise concerns or pose criticisms of budgetary systems, but it is the officials and technocrats who clearly have driven the reforms—sometimes in the face of indifference or even opposition from politicians. This is as true of the managerialist budget reforms of the 1980s as it is of the accrual reforms in the late 1990s. Most politicians do not understand the technicalities of the budget process—it is often as much a black box to them as it is to the rest of the community.

Budget reform is also continuous and unending. There is no nirvana or final resting point at which we can hope to arrive. Budget reform is a means, not an end in itself. As a set of processes separating powerful players and interests, the means must be continually revised. Budget processes must arguably be redefined and re-engineered continually to maintain their salience and efficacy. Nothing is more certain than that budgetary reform will continue into the future. Conversely, were a government to stop reform and freeze arrangements for a number of years then the instruments of budget control would quickly be of declining utility and effectiveness. More to the point, the political balance within the budget system would change in favour of spending departments. Claimants on the public purse would gradually exploit the 'gaming' possibilities and discover ways to circumvent or negate the intentions of the budget operators. Ultimately the government would find budget discipline threatened and restraint impossible. Politically, senior ministers back budget changes (even if they are not themselves particularly interested or convinced of their necessity) because it is a way of realigning budgetary relations within an adversarial system to their advantage.

Central agencies invest in budget reform as a continuous process of 'improvement' for two reasons: they genuinely believe specific reforms are needed to produce benefits to themselves and perhaps more broadly; and the process of reform is their main purchase on the relationship with all other claimants to the budget. Reform potentially enhances the political position of central budget agencies and has become their currency. They deliver value as a public institution to the political executive by controlling the process of putting budgets together and maintaining an upper hand in relations with their 'clients'. If central agencies give the impression that budget reform is an end in itself, this stems from an exuberant advocacy and a desire to proselytise. Of course, not all reforms work or are effective, and some prove counter-productive, but the need for change to the processes of setting adversarial public budgets does not diminish.

The main approach adopted in this study focuses on explaining changes to patterns of behaviour. The analysis revolves around the interactions and relationships between the actors, organisations and the rules involved in the budgetary and expenditure processes of the Commonwealth government. The relationships and interactions between the human actors are not only adversarial but are frequently imbued with personal animus. Such relationships stem not just from individual personalities, strong though many of them are especially in their bids for power, but from fundamental differences in perceptions over the goals to be set, as well as the means to attain them. There are disagreements about Australia's social and economic systems and the way they should operate. Differences also arise from the roles assigned within the system itself. Individual actors are assigned different roles and their behaviour is often to be understood in terms of those roles.

EXPLAINING BUDGETARY BEHAVIOUR

How budgetary behaviour more generally is explained depends greatly on the approach adopted and the aspects of budgeting

chosen for analysis. It is convenient to unpack the existing contributions to budgetary theory with reference to four analytic dimensions:

- the basic and often *a priori* assumptions made from the outset;
- the intended approach or analytical framework used in the investigation;
- the main events or topics of interest chosen for investigation; and
- the particular features prioritised or privileged in the account.

At the most fundamental level, research rests on the explanatory frameworks and basic assumptions adopted by researchers. This can involve the degree to which they believe social interaction is conflictual or consensual; the degree to which we are individuals or collectives; the degree to which we seek to maximise or share our utilities. For illustration, much of the strategic-managerialist literature assumes problems are solvable with sufficient planning and leadership, while sceptics are less sanguine, expecting unintended consequences to emerge and Murphy's law prevail. These assumptions shape and are shaped by the values held by the researchers themselves.

On the second dimension, the analytical approach adopted may be coherent or episodic, systematic or eclectic, rigorous or lax. A recognisable approach is often the result of intellectual training or disciplinary interest, as with political, historical, administrative, socio-anthropological or economic approaches. Analytical approaches relate closely to the research methodologies used to progress the investigation, perhaps using deductive or inductive reasoning, qualitative or quantitative methods of explanation, longitudinal analysis or case studies. Research may proceed according to chronological order or themes picked out for special mention. Political theories or ideological frameworks can enrich the analysis or inform the way researchers examine issues—perhaps drawing on the relatively coherent ideological dispositions available in liberalism, neo-liberalism, neo-marxism, or social democratic thought.

Third, the chosen topics of interest or main subject-matter investigated provide a body of evidential material which influence explanatory accounts. Whether focussing on budget reforms, official documentation, changes to inputs, results and outcomes or even on particular budgets, will partly predetermine the account developed. Researchers often select incidents or particular events (e.g. a single but difficult budget such as 1974 or 1993) and concentrate on explaining the aberrant. Others are apt to evaluate the tangible benefits or measurable outcomes when governments promise improvements; contrasting the rhetoric of the players with subsequent empirical reality.

Fourth, many studies privilege certain aspects of social relations in constructing explanations. For instance, the analysis of guardians and spenders prioritises the roles and behaviour of insider agencies relative to structural, economic or societal forces or where budgets occur in the election cycle. Researchers have also highlighted the roles of budgetary networks or insular 'village societies' within which shared knowledges and understandings develop. Weight may be given in the analysis to elected political elites over administrative ones or *vice versa*, or external pressure groups relative to key insiders. The conventional discourses associated with budgetary systems can be studied as a way of interpreting meaning and contrasting accounts of apparent phenomena.

These dimensions of research offer many alternative ways of conceptualising budgeting and the budgetary process. The particular orientations adopted by researchers over these four dimensions (the emphasis within each and the mix between them) provide an almost limitless variety of explanatory accounts. It must be noted that most of the existing contributions to the study of public budgeting are not organised around 'debates' where the merits of particular explanations are contested. Rather, most researchers or groups of like-minded scholars are engaged in separate endeavours, which only when taken together can be acknowledged as a range of debates on public budgeting. It is as true of budgeting as it is of many areas of social science that most writers on the topic are not greatly reflexive or sensitive to other representations, but tend to stay in well worn ruts. Having made these points, the most influential contributions to explaining budgetary behaviour are summarised below.

The public finance literature tends to be written by economists generally interested in the impact of budgets on the economy. They emphasise the fiscal and economic functions of public spending and taxing (and also the impact of public regulation on markets). Often public finance scholars face a dilemma in that they show a general preference for smaller government yet have to account empirically for increases in the size of government. Budget growth theories point to various contributing causes (such as economic maturity and meeting higher levels of need, productivity lags, social structure and demographic change, displacement effects due to crises and wars). Alternatively, critiques of public sector expenditure have emerged from neo-liberal or new right protagonists who favour ways of reducing government responsibilities and returning to a 'residual' state or notions of virtual government.[5]

Public choice theories extend these observations into a more robust model of the 'economics of politics'—but are heavily dependent on a set of narrow assumptions and ideological preferences. Public choice and institutional economics begin from notions of individuals or groups inside government who engage in self-interested behaviour to maximise their share of resources. Politicians and budget maximisers within government departments typically 'over-produce' public or merit goods while responding to voter choices or political pressures with consequent increases in taxation. Citizens are considered mobile between jurisdictions seeking out the lowest acceptable tax-benefit trade-off. Solutions include making governments more competitive and changing public sector incentive structures, with perhaps the imposition of constitutional or legislative strictures on budgets (e g. balanced budget legislation). Other views within this explanatory framework have argued that the fungibility of budget resources together with contractualism may empower the 'bureau-shaping' capacities of political executives—thereby

5 See Groenewegen (1990); Mikesell (1998); Rosen (1999); Musgrave (1959); Hyman (1990); Wilson (1998); Peacock and Wiseman (1967); Taylor (1983); Wildavsky (1985).

perhaps reducing the inherent bias toward budget maximisation within agencies themselves.[6]

An extensive literature exists in welfare economics investigating in positive and normative ways the most appropriate means of instituting allocative efficiency in public budgets. Their concern is to encourage the best use of funds and investigate how governments can decide on better ways to reallocate funds to maximise social well-being. Some models are technical, as with projects or programs assessed according to evaluation techniques (such as cost-benefit analysis). Others are more concerned with the distributional aspects of budgets over policy fields, citizen lifespans, asset maintenance, and patterns of spatial distribution.[7]

Theories of budgetary behaviour often stress the cyclical and incremental nature of budget decision-making in which groups and organisations vie for public resources. Incrementalism implies that budget decision-making is shaped by the politics of inheritance, the steady accruing of piecemeal decisions and marginal change. Governments are risk-averse and conservative, and so prefer regular adaptations to radical change. Such process theories focus on the analysis of the major and often repetitive stages of decision-making within which budgets are framed. Budget process theory tends to privilege the technical aspects of budgeting and usually emphasises the formulation stage of budget-making. Against these bottom-up depictions of budget formulation, strategic thinkers and managerial planners believe budgets can be driven by top-down prioritisation, involving formal relations and strict accountabilities between plans, budgets, operations and evaluation and feedback.[8]

Institutional theories (both traditional and new), by contrast, explore the roles of key actors and the ways they operate. Institutionalised actors may be motivated by concerns of control, propriety, secrecy or service to others rather than behave according to the assumptions of economic theory. Governments will often

---

6 See Niskanen (1971; 1975); Tiebout (1956); Buchanan and Tulloch (1962); Downs (1957); Tulloch (1970); Miller and Moe (1983); Blais and Dion (1991); Dunleavy (1991); Stretton and Orchard (1994).

7 See Mishan (1964; 1973); Samuelson (1954); Boardman *et al.* (1996); Rosen (1999); Self (1975).

8 See Wildavsky (1964; 1975); Rubin (1988; 1990); Caiden (1992); Schick (1990; 1997); Savoie (1990); Aucoin and Savoie (1994); Thompson, Meyers, Patashnik, Pitsvada, Jones, McCaffery (1996–97); Premchand (1993a); Forster and Wanna (1990); Walsh (1991); Keating and Holmes (1990); Pradham and Campos (1996); OECD (1997).

construct adversarial relations between major budget actors (central guardians versus spending departments) that serve to ration or control the provision of resources. Often their behaviour can be interpreted through the patterns of interaction including the development of languages, codes and rationales that give meaning to their actions. Insular networks like a 'village society' operating at the centre of government maintain a cultural but often unwritten understanding about budgetary practice. These relationships may serve to routinise or deflect conflict, minimise disagreement or internal disruption, or deal with 'easy options' so that more difficult ones can be avoided, put-off or dealt with at higher political levels.[9]

These very different approaches illustrate how problematic explaining budgetary behaviour can be. Although the existing literature on *budgeting* may not be extensive (and is particularly weak in relation to specific countries), it is nevertheless diverse; drawing on some of the main theoretical and ideological paradigms in the political, economic and social sciences. This analysis draws on this theoretical literature in analysing the changing *relationships* involved in budgetary and expenditure processes in Australia.

STRUCTURE OF THE BOOK—AUSTRALIAN EXPERIENCE FROM THE 1960S TO 2000

The structure of this book reflects the patterns and development of the Commonwealth government's experience in expenditure management. It covers changes from the 1960s to the present day, but traces some changes back to the late 1950s. Though there is an evolving reformist logic to the developments traced, such logic was also subject to the contingencies faced in political and bureaucratic arenas. The structure of the text, therefore, is episodic, covering periods of government incumbency while highlighting crucial themes within the chapters. This book should not be read as a linear progression enforced by a single rationality. Rather, the chapters are better viewed as scenes from a multi-act play where the twists and turns of the central characters bring topics into and out of focus, adding complexities to the account.

Consequently, the main chapters of the book are of two kinds. The majority are centred upon the lives of specific governments,

---

9 See Heclo and Wildavsky (1974); Thain and Wright (1995); Weller and Cutt (1976); Hawker, Smith and Weller (1979); March and Olsen (1989).

with an assumption that the survival and character of the government was generally determined by the content of their budgets. It is essential to base the analysis on specific governments because this provides the framework within which important changes of political ideologies and practice, and key ministerial personnel occur. Such analysis also allows the text to embody a historical approach while avoiding a simple chronology of events. Within the life of a single administration, individual changes may not be especially prominent or considered important, but the historical approach allows movements on a much larger time scale to be examined. We argue that the impacts of budgetary reforms are not always visible within the turbulence of a single administration, but are often significant over a period of a decade or more.

Nevertheless, *expenditure management* and *budget reform*, as opposed to the *content* of budgets, are rarely the flagship of any government. Both sides of politics periodically talk about reducing waste and increasing government efficiency, but it is often not significant in electoral terms. Expenditure management remains very much out of the public gaze and interest. It is prone to be tossed on the seas of parliamentary and ministerial uncertainty often without having much reciprocal impact on those forces. As a result, any changes or reforms in budgeting and expenditure management that occur, no matter how significant in the long-term, are unlikely to be articulated as the central political strategy of any government.

However, some events or problems require separate treatment. These are dealt with in thematic rather than government-based chapters—but still taking a largely historical form in a style consistent with other chapters. The first thematic chapter (Chapter 2) examines the statutory framework and introduces the basic characteristics of the Commonwealth budgetary system (budget cycle, timetable, functions, actors and processes). Chapter 5 deals with the institutional 'creation' of a specialist budget agency—the Department of Finance—although at the time this development was perceived more as the splitting of Treasury. Chapter 8 traces the development of the Financial Management Improvement Program and the adoption of 'one-line' running costs budgets—emphasising the competing aims and the importance of institutional dynamics frequently ignored or unknown outside professional budget circles. And in Chapter 11 the focus turns to the problems of cutting rather than controlling expenditure in the context of budgetary management—including problems associated with the politics of managing surpluses.

Chapter 3 commences with the early moves to improve budget information in the 1960s and early 1970s. With hindsight, these moves can be seen as timid but there were few in government for whom reform in this area was a burning issue. The Menzies' period (1949–66) saw a concern with probity but little enthusiasm for other reforms. The extant processes of expenditure control were almost entirely based on laborious negotiations over specific expenditure items between the 'guardian' agency (Treasury) and spending departments, with most budget allocations largely dependent upon the actual figures for the immediate year. Departments, therefore, regarded any additional expenditure increment as a strong base for permanent growth—and the reliance on additional bids between budgets merely exacerbated this problem. This decentralised process hindered overall planning and heavily favoured expenditure accountability over efficiency. Incremental predictability guided budgets rather than the ability to plan and manage expenditure.

Traditional budgetary mechanisms were gradually considered unsatisfactory for the needs of the time. The post-war expansion of the Commonwealth's role and spheres of activity was one reason for this. The Commonwealth government had gradually increased its activity compared to the states, and in addition had adopted interventionist Keynesian macro economic policies. Moreover, in the early 1970s the long post-war boom came to an end and public resources started to come under pressure. At the same time, governments in the early 1970s increased spending significantly, often without much scrutiny or consideration of the long-term consequences. All of these developments led to calls for greater control over expenditures and costs.

The limitations of the traditional budgetary system were hidden not only by economic growth, but by a conventional rule-bound administrative culture closely attuned to these controls. The seeds of a major shift in budget management were planted by Treasury's increasing frustration at its inability to plan forward expenditures against expected revenues. This created uncertainty in the business community and meant that revenues were always expenditure determined, rather than a more prudent process of revenues limiting expenditures. To cope with these problems Treasury began to prepare forward estimates of expenditure for its own planning purposes, but still based upon the assumption that expenditures determine revenues. The use of forward estimates gradually evolved, with much trial and tribulation, beyond their limited role inside Treasury to become a mainstay of budget management and expenditure control.

While Treasury was increasing its attention to fiscal management, its efforts and status in budget and expenditure management came under increasing attack. It is argued in Chapter 4 that while Treasury was interested in high macro-economic policy, it had little time for the more mundane tasks of the accounting and bookkeeping functions of government, even though these were assigned to it by the Constitution. Moreover, in the 1960s budgetary innovations were occurring around the world and Treasury was seen as having little interest in them.

Other political difficulties impacted on Treasury. The arrival of the Whitlam Labor government (1972–75) upset established political patterns and led to the government pressing for reform. Whitlam established a royal commission into government administration with very broad terms of reference. It was from a preliminary investigation into areas of concern that criticisms of the role and functioning of Treasury emerged (mainly from policy areas and spending departments which were often adversaries to Treasury). Both the roles and performance of Treasury were criticised as was the system of budgeting using detailed line-by-line appropriations. The overall impression of a hide-bound department was damaging to Treasury's position as the central economic and budgetary agency of Commonwealth administration. The constitutional crisis and ensuing demise of the Whitlam government diverted attention from this issue for a time, but once having emerged on the agenda, such concerns about Treasury's performance quickly returned.

The Whitlam government endured a torrid time in office, battling the Coalition, the unions and the bureaucracy (and some would argue even itself). Big spending together with the oil shock of 1973 and the debacles of the 1974 budget produced even higher inflation but slowed growth. The government's last budget in 1975 was blocked by the Senate, leading the Governor-General to dismiss the Prime Minister. Despite the controversies, the Whitlam government gradually began a process to change the relations between the political executive and the bureaucracy. It was clear governments now sought options from their officials rather than following the single line of advice the mandarins felt appropriate. Treasury in particular was slow to adjust to the new political environment and continued to consider itself having a monopoly on policy advice on economic and budgetary matters and an effective veto upon government policy. The Fraser government (1975–83) in turn became dissatisfied with Treasury's advice and poor performance—leading to a confrontation between the Prime Minister and Treasury. In a pre-emptive move, Fraser decided to split the Treasury into two departments, essentially to diminish Treasury internally. In doing so, he created the Department of Finance (DoF)—soon to become an alternative locus of bureaucratic power and specialist source of policy advice on public finance. As Chapter 5 suggests, Finance became a powerful central budget agency almost by default.

Chapter 6 documents the Fraser government's attempts to control expenditure and impose restraint. Under Fraser, the fight against inflation meant public expenditure had to be better controlled and reduced if possible. Finance with the support of the Prime Minister gradually began to modernise expenditure management. New budgetary processes and an appreciation of better management systems were all prototyped under Fraser and in this sense began their evolutionary histories. Fraser continued the pattern of bottom-up incremental budgeting with restraint imposed by top-down decrees. The emphasis remained on rules, with central gatekeeping institutions using overlapping controls to hold down expenditure. The paradox of the Fraser years is that while the government prided itself on its fiscal rectitude and genuine desire for greater budget control, the government threw this away in a spending breakout in its last year in office.

The Hawke Labor government (1983–91) wished to avoid the problems that had befallen the Whitlam government. As Chapter 7 recounts, the Hawke ministry was conscious of the failures of its predecessors in budgetary process and expenditure management. Consequently, this was an area of government in which the cabinet required themselves to succeed. Fiscal restraint became a priority and was seen as a major vehicle for staying in office for more than one term—and by surviving into a fourth term they were allowed a continuous period of budgetary reform. During the 1980s Labor did not attempt to implement a democratic socialist program but rather emphasised 'tight budgets' and the bottom line—which resulted in four consecutive budget surpluses in the late 1980s. Many factors contributed to their relative success in maintaining budget discipline. These included: the collective political will to be fiscally 'responsible'; the early popularity of Hawke and his ability to manage his ministry and cabinet; and growing recognition of the need for reform in the public service, including major reforms to the budgetary system. Powerful economic ministers and an assertive central budget agency (DoF) provided the catalyst to accomplish reform. Cabinet's Expenditure Review Committee emerged as a dominant player, imposing cuts, evaluating program efficiency and overseeing budgetary reforms. A plethora of reform ideas were promoted during this period and, by trial and error, a significantly changed budget system emerged.

Alongside the enthusiasm for pragmatic budget reform there were calls from line agencies for greater freedoms to manage resources, rather than merely administer. The wish for greater responsiveness to political direction and managerial autonomy to deliver was shared and sustained by many actors each believing they stood to benefit. As Chapter 8 demonstrates, the introduction of greater flexibility in resource management was a tortuous process. But, once in place, this managerialist budgetary phase made managers identify goals and then allocate resources in accordance with those requirements. Concepts of resource flexibility were limited by the thinking of the time where delivery by the public service was largely unquestioned. Cabinet and DoF were instrumental in imposing efficiencies and 'clawbacks' on departments, engineering resource agreements to save money, and the promotion of program evaluation was a means by stealth to cut costs.

After managing four budget surpluses and hitting a severe economic recession in 1991–92, Labor attempted to stimulate the economy and provide employment. As Keating wrested the leadership from Hawke, Australia embarked upon a spectacular roller coaster in budgetary management. Still targeting expenditure to areas of need or policy priority, the government recorded a series of a high deficits between 1991 and 1996, principally generated by increasing outlays while revenue declined sharply. The spending was politically-driven and not a result of budgetary mis-management. Initially the size of the deficit was widely accepted and only later became an electoral issue on which to attack the government. Keating won the 1993 election on the back of a campaign to discredit the opposition's proposed Goods and Service Tax (GST), but immediately struck difficulties in the Senate in getting the 1993–94 Budget passed. A number of 'big picture' spending programs together with increased unemployment levels again increased outlays as a proportion of GDP. Nevertheless, the Keating government kept a tight rein on the management of its own outlays and continued to devolve financial and managerial responsibilities, while awaiting revenues to pick up.

Chapter 10 discusses the new business of budgeting under the Coalition government led by John Howard (1996-). Although the Howard mandate has still to run its course, a new emphasis on the bottom line of public budgets and fiscal rectitude was apparent even before they came into office. A major issue in the 1996 election campaign was the deficit inherited from Labor. Following sizeable cuts in the first two years, a continuing theme was the Coalition's commitment to achieve and maintain a budget surplus. This return to parsimony on the expenditure side was aligned during the 1998 election with taxation reform and the introduction of a GST in 2000. At the same time the government moved away from cash appropriations and adopted a new budgetary framework using accrual accounting and accrual and price-based budgeting. Resources were explicitly allocated to 'outcomes' and 'outputs' as a way of 'pricing' services. Using price-based budgeting and results monitoring, the government hoped to become more empowered in the budgetary process—moving from being a 'price-taker' to a 'price-setter'. Together these developments represent a new 'business-like' approach in Australian budgetary politics. For all this, retaining the surplus proved more difficult than the government had expected, especially over the trade-offs associated with the introduction of the GST. Other events such as the Asian financial and currency crisis of 1997–99 and East Timor crisis of 1999–2000 or the 'revolt of the bush' also posed severe tests to budgetary discipline and, with economic growth slowing, the same problems that beset Keating suddenly loomed for the Coalition. The new business of budgeting again appeared to offer only temporary solutions to the intractable problems of budgeting.

In Chapter 11 the main themes of the previous chapters are picked up and two intimately related topics are analysed. First, expenditure cutting is examined as a non-routinised expression of expenditure control—for even the best managed budgets cannot escape the necessity of occasional cuts. The reasons for cuts, as is discussed, may arise from a variety of causes. Yet actual cuts to budgets are enormously difficult to make. Cutting is also difficult to situate within a coherent expenditure management framework. It is argued that the disguised manner in which cutbacks are usually made confirms this view. Secondly, the chapter examines the management of budgetary surpluses following periods of tight fiscal control. Long considered notoriously difficult to achieve, surpluses are now appearing under governments of different political persuasions in many advanced economies including Australia. The reasons behind this are explored—as are the real political problems associated with their retention. In some ways managing surpluses is more difficult and politically hazardous than coping with deficits.

Chapter 12 then poses the question to what extent, after decades of budget reform, can we say public expenditure is better managed today.

2 Understanding the Australian budgetary system

THE DELIVERY OF the Commonwealth Budget is a major event in the parliamentary year expressing the government's request for funds from the popularly-elected bicameral legislature. The presentation of the Budget is signified by the Treasurer's delivery of the Budget Speech in the House of Representatives. As the government's most senior economic minister, the Treasurer can use this speech to report achievements, outline the government's strategy, announce new initiatives and budget measures, or deliver revenue adjustments. The speech is crafted to have impact. It is short, to the point, and highlights the main topics the government wishes to identify. The Treasurer will present the Budget in the best possible light and usually with some hyperbole. Immediately after the Treasurer has introduced the government's main package, the Minister for Finance and Administration then presents a shorter speech perhaps outlining any changes to budgetary documentation or accounting processes. The Leader of the Opposition by convention has the right of reply usually two days after the Treasurer's speech after which the legislature commences the 'Budget debate' which is a relatively wide-ranging debate lasting several weeks.[1]

CONSTITUTIONAL AND LEGISLATIVE REQUIREMENTS—BUDGET PRESENTATION

The presentation of the Budget Speech by the Treasurer introduces the first appropriation bill to provide funds to the government. In

1 See Parliament of Australia, House of Representatives Fact Sheet No 10: The Budget and Financial Legislation, May 1999.

parliamentary terms, the second reading speech on the intended legislation initiates the wider budget debate in Parliament. Traditionally, *Appropriation Bill No 1* provided 'for the appropriation of sums from the Consolidated Revenue Fund for the *ordinary annual services of the government*', ending at 30 June the following year. The bill requests Parliament's authority for funds to enable executive government to administer laws and run its own administration. Traditionally, it covered the costs of administering departments—in cash terms or recurrent spending—and provision for the funds administered by them on behalf of the Commonwealth. More recently, under the accrual budgeting format, the appropriation bill now presents total *departmental expenses* by agency (the operational costs of delivering services in accrual format) and all funds by outcome and agency transferred to or from the community (*administered expenses*). The second appropriation bill introduced by the Minister for Finance and Administration (with the Treasurer) seeks authorisation of expenditure for new policies, capital expenditures, equipment purchases and payments to the states and territories. In the accrual format, this bill makes requests for administered capital, equity injections, administered expenses for new outcomes and specific purpose payments to the states. A much smaller third appropriation bill also presented by the Finance Minister provides funds for the operation of the Commonwealth Parliament. The legislative pattern is repeated when further appropriation bills are required (supplementary or additional estimates). Since 1994 the government has chosen to present its annual budget in May—prior to the start of the financial year. However, when the government decides or has to present its budget in August (perhaps because of election timing but after the start of the financial year), then supply bills are required to advance funds to the administration as an interim measure before the main appropriation bills are passed.

The reason for separate appropriation bills and the main differences between them derives from the Constitution and the legislative process. The Constitution stipulates that 'no money shall be drawn' from the public account by the Commonwealth 'except under appropriation made by law' (s.83) and that monies or revenues received 'shall form one Consolidated Revenue Fund, to be appropriated for the purposes of the Commonwealth' (s.81). Moreover, in an expression of majoritarian principles, 'money bills' for the 'ordinary annual services of the government' cannot be introduced in or be amended by the Senate (s.53). However, due to a compact between the Senate and the executive (dating from 1965) that agreed what should not be in Appropriation Bill 1, the government accepts that the Senate *is* able to amend the second a well as the third appropriation bills.[2] This does not prevent the Senate from making 'requests' in relation to the first bill, although the House of Representatives is at liberty to accept or reject the requests or negotiate an agreed outcome. To date, the Senate has not formally rejected an appropriation bill, but has delayed passage as in 1975.

Only the government can make requests to appropriate funds

---

2 Section 53 of the Constitution provides that the Senate cannot amend a bill either imposing taxation or appropriating monies for 'the ordinary annual services of the government'—and that a proposed law to appropriate funds for the 'ordinary annual services' of the government 'shall deal only with such appropriation'. The compact essentially agreed that what constitutes the 'ordinary annual services of the government' is for Parliament to determine and can change over time. Regarding the Compact of 1965, Odgers' *Australian Senate Practice* 3rd Edition (1967:280) states: 'The Government agreed that appropriations for new policies, not authorised by special legislation, should be included in the Appropriation Bill which was subject to amendment by the Senate. Subsequent appropriations for such items, however, would be included in the Appropriation Bill for the ordinary annual services . . . Members of both Houses can approach a consideration of the annual appropriations sure in the knowledge that only appropriations for services already approved are included [in the Appropriation Bill for ordinary annual services].' This compact came about as a result of a 'huge kerfuffle after Harold Holt agreed on 11 September 1963 to a Treasury submission that the Appropriation (Works and Services) Bill—which the Senate purported to be entitled to amend—be amalgamated with the main Appropriation Bill—for the ordinary annual services of the Government and thus not susceptible to amendment by the Senate' (Cyril Monaghan, former Treasury official, personal communication). The Leader of the Government in the Senate announced the government's intention to amalgamate the works and services bill in May 1964. Odgers maintains that Senators 'expressed concern at the effect of the new procedure on the powers of the Senate' (1967:278). According to Monaghan, when the Supply bills for 1964–65 were prepared on this basis, the Senate 'had apoplexy' and indicated they would not pass future bills in this form. A committee of Senators 'forced a rethink and a new split was proposed between the bill the Senate thought it could amend and the one for the annual services which it could not. Holt capitulated in the Supply bills for 1965–66'. The Prime Minister's acceptance of the new compact appeared in Hansard (13 May 1965:1484–5), in which Holt stated that 'there have been further discussions' with the Senate and that 'henceforth there will be a separate bill . . . subject to amendment by the Senate' containing appropriations for public works, sites and buildings, plant and equipment, grants to the states, and new policies not authorised by special legislation (p.1485).

(taxation or expenditures) and Parliament cannot make or increase appropriations beyond these requests. Hence, budgets are 'owned' and conceived by the executive. The government presents *its* spending plans to Parliament for authorisation, not *vice-versa*. This 'financial initiative' is enshrined in the Constitution where it states that money votes can only be passed when 'the purpose of the appropriation has in the same session been recommended by message of the Governor-General' to the house in which the proposal initiated (s.56). Technically the Governor-General 'procures supply for the government by recommending the purpose of the proposed appropriation by message to the House of Representatives' (DoF 1996:27). By convention the lower-house cannot increase the amount requested by the executive, while the Senate is expressly forbidden from amending money bills 'so as to increase any proposed charge or burden on the people' (s.53)[3]. The terms '*purpose* of the appropriation' or 'purposes of the Commonwealth' have also assumed importance on two accounts. First, the High Court has debated on occasions how the words should be interpreted—narrowly in restricting the Commonwealth to the specified areas of its legislative competence; or, broadly, allowing the Commonwealth to spend in areas beyond its limited set of legislative powers. Secondly, there has been concern that the term 'purpose' implies a very precise level of detail is required for all appropriations (perhaps detailing specific line items of expenditure such as salaries, numbers employed or office locations). Since a number of High Court cases have involved judgments on these issues, the view has emerged that the meaning of the 'purposes of the Commonwealth' is left to Parliament to decide.

While these appropriation bills consolidate spending intentions for the year ahead, by far the largest proportion of Commonwealth outlays are now contained and approved within special and standing appropriations. Such standing appropriations are not voted upon each year and are not limited in sum. They require funds be

---

3 The *House of Representatives Practice* (www.aph.gov.au/house/pubs/horpract/chap.1e.htm) describes the convention in this way: 'The Executive Government is charged with the management of revenue and with payments for the public service. It is a long established and strictly observed rule which expresses a principle of the highest constitutional importance that no public charge can be incurred except on the initiative of the Executive Government. The Executive Government demands money, the House grants it, but the House does not vote money unless required by the Government, and does not impose taxes unless needed for the public service as declared by Ministers of the Crown'.

allocated to specially approved purposes under enabling legislation (eg. pensions, benefits, transfers to the states), but are not considered part of the 'ordinary annual services' and so are termed 'amendment bills', able to be amended by both houses when presented. The enabling legislation stipulates the intent and criteria for entitlement while the annual Budget documentation presents the latest estimates of likely requirements. Around 25 per cent of Commonwealth outlays are appropriated through the annual appropriation process (for agencies and programs), while 75 per cent of outlays (or 'expenses') are authorised under the standing appropriations.

In recent years the Commonwealth has imposed upon itself the discipline of a *Charter of Budget Honesty*. Passed in 1998 (see Chapter 10), the act followed accusations of government subterfuge over the non-disclosure of information on the financial position and the size of a budgetary deficit. The act imposes requirements on the government's budget plans and fiscal strategy. It stipulates that budgets must be based on 'sound fiscal management' involving a 'sustainable medium-term framework', stability in public spending and taxing, the prudential management of debt levels, regard to savings levels, and the impact on future generations. The Charter requires the secretaries of Treasury and Finance to produce and release publicly a pre-election economic and fiscal statement and, if requested, cost the policy commitments of the political parties. The act does *not* require that governments either balance the budget or deliver surpluses (ie. it is not a 'balanced budget' law), but it is intended to improve the accountability and transparency of budget deliberations. It requires governments maintain 'the ongoing economic prosperity and welfare of the people'—which are essentially politically defined.

The *presentation* of the Budget is equally as important as the legislative provisions. Emphasis is placed by the government on the *selling* of the Budget via additional publications and through parliamentary and media promotion (including the media 'lock-up' of Budget Night). Alongside the appropriation bills, the government produces a wealth of accompanying budget documentation (known as the Budget Papers). The structure and content of the Budget Papers are essentially the preserve of executive government. Conventions tend to dictate the format even though the forms of presentation change over time. For instance, in 1983–84 the government produced 11 Budget Papers ranging from an overview *Budget Statement* (No 1) covering the broader economic context, to details of estimates of revenue and expenditure (No 5), civil works (No 6), overseas aid (No 9), national income (No 10) and income tax statistics (No 11). By the late–1980s Budget Paper No 2 presented the *Commonwealth Public Account*, while No 3 contained portfolio program estimates.

Moving toward an accrual budgetary framework in the late–1990s, the government made major changes in presentation to the budget statements. Budget Paper No 1 was retitled *Budget Strategy and Outlook* to better describe its purpose. Budget Paper No 2 presented the *Budget Measures*, while Paper No 3 outlined *Federal Financial Relations* and Paper No 4 indicated *Agency Resourcing* in an accrual format. This new format was preserved in both the full accrual budgets of 1999–2000 and 2000–01. In addition, three further batches of material are routinely produced. Individual portfolio budget statements are released (around 17—or however many portfolios exist) containing detail of the specific spending plans within each portfolio and agency. Ministerial statements present statements of government policy on particular topics (eg. regional issues, women's policy issues, cultural heritage); and finally a compilation of press releases are included for the media and interest groups. Contents of the budget documentation for 2000–01 are shown below in Table 2.1.

It may be an obvious point but there are no statements issued about what government is *not* doing or has chosen to eschew. So, for instance, tables showing changes to outlay measures (perhaps showing increased spending for priority areas) do not necessarily show or highlight other areas where no increases have been awarded, but savings or reductions are now identified as budget measures. Similarly governments do not use budget documentation to show where they have refused to commit funds to initiatives presented to them in the budget process (eg. on selected programs which did not receive support in cabinet). Their acts of omission are omitted.

BUDGET CYCLE AND TIMETABLE

Parliament's role in the budgetary process is to scrutinise and authorise expenditure and provide accountability. In presenting appropriation bills for consideration by the legislature the government opens itself to public scrutiny for its management of the public purse and potentially for any item or type of spending.

Table 2.1 Budget Presentation 2000–01

Budget Papers	Size, Structure and Preparation	Major Contents
Budget Speech	1[illegible] pages—prepared by Treasurer, Treasurer's Office, and Treasury with input from DoFA, PM&C	2nd Reading Speech of the 1st Appropriation Bill; the initial presentation and selling of the budget
Budget Paper No 1—*Budget Strategy and Outlook*	8 statements over 325 pages—prepared by Treasury and DoFA	Fiscal outlook and strategy (incl. fiscal balance), economic outlook, economic policy, financial outlook, revenue, expenses and net capital investment, budget funding, the public sector
Budget Paper No 2—*Budget Measures*	Contains tables of Measures for each portfolio over 212 pages—prepared by DoFA	New initiatives or budget measures—shown according to expenses, revenues, equity or capital injections
Budget Paper No 3—*Federal Financial Relations*	Four chapters and two appendices with 118 pages—prepared by Treasury	Financial relations with the states, territories, and local government; general revenue assistance, specific purpose payments, state fiscal contributions
Budget Paper No 4—*Agency Resourcing*	Includes Appropriation (Parliamentary) Bill; Appropriation Bill (No.1); Appropriation Bill (No.2); and *Resourcing Agency Expenses* in total 295 pages—prepared by DoFA	Details of agency resourcing by outcome, administered appropriations and departmental appropriations—linked to portfolio budget statements
Budget Related Papers		
Portfolio Budget Statements	Separate papers for each portfolio—prepared by DoFA and Agencies	Presents details of budget measures and significant changes in appropriation for each agency; financial and non-financial performance targets for each portfolio (intended outcomes and outputs shown in accrual format)

Budget Papers	Size, Structure and Preparation	Major Contents
Budget Related Documents		
Budget Overview	Media guide to the budget—2 sections and 5 appendices, in total 28 pages—prepared by Treasury and DoFA	Overview of the budget; overview of the economy; the budget priorities
Ministerial Statements	Prepared by selected portfolios coordinated by PM&C	Composite budgetary information and other policy pronouncements on specific topics of concern
Press Releases	Prepared by portfolio ministers—usually 1–2 pages each	Available for the media 'lock-up' and circulated to media outlets and key interests groups

Parliament scrutinises public expenditure both at a generic level and can delve down to specific levels of expenditure at the discretion of members.

Budgets are presented to Parliament according to a strict timetable. Appropriation bills are the only bills necessarily dealt within the same session of Parliament to which they are introduced. Detailed investigations of expenditure plans are conducted promptly through Senate legislation committees at estimate hearings. These committees are not only able to scrutinise the *intended* use of resources by the government, but also *previous* patterns of usage. Departmental officials are summoned to appear at these sessions and often grilled on administrative and resource issues. In many instances estimates committees will question ministerial decisions or policy intentions, conventionally the preserve of executive government. Committees are not restricted to the scrutiny of estimates, but members are able to question the agency on any matters of interest. The Senate has managed to extract greater latitude for itself in conducting these investigations, reflecting its increased political importance when not controlled by the government of the day (and over the past thirty years government has only managed to command a majority in the Senate for five years 1975–81). Once the estimates hearings are completed and the committees have presented their reports, the Budget proceeds to its third reading and is able to be passed by both houses. At this latter stage all three appropriation bills could attract further debate or tortuous negotiations before agreements can be reached and passage assured. Once passed the Budget empowers the Commonwealth to commit resources legally to its own purposes for the year ahead.

The annual cycle of appropriation serves both as a crucial accountability safeguard and provides a temporal structure to the budget process. Public funds are authorised only for a fixed period—approved prior to and authorised to the end of the financial year. Forward estimates or projections of expenditure may show intended commitments for future years but these do not constitute formal authorisations to spend. This annuality gives budgets both a temporal and cyclical character almost to the point of regimentation. Accordingly, budgets are divided into stages, processes and discrete functions repeated year after year according to the budget cycle. Many organisations in the public sector pace themselves according to the requirements and procedures of this annual timetable—both in consuming expenses and in making requests for new resources. For instance, new policy proposals (budget bids of the year ahead) generally have to be lodged to the central budget agency (the Department of Finance and Administration—DoFA; which succeeded the Department of Finance in October 1997) and cabinet by February/March. Monthly and annual reporting of financial statements are produced according to strict deadlines for compilation and publication. The budget cycle grinds on with repetitive regularity, although from time to time procedural adjustments may be made to the internal processes or schedules.

Notwithstanding the adoption of accrual reporting and accrual budgeting in the late 1990s (see Chapter 10), the basic budgetary timetable has not changed greatly over past decades (except for the timing of the presentation of the Budget moving from August to May). In the late 1970s governments followed a simple process involving cabinet but staged around *ad hoc* negotiations. Ministers were circulated with estimates for the coming years between October and April. Budget estimates were then set from April to July, with new policy being added as future commitments of expenditure prior to July, before the Budget was tabled in August. Supply bills in April-June authorised interim resources and additional estimates were added in the following March (see HRSCE 1979 for further details). The budget process in the 1980s followed the same timelines, but involved more formal cabinet bodies such as the Expenditure Review Committee (ERC) and a special ministerial strategy review and some external input from the Economic

Planning Advisory Council (see *Budget Reform* 1984). Increasingly, mini-economic statements were introduced around May to adjust revenues and expenditures over the following financial year. By 1989 a two stage internal process was adopted with consolidated portfolio limits imposed by ERC within which new policy proposals were considered often with 'offsetting savings' (Keating 1990b). For the most part, internal changes to budgetary procedure are within the executive's discretion. Adaptations applying to the formulation stages occur readily while the formal parliamentary steps remain relatively unchanged.

The current budget timetable commences with a fiscal strategy and review of policy priorities some seven months before the Budget is finalised. Table 2.2 indicates the activities in budget formulation through to the monthly reporting and final reporting of financial statements. The stages occur within compressed timelines, with multiple activities occurring simultaneously. It is also noteworthy that while the Treasurer still presents the Budget Speech to Parliament, it is DoFA that performs the majority of budget-related tasks (including reconciling revenues and expenses/ expenditures)[4].

While the process of legislative authorisation gives budgets an annuality, the decision-making process involved in the allocation, deployment and evaluation of resources takes place over a compartmentalised three year cycle—formulation, implementation and evaluation and review (HRSCE 1979). In the first year, decisions are made with respect to resource formulation, reflecting objectives or policy choices and program selection. The formulation phase concludes with the presentation of the Budget to Parliament. In year two authorised budget resources pass to agencies and citizens in the implementation phase of budgeting. Within implementation, choices can be made about modes of service delivery, but not usually about legal entitlements; which pass to recipients on the basis of statutory criteria. The third phase of budget management concerns review and evaluation. Auditing financial records and

---

4 The Department of Finance and Administration is responsible for advising on budget matters and coordinating public expenditure. In overall budgetary terms, Treasury retains responsibility for macro-economic parameters and revenue estimates. Treasury has aggressively expanded its empire since losing responsibility for expenditure in 1976 (see Chapters 4 and 5 in this volume). Treasury has turned its attention increasingly away from expenditure matters to national competition policy, micro-economic reform, and financial markets.

Table 2.2 Budget Timetable 2000–01

Month	Budget Activity
Oct–Nov	Review policy priorities and set fiscal strategy—sets budget parameters
Oct–Nov	Publication of the Mid-Year Economic and Fiscal Outlook (MYEFO)
Nov–Dec	Senior ministers' review (usually 4 ministers)—other ministers advised by Prime Minister of outcomes of the senior ministers' review; provides guidelines to ERC and priority setting for ministerial submissions
Jan	Draft-Portfolio Budget Submissions (PBS) to central budget agency (DoFA) for costing
Feb	Pre-ERC review and up-date of estimates by DoFA
Feb–March	Ministers' bids for resourcing and PBS produced by agencies and spending departments
March	Final PBS lodged, DoFA prepares 'green briefs' on each agency/proposal; ERC systematically considers bids and decides budget measures—separates between major/sensitive and minor proposals (major or sensitive proposals are considered by ERC while minor ones are handled bilaterally between portfolio ministers and the Minister for Finance and Administration in the first instance)
March–April	Cabinet Revenue Committee meets as required
March–May	Budget Papers and other documentation drafted principally by Treasury and DoFA with input from PM&C
April	Budget Cabinet approves final package and budget measures; pre-budget review of estimates—sensitivity analysis and assurance of agency estimates by DoFA. Consolidated budget figures (revenue and expenses) with projected bottom lines are agreed between DoFA and Treasury. Any late parameter changes are adjusted in budget figures by central agencies according to 'rule of thumb' measures
May	Budget presented to Parliament—Treasurer's Budget Speech
June	Senate estimates hearings and parliamentary questions on Budget—before passing of Budget
June–Oct	Review internal processes and prepare for next year (including one up-date of the estimates prior to the MYEFO)
Monthly—July-to-June	Reporting cycle of actual financial position by agencies and whole of government—consolidated financial statements
End of Sept	Final budget outcome—consolidated financial statements—to Auditor-general and JCPAA

procedures for compliance is a statutory provision, while other reviews covering efficiency, effectiveness and appropriateness are usually subject to negotiation or executive discretion. The Auditor-General is empowered to undertake performance audits on operational areas, but not engage in policy reviews.

There are two significant consequences of this three-year formulation-implementation-evaluation cycle. First, the experiences derived at each level may not be transferred to other levels—hence knowledge, information and expertise at any level may remain compartmentalised. Second, there is a long delay and poor feedback mechanisms between the evaluation phase and the formulation process. Lessons gleaned from the review process may take some three or four years to filter back after the initial budget decisions were made. Reporting on compliance and actual performance have traditionally been seen as the weakest links in public budgeting—and a number of governments have attempted to insist on performance data being formally integrated into the budget formulation stages. While 'in-year' budget problems generally receive on-going attention, the problems 'between years' have yet to be adequately addressed by budget reformers.

BUDGETARY FUNCTIONS IN AUSTRALIA

Budgets 'brought down' in Parliament are not necessarily aimed at a parliamentary audience. Rather, the likely audiences are manifold, each with different interests and expectations. Some audiences are inside government (agencies and departments may wish to see how well they fared), while others are outside government, including those located abroad. State governments remain anxious to discover how much the Commonwealth has agreed to provide. Banks, money markets and international traders have interests in the projected levels of government spending and borrowing. Businesses and investors have interests in economic growth rates, fiscal settings, and revenue adjustments. Social and community welfare groups and sectional lobbyists seek concessions or redistributive assistance. There is no single way in which the 'Budget' is understood and no agreed interpretation among the respective audiences.

One of the distinguishing characteristics of government budgeting (compared to household budgets or budgets in private firms) is that they operate as complex and multifarious plans produced to achieve a number of different ends. Public policy involves non-market mechanisms to acquire and allocate collective resources throughout the community. Budgets are a way of organising by political choice the distribution of desired merit goods and public services to recipients and the costs of provision to the community.

Hence, we should recognise government budgets are not uni-

functional phenomena. They fulfil a number of discrete and broad functions, some of which can be contradictory. Some functions exist but we pay little attention to them, some are emphasised greatly, while others change in importance over time. The functions we tend to emphasise will influence the types of expectations we have or questions we ask of budgets. For instance, focussing on the *financial aspects* of budgets will lead to questions about whether budgets add up (are balanced budgets or have a healthy bottom line); focusing on *allocative issues* will raise questions of efficiency or fairness and social equity. Attention to the *economic function* of budgets usually concerns the degree to which budgets stimulate or deflate the economy through fiscal strategies; those concerned about public infrastructure are raising questions of *investment* or replenishment of public assets though equity and capital injections. Those demanding evidence of strong propriety and probity in the discharge of public funds will emphasise functions of *accountability*. A composite list of the main functions budgets address is shown below in Table 2.3.

As many have argued when investigating budget outcomes, there is no necessary correlation across these functions between government intentions and consequences (Wildavsky 1964). Rather, while governments feign control over these functions (often seeking to use them authoritatively as policy levers of instruments of social engineering) unintended consequences tend not to be considered, yet frequently occur.

Table 2.3 Budgetary Functions

Key Budget Functions	Instruments	Main Aims / Concerns
Economic function	Mid-year Economic and Fiscal Outlook (MYEFO), medium-term fiscal strategy (ie, no overall call on private savings); Fiscal Balance	Fiscal discipline and stability; reception of the economic statement aimed at financial markets and business; budgets are becoming less important in macro-economic settings
Political function	Budget Speech and documentation; ministerial statements; press releases and media engagements; parliamentary debates	Reception and spin—selling a message—writing the headlines for the media; highlighting the government's record, strategies and plans
Revenue/Income function	Taxation authority and types of tax instruments, some user-charging and sale of services	Provision of resources for collective needs; notions of tax efficiency, non-arbitrariness, simplicity; fairness, compliance
Financial/outlay function	Agency resourcing (revenues and expenses); Measures; and intended outcomes	Public sector; agencies and departments; performance and financial management; compliance
Accountability function	Appropriation bills and associated documents, public scrutiny; parliamentary debates	Electorate; Parliament and JCPAA; ANAO; media; pressure groups
Allocative function	Strategic review; current priorities; policy review; contestability and CTC; revenue retention; expenditure shares;	Priority need; redistribution; services or targeted assistance; service providers; agencies; range and type of public/merit goods to the community
Investment function	Capital statements; specific policy statements/commitments	Capital works; economic and social infrastructure; asset base; equity injections
Technical efficiency function	Resource management, purchaser-provider models; price reviews, efficiency audits, best practice guides	Productivity improvement; offsets/ savings; cost effectiveness

Key Budget Functions	Instruments	Main Aims / Concerns
Exchequer function	Issuing of warrants on the availability of funds, receipts to consolidated revenue; previously a separate function to mid 1980s; now within executive (FMA Act)	Central funds management; guaranteeing the availability of money; vouching the government can honour payments; ensuring consistent practices in the collection of receipts
Territorial-jurisdictional function	Appropriation Bill No 2; plus Commonwealth-state negotiations; post-GST deal; adjustment recommendations by the Commonwealth Grants Commission	Fiscal federalism; financial assistance grants and specific purpose payments; elements of purchaser-provider relationships

BUDGETARY ROLES, ACTORS AND PROCESSES

There are a large number of actors in the Australian budgetary system. These include both key individuals and significant organisations with budgetary responsibility. One way of categorising these actors is according to the roles performed *vis-à-vis* resource allocation. Wildavsky (1964; 1975) argued that in traditional, democratic budgetary systems, two types of institutions could be detected, each of which performed specialist functions. *Guardian* actors guarded the public purse while *spending agencies* found new ways to spend more. These adversarial institutions were locked in ongoing conflictual relations over budget formulation. One set of actors, the guardians, would 'push' and seek to impose discipline knowing the spenders would 'push back' finding justifications to request more resources. Typically the guardians were the senior ministers and the central agencies with an interest in the overall fiscal strategy of the government and in issues of expenditure control or targeting. Their routine actions were often invisible to outsiders and because of their roles in holding the purse strings were often regarded as harsh or uncaring. Australian guardians include the Treasurer, Minister for Finance and their respective departments and specialist cabinet committees used explicitly to perform guardian roles (eg. the Expenditure Review Committee). On occasions the Prime Minister, as the overall coordinator of government policy, can also perform this role, but equally can be an advocate of big spending initiatives.[5] The Prime Minister's priorities or fiscal stance will depend on a range of political and economic factors, but the Prime Minister does not perform an exclusively guardian role. All these actors are central agencies and typically have little direct operational responsibilities or service delivery functions but have an overall interest in the quality of services throughout government.

By contrast, spenders include the vast array of budget-dependent agencies that each year compete for funds from the public purse. They may be 'budget maximisers' interested only in expanding their resource base, but more likely they are task-focused, service delivery agencies faced with wide and often increasing responsibilities and yet provided with what they see as insufficient resources to do the job properly. Their role is not in rationing public resources or allocating between different policy objectives, but in claiming and then deploying public resources within their own sphere of operations. If guardians perform a necessary role restricting resources, spenders perform the equally necessary task of delivering real services and handing out largesse. Governments tend to be elected and re-elected by their policy actions and service delivery record—and spenders rather than guardians tend to be their vote-winners. A government entirely of guardians would probably not survive for long (nor would it have much to do)!

The Australian budgetary system may be assessed as one in which the guardians are generally more powerful than spending agencies, but nevertheless, spenders occasionally turn the tables. Certainly, some international evidence suggests that Australian guardians are relatively stronger and more able to impose their preferences and procedures than their counterpart guardians in some other countries (Kelly and Wanna 1999). But the balance of power in guardian-spender relations vacillates and shifts over time, and a win in one year may lead to other types of compromises or defeats in subsequent years. Certainly, as will be seen in later chapters, some aspects of evolving guardian-spender relationships remain significant and change very little. Other aspects of the relationship are subject to major change and redefinition—leading to new sets of politics and game-playing.

For instance, prime ministers and their immediate staff continue

---

5 A complete list of senior ministers from 1949 (Prime Minister, Treasurer and Finance Minister) is included in Appendix A1 in this volume.

to play a large role in budget formulation and the determination of fiscal strategies—when disagreements occur amongst the guardians their personal preferences may hold sway even in the midst of serious opposition. The importance of prime ministerial power when exercised over expenditure management and budgeting is one reason for the structuring of this book into periods reflecting the tenure of heads of government. At times prime ministers have shown little interest in issues of public finance and, arguably, most are focused on issues other than budgetary management. Two examples can be used to illustrate the different outcomes that can occur. It can be argued that Gough Whitlam's lack of interest in expenditure control and public finance in general helped to precipitate the events that led to the morass in which his administration (1972–75) eventually found itself. By contrast, Bob Hawke was more economically literate but not necessarily interested in government budgeting; yet being assisted by a group of powerful economic ministers, he presided over a period of tight fiscal management leading to successive budget surpluses in the late 1980s. Leadership style, interest and personal preferences are particularly powerful parameters within which public budgeting occurs in Australia. Moreover, as illustrated successively through the terms of Fraser, Hawke, Keating and Howard, the agendas and preferences of prime ministers on budget matters are far from consistent throughout their period in office, fluctuating markedly according to their assessments of the economic and political circumstances faced from year to year.

Other features shaping the relations between guardians and spenders can also change markedly and some repeatedly. The Fraser government in the mid-1970s restructured the guardian actors by creating new arrangements and specialist roles. While Fraser's interest was not centred on the role of budget guardianship, but much more on broad economic policy, his almost incidental creation of the Department of Finance is arguably one of the pivotal administrative changes since federation. It is ironic that the establishment of a new budget guardian was a by-product of attempts to temper the influence of Treasury. Nevertheless, in many ways the decision to create a discrete budget guardian began a new era in public financial management—with some global repercussions in the ways Australian reforms have guided other nations.

Subsequently, a further budget actor was added—the Minister for Finance. For a quarter of a century the role of Finance ministers has varied enormously with the personality and interest of the person. Perhaps the most important characterisation of Finance ministers is whether they were active or passive in pursuing the duties of their office. Some, such as Senator Peter Walsh, 1984–90, occupied centre stage and saw it as a matter of honour or a crusade to enhance the department's expenditure restraint role. Alongside the financial management initiatives pushed by the guardian technocrats in his department, Walsh used his political influence in cabinet and its powerful budget committee to impose fiscal discipline. Other Finance ministers have been more passive. On occasions even passivity has its advantages; in Finance's case enabling departmental administrators to experiment relatively freely with different forms of resource management, evaluation or contestability. Ministerial commitment and support for technocratic endeavours, rather than personal involvement in initiatives are often one of the signs of an effective guardian in the Minister for Finance.

Hence Australia, like Canada, now operates with two central agencies responsible for guarding the integrity of the budget. The Department of Finance and Administration coordinates expenditure—overseeing the financial, allocative and technical efficiency aspects of the budget. It collates and 'validates' estimates information from spending departments on expenditure commitments, advises on new spending proposals, and oversees the budget process and final consolidation of most budget papers. As one of the original departments dating from federation, the Treasury maintains a role in budget policy and advising on fiscal strategies. Treasury also advises cabinet on budgetary matters and taxation policy and intergovernmental transfers. It has a much wider role in economic policy matters more generally. Along with the Department of the Prime Minister and Cabinet, the guardian departments of Finance and Administration and Treasury are key advisers to the Expenditure Review Committee of cabinet.

Budget processes prescribe the ways in which certain tasks are organised or accomplished. Processes may be descriptive in the sense that they describe a sequential order in which events or tasks occur. They may also be prescriptive in the sense that they dictate ways in which tasks must be ordered or related. The public sector and the many forms of public provision are both organised and operationalised according to such processes and rules. In some circumstances rules may offer routine and order in place of confusion or chaos. But equally it is also recognised that existing rules place constraints on the ways departments can organise resources and so place further constraints upon the ways in which managers can act. Hence, the rules and routines of budgeting governing the behaviour of participant actors have been subjected to major and successive waves of reform.

The history of public expenditure management in Australia since the 1960s can be seen as a series of attempts to re-define the rules that govern the behaviour of both spending departments and individual managers in their resource decisions. Traditionally, the primary tool of guardians was to impose detailed financial controls over departmental expenditures. Reform initiatives introduced greater operational flexibility while imposing strict performance requirements on agencies and managers. Guardians became less concerned with controlling detailed input amounts (expenditure items and new claims) and more focused on resource management frameworks, results monitoring and the reallocation of resources to new priorities. Mostly Australia's moves towards new public expenditure management systems can be seen as attempts to free-up and better utilise these resources from a guardian's perspective to allow policy goals to be achieved.

Because guardian-spender relations are themselves contestable, processes are frequently used to disturb or dismantle rules and predictable routines. Guardian actors such as DoFA repeatedly seek to change routines that they consider to have few remaining benefits; especially if spenders have become comfortable or complacent. As argued in Chapter 1 there is no perfect system or set of processes. There is no necessary science to a system of budgetary rules and many processes could conceivably be located or operated at various points in the system. Over time and with the increasing utilisation of information technology (with comprehensive budgetary information available instantaneously), new possibilities emerge and the nature and location of processes can be periodically reconsidered.

The devolution of financial management was undertaken for two main reasons: because central controls were eventually considered to have become ineffective and because devolution also imposed a rationing function on the spenders—forcing them to become more guardian-like (Kelly and Wanna 2000a). Financial resources are also fungible in the sense that they are movable, flexible and transferable, and can be deployed in a great many potential ways. Transaction costs and incentive structures can be re-considered and trade-offs made over the forms of budgetary processes with some disappearing and others being transferred to spenders. The guardians meanwhile will move on to introduce new processes they deem to improve their ability to monitor resources or impose efficiencies on the use of resources. In addition, given the unequal nature of the power relations between guardians and spenders, any devolved processes can be reclaimed if necessary. Hence, Australian central agencies have held onto or relaxed the control of processes and in many ways this is a crucial part of their power as guardians.

Other actors are particularly important in selected aspects of the disbursement of Commonwealth funds. State Premiers and Treasurers meet annually or as required with the Commonwealth in *councils of ministers* (previously Premiers' Conferences). These play a role in allocating intergovernmental transfers and reporting the performance of service delivery in sub-national governments. These *ad hoc* institutions form to negotiate amounts either as general financial assistance grants or as tied grants (special purpose payments where the Commonwealth has a major say in the uses of the funds). In 2000–01 total Commonwealth grants to the states including the GST were $44 billion or 25% of total outlays. The Commonwealth government can also negotiate with states and territories separately, but not so as to disadvantage any state relative to others. The Australian Loan Council, formed in 1927 as a joint council of Commonwealth and state governments, exists to regulate the amounts of public borrowing occurring in any one period. This body essentially prevents the states from borrowing to supplement their recurrent costs or over-committing themselves with debt.

Finally, some mention should be made of the non-guardian/non-spender institutions that oversee public expenditure, authorise its use and improve accountability. Parliament, but not the Constitution, insists on an *annual* appropriation of resources (rather than for shorter or longer term—perhaps to the full term of the Parliament). In place of guarding, the Parliament authorises and scrutinises expenditure proposals presented to it by the guardians. Although the process of public scrutiny is fundamental to our democracy, parliamentary influence or criticism tends to have little impact on the annual Budget. On occasions Parliament has complained of being under-represented in budget deliberations and marginalised from the process (Uhr 1999; HRSCE 1979:10–12; Walsh 1991). Parliamentary budget debates are too late to exert influence on the current budget and too early to impact on the next. However, general parliamentary debates and ongoing scrutiny given to particular activities or budget measures may have significant influence on the executive's formulation of the next budget.

In this sense, parliamentary scrutiny is both important and influential in holding the executive to account over the use of public funds.

Since the 1970s Senate committees (organised to investigate estimates and public accounts) have become more active in reviewing the budget, government finances and operations. Their deliberations and audit reviews of compliance and performance occur in public in the implementation and evaluation stages of the budget cycle. Estimates hearings have a wide brief to question ministers and officials on policy issues as well as intended expenditure plans. A Joint Committee of Public Accounts and Audit regularly examines the financial activities of government focusing not only on issues of compliance but also managerial practices, efficiency and effectiveness in public administration. It relies on expert opinion from the Auditor-General on the financial statements of government and agency performance. The committee receives reports of the Auditor-General and is regularly briefed by the Auditor-General and staff of the Australian National Audit Office. The committee has also closely scrutinised the role of auditing in terms of audit independence, integrity, and the use of private sector auditors within the public sector. A major overhaul of the audit and financial legislation was undertaken in the early 1990s largely at the behest of the public accounts committee.

The last actor arguably with an eye to accountability is the media and some interest groups with a concern in holding the government to account. Their dissection of the political and financial aspects of government budgeting can provide a powerful and testing forum, simultaneously allowing government to sell its message while subjecting it to criticism or approval. These actors have no formal role and their interest may be variable from time to time, but they assist in the accountability of public budgets.

The discussion in this chapter presents the Australian budgetary system as it currently operates. Although the basic constitutional constraints were in place from federation, many of the elements of this system have emerged since the 1960s. It is argued that the 1960s represents an important watershed in the development of government budgeting in Australia. It is to the 'great expectations' of the 1960s that we now turn.

3 Great expectations: the promise of early budget reforms

In the 1960s and early 1970s public expenditure was increasing rapidly both in real terms and as a proportion of GDP. Expenditure growth was fuelled by government activism and an inability to withstand political pressures. The policy appetite of government had been whetted and ministers were increasingly interested in 'program' options to ameliorate social and economic problems and further national development. Resource needs burgeoned as governance became more expansive with wider responsibilities. Revenues rose and with additional expenditure available successive governments competed with each other to do more with more. As the apparatus of state became more complex and more adventurous, pressure was placed on the traditional ways of forming budgets, allocating resources and controlling expenditure. Bigger government needed better and more appropriate resourcing systems. Governments in this period were unclear about the nature of budget reform and ways to achieve expenditure control—in this context the system of forward estimates evolved as the main instrument of budget reform to the mid–1970s.

'BOTTOM-UP' BUDGETING IN THE 1960s AND EARLY 1970s

Budgets present the collective expenditure decisions of government; or more accurately bundle up the many 'items' of spending covering the range of activities ministers have wished to pursue or could not refuse. Budget allocations are statements of commission, recording what is intended. Conversely, they communicate by omission the areas governments feel less able to support or in which they have less interest. Over time budgets chart the triumphs and occasional defeats of ministers, agencies and interest groups, and each increase establishes a new base-line from which they could hope to secure further resources. While politicians are one cause of increased spending, the budget system itself has tended to have an upward ratchet-effect on expenditures.

The system of government budgeting evolving over the post-war years consisted of disaggregated and dispersed processes of incremental decision-making brought together both by and for the annual cycle of parliamentary appropriation. Annual budgets were by definition approval-oriented documents oriented toward the short-term. They consisted of very detailed cash allocations classified into 'line items' (separate amounts listed for each item of expenditure). Parliament then approved these items as identifiable objects of expenditure rather than for any purpose for which they may have been intended. Spending departments received 12 months funding which had to be spent within the time frame—and many routinely overspent. Supplementary funding midway through the budget year also allowed for regular top-ups. If departments conserved resources or spent too slowly during the year, those surpluses remained in consolidated revenue. There were no rewards for conserving resources. Consequently, departments felt obliged to conduct a big end-of-year spend-up in the last months of the financial year.

Preparing budgets in the 1960s involved sequential bilateral negotiations between 'guardian' and 'spending' agencies. Resource allocations largely followed inherited patterns that were augmented year-on-year by some annual inflation factor or estimated cost adjustment. New policies and requests for additional resources were presented as new bids and regularly transmitted to cabinet and budget agencies throughout the year. The budget was formed by 'bottom-up' incremental processes that were both laborious and time-consuming. Budget information was gathered together manually to enter into a centralised budget ledger system that had been computerised in the early 1950s (using a central mainframe computer).[1] But it was often difficult to get timely information and in

1 The term central ledger was used to describe the record of cash receipts and payments for the government as a whole, and was centralised in Treasury. From the 1950s data was transmitted by tape from the sub-treasuries (state offices) to Canberra, and then converted into punch cards and processed by Stats main-frame calculators and later by the Treasury's main-frame computer. Details

some cases impossible to get any (e.g. on asset holdings). There was no coherent overall fiscal framework into which the pieces must be shaped to fit. The control problem was thus two-fold: not only were expenditure levels continually moving targets against which to plan and match revenues, but the process created a situation where it was hard to discipline spending departments and keep them to their budget intentions. Profligate spending at the ministerial level simply compounded these problems.

The consequent lack of consistent and detailed knowledge of expenditure commitments made any overall budgetary planning and prioritisation difficult. Although cabinet first considered issues on the 'expenditure side' of the budget and then adjusted the 'revenue side', they had little notion of the magnitude of expenditure commitments for the year ahead or likely revenue requirements in the future. Putting the budget together was less a matter of foresight and planning than conjecture and supposition. Not knowing the costs of commitments for the period ahead, made it difficult to determine the total level of expenditures or revenues needed. Public sector borrowing and deficit financing were often required to make government revenues and expenditures balance.

Under such circumstances the best and most reliable indicators available for formulating budgets came from the actual levels of expenditure in the previous year's budget aggregated on an agency by agency basis. Precedent was thus the best predictor of future resource needs. In turn, this encouraged departments to both avoid underspending at all costs and occasionally overspend to demonstrate they had greater needs.

Few politicians of the late 1960s showed any great interest or concern in over-spending or debt levels.[2] There was also no great knowledge among politicians about either expenditure management or the consequences of long term debt repayment obligations. There was far more electoral kudos to be gained from initiating projects and building empires—variously called the 'ribbon cutting' mentality or the even more cynical view of 'spend today and leave the debts to one's opponents'. Ministers loved to over-estimate their expenditure needs as a way of advertising the government's

---

of total expenditure could be produced at the end of a given period (month, quarter, year) and was generally available about two to three days after the close of the period.

2 There were some exceptions: for example Les Bury and Paul Hasluck. The issue of deficit spending is treated separately in Chapter 11.

'good intentions'. Cabinets frequently committed to policy decisions without either any knowledge of the real costs or future financial implications. Governments appeared sanguine that there would always be sufficient resources for their purposes regardless of the consequences.[3] An ideology of Keynesian demand management and pump-priming seemed appropriate in an era of high economic growth, a buoyant world economy and favourable commodity prices (Whitwell 1986).

Even ministers with direct oversight of the budget were not necessarily cognisant of their responsibilities. Records show that cabinet rarely became involved in debating budgetary parameters or debating medium term strategies. Overall budgetary responsibility was the province of a single minister—the Treasurer—and the appointment of such a 'guardian' minister did not guarantee capability or interest in the portfolio. Within cabinet the position of Treasurer was a prized ministerial appointment, but often the lucky incumbent was inexperienced and ignorant of the requirements of the portfolio (especially in the case of Treasurers Arthur Fadden, Harold Holt, William McMahon and Billy Snedden). Treasury officials considered it fortunate if such ministers could 'follow the Treasury brief' and stick to it. It is perhaps an extreme example, but on his first day as Treasurer in 1971 Snedden asked what the letters *cr* and *dr* meant when provided with briefing papers and financial statements from Treasury officials (Craik Interview 1996). Post-war ministers indubitably relied on Treasury for instruction and advice.

THE SEARCH FOR EFFECTIVE INFORMATION ON EXPENDITURE PROJECTIONS

The Accounting and Supply Division of Treasury traditionally produced *budget estimates* for the year ahead. Such annual estimates were the basis of the appropriation bills and Budget papers presented to Parliament, where they were often the subject of

---

3 One former Treasury official recalled that in the early 1960s 'when a department wanted funds in the Additional Estimates during the year, all it really had to do was convince Treasury that it would in fact spend those funds. I do not recall any cases where a department was told it would have to reduce its expenditure so that it would remain within the Budget figure' (Monaghan, written correspondence 2000).

criticism. The Joint Committee on Public Accounts made numerous criticisms between 1954 and 1962 about the inaccuracy or the annual estimates and the practice of 'over-estimating' expenditure to allow some scope for new activities in the year ahead. Treasury responded in 1963 (Minute 63/703) by adopting three principles on which to construct estimates:

- The estimates figure for any item should be the sum that is expected to be spent;
- It should not include amounts for proposals that are so far from firm that it is not possible to know what payments, if any, will be made; and
- But where the item is for a type of recurring expense (for example office services, travelling expenses) it is appropriate to budget on the basis of experience.

Such principles were intended to give greater rigour to estimates preparation. Treasury also sought to advance the agenda by gathering information together about the likely expenditure requirements *beyond* those collected for the immediate budget round. Yet, if the determination of annual estimates was fraught with problems, the process of projecting estimate needs for future years was a minefield.

When *forecasted estimates* of expenditure were first introduced, they were *not collected for expenditure control purposes*, but to provide an idea of the projected magnitude of expenditure and the available scope for new initiatives. Such 'informal' Treasury projections, however, were not incorporated into the budgetary process nor were they used as a basis for departmental claims for on-going or further budgetary resources. Although expenditure estimates later became a favoured procedure for limiting expenditure, at the time they were intended to enhance the information base of Treasury for planning purposes—particularly for fiscal policy and macro-economic settings. Yet, acquiring such knowledge and information was an evolutionary step in the eventual quest for expenditure control.

It now seems remarkable that the demand for accurate information on expenditure requirements is a relatively recent phenomenon in the history of public finance. In general government accounting, Treasury traditionally performed the essential functions of overseeing the provision of funds to spending agencies and then monitoring amounts spent over the time period of the budget as implied in the Australian Constitution.[4] By the mid–1960s Treasury began to argue that if they could shift emphasis from a *fait accompli* mentality to expenditure prediction and planning, then there was a better chance of holding budgets in balance. At the time, showing a budget apparently in balance was often politically more important than eliminating deficits or reducing debt. Public pressure to prevent revenues from continually snowballing, especially as high inflation began to bite, further underscored the need to balance budgets.

Treasury became particularly interested in extending its budgetary functions to include the production of expenditure forecasts based on information about prospective outlay requirements. Interest in producing forecasts did not arise from political or public pressure but came from *within* the Treasury. Forecasting was undertaken for its own benefit in framing economic policy advice. The collation of confidential estimates signalled that Treasury were increasingly becoming frustrated by their demonstrable lack of fiscal control and consequently were anxious to adopt a more pro-active role in planning and preparing for expansions or emerging commitments.[5]

To assist in determining fiscal policy and preparing for likely revenue/borrowing levels, Treasury began to collate projected resource requirements so that future trends could be factored into the fiscal planning for next year's budget. Projections involved assuming an ongoing policy context subject to minimal change or review. Ministers were *not* involved and Treasury generally refrained from attempting to predict how cabinets might respond to new submissions or unfolding events. And, part of the purpose in collating these estimates was to indicate to governments the projected costs of known commitments in order to impress on cabinet the need to restrict the scope to commit to new initiatives. Forecasts were intended in part to quell the appetite of politicians for additional spending—or as one former Treasury official put it 'to scare hell out of them'.

Initially, Treasury sought better information on outlays purely for its internal purposes. The information was not intended for government or Parliament, nor was it used for planning purposes in spending departments. Gradually, centrally collected information

---

4 Section 83 of the Australian Constitution states that 'no money shall be drawn from the Treasury of the Commonwealth except under appropriation made by law'. This section has often been interpreted to mean that Treasury has a special responsibility over public funds.

5 See Treasury's submission to RCAGA 1975.

allowed Treasury to appear more authoritative and professional in its preparation of budgetary figures and, potentially, more powerful in its relations with other departments. So forecast information was sought, not essentially to enhance the role or decision-making capabilities of government, but to enhance the role of Treasury in budget formation. Although expenditure estimates were a 'minor undertaking' for Treasury (Weller and Cutt 1976:70) they offered the budget agency the prospect of moving onto the front foot in dealing with spending departments. Unfortunately, they could also arouse the ire of treasurers and prime ministers when forecasts were wrong (and in the late 1960s expenditure forecasts were generally too conservative), or when Treasury itself decided which projections to let governments see and which to withhold, as they did in 1974 (see Hawker *et al.*1979).

The motivation to forecast future outlays and construct estimates of likely expenditure needs came *before* the real onset of fiscal stringency and demands to cutback the size of the public sector. In the late 1960s Treasury's rationale for undertaking expenditure projections was largely about ensuring adequate resources were available for the expanding state. In their Keynesian paradigm, the public sector was committed to keeping unemployment low, and levels of government expenditure were necessary to avoid recession (including resorting to deficits). Hence, estimates of expenditure needs were useful to Treasury in deciding whether adjustments in levels of taxation were necessary through the budget process or in gauging the magnitude of borrowings to be negotiated. Estimates of future commitments were *not initially about imposing cuts to expenditure* or tailoring expenditure levels to resource intakes. Governments simply needed better expenditure information in order to adjust revenue or borrowing.

FROM GUESSING TO BIDDING—TREASURY'S INTERNAL ESTIMATES OF EXPENDITURE

So, from 1965 onwards Treasury began to collect informal information on expected or anticipated future outlays using 'bottom up' assessments of expenditure needs.[6] The process of assessment remained centralised in the sense that Treasury did not consider

6 For a summary of the stages of development of the forward estimates system from 1965 to 2000 see Appendix B in this volume.

that the active involvement of spending departments would greatly assist the process, feeling such involvement would only serve to complicate estimates with ambit claims, pre-emptive bids or padding. However, departments often contributed raw figures for existing policies and provided other information as requested. Not surprisingly, the resulting estimates were influenced by Treasury's own biases as well as its partially self-imposed lack of detailed knowledge of specific policy and administrative areas.

Prior to 1971 the 'informal' estimate projections were gathered and collated by the economic policy officers in the General Financial and Economic Policy Division of Treasury. They were also sometimes asked to forecast likely needs. Treasury originally projected these figures forward over three years, estimating 'known' expenditure requirements and adding any other predicted changes (e.g. demographic shifts) onto the range of budgetary line items. But these bottom-up forward estimates costed only 'existing policies' and were assembled without the inclusion of any new policy priorities cabinet might be considering or were likely to decide in the near future. Projections did not include any new initiatives departments were intending to submit. As well, these early projections (as a later Treasury Circular 1971/8:20 explained) were 'prepared on the assumption that all prices, wage rates and costs will remain at levels prevailing at the time the estimates [were] prepared'. As inflation began to rise at the onset of the 1970s, this methodology could not be sustained.

The figures did not need to be precise as they were simply produced for internal working purposes and even through to the mid–1970s some senior Treasury staff remained dismissive. Only a few officers were involved in preparation and the department regarded the process as a 'comparatively minor undertaking'. Treasury's 'unofficial' estimates, therefore, did not constitute commitments to fund activities. Indeed, 'expenditure trends were calculated only for existing programmes and were not regarded as any sort of commitment' (Weller and Cutt 1976: 70). Significantly, these early projections were not part of the budget process, and given the limitations on the information served as little more than informal guides.

In the course of time these projections became known as 'forward financial estimates', and as the process of calculating and producing them evolved, the meanings and implications of the term markedly changed. From the early days the primary function of forward estimates, from Treasury's perspective, was to assist in macro-economic planning. Some speculation on the magnitude and scope of public expenditure was seen as necessary for fiscal policy planning and used for incorporation into the department's macro-economic projections/scenarios. Estimates of expenditure were gathered to provide Treasury with the guesstimates necessary to formulate general economic policy advice. Any other function the estimates might then serve was purely of secondary consideration.

Consequently, as Treasury explained publicly to the Coombs Commission in 1974, macro-economic planning was the original and principal reason why a system of forward estimates was developed. They were not initially central to expenditure management as they would later become. It was argued that the only possible way for Treasury to be able to fulfil its responsibilities, as the central agency responsible for economic policy, was to incorporate detailed knowledge about expected expenditure patterns in the public sector. Treasury also argued to Coombs that general economic policy advice required information from the supply divisions which then provided them with the capacity to judge future borrowing requirements, as well as the size of government deficits and surpluses. Treasury also suggested the preparation and use of forward estimates provided compelling arguments opposing any suggestion of splitting the department. Paradoxically, the Treasury's post-war preoccupation with short-term macro-economic management deflected it from its core role of controlling government expenditure.

Speculative information on estimates was initially regarded as confidential and only likely to exacerbate budget planning problems if released. In response to this confidentiality, some spending departments began producing their own internal estimates for planning purposes. Treasury's cautious and secretive nature inevitably shaped the way in which budgetary instruments were devised and used. For instance, early estimates were not in any sense 'authorised' as official figures and Treasury was not prepared to allow them to be used as base budget figures. Indeed, Treasury was often reluctant to divulge these speculative, informal estimates of expenditure even to cabinet ministers. Moreover, when estimates were used as part of the briefing process, Treasury was not prepared to endorse them as accurate indicators. Such reluctance derived from the department's understanding of its continuous guardian role over public finance. Treasury regarded itself as a permanent institution of state, whereas elected governments came and went.

Senior officers within Treasury did not necessarily see or ask to see the estimate figures, particularly if they were not heading one of the supply divisions. The Treasurer rarely if ever saw a composite picture of all estimates although was often briefed on matters where departmental advice was shaped by these projections. The Prime Minister and cabinet were not routinely informed on the details of Treasury's estimates or how they were formulated—a situation that eventually led to demands for information and political tension with elected governments. Relations between the Treasury and the Coalition governments led by John Gorton and William McMahon began to cool in contrast to the relative closeness (and tightness with expenditure) that distinguished relations with the Menzies government. Certainly some officers in Treasury considered cabinet ministers as potential enemies with different motives and agendas from the national interest. Senior politicians often saw Treasury in the same light.

UNCERTAIN EXPECTATIONS: FORWARD ESTIMATES AND BUDGETARY CONTROL

During the early 1970s the construction of forward estimates became more sophisticated as their role evolved. They became more systematic and the method of producing information became more technical and thorough. Cabinet ministers were now routinely circulated with Forward Estimates Memoranda (usually in

October-November and between March and May). More reliable forward estimates offered a way to plan and control expenditure outlays—along perhaps with other potential initiatives such as program-based forms of budgeting which were under discussion in Treasury around the same time (Minute 68/946).[7] Certainly from a central agency's perspective, forward estimates provided some forecast of line item expenditure levels which could be used to help limit or frame departmental levels of expenditure. If forward estimates could be made accurate and then fixed, they opened the possibility of allowing greater control of future expenditures.

This potential for increased control served as an incentive to Treasury to further the evolution of forward estimates as a *budgetary* instrument. Control as opposed to forecasting began to be their motivator, but while forward estimates remained internal working calculations and not intended for public disclosure their effectiveness was inevitably limited. Confidentiality restricted the usefulness of forward estimates, confining their role to the informal budgetary processes. They became part of a specialised language practiced by budgetary mandarins, but not yet a component of a publicly disclosed system of control. There are parallels here with the account Weber provides of the ancient Egyptian bureaucracy who employed a secret language for budgetary purposes so that others would not know their books.

In March 1971 the Treasurer, Les Bury, with the support of Prime Minister McMahon, wrote to ministers announcing a revised and more open system of collating forward estimates. His letter and subsequent Treasury circulars explained the revised format and new procedures. The Treasurer wrote of 'treading new ground during the first exercise' and taking a first step 'towards improving

---

7 Treasury had been studying program budgeting and the US experimentation with Planning, Programming and Budgeting Systems (PPBS). Well over a decade before Australian governments became interested in program budgeting, Treasury produced a briefing paper to the Treasurer recommending a 'program budgeting' trial be undertaken in one department. A draft cabinet submission was produced in December 1969 which advocated budgets based on outputs, long-term planning estimates, measurements of program effectiveness and systematic analysis of policy issues. The draft was given to the Treasurer Les Bury who reputedly carried the submission around in his brief case for 'many weeks' before returning it 'soaked in whisky' with his approval. However, the program budgeting initiative was sacrificed to the apparently more pressing needs of getting the forward estimates system up and running (Monaghan, written correspondence 2000).

our procedures and towards the provision of more adequate information upon which the government may base its policy decisions' (Treasury Circular 1971/8). The revised procedures allowed departments to submit estimates for *new proposals* as well as for existing activities. Bury agreed that over time forward estimates 'will become an integral part of our budgetary procedures and economic analysis. They will enable ministers to consider policy and expenditure proposals within a framework of the government's known and anticipated forward commitments and the resources possibly available over the period of the forward estimates to meet these commitments'. Moreover, responsibility for producing the new forward estimates was given to the departmental expenditure specialists within Treasury—the Accounting and Supply Division—which routinely worked through the details of spending requirements with departments.[8]

The desire for greater reliability in the final figures necessarily saw the spending departments and authorities become more involved in the process of collation of data for the estimates, if not their actual construction. These departments had a better idea of the prospective expenditure requirements (and new policy proposals) within their specific spheres of activity. Once the method of constructing forward estimates gave more weight to input of spending departments, their respective ministers had to 'approve' the estimates-information communicated to Treasury. This reform was originally welcomed by spending ministers and embraced as a device to help them retain control over the policies and agendas within their own departments. Yet, the formal approval of estimates also implied a formal commitment by ministers and their departments to which they would generally be held. The evolution of public management is full of such unintended consequences.

The process of compiling forward estimates was expanded in 1971 to include *anticipated* expenditure information *from* departments—a process open to some abuse. Estimates went from being

---

8 One option had been to convert the 'informal' future estimates produced by the General Financial and Economic Policy (GFEP) Division into official forward estimates. This was recognised by Treasury but in March 1968 the head of GFEP suggested the production of official 3-year estimates should be undertaken by the accounting and budget supply people. At the time nothing directly came of this, but the proposal suggests that even inside Treasury there was beginning to be an awareness that the economic policy section may not be the best unit to collate the official forward estimates.

informal projections to a system of declared bids. Treasury was keen to restrict the figures for new proposals to 'foreseeable expenditures for which ministers intend to seek government approval'. New proposals, in Treasury's view, did not include a list of everything departments would like, but only the costs of proposals 'the minister firmly intends to put forward over the period'. Departmental figures also had to distinguish costings for existing policies from those attributed to new policy proposals, as well as securing ministerial endorsement for both sets of projections. In theory, spending ministers had some reason to limit the out-of-budget-year demands for resources from within their own departments.

There was another reason for involving spending departments in the setting of forward estimates: previously they did not have to consider the full *future* expenditure implications of policy proposals. Treasury officials had long been concerned that new bids and changes to policy were approved by cabinet without much analysis of the long-term implications. Spending departments relied simply on the argument that government would have to provide for whatever actuals or entitlements would subsequently occur. However, Treasury believed that if departments were forced to calculate and consider the future implications of their submissions, and then defend the implied medium-term impositions in their submission, cabinet would then have better information from which to make its decision, and perhaps offset or limit future exposure. Urging departments to take a multi-year view was intended to help reduce major cost blowouts or other foreseeable hikes in outlays.

Nonetheless, Treasury was not overly optimistic about the success or accuracy of the new estimates. A circular from the Treasury Secretary, Sir Richard Randall, to other departments was frank, admitting 'it will be appreciated by all that the first forward estimates of Commonwealth expenditure to be collected shortly after the Budget this year [1971] may not be as accurate or as fully indicative of ministerial intentions as we expect they will later become'. He acknowledged that there could be 'difficulties in distinguishing what is continuing commitment covered by "existing policy" and what represents a new proposal that has yet to be approved by the Government'. He also warned of the dangers of losing some flexibility in allocating resources to meet changing priorities. Even at this stage Randall foresaw ministers being locked-in to their intentions as forward estimates became approved. Thus ministers had one rationale in 'approving' estimates information while Treasury was already warning of 'locking-in' resources.

The new process of constructing forward estimates in the days before desk-top computers was laborious. Estimates were put together by hand involving frequent revisions and adjustments (even with a computer-assisted central ledger system). Estimates for one, two and three years ahead were required from departments in January of the year of submission, and then assembled centrally by Treasury. The preliminary input data were then compared with previous allocations adjusted for any known variations or changes in legislation/policy. The formal process then intended that 'estimates submitted by departments will be examined by Treasury and talks will proceed with departments with the aim of reaching a mutual understanding of the costing of proposals and the split of expenditure between that covered by "existing" policy and that still requiring government approval'. After the delivery of the Budget to Parliament the estimates for the second and third years were revised, and towards the end of the calender year the estimates of the immediate budget year ahead were revised in light of developments and changing conditions. These revised estimates were then used as a guide to the next round of three year estimates due in January.

Meanwhile, once Treasury had 'clarified' items in discussions with departments (usually by March), the Treasury was in a position to aggregate the estimates, known as the 'draft estimates', and present them to government along with a 'commentary on their implications for trends in Commonwealth expenditure and economic conditions'. At this early stage in their evolution, draft estimates were still not automatically the base for the real budget estimates, nor were they a substitute for the budgetary submission process (the round of bids coming from departments). Rather, the eventual estimates used to form the budget (the actual 'budget estimates') still had to be re-negotiated with Treasury separately and in greater detail than the forward estimates process. This was a more exacting process as these *budget* estimates would form the basis of the itemised funding for the agencies.

Three types of estimates were produced for expenditure planning purposes—expenditure, revenue and staffing. Departments submitted estimates on both expenditure and revenue. However, unlike budget estimates, forward estimates for staff included provisions for approved 'establishment' numbers whenever they were approved (and not subject to a set date, such as 1 July)[9]. Between 1972 and 1973 Treasurers Billy Snedden (Liberal) and Frank Crean (Labor) both nudged along the estimates process, by requiring that expenditure estimates should be presented in a functional classification of outlays indicating the 'purposes' for which it was intended. Such functional presentation was not intended as a form of *program* allocation (a related initiative that had some early support in Treasury), but simply to identify 'recognisable and meaningful groupings which lend themselves to discussion and analysis' (RCAGA 1976: 1/81). Crean announced in May 1973 that a more ambitious system of *program budgeting* would be devised, within which functional estimates would be a key pillar (see Weller and Cutt 1976). Yet it would take until 1985 for forward and budget estimates to be structured on a program basis (DoF 1984f), while *program budgeting* remained an illusive 'holy grail' for successive governments—constantly sought but never actually acquired.

Treasury produced its first *Forward Estimates Report* in 1972, an internal report summarising expenditure commitments and prospective budget outlays. These confidential reports were produced for Treasury and were available to the cabinet, usually coinciding with the Budget Cabinet meeting held in July (Groenewegen 1973). However, the reports contained only aggregate estimates and after 1973 were typically presented according to 'functional classifications' rather than on the basis of detailed 'line items' by department. Other more detailed estimates remained internal Treasury documents. For over ten years this annual report was produced within the central budgetary agency, before it was authorised for release beyond the agency's walls.

Initially, the Whitlam government endorsed Treasury's revised procedures in collecting forward estimates, and established a special ministerial committee to oversee the development of these initiatives (which met just once in February 1973). Labor also linked the estimates process to the Priorities Review Staff for the purposes of helping create strategic guidelines for expenditure policy (Boston 1980; Weller and Cutt 1976:111–117). Greater attention was also directed to expenditure matters after the establishment in January 1975 of a special cabinet sub-committee—the Expenditure Review Committee—with six ministers accompanied by their heads of department.[10] This 'inner cabinet' attempted to bring some overall discipline to expenditure decisions in the heady days of 1975.

---

9 Establishment figures for departments were approved staffing levels based on profiles calculated and set by the Public Service Board.

10 With hindsight, Whitlam described the ERC as 'the most significant reform in the policy making process established by my Government' (Whitlam 1985:690).

However, as discussed in Chapter 5, relations between the Whitlam ministry and the Treasury deteriorated rapidly after 1973. Arguably, Treasury began to see its role as separate from serving the government of the day, as if it had a special charter bestowed on it by the Constitution to protect the public purse even from government. Indeed, there is evidence of an erosion of confidence between Treasury and government. In particular, a stand-off arose with the 1974 Budget over the release of detailed forward estimates, when Treasury refused to show projected figures to the Prime Minister's department. The government insisted on seeing them. Eventually the Prime Minister's economics adviser Fred Gruen was permitted by Treasury to see the detailed estimates, but only on condition that he consult them in the Treasury building and not take any documents away. Such a stand-off arising from the intense political circumstances of the day would seem inconceivable in years to come.

DEFICIENCIES AND DISILLUSIONMENT WITH FORWARD ESTIMATES

Criticisms and critiques of the value of forward estimates arose almost from their introduction. Although the idea of forward estimates was often welcomed, the figures initially were poorly developed, inconsistently used and (contrary to some claims, for example, to the Royal Commission into Australian Government Administration) not well integrated into decision-making systems. Because estimates were not a formal part of the budget process it is difficult to judge how far estimates were useful in arriving at budgetary decisions. The accuracy of the estimates was also problematic in two ways: Treasury's estimates were not necessarily realistic projections of actual spending patterns, and once spending departments had the chance to inject their own figures they often inflated them or treated them as ambit resource claims. By the

---

Whitlam's ERC was balanced between 'spending' and 'monitoring' agencies and included a two-phase process with an officials' committee meeting ahead of the ministerial committee (at which the same officials were also present). Commenting on the arrangements, Whitlam stated 'even if we did not see the lions actually lie down with the lambs, we were able to supervise the conditions in which the lions roared at others and at each other' (1985:690).

mid–1970s forward estimates were little more than exaggerated projections of anticipated budget bids.

Accordingly, the estimates process suffered because it was not taken seriously by Treasury, cabinets, and spending departments (Weller and Cutt 1976:72–73). Forward estimates were certainly not intended or used as a firm budgetary base. As long as forward estimates were 'disconnected' from the annual budgetary system, they remained a marginal exercise. Moreover, because expenditure estimates were not intended as a base for the budget estimates, those responsible for constructing the figures did not have to be sticklers for precision. Some concessions and guesstimates could be accepted precisely because the figures were not intended to roll into the budget figures. Hence, the estimates initiative became locked in a vicious circle: the estimates process was not tied to the budgetary process, so forward estimates were not taken seriously, and because they were not taken seriously there was reluctance to incorporate them into the budgetary process.

There was a further argument that the production of forward estimates consumed considerable amounts of time and resources, and if they were not to be used to set expenditures then one could question why the public service bothered producing them. Projections of spending extending three years out from the budget year were regarded as dubious and little more than pure speculation. Weller has argued that the estimates became 'pre-first bids' and 'mere wish-lists . . . unrestrained by budget parameters' (Weller 1977:32). Treasury 'regarded them with derision' and gave scant attention to figures for the second and third years. These points were echoed in the report of a Task Force on Forward Estimates (1977) which argued:

> Estimates for the second and third years can . . . have a bearing on the decisions taken in relation to year one. But it remains true that the forward estimates have not really been used for longer-term planning purposes. It is said that the forward estimates simply are not good enough for planning purposes and this view certainly appears to be true of the estimates collected in the past. There would however seem to be scope for improving the quality of estimates for the second and third years.[11]

Such criticisms reflected the concerns of many Treasury officials

---

11 See Report of the IDC Task Force on Forward Estimates February (1977:6–7).

who regarded forward estimates as notoriously inaccurate and not a good guide to eventual outlays (see RCAGA Appendix 1C). If rational managerial behaviour in the spending departments implied that estimates tended to be inflated, then it was unlikely that much detailed work would go into their production or that much credibility would be invested in their accuracy.

Treasury also became disillusioned both with the bottom-up method of constructing reliable forward estimates and the opportunities (and imperative) given to spending departments to 'gild the lily' and exaggerate claims. Hence, although the concept of estimates becoming more generally used as a planning device was widely applauded, the actual process of formulating forward estimates was considerably flawed. Treasury increasingly returned to the view that input from the spending departments was, on balance, counterproductive. It was considered far more preferable to rely on spending departments only for the raw data on expenditure while exercising strict central control and scrutiny of the eventual estimate figures. They adopted the view that forward estimates had more potential to become an effective instrument of expenditure control when imposed, perhaps as limits, by central agencies through cabinet, rather than being jointly agreed with line agencies.[12] But even at this stage there was no intention to officially authorise estimates, and forward estimates were still not publicly available in published form.

Other reservations over the effectiveness of the estimates system were voiced to RCAGA in 1975. In submissions and research presented to the Commission, a number of commentators put forward arguments in favour of the development of a more effective system of forward estimates. Academics, in particular, argued improvements were necessary to the formulation of estimates and their application to the budgetary process.[13] Treasury was similarly hopeful that a revamped forward estimates would improve their capacity in the management and control of public expenditure—

12 A decade later in the early 1980s, the Department of Finance proposed again to devolve the generation of estimates, on the logic that more accurate bottom-up information would enhance the accuracy of the figures. Finance's proposal to broaden input into the estimates process brought forth a predictable warning from Treasury that this was not the way to go. Finance apparently heeded this advice and at the behest of their new Secretary, Dr M. Keating, a decision was made in 1986 that the determination of estimates was to be centralised in Finance.

13 See submissions to RCAGA by G. Caiden, J. Cutt and G. Terry and P. Weller.

extending the role of estimates beyond merely providing information for planning. Increasingly, reforms to the forward estimates were perceived as solutions to innumerable problems. However, while dissatisfaction was common, the various proposals aimed at reforming the estimates differed, sometimes dramatically.

Proposals for improvement were frustrated by understandable responses from departments. When the government conducted a diagnostic study of financial management in 1983 it produced evidence of widespread disillusionment with the forward estimate process from departmental staff. The study found that 60 per cent of departmental executives agreed that managers had to exaggerate their bids for the purpose of forming estimates in order to get the funds they believed they really needed. Half the respondents also believed that the procedures used by central agencies to determine estimates encouraged rational department managers to attempt to manipulate the system. The Secretary of Treasury, John Stone, candidly admitted these findings pointed to widespread deficiencies in the estimating process. For Stone the study indicated a 'systematic lack of zeal in pursuing efficient estimation' (Stone 1984).

CASH LIMITS ON DEPARTMENTS: IMPOSING CRUDE EXPENDITURE CONTROLS

Paradoxically, Treasury became increasingly interested in using forward estimates to provide expenditure control at the time the deficiencies with the estimates process began to emerge and be acknowledged. The main problem with the system of 'disconnected' forward estimates was that simply setting them did not in itself lead to a better management of expenditure nor did it particularly assist in the next budget round. By the mid-late 1970s cabinet and individual ministers would consume considerable amounts of time once the budget planning process commenced attempting to agree on a base-line set of budget estimates (which may have borne only distant relation to the figures released in the forward estimates). Forward estimates did not necessarily assist and could actually hinder decision-making.

With the intention of imposing greater control, two top-down capping devices were introduced from 1975 under the auspices of the Expenditure Review Committee. Staff ceilings and cash limits imposed restrictive parameters on the spending patterns and demands of departments. Staff ceilings had been intermittently used by the Commonwealth since the 1960s, but were 'applied in a continuous fashion' from 1975 as a way of reducing the number of public servants (and other employees covered by the 'ceilings'). The numerical restrictions on staff were imposed by the Prime Minister on advice from PM&C and Treasury, but departments typically invented a myriad of ways of getting around them. Secondly, cash limits were imposed on departmental spending as a mechanism to rein in expenditures and attempt to prevent over-spending. Cash limits applied to budget allocations for the year ahead plus also limits on 'undischarged commitments outstanding at the end of a financial year payable in future years'. Once introduced their success was mixed, but governments continued to believe in their effectiveness, seeking to tighten the limits when the opportunity arose.

THE SEEDS OF REFORM

Although the initial experimentation with forward estimates was not an unqualified success, there was never talk of abandoning them and over time the evolution of the process underlined the importance of a more disciplined estimates process. Central agencies accumulated significant expertise and experience in calculating information about future commitments which was indispensable to the achievement of improved budgetary control. If the estimates process was judged from results achieved by the mid 1970s it would have to be deemed a failure; however, if it were assessed a little over a decade later it was by that stage trumpeted as one of the most successful budgetary reforms.

By the mid–1980s forward estimates had become a firm basis for future year budgets. The Commonwealth agreed to publish their *Forward Estimates Reports* in 1983, essentially as a means of declaring estimates as firm budget targets. This added a degree of accountability both to the estimates and to governments themselves. Gradually forward estimates became integral to the 'four year rolling budget' forming a precise indicator of known commitments where no policy changes were foreshadowed. Subsequent changes to policy could readily be augmented to the 'hard' estimates as approved by cabinet. As the transformation of the estimates occurred, it was argued that if they were to become the baseline for the next budget, then it was imperative the estimates were precise and that the department responsible for producing the estimates was held accountable for the precision of the figures. But by this stage Treasury had been divided and moved from centre stage to the wings and the Department of Finance was left to make the running on a harder estimates process—a task they approached with some relish.

4 The enduring 'problem' of Treasury

FROM FEDERATION THE Commonwealth Treasury essentially performed the constitutionally mandated role of accountant to government. For a number of decades it did little else; it kept the books, funded approved activities, marshalled revenues and (after 1910) directed tied funding to the states. From the 1940s onward this limited role gradually expanded to include macro-economic policy advice: a role it had to fight to secure. Guided by the tenets of Keynesianism, the ideas associated with the policy field of 'economic policy' gradually developed, and this increased the need for Treasury's involvement in advising on the 'economics' of government policy generally. Treasury officials, after undertaking financial and economic analyses, began to comment on the *appropriateness* of policies across government often to counter the expenditure claims of departments. As a result of this involvement, Treasury expanded in the post-war period beyond its constitutionally stipulated and traditional function to create three distinct but over-lapping roles:

- accounting and bookkeeping functions of government;
- general financial and economic policy advice; and,
- control and management of public expenditure.

These distinct roles were not given equal attention. Senior officials in Treasury focused increasingly on general financial and economic policy advice—under the rubric of macro-economic policy. Behind the scenes the task of controlling departmental expenditure went largely unnoticed.

By the 1960s, however, the adequacy of traditional line-item budgets and their underlying premise of detailed financial control were being challenged by practitioners and academics throughout the world. In America, Canada, Britain and elsewhere debates about how to improve budgetary systems shifted from the conceptual level, leading to experimentation with new budgetary systems (Thain and Wright 1995). By contrast, in Australia the issues of public finance, and in particular questions of budgetary and financial reform, escaped wider public debate. Those showing any interest were largely confined to small groups of public servants and a few interested academics. Ignorance appeared bliss in the expanding Australian state of the post-war 'long boom'.

The findings of the Royal Commission on Australian Government Administration (RCAGA 1976) threatened to disturb this complacency. As the Commission's inquiries progressed the role and behaviour of the Treasury increasingly began to be identified as a 'problem', and important questions were raised about the processes, institutions and mechanisms of Australian public expenditure management—although few solutions were offered. This chapter traces the process by which Treasury emerged as a 'problem' with respect to its overseeing of public finance and how this then prompted debate over the entire system of public expenditure management. The issues that emerged remained central to the debate over public expenditure management for the next two decades. Indeed, a senior officer responsible for resource management across government reflected after twenty years of subsequent reform that 'everything dates back to Coombs' (Bartos Interview 1996).

TREASURY'S THREE DISTINCT ROLES

(i) Accountant to the Government

The Treasury served as the government's accountant from 1901, and this became the department's *raison d'être*. The *Commonwealth of Australia Constitution Act 1900* and the *Audit Act 1901* jointly established the legal framework for this role. The former required Commonwealth revenues be deposited exclusively into the Consolidated Revenue Fund and stipulated that money could only be drawn from this fund with parliamentary approval. The *Audit Act* allocated responsibility for the management of government accounts to Treasury.[1] It authorised the Treasurer to issue funds for parliamentary appropriated expenditure, with Treasury able to open and operate subsidiary accounts. It was also required to publish expenditure and revenue statements for government accounts.

Treasury's accounting function was ongoing and involved the department in continuous and detailed procedures in relation to other departments.[2] Many of the controls imposed on departments were aimed at enforcing parliament's legislated expenditure levels while seeking to eliminate opportunities for fraud. Treasury instructions, directions, and regulations formed a 'manual of guidelines on accounting matters' which retained control and uniformity in accounting matters (Treasury 1974, D:4). Some regulations included a requirement for Treasury approval before amounts could be spent. Treasury delegated little of its authority. Legislative provisions partially qualified Treasury control over expenditure in statutory authorities, but borrowing, contractual and reporting arrangements remained under Treasury control.

Treasury's objective in this *gatekeeper* role was to ensure expenditure accorded with parliamentary appropriations and remained consistent with traditional bookkeeping and budgetary practices. But expenditure controls were cumbersome. While detailed information was required, spending departments lacked discretion and flexibility. Treasury was often criticised for delaying or preventing government initiatives. Not surprisingly, these arrangements irritated departments whose operations were constrained by Treasury's officious routines.

(ii) General Financial and Economic Policy

During the Second World War a new orthodoxy of economic intervention was accepted by Treasury, significantly expanding its role. In Treasury's early years, the provision of economic advice was a relatively minor function. This was reinforced, even through the depression years, by the dominance of a non-interventionist economic ideology. The defeat of attempts to counter mass unemployment

---

1 Commonwealth finances are managed through three different funds: Consolidated Revenue Fund, the Loans Fund and the Trust Fund. For further discussion, see various Department of Finance publications including (DoF 1992:36–9).

2 Some of Treasury's behaviour involved almost trivial arguments when additional funds were requested. For instance, Treasury had arguments with Foreign Affairs over funding of diplomatic residences overseas which involved such things as the length of curtains to be installed in residences; and with other departments over the installation of phone points and the length of telephone cable they were allowed (Monaghan written communication 2000).

remains a significant part of Australian economic history. The significance and impact of macro-economic policy advice grew along with the advent of Keynesian 'demand management' economics, and preferences for full employment and economic stability. The *Full Employment White Paper* (1945) became a key turning point in government thinking. Post-war development and reconstruction increased the complexity and breadth of government economic activity. Government borrowing and budget deficits became legitimate and essential options in economic management. Taxation and expenditure aggregates were manipulated to achieve short-term economic goals and to even out the trade cycle. Such 'fine-tuning' required extensive information about prevailing economic conditions. Thus, Treasury began to undertake macro-economic model building and analysis in order to help predict future economic conditions and frame budgets. Interest in aggregate public expenditure levels became firmly located in the context of short-term economic management by the mid–1950s.

By the mid–1970s, however, both inflation and unemployment were rising inexorably and the post-war economic theories no longer appeared to work as well as they had done. A new wave of neo-classical economists and monetarists in Treasury, economic think tanks and universities, began actively questioning the theoretical bases of government intervention and the underlying principles of Keynesian demand management. They became less convinced governments had the capacity to anticipate changes in the economy, or of the benefits of short-term 'fine-tuning'. 'One-sided' Keynesian macro-economic management, in the hands of politicians and bureaucrats, expanded the public sector through fiscal injections in times of recession but was unable to reduce public outlays in times of full employment, high growth and inflation. Under such circumstances, Treasury's capacity to provide long and short-term economic policy advice, and maintain expenditure control was increasingly coming under challenge. Whitwell (1986) argues that Treasury not only began to question the previous assumptions of economic orthodoxy, but also its own role as an economic manager.

(iii) Control and Management of Public Expenditure

Treasury's interest in the control and management of public expenditure occurred largely by default. The expansion of government commitments in the post-war period gradually increased sensitivity toward the magnitude of expenditure and need for aggregate controls. While Keynesian ideas were dominant and the economy continued to expand and revenues grow, public expenditure growth continued largely unfettered. But as the complexity, scope and diversity of public spending increased, so did the demand for improved methods of policy coordination. This responsibility fell to Treasury primarily because of its involvement in the budgetary process and ongoing funding roles. Yet, Treasury was becoming much more sceptical of the inherent benefits of public expenditure as serious economic problems arose in Australia. This sceptical view emphasised the costs of public spending, especially 'the burden of taxation', and the 'crowding out' effect on private investment. The supply divisions of Treasury accepted this broader contextual view and actively sought to control the level of public expenditure within their own policy jurisdictions. Expenditure projections began to be grouped functionally to indicate aggregate expenditure in policy areas. Treasury was able to undertake economic and financial analyses of *policies*, rather than of specific line-items, and provide cabinet with this information. Thus, Treasury gradually extended its traditional roles and became increasingly involved in policy management and evaluation—areas previously considered the domain of line departments, coordinating policy units and politicians.

As Treasury's attention focussed on the *control and management* of public expenditure, major disagreements occurred with the spending departments. Treasury often felt it appropriate to provide advice with respect to the efficiency and effectiveness of selected policy proposals; this included the appropriateness of the policy instruments, the continued relevance of specific policies and the relative efficiency of departmental operations. For many departments this constituted meddling, and Treasury officers increasingly came into conflict with their departmental counterparts. The implications of Treasury's expansion into public expenditure management and its own perceptions of its increased role did not become evident until after Labor won office in 1972.

Given these three competing discrete roles, Treasury accommodated them as functionally discrete responsibilities, the legitimacy of which was increasingly recognised both inside and outside Treasury. These functional splits were increasingly incorporated into the formal divisional organisational structures of Treasury.[3] The divisional structure thus evolved *organically* as it followed the functional evolution and broadening of Treasury's roles, rather than being the outcome of deliberate organisational design. Such divisional arrangements not only allowed for functional specialisation and efficiency, but also helped avoid internal or ideological splits within Treasury—and a cohesive and dominant Treasury culture could be maintained. Paradoxically, these formal divisions made the implementation of the splitting of Treasury that much easier and, ultimately, perhaps more successful.

WHITLAM, TREASURY AND COOMBS

In December 1972 Gough Whitlam led Labor to government after 23 years in opposition. The new government moved quickly to implement its agenda for big spending social and economic reform. This involved an extended welfare role for the public sector in areas of education, housing, social security and health (McLaren 1972). Problems of implementation soon became apparent. Many within the ALP believed that the inherent conservatism of the public service both implied and generated antagonism toward Labor policies (Hawker 1980). Up to a point, this argument is sustainable. The public service and the Labor government did not work well together even in departments sympathetic to the government's agenda. Treasury increasingly was singled out for much criticism, particularly for its preoccupation with the inflationary impacts of government policies (a concern since 1970) and increased public sector borrowing requirements.

To a large extent the implementation problems were symptoms of 'sudden overload', and in many respects the Labor government brought problems on itself. Departments required additional resources to implement Labor's policies. Policy ambition demanded a commensurate increase in the size and capacity of the public service, particularly at managerial levels. Yet the then dominant public service culture was not designed for rapid policy and implementation responses. Mutual distrust flourished. Outdated administrative practices and structural rigidities slowed the speed of change. Recruitment and incremental progression limited the range of people competent at managerial levels, and some staff were promoted into managerial positions before they acquired the necessary experience and skills. The Whitlam cabinet was too large

3 Treasury's internal divisions were not entirely organised around discrete functions. Some divisions, such as the Revenue, Loans and Investment division, for example, included federal-state relations but also had some supply functions.

and cumbersome, and ministers were often ambushed in cabinet as objections to their submissions were raised without prior warning. Before the ERC was established in January 1975, the entire cabinet was not particularly interested in constraining resources or considering the longer-term costs of new initiatives.

Whitlam's impressions of the public service were in part shaped by the difficulties experienced with some sectors of the service. He was convinced the existing systems of public administration needed to be reformed to cope with the demands of modern government. The Commonwealth would become a 'model employer'. Responding to demands for an inquiry into the public service from his own party, Whitlam announced his intention to establish an inquiry in his 1974 electoral policy speech. Returned to office with a reduced majority, Whitlam established RCAGA on 6 June 1974. The Commission was asked to undertake a comprehensive review of the Australian public sector reporting back to the Parliament in two years. In opting for a royal commission, rather than a task force or other review mechanism, Whitlam hoped to mitigate the impact partisan and bureaucratic politics would have on the inquiry's operation and findings.

Five Royal Commissioners were drawn from a range of fields and backgrounds. The Chairman Dr Herbert 'Nugget' Coombs, then with the Council for Aboriginal Affairs, had been a consultant to a succession of prime ministers. Although devoting his career to public service he was not generally recognised as an advocate for public sector reform. Early in 1974, Coombs had produced a *Review of the Continuing Expenditure Policies of the Previous Government.* This examined existing programs in an effort to reduce the problem of budget 'lock-in'—a forerunner of the later 'audit commissions'—but not principally directed to public sector reform. The public service was represented by two very different commissioners: Peter Bailey (Department of Prime Minister and Cabinet) was recognised as a conservative who sought to maintain traditional public service values; while Paul Munro (Secretary of the Council of Australian Government Employee Organisations) was relatively more progressive, although likely to reject proposals which threatened existing workplace conditions. Both of the remaining commissioners had experience in legal and academic fields. Professor Enid Campbell of Monash University had an interest in administrative law reform and equal employment opportunities. Dr Joe Isaac, a Deputy President of the Conciliation and Arbitration Commission, had previously been Professor of Economics at

Monash University. Collectively the five commissioners contributed extensive experience, albeit with a pronounced bias in their collective expertise toward law and industrial relations fields.

THE DIFFICULTIES IN DETERMINING THE AGENDA AND FOCUS FOR RCAGA

The particular problems to be addressed by the Commission were not immediately apparent. There was no consensus on the mischiefs to be remedied. Although many believed that 'something needed to be done' in the public service, there was little agreement on the core issues to be addressed. Part of the problem was that no one composed a discussion paper on what *were* the problems. Some believed the problems facing the public service were so complex they defied definition, largely due to the fact that no systematic and overall review of the public service had been undertaken in almost 60 years. Two world wars, depression and the Menzies conservatism had ensured this was the case. Throughout that period, nevertheless, the responsibilities of the federal public service had increased massively in an *ad hoc* and incremental way, and the institutions and bureaucratic procedures used to administer the system had developed in a largely consequential manner. Arguably, RCAGA ought to identify and explain existing systems, recommending any changes or reforms.

The level of uncertainty over the Commission's *purpose* was reflected in the very broad terms of reference. The government appeared more interested in a trawling expedition—aiming to catch whatever good ideas were around—than a more narrowly focused enquiry. The Letters Patent (RCAGA 1977:1) directed the Commission to:

> inquire into and report upon the administrative organisation and services of the Australian Government, and in particular:
>
> 1. the purposes, functions, organisation and management of Australian Government Departments, statutory corporations and other authorities and the principal instruments of coordination of Australian Government administration and policy; and
> 2. the structure and management of the Australian Public Service; and to make recommendations for improving efficiency, economy, adaptability and industrial relations and the dispatch of public business.

These broad terms of reference left very little out. In addition to these general responsibilities a wide range of specific topics were nominated for particular attention. The mention of 'statutory corporations and other authorities' signified that the entire public *sector* was to be reviewed, not just government departments. Particular aspects of public sector administration were also expressly nominated in the terms of reference. These included the evaluation of centralised control mechanisms and institutions, the adequacy of policy making and evaluation techniques and the appropriateness of human resource policies and staffing practices. It was also clear the review was intended to extend beyond administrative mechanisms to include relations with parliament, ministers and the community in general. Indeed, very few areas of government administration were excluded by the inquiry's terms of reference.

The expansiveness of the Commission's terms of reference meant the first challenge of the commissioners was to determine a clear direction for the inquiry. Rather than impose their collective prejudices on the inquiry from the outset, RCAGA attempted to 'inform itself about where the shoe was pinching' (Hawker 1978:46). Within the first six months of the inquiry submissions were received from a wide cross section of government departments, community groups, academics and individuals. A series of meetings and background discussions were held by the commissioners in Canberra to 'establish informal contacts with individuals and organisations whose wisdom and experience it felt would assist it to determine the directions its inquiries should take' (RCAGA 1976:4). Between November 1974 and April 1975, the commissioners undertook an extensive program of public hearings, community consultation and a number of 'work-place visits' to enable agencies to expand on their written submissions. Two advisory committees were set up to secure participation from both business and trade union representatives. From this 'bottom up approach' some of the primary issues of subsequent research projects were identified.

It was somewhat serendipitous that expenditure management and the role of Treasury emerged as a central issue during the inquiry. Initially, questions about the budgetary and financial management systems used by Treasury were subsidiary to the inquiry's direction. This changed as submissions from government departments were received and the structured discussions began. Interest initially focused on the impact Treasury practices had on the public sector's efficiency, but this gradually developed into a more comprehensive examination of existing systems of public expenditure management in Australia.

TREASURY RECOGNISED AS AN ENDURING 'PROBLEM'

Considered in isolation, Treasury's submission to RCAGA appears a factual document. It articulated the department's perception of its proper role within the federal public service; described existing Treasury practices, organisational structures and the various roles and responsibilities of specific divisions; and explained cogently why all these continued to be necessary. Overseas initiatives in public expenditure management were acknowledged, but with characteristic scepticism. However, when read in context against the debates and external reviews conducted by RCAGA, the Treasury submission assumes a different status as a rather political document that was both self-serving and self-congratulatory.

Despite the formal language and ostensible neutrality, Treasury's written submission to RCAGA was a considered defence of the *status quo* that ignored many emergent issues. As the inquiry progressed, the focus of the investigations shifted, allowing critical and diverse opinions to surface. Senior public servants and other consultants challenged many of the issues reported as 'facts' in Treasury's submission. For example, questions were raised about the legitimacy of Treasury's involvement in detailed financial control—then the basis of existing accounting mechanisms. This precipitated debate over the efficiency of centralised accounting mechanisms; the line-item appropriation system and departmental financial systems. Such issues were then investigated and debated in a series of research papers[4] and task force reports[5] (although attention here fell mainly on the provision of financial and economic policy advice). As it defended its stated position, Treasury was drawn into issues and debates it had sought to avoid. And so, somewhat unexpectedly, the 'problem of Treasury' was placed high on the public agenda as a result of the Coombs' Commission. The ensuing debates both highlighted the inadequacy of existing systems of expenditure control, and helped define discourse on public expenditure management for the next two decades.

RCAGA received Treasury's written submission on 17 November

---

4 See for example: Emy (1975); Kasper (1975); and Terry and Weller (1975).

5 See particularly: Caiden (1975); Task Force on Economic Policy (1975).

1974. It included a short introductory letter by the Secretary to the Treasury, Sir Frederick Wheeler and five attachments. In the letter, Wheeler (1974:1) discussed briefly the Treasury's history and identified its primary function *inter alia* as to 'advise and to assist the Treasurer in the discharge of his responsibilities in the economic, financial, budgetary and accounting fields of government'. He went on to list the department's nine major divisions and their ten main activities. A series of attachments constituted the bulk of Treasury's submission.

Treasury acknowledged its primary responsibility was in overseeing the public purse, and the department relied on the Accounting and Supply Division to provide advice 'in relation to the Public Account'. Treasury further argued that this responsibility necessarily translated into a coordinating role in the preparation of the annual budget. The division collected forward estimates from departments, prepared the annual estimates for revenue and expenditure and prepared the Appropriation Bills. In addition, the division developed service wide accounting rules and regulations ensuring that uniform information was collected from departments. This information was used by other divisions within Treasury and was also available to the Treasurer, Prime Minister, Cabinet and even relevant parliamentary committees. The division also claimed to be engaged in research to ensure that contemporary accounting techniques were adopted within the public service. The accounting function of this division was based in Canberra but assisted by regional accounting offices of the Treasury in the state and territory capitals and in London, New York and Geneva.

Detailed accounting functions were carried out by the four 'supply' divisions[6]—which maintained general oversight of departmental finances, including estimates of receipts and expenditures. These supply divisions scrutinised each line of proposed expenditure and ensured that spending departments adhered to Treasury accounting directives and prepared budget estimates properly. In addition, the supply divisions were responsible for providing advice on 'financial and economic aspects of policy matters' in nominated policy areas. Wide *functional* policy responsibilities were given to each supply division rather than *departments* being allotted to each supply division. The Social Security Division (SSD), for example,

---

6 In 1974 these were the Social Security Division, Transport and Industry Division, Defence and Works Division and the Overseas Economic Relations Division.

was responsible for social services, repatriation, health, education, housing, migration, scientific research, recreation, arts and culture, Aboriginals, the environment, labour conditions and employment throughout the Australian government. Ten departments fell entirely within the SSD's jurisdiction while another five departments were partially covered (Treasury 1974, A:2–3). This was a crucial device in Treasury's power with respect to spending departments. Treasury had at its disposal centralised information in relation to the whole of government and so was able to speak with one authoritative voice. If other departments were seeking to expand their policy influence or bureaucratic empires, or challenge one another for ownership of policy areas, Treasury could claim neutrality with respect to such 'turf' issues; adopting tactics of divide, conquer and rule.

In macro-economic areas, the General Financial and Economic Policy division (GFEP) provided advice on domestic economic and financial policy and was considered among the elite of Treasury's divisions (along perhaps with the Revenue, Loans and Investment division and the Overseas Economic Relations division). Treasury argued GFEP was its 'policy initiator' and so its role necessarily contrasted markedly with the operationally-focused supply divisions that typically commented on policy initiatives originating from other departments. The GFEP division focused on the 'broader aspects of domestic economic and financial policy'; especially general economic management including fiscal, monetary and general taxation policy advice. The division also undertook 'research into Australia's long term potentialities for economic growth' and assessed information about economic trends to develop economic policy advice for the Treasurer (Treasury 1974, A:4). GFEP then ostensibly set the framework for budget aggregates. Treasury, therefore, saw the functions of economic policy and expenditure management as inextricably related. When asked to explain Treasury's *advisory* role, Wheeler ventured (in RCAGA 1974:432):

> *the Treasury field is concerned with expenditure; it is concerned with revenue;* it is concerned with notes; currency; it is concerned with money in general, and so on, but we do not collect taxes. We do not print the notes; we don't in any sense perform banking functions and *it is in the nature of things that our concern is with the* ***general*** *aspects of all these topics . . .* (emphasis added).

Treasury's own assessment of its functions saw the Revenue, Loans and Investment (RLI) division as advising the Treasurer on both borrowing issues and on the financial and economic impacts of various forms of financial assistance. The division was responsible for overseeing and coordinating revenue raising by the Commonwealth, state and local governments. RLI provided the secretariat for the Australian Loans Council and the National Debt Commission and administered agreements made by these bodies. At a more specific level, the division evaluated the financial implications of those developmental policies and projects with significant borrowing requirements—for example, the public works infrastructural projects associated with the Snowy Mountains scheme and the Ord River project, but also increasingly with urban development projects. The appropriateness of different financial instruments was assessed in terms of Australia's overall economic and financial objectives. The policy initiatives coming under investigation usually originated from *outside* the Treasury, generally from infrastructural departments like the Department of Urban and Regional Development (DURD) an emerging rival to Treasury on domestic economic planning in the Whitlam years.

The remaining three divisions of Treasury were only briefly mentioned in its submission. The Financial Institutions division played a similar role to the supply divisions in providing 'advice on financial and economic aspects of policy matters'. While its main focus was the banking and financial institutions, the division also provided advice on exchange control, insurance and relevant aspects of company law. As its name suggested, the Foreign Investment division advised on policy matters associated with foreign ownership and control of Australian industry and resources. Finally, the Management Services Branch of Treasury was responsible for internal corporate service provision and the department's internal practices and procedures.

The interrelated nature of the 'economic, financial, budgetary and accounting' functions was continually emphasised in Treasury's submission. It suggested the department's two major responsibilities of providing policy advice and exercising financial oversight were coterminous. Treasury argued that most divisions combined both advisory and overseer roles but the activities of each division were integrated by shared information needs. Financial data gathered in the supply divisions, for example, was aggregated to provide base data for the general economic policy divisions. Treasury could not hide the fact that quite separate organisational domains had emerged within the department separating those divisions providing general economic advice from those that routinely assessed expenditure

proposals generated by other departments. As a single institution, Treasury could be perceived to have competing priorities, and critics began to claim that the Treasury could not perform each of its roles equally well.

RCAGA'S CRITICISMS OF TREASURY'S THREE ROLES

RCAGA criticised Treasury's performance across each of the three roles. For the purposes of this analysis, however, we discuss the criticisms levelled at Treasury's accounting and expenditure management roles, and pay relatively less attention to the other criticisms made against Treasury's economic policy responsibilities.

(i) Accountant to the Government

Most submissions to RCAGA accepted the legitimacy of Treasury's accounting role. There was recognition of the need for some form of control, oversight and coordination of ongoing public expenditure. However, the mechanisms used by Treasury to perform these tasks were criticised extensively, especially the systems of budgetary and financial management. Anecdotal evidence in departmental submissions repeatedly highlighted operational inefficiencies resulting from Treasury's accounting regulations. Professor Gerald Caiden (1975:89–104) commissioned to investigate efficiency of the public service produced a critical commentary on 'Treasury control':

> Treasury attempts to do too much through highly centralised operations. As a result, other ministers complain about the dominance of the Treasurer in determining public policy and Treasury's interference with the operation of government organisation beyond purely economic and financial consideration. Government organisations are bitter in their denouncement of Treasury rigidity and arrogance. Treasury officials are unduly discriminatory in their review of budget proposals submitted by government organisations. In anticipation of Treasury negativism, governmental organisations have devised various strategies to get their way, strategies which are uneconomic, inefficient and ineffective from the public viewpoint and damaging to Treasury objectives. As long as Treasury and the governmental organisations view public finance administration from different directions, these defects are likely to persist and the more Treasury imposes restrictions to prevent abuse, the more governmental organisations will seek ways and means of getting around them. The system is self-defeating.

His argument consisted of two main points: Treasury needlessly involved itself in detailed controls which constituted a 'drag on efficiency' and could be better left to departments; and the inherent inflexibility of line-item budget controls locked operational managers into patterns of expenditure, which did satisfy authorisation requirements, but were inefficient and not geared to actual delivery concerns. Departments argued that increased resource flexibility would enable them to apply funds where they were most required and facilitate a more strategic management style. In other words, the criticisms found Treasury, as much as the spending departments, bound by the existing multi-line-item budgetary system, yet complacent about the operation of that system and reluctant to make changes to improve the system. Not surprisingly, Treasury's efforts to research new budget management and accounting techniques were deemed insufficient.

RCAGA recognised that budgeting and reporting systems tended to become self-reinforcing over time. Enforcement of line-item budgeting necessitated a centralised system of detailed expenditure control incorporating stringent accounting rules and regulations. The existing accounting procedures developed by Treasury were aimed at satisfying the requirements of this compliance system. The prevailing belief that parliament could only appropriate highly specified items of expenditure also underscored the logic of this system. Complaints from departments about apparently minor inconveniences, such as the frustration at being unable to transfer funds between postage and telephone expenditure line items, were simply an unfortunate but necessary by-product of the system. At another level, such criticisms of Treasury's stringent regulations suggested deeper frustrations with the budgetary system as a whole. One critic interpreted Treasury's reluctance to move away from line-item budgeting as confirmation of the department's reputation for 'stubbornness, rigidity, narrowness, inflexibility . . . lack of initiative and negativism' (Caiden 1975:90).

The majority of critics argued for a less detailed system of appropriation. Indeed, two RCAGA consultants found that 'on no single issue in the area of Treasury control is there greater unanimity among departments than on the need for a different system of appropriations giving greater flexibility between votes' (Terry and Weller 1975:37). Of course, such reform proposals would still have to satisfy the appropriation conventions of parliament where backbenchers in particular saw individual line items as detailed indications of *where* public funds were spent. There was always potential for tensions to exist between a department's desire for increased managerial flexibility and the requirements of parliamentary accountability. DURD's submission, for example, suggested that 'departmental estimates in the Appropriation Bills were presented in the existing way but the Appropriations were made under a limited number of division headings' (RCAGA 1976e:109). Detailed *ex-post* financial reporting was recommended to maintain parliament's capacity to review actual expenditure. In this way, it was hoped decisions about actual expenditure could become the province of operational departments and the parliament rather than of Treasury officers. Need and policy preference could become the basis of budgetary decisions, rather than precedence and inherited levels of expenditure. Such ideas aimed to eliminate the perverse logic whereby departmental heads were given tight line-item appropriations (to limit their spending), but chastised for underspending any line of appropriations.

Treasury did little to counter these claims, and some officers within the department accepted that increased flexibility would, theoretically, enhance public service efficiency. They concurred on the problems associated with line-item budgeting and could see merit in reducing the level of detailed expenditure control. They pointed to instances were Treasury had devolved accounting responsibility to departments and where they had endorsed single line consolidated appropriations (later called 'one-line' budgets). There was also evidence that Treasury was studying the possibility of merging some lines of appropriation, especially in relation to administrative costs. A study into the applicability of 'broadband' appropriations had recently been undertaken (it examined, for example, funding 'office expenses' rather than separate line items for individual expenditures). In short, in response to its critics, Treasury argued it was aware of the problems inherent in the existing budgetary system, perhaps more than the client departments.

Nonetheless, Treasury remained unconvinced of the merits of devolving financial responsibility to the operational departments in the short term. According to Treasury, the major impediment to adopting less stringent control mechanisms was the relatively junior position of departmental finance officers (DFO) in spending departments (Weller and Cutt 1976:52–54). Treasury argued they would only relax financial controls if DFOs became more capable of accepting such responsibilities. They proclaimed a 'growing concern in the Treasury at the scarcity of knowledgeable and experienced accounting officers in departments leading . . . to the appointment of "raw" staff to exercise important accounting responsibilities' (Treasury 1974, D:9–10). Short of seniority and skill, DFOs were in Treasury's view unable to adequately perform an enhanced accounting role or assist in the development of departmental estimates. With hindsight it is debateable how far Treasury overstated its case, especially as departments had been given little incentive or opportunity to enhance their capacities in this regard.

Although Terry and Weller (1975:68–70) corroborated Treasury's claim, they highlighted a more complex problem. They argued that DFOs had historically focused on ensuring compliance with accounting rules and regulations. In a decentralised financial management system, such responsibilities would expand to include many of the functions undertaken by Treasury officials. Consequently, DFOs would become increasingly caught between contradictory pressures for *operational expansion* and *financial restraint.* The DFOs would be incapable of fulfilling such contradictory responsibilities under the existing budgetary arrangements.

The 'financial services' section of most spending departments were generally located in 'managerial services' or 'corporate services' divisions. They were usually 'isolated from the policy areas' and marginalised from the 'main game' of policy development (Weller and Cutt 1976:53). Frequently DFOs only heard of policy initiatives that had already been decided, and this information often came third-hand through Treasury supply officers. As a result, DFOs had little input into new policy development within their departments and, on the rare occasions they were involved, were usually powerless. Moreover, 'permanent heads, usually former policy officers themselves, tend[ed] to support the policy area in disputes over resource allocation' (Terry and Weller 1975:68). Together these factors meant that DFOs lacked sufficient standing to influence decisions or impose discipline on departments. This suggested that existing financial controls were unlikely to maintain expenditure control in a more devolved budgetary environment.

These problems were compounded by the ambivalent (and sometimes hostile) relationships between Treasury supply officers and DFOs. At one level, DFOs gained a semblance of authority within their own departments from their close relationship with Treasury officers. But, demands for additional funding within departments were typically rejected by Treasury officials sometimes using the DFOs as their conduits. Hence, such relationships were uneven, especially given the relatively junior position of most DFOs. Treasury officers also scrutinised departmental accounts, for which DFOs were responsible, in an attempt to discover inaccuracies—perhaps 'obsessed with catching out the finance officers and destroying their arguments for the pure joy of doing it' (Weller and Cutt 1976:53). While this was a legitimate role for Treasury officers, it often bred a competitive and distrustful relationship. For example, a senior supply officer in the Social Security Division recalled that Treasury during the 1960s 'never believed a word of what Health said' (Craik Interview 1996). Departmental expenditure estimates were similarly analysed, typically on a line-by-line basis. Treasury officers frequently focused on symbolic items or new proposals for expenditure which may have been minor relative to overall outlays (Craik Interview 1996). Terry and Weller found personality and trust were the major factor determining the extent to which Treasury officers analysed departmental estimates. Supply officers divided DFOs according to their 'track record' into those they could trust and who were 'reliable' and those who were 'shifty and unreliable' (Weller and Cutt 1976:43). There was also the issue of the general reputation of the spending department to consider, and which ones would 'stand firm and which will give way' in a fight (Weller and Cutt 1976:44). The consequence of this interaction meant that unproductive relations developed between policy staff, DFOs and Treasury officers; many of whom regarded each other with mutual suspicion.

To overcome these problems, Terry and Weller (1975:90) recommended two minor modifications to help address the difficulties faced by DFOs. The first aimed at the marginalisation of DFOs and the power imbalance between them and the Treasury officers with which they dealt. They proposed 'finance officers in departments be upgraded in rank and that departments should consult these officers before cabinet submissions are lodged'. Second, they attempted to reduce the uncertainty and arbitrariness that characterised relations between Treasury and departments. Treasury was asked to assist DFOs prepare estimates and accounts by circulating 'a check list of information required, and explanations necessary, for all administration, ongoing and new programmes' (Terry and Weller 1975).

The conclusion from RCAGA's inquiries tend to suggest that the accountant role had become increasingly reactive and combative, perhaps reflecting that very little 'after the event' evaluation of expenditure occurred except for the compliance reports of the Auditor-General. Treasury had exploited its power over the purse to become a 'gatekeeper' over what departments were allowed to do. Thus, the accountancy role had become progressively counterproductive and irksome to spending departments especially as responsibilities and government intervention had increased.

(ii) General Financial and Economic Policy

RCAGA's analysis of Treasury's role in economic policy making, which is only briefly touched on here, was assisted by a special taskforce on economic policy headed by Professor Wolfgang Kasper. The taskforce had been commissioned to investigate the adequacy of the existing policy process, and in its report questioned Treasury's capacity to integrate short and long term economic analysis with budgetary management (TFEP 1975). Two impediments to better policy making and advice were identified. First, Treasury's dominance in the provision of economic policy advice did not allow for other assessments or viewpoints.[7] Previous

7 It must also be recognised that ministers could go outside the Treasury and look for advice from other regulatory bodies but by the late 1960s and early 1970s ministers tended not to do so. While McEwen had built the Trade department into a powerful economic ministry its significance was declining by

attempts to provide alternative economic advice through departments such as the Trade or the Prime Minister's portfolio had not succeeded or had been defeated by Treasury. This meant the only competing advice tended to emerge episodically from outside sources (e.g. business, media or academia).

Second, requirements of the annual budget cycle meant that short term financial and economic issues tended to dominate Treasury's advice which typically shunned long-term economic planning. The taskforce argued that budgetary parameters were directed by short-term considerations, and critics maintained Treasury's economic policy advice did not take into account the economy's long term well being when developing GFEP advice. In essence, Treasury did not have a strategic view of the Australian economy gradually losing force to the global economy. Critics also claimed that the department's traditional roles of controlling public expenditure had resulted in an institutional bias favouring low levels of expenditure. They were not alone in claiming that fiscal and financial stringency was Treasury's overriding instinct; even ex-Treasury officials admitted that if there was 'a Treasury view' it was 'no' (Weller and Cutt 1976)—sometimes represented by outsiders as 'the Abominable No Man'.

Treasury's official response to these criticisms was a conventional Keynesian defence that responsible economic policy should be directed by the short-term needs of the economy. However, at the time there was also vigorous debate occurring within Treasury and elsewhere between Keynesian and neo-classical economics. Neo-classical views which were gaining ground insisted that short-term policy tended to distort market outcomes and that government's influence could and should only have impact in the long-term. Monetarists went further, arguing that governments could have virtually no benign influence in the self-correcting mechanisms of the economy.

(iii) Control and Management of Public Expenditure

In its submission to RCAGA, Treasury articulated a more activist stance towards the control and management of public expenditure. It explicitly rejected the narrow interpretation of its functions implied by the terms 'expenditure control' and 'expenditure coor-

---

the late 1960s and ministers were not looking to the Reserve Bank for independent advice as they did in the 1980s under Treasurer Paul Keating.

dination'. Instead, it opted for an all encompassing definition of 'financial control' used in a 1962 New Zealand Royal Commission. This stated that, in addition to ensuring value for money, 'financial control' involved:

> expertly appraising the public financial resources; directing these resources towards specific policy goals . . . balancing competing claims; planning and controlling to ensure that expenditure is contained within the limits determined by the Government; and finally, coordinating public expenditure with the Government's broad economic and social aims and with the economic development of the country (Treasury 1974, C:1).

In a sense this was Treasury's ambit claim to RCAGA urging its roles and powers be increased. Treasury believed that its financial control activities complemented 'its role in relation to management and control of public expenditure' (Treasury 1974:4). Aggregate expenditure levels were controlled and managed through general financial and economic policy. Detailed expenditure control of appropriated funds was maintained through the department's accounting function. In addition, Treasury's information requirements provided the 'machinery for verification that expenditures have been carried out as intended and that relevant rules and requirements have been observed' (Treasury 1974, C:8). These were the essential features of 'Treasury control'.

Treasury had ambitions for further control. It argued that Treasury supply divisions should more actively 'manage' public expenditure through the budget process for two major purposes: to ensure that expenditure 'fits within the overall economic strategy', and to bring 'the elements of the expenditure together in a coherent, consistent and well-balanced fashion'. Treasury noted that within their policy areas, supply officers were starting to evaluate new proposals and 'scrutinised' on-going expenditure to 'promote review of programs and activities that might no longer be justifiable' (Treasury 1974:18). Supply officers were thus beginning to analyse the content and the objectives of departmental programs, not just calculate the 'economic and financial implications'.

It became clear during the RCAGA review that opinion was divided over the appropriateness and legitimacy of Treasury's involvement in 'managing' public expenditure. Spending departments typically argued that an 'accountant's mentality' pervaded Treasury analysis of departmental expenditure and that the overriding motivation of Treasury supply officers was to minimise expenditure wherever possible. They argued Treasury's focus often had economic costs which outweighed any costs of additional expenditure. Treasury's expertise was also questioned; with Caiden (1975) reporting perceptions of 'pretend experts in their ivory towers'. Not surprisingly, Treasury rejected these claims and insisted that as 'guardians of the public purse', their role was to stop unwarranted public outlays and ensure money was spent in the most efficient manner. Analysis of policy instruments, past performance and program appropriateness were to Treasury all within the ambit of their 'guardian' role. Spending departments should not criticise Treasury but follow its example and provide sound counter-arguments to support preferred expenditure proposals within the government's overall economic framework.

While Terry and Weller accepted the need for Treasury's expanded 'manager' role, they argued Treasury's existing practices necessarily resulted in arbitrary decisions often being made and the merits of policy being ignored. As part of their research, the consultants obtained an informal list of Treasury questions likely to be asked by supply officers to their counterpart DFOs when evaluating proposals. These questions were not consistent across or within supply divisions, nor were they comprehensively applied to expenditure proposals. Treasury admitted that no formal guidelines for evaluation existed. Such evidence reaffirmed the conclusion that the personality and previous performance of DFOs remained the most important determining factor in the nature and depth of Treasury analysis.

Rather than recommending Treasury reduce its involvement in this area, Terry and Weller advocated supply divisions develop a uniform consultative approach. To facilitate this change, they recommended a *functional separation* of the economic policy and the financial control functions of Treasury. They suggested that economic and financial functions would be more effective if divided and a new division formed to coordinate financial operations (they rejected arguments in favour of separating Treasury functions between two departments). These recommendations aimed to promote consistency in resource allocation across each of the divisions and ensure processes and information demands were tailored specifically to financial control, rather than macro economic policy making. Acknowledging the increase in the Treasurer's workload, they recommended a second minister be appointed to take sole responsibility for overseeing financial control. Significantly, they felt this minister ought *not* be subordinate to the Treasurer.

INTEGRATION BETWEEN TREASURY DIVISIONS: FACT OR FICTION?

Treasury had argued to RCAGA that the interrelated nature of its economic, budgetary and accounting functions meant it was essential to preserve Treasury intact as a single department. Their main argument was that policy advice and financial oversight were coterminous and one could not be undertaken without the other. Supply divisions necessarily combined advisory and overseer roles, and the information gained in these processes was indispensable to the department's wider responsibilities. For example, Treasury argued that financial data and expenditure estimates provided a base for general economic policy projections (despite, as discussed in the previous chapter, many in Treasury being dismissive or sceptical of such speculative estimates).

But Treasury could not hide the fact that separate functional domains had evolved within the department. On the one side were the general financial and economic policy functions (GFEP, RLI and OER divisions), and on the other the supply divisions that routinely assessed proposals from other departments. As a single institution Treasury was accused of having developed competing priorities, and critics began insisting that it could not perform each of its roles equally well.

Arguments favouring a formal separation of Treasury were put to RCAGA. The economic policy taskforce considered various restructuring proposals including one advocating a new institution dedicated exclusively to long term economic analysis and advice. This was seen as a means of redressing Treasury's bias toward short-term analysis (and such a move would have wound Treasury back to its original function). Despite apparent benefits, the taskforce rejected this option. They reasoned that a new institution with a long-term focus would find it difficult to develop a power-base in cabinet and as a marginalised body would be unable to challenge Treasury's dominance in economic policy advice. Others on the taskforce, such as Wolfgang Kasper and Ian Castles, argued Treasury's discrete roles should be split into two separate departments. They envisaged major problems ahead if all three roles of Treasury continued to be performed by the same department. In particular, the interconnection between economic policy and expenditure control was seen to distort sound expenditure advice offered by operational departments. This proposal to split Treasury had the merit of allowing greater specialisation and sense of purpose. Research showed that although the economic policy divisions were staffed by 'elite personnel within an elite department', they were severely under-resourced and incapable of producing the breadth or depth of analysis required by government. It was also 'logical' that financial and economic policy functions would need to become stronger over time. By contrast, the supply divisions had sufficient personnel, but were less elite and suffered from lack of coordination and guidance. Yet, although the option of splitting Treasury was canvassed, the taskforce cautioned against an immediate institutional separation as 'further substantial disruption to departmental organisation in the short term is likely to be costly' (TFEP 1975:14.38).

Other submissions to RCAGA also stopped short of advocating a complete institutional split. Terry and Weller rejected separation because of the disadvantages this would imply for coordination and information flows. Their 'bob-each-way' proposal of appointing a second minister to the portfolio sought to improve the rationality of resource allocation within government without disrupting existing information systems necessary for the provision of economic advice.

The Commission implicitly (or partially) accepted Treasury's central argument that economic and financial functions were necessarily integrated. The final report of the Commission stopped short of recommending the division of Treasury, despite the personal preference of its chairman, Nugget Coombs, in favour of separation. RCAGA's final report acknowledged Treasury's appropriate central role in the budgetary process, but suggested that its responsibilities in relation to *public expenditure management* were emerging as a distinct function in addition to Treasury's roles in economic policy making, financial control and accounting. The report recommended that Treasury separate its internal functions within the department and appoint a second minister assisting the Treasurer. Treasury would therefore retain responsibility for public expenditure but develop a more focussed interest in financial control and efficiency.

However, RCAGA did attempt to end Treasury's near-monopoly over economic policy advice by advocating the establishment of a Department of Industry and Economy (DINDEC) which would have responsibility for long-term economic planning. The economic policy capacities of related departments were also in need of enhancement—especially Prime Minister and Cabinet, and Urban and Regional Development. Finally, to provide freer access to economic data and statistical information, the Commission advised that the Australian Bureau of Statistics be transferred out of the Treasury portfolio.

In general, issues of efficiency and improved resource management were prominent in the final report, with recognition of the need to develop a more comprehensive system which classified government activities into functional areas and provided a better system of calculating forward commitments and expenditure estimates. RCAGA argued that functional classifications would assist a focus on ends instead of inputs, while better forward estimates would inform government about the future financial implications of policy decisions. The report also emphasised the importance of developing the capacities and roles of DFOs as a prelude to devolution and more systematic financial management improvements.

CONCLUSION

Through to the mid 1970s Treasury regarded itself as the premier agency in the Commonwealth bureaucracy; certainly its primacy was recognised as '*primus inter pares*'. Its power over the public purse gave Treasury a commanding position, and despite occasional challenges from rival players, its dominance remained intact for almost seventy years. By the mid–1970s and arguably at the height of its power, Treasury came under direct challenge.

Prior to the RCAGA exercise, debates about the merits of various aspects of expenditure control had been kept off the public agenda, and only occurred episodically within the higher echelons of the public service. The external inquiry into government administration drew attention to Treasury's shortcomings and its competing priorities. It also highlighted major problems in existing budgetary and financial management systems. Treasury's stringent control mechanisms revealed significant inefficiencies in the use of public expenditure. Complaints from operational departments were apparent symptoms of a broader problem with the existing system of line-item budgeting and the adequacy of departmental financial management. Their complaints could not just be swept away.

Once Treasury had been defined as an enduring 'problem' the debate intensified and Treasury could neither contain nor control the direction of the agenda. Indeed, its own actions and commentaries tended to fan the controversy and excite further criticism.

Treasury felt compelled to justify its position and defend its systems and internal practices; and Treasury was not used to defending itself on its budgetary and management performance. Despite its claims to be a central agency with economic policy responsibilities, Treasury was beginning to be judged according to the impacts its controls had on the nature of public administration. This was a new environment for Treasury, and one to which they were not well suited. The argument put to the Commission that Treasury's centralised control mechanisms reduced the efficiency of the entire public sector could not be ignored by a department purporting to promote efficiency, or by governments increasingly interested in value for the public dollar (Caiden 1975).

Ultimately, the various recommendations proposed by RCAGA were overtaken by political events and the dismissal of the Whitlam government in November 1975. A political stalemate developed while the Coalition settled into government and the Coombs' Report was slowly digested. Where recommendations could be incorporated (such as the development of a more effective system of forward estimates), Treasury was hopeful that progress could be made to improve their capacity in the management and control of public expenditure. Where the report's recommendations (or criticisms) threatened its powerbase, Treasury hoped the change of government would alleviate the need to make changes and a welcomed return to normality would prevail. Certainly, Treasury was hostile to any suggestion of surrendering control of the public purse, as this guardianship was one of its prime sources of institutional power. However, the demise of the Whitlam government did not end criticism of Treasury, and its successor somewhat surprisingly decided to exploit the opportunity to make institutional changes that suited its own agenda.

5 Splitting the Treasury: Humpty's great fall

MALCOLM FRASER ANNOUNCED the splitting of Treasury on 18 November 1976. This decision arguably remains the most profound in the history of public expenditure management in Australia. Its corollary was the creation of the Department of Finance, an agency devoted to public expenditure issues. In one fell swoop expenditure management was removed from its Cinderella existence within Treasury. Although speculation about a split had been around for some time, the announcement came as a shock. A decision conceived and executed in the Prime Minister's office, the split caught all but Fraser's closest confidants by surprise. As Kelly (1978b:22) suggests:

> The splitting of Treasury shows Fraser as the most ruthless and power-conscious Prime Minister seen in Australia for many years. This was Fraser telling Stone and Treasury that he was tougher than they.

While Fraser's actions were backed by sound arguments and by international experience, the decision owed much to ongoing tensions between the ministerial and bureaucratic arms of government.

The option of splitting Treasury, in part to end its dominance over economic advice and expenditure policy, had been debated at length by RCAGA. Many believed, however, that rejection of this option in the final report, and Fraser's electoral victory, had closed the issue. Clearly, this was not the case. Treasury's reluctance to canvas wide-ranging economic policy advice and provide options continued under Fraser and, as a result, the department quickly offended the new government—creating exasperation on both sides of politics.

Fraser publicly justified his decision to split Treasury on the grounds that the creation of Finance as a specialist department would improve the government's capacity to manage public expenditure, and improve financial management within the public service. To back his arguments, Fraser cited the Canadian experience where two separate central agencies administered expenditure and economic policy (respectively, the Treasury Board Secretariat and Ministry of Finance—but Fraser reversed the Canadian convention in labelling the departments). Most commentators at the time dismissed such argument as *ex post* rationalisations, and focussed instead on the political implications of the split and its potential to improve economic policy advice. They concluded that little would change and even among those who acknowledged the *potential* for longer-term improvements in public expenditure management, many concluded substantial change was unlikely.

As the government's new 'accountant', the Department of Finance assumed responsibility for the control of the public purse; particularly expenditures. Consequently, Finance acquired some of the most contentious (though 'invisible') aspects of Treasury's operations. Significantly, the embryonic agenda of budgetary reform was also transferred to Finance. This meant it was a new department that now had to grapple with issues such as what to do with forward estimates; how to achieve and sustain expenditure control; and what further reforms to make to budget formulation. As it transpired, inheriting an embryonic set of resource-related reforms provided the new department with an opportunity to develop an independent identity and role—both of which were essential for the department's subsequent survival. Over time separate departmental status allowed Finance to develop a specific focus. For Finance, the demands of general economic management which had dominated Treasury were no longer a competing responsibility. Instead the issues of increased efficiency and effectiveness in public expenditure and public sector management became their prime objectives.

Gradually, Finance shook off its humble origins as the mundane beancounters of supply inhabiting the 'saltmines' of Treasury, to become an independent central agency with distinct functions and its own culture. Indeed, within ten years of its establishment the Department of Finance had emerged as the principal reform champion for resource management in the Commonwealth. The

Department eventually introduced wide ranging reforms to public expenditure management practices; reforms that were often strongly opposed by the Treasury. With hindsight, the split of Treasury was one of the most significant changes in the institutional composition of the Commonwealth public service in the post-war period.

THE LEAD-UP: POLITICAL EXASPERATION WITH TREASURY

Treasury was typically single-minded, if not decidedly ideological, in its approach to economic policy advice. It jealously guarded vital information on the economy and used the budgetary role to impose its own opinion on the policy proposals from other departments and even upon governments. The resulting tensions were exacerbated late in 1971 when John Stone was appointed as Treasury's Deputy Secretary (heading the economic divisions). Stone adopted the 'Treasury line' with zeal. He was described as 'Australia's most brilliant economic overlord, or as a dangerously aggressive, right-wing ideologue' (Kelly 1987a:8). Defending preferred policy positions with intelligence, arrogance and passion, he quickly provoked intense emotional responses—both positive and negative. Stone resolutely refused to provide governments with alternate policy positions, believing that politicians would always choose the 'easy option' if one was available, and encouraged the officers within his division to adopt a similar stance. Given Treasury's command over economic advice, this left government in a difficult position; they either accepted Treasury's advice, or sought out and acted upon alternative advice in the knowledge that Treasury would vehemently oppose and would be publicly known to oppose.

The political and philosophical tensions between the Treasury and the Whitlam government are now notorious (Hayden 1996; Weller and Cutt 1976:24–27). While this was not the first time tensions had erupted between Treasury officials and government ministers, it was perhaps the most acrimonious. Treasury considered the Whitlam government fiscally irresponsible and opposed in principle many of the expansionary policies pursued by the new government. Whitlam ministers felt Treasury advice was entirely discredited after attempts to deceive the government over the two mini-budgets and budget of 1974 (Hawker *et al.* 1979: Hayden 1996: 174–180). Treasury was so determined to restrain expenditure that it 'obscured the situation', and according to ministers 'had deliberately sought to mislead' (Hawker *et al.* 1979:267–8).

The unfolding of the amateurish 'Loans Affair' (1974–75) exemplified the distrust between some in the government and Treasury. To senior ministers such as Jim Cairns (Treasurer for 6 months—the only one never to bring down a Budget) and Rex Connor, Labor was attempting to displace Treasury's long-held conservatism in economic policy with more expansionist infrastructural plans to revive the economy. But the bungled 'Loans Affair' also demonstrated the entrenched institutional power of Treasury—expressed both in ways to defend Australia's reputation overseas (saving the government's skin, as in their rearguard action in 1975 to prevent a credit rating downgrading) and in bringing to heel ministers considered wayward in economic policy. Treasury showed how effective its power could be when challenged.

The genesis of the 'Loans Affair' occurred on 13 December 1974. On that date, the Minister for Minerals and Energy, Rex Connor, received authorisation to negotiate a $US4 billion loan on behalf of the government. The authorisation was signed by the Governor-General in Executive Council and senior government ministers: Prime Minister Gough Whitlam; Treasurer Jim Cairns; Attorney General Lionel Murphy; and Rex Connor. From the outset Treasury opposed the initiative—'the Secretary to the Treasury, Sir Frederick Wheeler, fought against the authorisation to the end, and even urged his minister, Jim Cairns, not to sign. Wheeler was alarmed about both the policy and the process' (Kelly 1995:89). The resultant 'cat and mouse' game between Treasury and the government became legend, and is well-documented (Kelly 1976:155–177; 1995:86–103; Whitlam 1979a:47–59; Kerr 1978:223–40; Freudenberg 1977:342–65; Reid 1976:1–28; Hayden 1996:214–267).

Bypassing Treasury, the proposed loan moved the government outside accepted loan raising mechanisms. Treasury's established New York bankers were overlooked for a little known intermediary, Tirath Khemlani, who promised petro-dollars.[1] The state governments were also by-passed when Loans Council authority was not sought due to the ostensible 'temporary' nature of the loan. Treasury's opposition was immediate: Stone wrote a confi-

---

1 It should be remembered that this was shortly after the first oil price shock with OPEC nations 'awash' with dollars for which they were seeking safe and profitable outlets. Their own economies were too small to accommodate them. Consequently there was a plausible alternative supply source at that time, overlooking the dubious character of the intermediaries involved.

dential memo to the Treasurer (Cairns) in December 1974 raising a series of questions about the proposed loan (such as the wisdom in dealing with 'virtually unknown commission agents', the high cost of the agent's commission, the repayment costs, and the legal aspects of the deal) (see Reid 1976:9–11). Wheeler and Stone both led Treasury's attack, opposing 'the undertaking at every point, to the extent of asking Scotland Yard to check on Khemlani' (Kelly 1995:87). Treasury officials classified Khemlani as a 'carpet bagger' (Hayden 1996:245).[2]

Treasury's reaction was based in part on not knowing what the money was for as well as on the unorthodox means of acquisition. Whitlam (1979b) later claimed that Rex Connor intended to use the loan to re-purchase foreign-owned Australian resources and develop expensive infrastructure (a national pipeline); in other words, to 'buy back the farm'. Treasury argued that not only was the loan to be used for 'dubious' purposes, but its repayments would put future generations of Australians in massive debt. To many observers, departmental rivalry was another reason for Treasury's objection to the loan: acquiring funds unilaterally would free the Minerals and Energy Department from Treasury control, enabling it to become a 'rival empire'. There was much speculation that Treasury officials 'openly set out to discredit the government by a series of calculated leaks to the Opposition and the press' (Freudenberg 1977: 349). Hayden as the last Labor Treasurer under Whitlam disputed such allegations arguing that there was no evidence Treasury had leaked the documents. He insisted that there was ample opportunity for the leaks to have occurred overseas and that most leaked documents had not been seen by Treasury (Hayden 1996:256).

Whitlam's initial response was to act directly against Wheeler by trying to remove him from Treasury. The Prime Minister offered Wheeler the position of Governor of the Reserve Bank,

2 In March 1975, Treasury had learned that Cairns was involved in a second loan raising exercise. In a series of letters, Cairns authorised Melbourne businessman George Harris to negotiate loans on the government's behalf. The Treasury had not been informed. When the authorising letter was directed to Treasury from a London representative, Wheeler immediately arranged a meeting with the Treasurer asking him to explain. Apparently dissatisfied with Cairns' response, Wheeler sought legal advice from the Attorney General's department on the legal status of the documents in his possession. The Attorney General 'shuddered away' from providing the requested advice, knowing that it had been neither discussed with or authorised by the Treasurer.

proposing Sir Lennox Hewitt (then Secretary to the Department of Mines and Energy) as his replacement. Wheeler did not accept. Reputedly, in one argument with Whitlam he insisted 'I'm the permanent head. I intend to remain permanent head. And so you'll just have to live with me' (Craik Interview 1996). In response to the growing tensions between Treasury and the government, senior officials within the PSB, at the insistence of Whitlam and Cairns, worked up a plan to divide the Treasury in case 'push came to shove'.

In May 1975, Treasurer Cairns secretly instructed RCAGA to examine the possibility of splitting the Treasury. There were already international precedents for splitting economic policy between two departments. In the UK, the Wilson Labour government had split the British Treasury in 1964 and established the Department of Economic Affairs.[3] Aware of the request's political implications, the commissioners responded by asking the taskforce on economic policy for recommendations (Schaffer and Hawker 1978:38). Treasury personnel were notably absent from the taskforce's staff, which was led by the senior economic adviser in the Department of Prime Minister and Cabinet, Ian Castles. Reporting in mid–1975, the taskforce supported the option of splitting Treasury's financial control and economic advisory roles—but felt the time was not yet ripe. The findings and evidence were written in a way that was broad enough to support whatever decision a future government would choose to make.

Meanwhile, in February 1975 the federal Labor conference at Terrigal (NSW) endorsed a proposal demanding the establishment of a department responsible for long-term economic planning and thereby the division of the Treasury into two departments (an option much closer to the UK model). During June 1975, discussions were held by cabinet over splitting the Treasury—Connor and Cairns 'urged that it be done' (Cutt and Weller 1978:26). Before any action could be taken, however, the 'Loans Affair' became public and both ministers were removed from the cabinet. The government was forced into defensive action—any move to split Treasury would smack of desperation and vindictiveness. When the government was dismissed on 11 November 1975, the plans to split Treasury still lay locked in a safe at the PSB.

---

3 The Wilson Labour government's attempt to provide alternative advice is not directly similar, as the establishment of DEA was undertaken in a very different manner, with very different functions hived off from the UK Treasury.

The change of government appeared to improve the relationship between Treasury and the government. As Treasurer, Phillip Lynch established an amicable relationship with his department and things appeared to return to 'normal': Treasury's power now seemed beyond assail. This prompted Weller and Cutt (1978:27) to state that Treasury 'has regained its position of strength. The pendulum has swung back'. Treasury appeared not only to have survived but to have carried the day.

However, by the middle of 1976, Treasury was again making enemies. One of these was the Prime Minister. Malcolm Fraser was increasingly unhappy with the quality of economic advice from Treasury. It was not providing the government with the information that he and officers of PM&C requested, and he believed that Treasury was providing poor analysis and recommendations on the twin problems of inflation and unemployment, a relatively new phenomenon for post-war Australia. Perhaps the most significant point of departure between Fraser and the Treasury related to international economic and currency advice. As a primary producer in private life, Fraser had strong views on the impact currency levels had on Australia's rural exports and, hence, the economy. It appeared to Fraser that Treasury was oblivious to such concerns and impacts, refusing to even contemplate the negative impacts of their advice. Indeed, he argued:

> On the question of devaluation, I've always regarded Treasury as dogmatic and doctrinaire . . . They would never give a breadth of advice (Fraser Interview 1997).

Fraser was also frustrated at Treasury's reluctance to be more forthcoming with details of forward estimates, economic information and advice on economic policy. According to many close observers at the time, he was concerned at the institutional power of Treasury, as well as the difficulties in obtaining appropriate advice. According to one inside source, the 'Prime Minister mentioned that he was unhappy with certain aspects of performance by the Treasury and expressed the view that additional emphasis and resources should be directed to budget management, forward estimating and the provision of timely information for decisions by Government' (for an account based on internal cabinet files see Weller 1989:73–4).

Behind the scenes other officials and key advisers to the Prime Minister were expressing concern over the need for better evaluation of public expenditure programs. In particular, Ian Castles advocated an increased emphasis on budget management and evaluation of expenditure use. As Fraser's 'economic guru', Castles had influence and could be considered the champion of the final decision (Kelly 1978b). His arguments provided an additional impetus to the creation of a separate Finance department.

In November 1976, Fraser was again confronted by the inflexibility of crucial Treasury advice. This time the situation was a pending currency crisis impacting on Australia's fixed exchange rate regime. The government, including Fraser personally, favoured devaluation, but the Treasury favoured holding the currency's existing exchange rate. Deputy Secretary Stone ferociously defended the Treasury view, refusing to consider compromise or alternative options; finally, the government followed Treasury's advice. The interchange left Fraser shocked by Treasury's intractability and convinced that the government required an alternate source of economic advice.

Fraser took the initial steps toward reducing Treasury's unrivalled power over economic policy advice on 5 November 1976. Five days later, a confidential cabinet document, which revealed the Prime Minister's attitude to devaluation, was leaked to the press. Fraser was convinced that Treasury was responsible for the leak and 'decided to engage in massive retaliation' (Kelly 1978b:22). Fraser personally decided to split the Treasury, and went looking for arguments to support his decision.

THE SPLIT: A CASE OF PRIME MINISTERIAL AUTONOMY

Wettenhall (1986) has argued that machinery of government changes or departmental reorganisations were difficult for all but the prime minister to achieve because of the multi-stage process required. Ordinary ministers must first convince the prime minister, then other members of cabinet, and (at that time) the PSB. Crucially it involved stepping beyond their portfolio, which ignited suspicion at political and bureaucratic levels. In contrast, the prime minister had exclusive responsibility for the machinery of government and could therefore make and implement unilateral decisions in this area. The prime minister was able to initiate changes from 'on high' consulting only those that needed to know or be involved. Only the prime minister could accept this responsibility for machinery of government decisions, and in Fraser's case it enabled him to achieve the split of Treasury quickly and in virtual secrecy. The tactics adopted by Fraser throughout the lead up to the split suggest recognition that this potential for unilateral action, and its exercise, was crucial to the outcome. As he built concentric circles of support for his decision, Fraser effectively removed likely opponents from the decision-making process. When the decision was announced on 13th November 1976, the split was called 'Canberra's best kept secret' (Beeby 1976:3).[4]

On 5 November Fraser requested that Sir Alan Cooley, Chairman of the PSB, speedily develop options to increase the sources of economic and financial advice available to the government. The Chairman was told to select a small project team and to maintain strict secrecy. A member of that team recalled at the time that 'the Chairman stressed secrecy aspects and indicated that only the Prime Minister, the Treasurer [Phillip Lynch] and Mr [Alan] Carmody were aware of the Prime Minister's intentions' (Woodward 1976:1). Alan Carmody from PM&C and with a background in the Trade portfolio was no friend of Treasury. The team initially consisted of five members of the PSB (John Taylor, Bob Young, Bob Hamilton, Lionel Woodward, and Alan Cooley) who produced a number of possible options for the Prime Minister's consideration. No one in Treasury was informed of these discussions.

Cooley presented three options to the Prime Minister on 12 November, only one week after the initial request. While the option of splitting the Treasury was submitted, it was clearly not the Chairman's preferred course of action—and he strongly recommended that the head of Treasury Fred Wheeler be consulted. In submitting the proposals to Fraser, Cooley warned:

> I suggest that you need to carefully weigh the issues in all options. This is particularly so in relation to the option of splitting the Department of the Treasury. The splitting of Treasury is a controversial subject. Attachment D (an extract from the Treasury submission to the Coombs Commission) describes the close interaction of the various Treasury Divisions in the formulation of the Annual Budget. The Coombs Commission concluded that any attempt to split the economic policy and budget functions of the Treasury would be damaging (Letter from Cooley to Fraser, 12 November 1976).

Undeterred, Fraser acted quickly. He examined the submission over the weekend of 13 and 14 November 1976 and on the following

4 Finance was formally established on 7th December 1976.

Monday morning advised Cooley of his preference for splitting Treasury into two departments under a single minister. He had already decided on the departmental leadership of both departments and on the ministerial head. Wheeler was to continue as the Secretary to the Treasury[5] and William Cole (Australian Statistician) was nominated as the Secretary to the new Department of Finance. Cole had been 'stunned' by the news of the split, but had come to expect the appointment. The Treasurer, Phillip Lynch, retained ministerial responsibility for both departments (and advice from the Attorney General's department urged this as an interim arrangement on legal and legislative grounds). But his appointment to head both departments was a temporary arrangement. Indeed, the creation of separate Ministers for the Treasury and for Finance was a crucial part of the original reasoning for the proposed institutional separation—allowing *two* economic portfolio ministers to be influential in cabinet, and on occasions 'singing the same tune'. In the short-term Lynch was personally opposed to the split, perhaps because it meant surrendering a part of his existing empire and responsibilities. When Cole 'expressed doubt about the wisdom' of a single minister, Cooley explained that the 'the PM had to throw that sop to Lynch to keep him onside with the split'. Thus, although Lynch became the minister for both departments, the arrangement was clearly a stopgap measure designed to keep him on side, especially in the lead up to the next election.

Led by Lionel Woodward, a small team of PSB officials set about designing the new departmental structures and allocating the key functions between the two departments. The team envisaged a functional separation similar to the Canadian model, albeit with the names of the two departments reversed (and with the Australian Finance department having a much smaller range of functions than the Canadian Treasury Board Secretariat). It is significant that Treasury, on the Prime Minister's expressed instructions, was not involved in the decisions on the actual separation of its responsibilities. The areas of public expenditure, financial management and accountancy were allocated to Finance, while Treasury retained all functions related to the more general field of economic policy, as well as the formal right (as provided in the Constitution) to present the Budget and receive appropriations. Other areas of

5 Fraser had little choice as Wheeler was permanent secretary and the continued existence of Treasury was formally guaranteed at federation.

Treasury not directly related to either broad sets of functions were allocated following Fraser's directive that 'as much as possible should be put into Finance'. Nonetheless, the team's efforts to develop detailed proposals were hampered by their relatively limited knowledge of Treasury's operations. Cole, who had lengthy and recent experience as a senior Treasury official, was directed by the Prime Minister to assist in the deliberations. Less than enthusiastic about the task, Cole argued that his knowledge was limited and urged Cooley to include someone from Treasury on the team. Although Cooley agreed with Cole, he argued this was not an option because the Prime Minister was 'insistent that Treasury could not be consulted' because he 'was fed up with Treasury and in particular with Wheeler and Stone'. Humpty-dumpty did not simply topple, he was pushed.

Late on Monday, 15 November, after only Cooley and Cole had been told, Sir Frederick Wheeler was informed of the decision. As expected, he was stridently opposed to it, even though confronted with the *fait accompli*. Although he and the deputies in Treasury (Roy Daniel and Jack Garrett) were instructed to work on the implementation arrangements for the split, they simultaneously composed a memorandum arguing against the proposal and continued to work on it until the night before the split was announced. Wheeler's counter-proposal suggested that if the government wished to devote more resources to 'economic policy advising and control of expenditure', then this could be achieved not by splitting Treasury, but 'by the creation of a fourth Deputy Secretary position in Treasury thereby enabling me to allocate two Deputy Secretaries full-time to the top level handling' of both functions. He also suggested that economic advice 'could be strengthened by the provision of some additional senior positions within the existing divisions' and by the establishment of a 'bureau of expenditure control' within Treasury (Wheeler to Treasurer 17.11.1976).[6]

After the public announcement, the project team expanded to include Jack Garrett and Roy Daniel from the Treasury; Clarence

6 Wheeler also wrote in a second minute to the Treasurer that 'in my considered judgement the advantages would be greatly outweighed by the disadvantages and a split of Treasury would produce very substantial confusion and inefficiencies in the period immediately ahead and continuing inefficiencies in the longer term' (Wheeler to Treasurer, 17.11.1976). He appended a list of both advantages and disadvantages.

Harders and Ewart Smith from Attorney-General's Department; and Ian Castles, Brian Cox and John Rose from PM&C. This expanded group negotiated the legal and organisational discussions related to the split and, according to one insider, 'the work became a hard and detailed grind'. Importantly, their involvement came only after the Prime Minister had effectively made and announced his unilateral decision to split the department.

THE 'EXPENDITURE MANAGEMENT' RATIONALE

Fraser announced the establishment of the Department of Finance to the House of Representatives at 5.45pm on Thursday 18th November 1976. Cabinet had learned of the decision less than three hours earlier at 3.00pm. In his parliamentary speech, Fraser focused almost exclusively on the expenditure management implications of the new structure, ignoring the more political issue of economic policy. In a *Ministerial Statement on Administrative Arrangements*, Fraser announced to the House of Representatives that:

> Particular emphasis is being laid on improving capacity to service the government's requirements for forward planning, priority setting and the strategic planning of government initiatives . . . it is crucial that there should be more orderly and effective scheduling of Government business through the various stages of research, objective setting and policy formulation, program design and the evaluation of program effectiveness. The new arrangements involve separation of the financial management and control activities of the existing Department of the Treasury from its role in broad economic policy analysis and advice to government. For the future, the financial management and control functions will be performed by a newly created Department of Finance. The new departmental arrangements are designed to help make more manageable the heavy workload of economic and financial expenditure management which necessarily falls to the Treasurer and senior officials. In addition it will be possible under the new arrangements for more concentrated attention to be given at the departmental level to the functions of financial budget management and the development of forward estimating, as well as the analysis of economic issues and the formulation of economic strategy proposals for consideration by Government (Parliamentary Debates 18 November 1976:2898).

A press release issued together with this announcement made reference to the Ottawa model where separate ministries were responsible for economic policy (the Ministry of Finance) and government expenditure (the Treasury Board Secretariat). A few days later, Treasurer Lynch (1976:3369) in a striking example of cabinet solidarity, told Parliament the 'creation of a new Department of Finance will enable more concentrated and specialised attention to the financial management area of government . . . particularly of expenditure control and review procedures, and associated activities including forward estimating and program analysis'.

Together these statements suggest Finance was established with a clear direction and rationale but the reality was somewhat less clear-cut. The project team's perception of Finance's functions was, in part, constrained by existing budgetary and financial management arrangements. The decision to split was orchestrated principally with the diminution of Treasury's power in mind, and much less concern was given to determining what Finance itself would do. Nonetheless, the new department's responsibility in the area of public expenditure management was indisputable. For the first time in Australia's history, a Commonwealth department was dedicated to the on-going management of public expenditure. This provided a functional basis upon which the new department could forge a distinct identity—essential if the department was to thrive.

Figure 5.1 The Split of Treasury

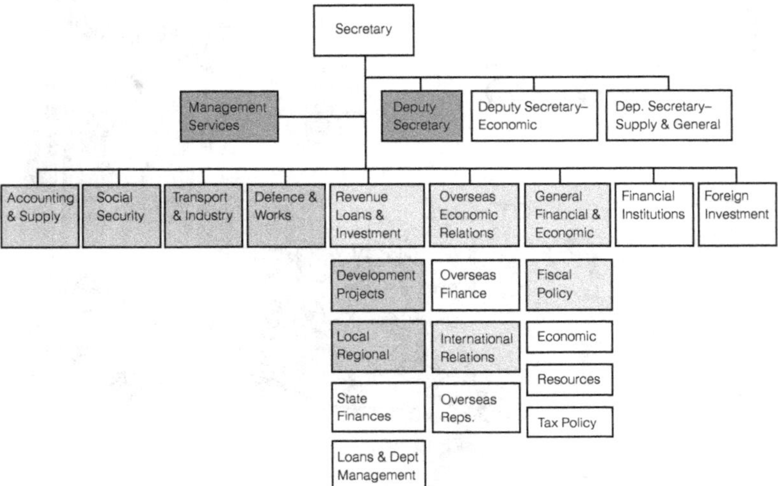

TREASURY SPLIT AND FINANCE CREATED

Once agreement was reached about the distribution of responsibilities, the process of splitting the Treasury was relatively straightforward. Treasury retained the entire Financial Institutions and Foreign Investments divisions, and large parts of the OER, RLI and GFEP divisions. Treasury also kept the Australian Taxation Office, the Australian Bureau of Statistics and related offices under its jurisdiction. Following Fraser's directive that 'as much as possible' go to Finance, the Royal Australian Mint, Actuarial Services, General and Life Insurance and AIDC were transferred to Finance—despite these functions having little to do with detailed public expenditure management. More importantly, Finance assumed total control of the Accounting and Supply, Social Security, Transport and Industry, and Defence and Works divisions, and the sections responsible for development projects, and local and regional affairs in the RLI division. After some debate, the areas responsible for foreign aid and expenditure policy were also allocated to Finance. The separation gave Finance responsibility for two of Treasury's three roles: the 'accountant to government' and 'control and management of public expenditure'; only general economic and financial management remained with Treasury. Figure 5.1 illustrates the initial division.

The transfer of Accounting and Supply gave Finance responsibility for administering the Commonwealth's Consolidated Revenue, Trust and Loan Funds. This entailed developing and prescribing accounting rules and standards throughout the public service, researching and developing accounting and management techniques, and administering the Audit Act 1901. The transfer of this division also gave Finance overall responsibility for certain crucial aspects of the budget formulation process: forward expenditure estimates, budget expenditure and revenue estimates, and the preparation and development of the annual appropriation bills.

Finance also inherited the 'saltmines' of Treasury, acquiring the three existing supply divisions—Social Security, Transport and Industry, and Defence and Works—and sections within OER and RLI divisions. Together these divisions oversaw the day-to-day financial management of every department in the public service, and provided economic and financial analysis of policy in all areas of government. They maintained records of individual departments' spending, commented on and assessed the accuracy (or otherwise) of departments' budgets and forward estimates.

The transfer of these divisions also gave Finance responsibility for advising the government on the financial and economic implications of new and on-going expenditure commitments. Responsibility of the supply divisions meant, therefore, that Finance—rather than Treasury—provided governments with the main advice on the formulation of budgets. By emphasising a role that had lain dormant under Treasury, the new department assumed a procedural power within the budgetary process that would be enhanced over time.

The power shift led to one of the first struggles between the new secretaries Bill Cole and Fred Wheeler. Those involved in separating Treasury supposed that Finance would assume overall responsibility for advising government on new expenditure programs proposed by spending departments. The function clearly fell within the overall ambit of expenditure management and the more specific role of budget formulation. The Prime Minister's instructions allocated both functions to Finance, and limited Treasury's advisory role to policy with 'significant national economic and fiscal policy implications'. Wheeler, however, was concerned about the potential decline in Treasury's capacity to comment on expenditure proposals, especially those with long-term economic implications.

He proposed, therefore, that Treasury's responsibilities be explicitly articulated as the capacity to provide 'advice on economic and financial policy aspects of expenditure programmes and proposals' (Wheeler 1976: 2). Taken literally, Wheeler's proposition sought to give Treasury the right to comment on all expenditure programs whether new or existing, presenting the opportunity for over-lap and conflict between Treasury and Finance. Eventually Wheeler gave way on this issue, arguing that he had never intended to introduce overlap into the system but was concerned to retain Treasury's control over issues with serious implications on the direction of Australia's economy.

Overall responsibility for fiscal policy remained the most contentious issue and another row quickly erupted over the organisational separation of the GFEP division. Most of the GFEP stayed with Treasury; the economic, resource and taxation policy areas were all outside Finance's jurisdiction, but the responsibility for fiscal policy was less apparent. Clearly, aggregate levels of public expenditure were of central importance to both the operations of Treasury and Finance. Treasury was allowed to retain responsibility of 'matters relating to expenditure, revenue and deficit/surplus and means of achieving overall budgetary objectives' (Fraser 1976:2898), while the fiscal section of GFEP was allocated to Finance. Although functional responsibility was transferred to Finance, the Treasury continued to operate a General Expenditure Division, which focussed on determining appropriate levels of aggregate public expenditure within the context of general economic policy. This meant the issue of who controlled fiscal policy was left unresolved by those effecting the split, creating the possibility for conflicting advice and functional overlap between the two departments, but also allowing for competing advice to government—one of the aims of the split.

Existing Treasury personnel were allocated between the two departments by Cole and Wheeler. Although most personnel were allocated according to their position, some disagreements did erupt over some of the senior officers. One dispute concerned the position of Bernie Fraser. As head of the Treasury's Fiscal Policy Division, Fraser's 'natural' appointment was to Finance. However, his interests lay in the general economic policy area much more than public expenditure management. In this instance, Cole won out and Bernie Fraser was appointed to head Finance's General Expenditure Policy Division. The second dispute concerned the number and allocation of existing Treasury deputy secretaries—Jack

Garrett, John Stone, and Roy Daniel. At the time, Treasury was one of only two departments in the APS with three deputy secretaries (the other was PM&C), and the prospect of losing two senior positions in the split would cause an even greater dent in the department's status. Treasury won this fight and kept two of the three deputy secretaries (Stone and Daniel). However, the appointment of Jack Garrett as Deputy Secretary to Finance was curious. Roy Daniel, not Garrett, had held responsibility for Treasury's accounting and supply operations. Given that these operations were entirely transferred to Finance, it appeared logical that Daniel should also move to Finance. These and similar events suggest that personality played a very important role in the split of Treasury personnel (Weller 1977).[7]

On paper the relative carve-up of resources between the two departments suggested an imbalance with Treasury controlling a much larger share of the budget allocation. In the 1978–79 budget, Treasury's total appropriation ($318.8 million) remained almost ten times larger than that of Finance ($16.9m). However, this figure included the appropriations for the ATO ($241m) and the ABS ($60m) both of which were in effect separate departments with control over their own budgets. Excluding these, the core departments of Treasury and Finance were of relatively similar size and responsibility, and the money appropriated to each department for administration was relatively similar: Treasury received $17.9m to Finance's $16.96m. Treasury did slightly better in terms of the seniority of staff allocations, even though Finance secured more staff (840 to 640) due to the labour-intensive functions it inherited. However, most of these officers had relatively low classifications and performed routine functions. The new Department of Finance and its officers remained housed in the Treasury Building, rather than being given separate accommodation. Although Treasury had been publicly reprimanded, it clearly retained seniority over the new housekeeping department.

---

7 Weller (1977:35) quotes Wheeler as not wanting to lose Garrett and still hoping the 'Treasury team' would survive under the new 'order of things' especially as both departments would be under the same minister and working in 'close collaboration with each other'.

THE REACTION TO HUMPTY'S GREAT FALL

Paul Kelly reported a stunned silence around Canberra when the split was announced (1978b). Certainly, public reaction to Fraser's decision to split Treasury was muted. Many public servants believed the separation would not last—and rumours circulated of 'Humpty-Dumpty' being put back together. This feeling was reinforced by the fact that Lynch remained minister of both departments, which continued to share facilities. A former senior public servant from both PM&C and then PSB summed up the feeling of many people at that time when he recalled (Taylor 1996):

> certainly in the earlier days I didn't see any great justification for it [the split]. I mean it's like cutting the head off the hydrozoan . . . they're bad enough as it is but why make it even more complicated and dangerous.

The Labor opposition, instead of welcoming the split of their institutional *bete noir,* castigated the move as a 'misinformed' and 'hasty' response to political problems within the government (Whitlam 1976:2990). Only one year out of government, Labor seemed to be ignoring the evidence presented to RCAGA. They also attempted to gain some political mileage out of the reorganisation by suggesting that the leak on exchange rates had motivated the split. Labor's suggestion was greeted with indignation by the Treasurer. Generally, however, the opposition's response was somewhat blunted because it was difficult to formulate a sustained attack over changes they had countenanced twelve months earlier. Discussion of the split vanished from the parliamentary arena within a matter of days.

Not surprisingly journalists at the time highlighted the political implications of the split. Brown (1976:2) when comparing the Fraser and Whitlam government's concluded that, 'Big Mal had done what Big Gough seriously thought of doing, yet never quite dared to do—moved to break the power of Treasury'. Beeby (1976:3) argued that the split was 'designed to overcome the hostility, bordering on hatred, of other government departments for the Treasury bureaucracy'. Grattan (1976:1) suggested that 'the arrangements are unpopular with the Treasury people', while after surveying opinion in Canberra, Davidson (1976:1) reported that 'Treasury officers were divided last night in their reactions, but several senior Government backbenchers were strongly opposed to the new arrangements'.

Many media commentators focused primarily on the impact these new institutional arrangements would have on economic policy advice and, measured against RCAGA's extensive recommendations, concluded that little would change. The government had not followed RCAGA's advice to establish a long-term economic policy agency because of a possible 'conflict of advice to the Government'. Grattan (1976:1) argued that such conflict 'could be a healthy development' but nevertheless dubbed the decision as 'shortsighted'. McGuiness concluded that: 'this division will achieve little beyond the weakening of the excessive power wielded for so long by Treasury officials. It will not improve the quality of advice, or even the range of options offered. Nor will it improve the financial management procedures' (McGuiness 1976:59). For Juddery (1976:1–4) the split was a lost opportunity for change which promised to 'almost certainly further entrench the Treasury approach to economic planning'. The general scepticism in the media was summed up in a simple cartoon shown below.

Some academic writers were also less than convinced about the benefits of the split. Hazlehurst (1978:303) lamented that:

> Instead of the creation of a Department of Industries and the Economy (DINDEC) as recommended [by RCAGA] . . . we have a bifurcated Treasury, and administrative arrangements likely to further entrench rather than remedy some of the defects RCAGA sought to eradicate.

Echoing this sentiment, Self (1978:329) observed that:

> The Fraser government has . . . chosen to divide Treasury, more with the idea of strengthening Treasury's financial control than sharing financial decisions with other departments. However, the logical Canadian device of combining financial and manpower planning, which might have accorded with the RCAGA approach although not their actual proposals, has not been adopted.

Nonetheless, other academic reactions to the split produced measured enthusiasm. Weller (a consultant to RCAGA, who had the misfortune to launch his book *Treasury Control in Australia* on the very day the split was announced), certainly did not object to the split, and highlighted a number of potential benefits in the new structure. More than most commentators, he argued that a department focused exclusively on public expenditure management had the potential to improve consistency and equity in budget deliberations, and to improve on-going financial management (1977).

But he was sceptical about the extent to which real change was possible under the new system *if* Treasury's existing culture was replicated in the new satellite of Finance—a likely event given the wholesale transfer of Treasury divisions and the sharing of the same minister. Unless the new department moved quickly to establish its own charter and culture, he believed, the restructure was unlikely to achieve the claimed benefits or improve systems.

PRIORITISING REFORM

Despite the prognostications, the decision to split Treasury had far-reaching consequences for public expenditure management in Australia. The most apparent and immediate consequence was the creation of a specialist institution. Built out of the accounting and supply divisions of Treasury, Finance was given the mundane, routine and non-glamorous functions of expenditure control. Observers at the time soon came to regard Finance as Treasury's poor cousin. Nonetheless, by establishing the new department the government had created for the first time since federation a specialist public expenditure management agency.

The political circumstances of the department's creation meant that it was free to establish its own role and shape a unique future to ensure survival. Despite Fraser's pronouncements over the reasons for the split, the political motivations of the main players clearly suggest the separation was the result of a decision to discipline Treasury, rather than the principal *raison d'etre* of the decision. Rational arguments favouring the split had previously been presented in a number of forums, but were rejected essentially for political reasons or timing. After the decision was made to split Treasury, many of the arguments presented to RCAGA were then adopted by Fraser's team to justify the decision. When asked why little mention was made of Treasury in announcing the split, Fraser (Interview 1997) replied: 'well you're not going to get up in Parliament and say you're cutting them down to size'. Hence, government arguments on the record should be treated with caution. Perhaps they were convenient *ex post* justifications for a decision made with political and personal motivations, rather than considered arguments guiding a rational decision. This does not mean that the decision was a bad one or that it did not accomplish prudent institutional changes.

Nonetheless, these debates provided a clear departure point

from which both departments could develop their own identities. Fraser's argument that Finance was established for the broad purpose of public expenditure management gave the department an operational focus. The expertise of experienced officers transferred from Treasury gave it the capability of achieving that focus. The immediate debates and arguments over public expenditure management presented during RCAGA provided Finance with an agenda for reform which could now be accorded higher priority. By taking the reform agenda away from Treasury, the split enabled the department to develop expenditure management techniques that were designed to facilitate efficiency and effectiveness within the public service.

6 More control . . . more spending: the paradox of the Fraser years

WITH FINANCE ESTABLISHED as the central budget agency responsible for public expenditure, the Coalition government hoped for a better grip on the control of the public purse. If the great expectations associated with the early forward estimates processes had been thwarted, the in-coming conservative government now turned to new institutional arrangements to impose budget discipline and tighter expenditure restrictions. Initially there was not much sense of how the institutional arrangements would achieve fiscal stringency or how future controls would evolve. The Fraser years, instead, indicate a period of experimentation with various types of control initiatives—some regarded as effective (and subsequently built on) while others were jettisoned with little ceremony. But an emerging pattern of institutional control gradually begins to emerge over these years. Cabinet budget committees and senior ministers begin to function as strong guardians of the public purse, Finance becomes a powerful advocate for restraint, and budgetary processes are progressively revised to increase central budgetary control of financial inputs. To this pattern we can add occasional forays into other forms of imposing restraint such as the notorious 'Razor Gang' exercise of 1980–81 which tried to reduce Commonwealth functions as a means of reducing outlays. The 'Razor Gang' attracted considerable attention but was perhaps more significant in its long-term influence on government agendas rather than its immediate cuts to the bottom line. Eventually, the government came to promote program-based reporting of expenditure and the adoption of more managerial approaches to resource utilisation. But the Fraser government fell before these reforms were to be fully implemented.

The seven years of the Fraser government (1975–83) were marked by a desire to impose expenditure control on the public sector. This chapter recounts those attempts at expenditure control and charts the effectiveness of their achievements. It is argued here that, in retrospect, the end of the Fraser period can be seen to provide a platform on which later budgetary reforms were often based. As the limits of crude *ex ante* controls were increasingly realised, key actors and central institutions began to reassess their control systems and their thinking about budgetary processes. And yet, toward the end of his period in government Fraser allowed a significant departure from his regime of austerity and tight control. His final budget suddenly increased spending and recorded a substantial deficit. This is the paradox. Here was a government that was almost obsessive about restraint, that designed and implemented many instruments for tighter control, but then after years of practising financial stringency failed to stem a major budget blow-out and allowed the budget process to become a quagmire. This paradox highlights not only the wider fiscal and economic nature of public expenditure, but also the sometimes conflicting imperatives operating between formal mechanisms of control and the exigencies of political will. The Fraser paradox signifies that even extensive formal controls can produce very differing results year to year as the exigencies of political office change.

INSTITUTIONAL AUTONOMY FOR THE CENTRAL BUDGET AGENCY

Government expenditure and the supply of resources to spending departments was a fundamental responsibility of Treasury up to 1976. Nevertheless, the evidence is that inside Treasury these matters were often seen as less important than macro-economic policy (Whitwell 1986). Weller and Cutt (1976:30) wrote that 'all other functions are considered subordinate' to the objective of economic management. Expenditure patterns and issues associated with the supply of funds to the Commonwealth's main portfolios were handled at the first assistant secretary level in the Treasury (under the four divisions of Accounting and Supply; Defence; Social Security; Transport and Industry). But these functions were largely separated from the 'main game'. According to officers who served in Treasury at that time, other senior officials in the department were only interested in this area to the extent it related to macro-economic policy concerns (Visbord Interview 1997; Craik Interview 1996). Other ministers and cabinet as a whole were also typically not much interested in the specifics of supply issues (except in relation to the fate of their own resourcing bids).

This neglectful attitude persisted within the core executive despite Commonwealth expenditures rising from 23.8% of GDP in 1972–73 to 28.6% in 1975–76. For two main reasons the lack of attention to the expenditure side of the budget was about to change. First, the rapid increase in Commonwealth spending occurred at the same time as the Australian economy moved into recession and experienced rising levels of unemployment. This increased the political significance of both government expenditures and the size of government. Second, dedicated attention was focussed on restraining expenditure through the new institutional arrangements that had almost by accident created a central agency with principal responsibility for the expenditure budget. The control of expenditure became a prime objective of the Fraser government, even if initially the means to achieve such control remained inchoate.

Splitting Treasury into two organisations was a relatively straightforward exercise because the old department had identifiable divisions which largely fell into one camp or the other. Those transferred to Finance had no previous experience of operating as an independent department (as opposed to a set of identifiable but subordinate functions within the confines of Treasury) and took some time to develop a corporate identity and find their niche. Institutional autonomy meant the new department had to define its separate role and objectives, both for its internal functioning and in terms of its relations with other Commonwealth agencies. Finance's immediate ability to define its own role was to a degree impeded by the widely held view that the experiment of forming a new department would be short lived and Finance would return to the fold of Treasury. Officials in both departments thought re-amalgamation was most likely. The talk of putting Humpty Dumpty together again was a rather unfortunate analogy given that 'all the King's men couldn't put Humpty together again'. Gradually the view developed in Finance that to survive in its own right the department needed a discrete and defensible role, and it needed additional staff recruited from outside Treasury, as well as some political protection (Cole Interview 1996).

Once it became a stand-alone central agency, the Department of Finance gained the advantages of its own bureaucratic and then political leadership. From the outset in November 1976 Finance was provided with a respected permanent head (Bill Cole 1976–79) and competent deputy (Jack Garrett). Both Cole and his immediate successor as departmental head, Ian Castles (1979–86), began to augment the senior staff of the new department. They selected recruits often from outside the Treasury culture, many of whom were to have a major influence over agendas of public sector reform in the Commonwealth. Neither Cole nor Castles were hard-nosed political infighters within the bureaucracy and to a large extent Finance remained in the shadow of Treasury—a situation which avoided the possibility of an enervating turf war with the more senior department. Both heads played a more important role behind the scenes in forging a new institutional culture for the central budget agency. Malcolm Fraser, in particular, was personally close to Castles and held his advice in high regard; his appointment as department head in January 1979 meant the Prime Minister and cabinet could be provided with advice separate from the Secretary of Treasury.

A distinctive political leadership of the new budget ministry was slower to eventuate. As an interim measure the Treasurer Phillip Lynch continued to hold responsibility for the two departments and was appointed the first Minister for Finance—probably to offset any impression that the deputy Liberal leader had been demoted and to avoid the need for a ministerial reshuffle prior to the federal election of 1977. But, as of December 1977 Finance gained its own cabinet minister, Eric Robinson (a senior Liberal party operative from Queensland), who had served as Minister Assisting the Treasurer since February 1976. Fraser's decision to promote Robinson reflected the Prime Minister's faith in his capacities—despite any formal training or interest in finance matters (Fraser Interview 1997).[1] His decision also indicated a need to accommodate the influential Queenslander, as well as his desire to retain the two divided economic/budgetary portfolios under the Liberals' control.[2] Robinson held the portfolio virtually continu-

---

1 Robinson had been company director of a Brisbane sports store—and after being appointed to the Finance portfolio one of his Queensland federal Liberal colleagues reputedly said to him: 'there's more to understanding government finance than selling tennis balls'.

2 Dame Margaret Guilfoyle, the fourth Minister for Finance, argued that it was crucial for Finance to have its own minister providing departmental views directly to cabinet. However, she later recalled that although the appointment

ously for one term until November 1980 when, rather than accept a demotion, he finally chose to quit the ministry.[3] At this stage the Finance ministry was given cabinet rank probably due to a combination of reasons: political considerations in the Liberal party; recognition of the need for another economic minister at the cabinet table; and recognition of the potential role of the fledgling Finance department. Finance ministers have since continued to enjoy cabinet rank except for three months under the Hawke Labor government in 1983.

One of the initial reasons, therefore, for the rise in importance of Finance as a guardian of public expenditure was that it soon attracted recruits with a vested interest in developing the roles and institutional autonomy of the department. Released from Treasury and with its own cabinet minister and a cadre of senior officials, Finance increasingly focussed on expenditure control and resource constraint. It is one of the paradoxes of the Fraser years that Finance was to some degree helped by Robinson's lack of interest in the department. This meant the minister had no personal barrow to push, and so let Finance develop according to its own lights. Had the senior executives of the new department been less able, Robinson's benign neglect could have been a costly mistake, but under the circumstances his tenure allowed for consolidation and the development of an agenda of tighter controls. Nevertheless,

---

of Eric Robinson in 1977 as the minister solely in charge of Finance was an important transition, Robinson 'probably hadn't had as much experience as might have been desired to run [Finance] at that time—his experience was more limited'. Both Guilfoyle and Fraser found Robinson more interested in politics than administration; Guilfoyle found 'he was interested in the politics of government and particularly from the state of Queensland . . . he represented the Liberal party from Queensland rather than being a coordinating minister who was the Minister for Finance . . . he played a different role from the one that I played' (Guilfoyle Interview 1996). Fraser (Interview 1997) similarly agreed that his faith may have been misplaced in Robinson as he showed little interest in the portfolio and, compared to Guilfoyle, displayed less initiative in pushing agendas of reform. Another official from the Department of Finance remembered that Robinson 'wanted to be a minister but he didn't really care about Finance'. Weller (1989:75) recounts in his study of Fraser that Robinson was often 'not briefed on issues when they were discussed; he was a lazy minister and not held in high regard'.

3 Eric Robinson's tenure as Finance minister was interrupted by his sudden resignation in February 1979—an interregnum never fully explained. John Howard (then Treasurer) became the third Minister for Finance for five days from 23.2.1979 to 27.2.1979 until Robinson was reappointed.

the growing political influence of Finance was assisted because it had a minister sitting inside the cabinet room or on budget review committees arguing for resource stringency and greater efficiencies in the public sector. This emerging visibility stood in stark contrast to the Public Service Board, which had nominal responsibility for management in the public service but had no such representation at cabinet and was fast losing influence. The Board operated as a resource gatekeeper in staffing matters, but had not shown much interest in managerial reform or resource efficiency.

REFINING THE OBJECTIVES OF THE DEPARTMENT OF FINANCE

From its inauspicious beginning the Department of Finance inherited many customary practices and traditional 'line-item' control orientations from the former Treasury. But simultaneously, Finance was charged by the Prime Minister with giving greater emphasis to a series of generic functions. On paper, these appeared a coherent set of functions, but whether they could be welded together into a coherent and effective department remained to be seen, and largely could only be achieved within the organisation itself. Conscious of this problem, Cole as the first secretary suggested his main role was developing a cohesive department, and he quickly came to the view that one of his initial goals was to establish a coordinating division within Finance to oversee public expenditure (Cole Interview 1996). Others were also cautious of the new department's capacity to fulfil these intended roles. Immediately after the split Weller (1977:31) argued: 'new structures do not necessarily lead to new styles . . . if the old system of Treasury control is to be improved, new styles are required'. Again, Robinson's personal manner, and that of his successor Senator Margaret Guilfoyle, allowed such styles to emerge gradually from within, rather than be imposed from without.

Both documentary and interview evidence indicate the early department continued to regard its principal objective as 'hands on' expenditure control—often involving traditional detailed controls on spending departments following from its supply orientations under Treasury. It was interested in a range of reforms or possible innovations, but these were primarily directed toward upgrading and improving existing scrutiny systems, rather than the creation of new structures and processes. The department's own sense of its purpose could be regarded as somewhat hazy and constrained by the 'accountants' view' that still dominated the department. This view is indicated by the statements of purpose in the departmental annual reports and ministerial statements and speeches.

For instance, the Department of Finance's first *Annual Report*, published almost three years after the split, suggests its activities were primarily directed toward expenditure control. Explaining the role of the department, the report states that the 'principal activities of the Department relate to the central financial and accounting functions of the Government' (DoF 1979:1). This is repeated in the 1979–80 *Annual Report*, which also identified the department's two central functions: coordination of financial administration, and the provision of 'accounting services for the Government' (DoF 1980a:1). Relative continuity of the department's purpose and function is also suggested by its stable organisational structure from its establishment in 1976 until 1984. Such freedom from political or administrative pressures, fostered not only a sense of purpose and more focused roles, but also departmental energy and internal debate (Castles Interview 1997).

In these early years there is little mention in official publications of the department's functions extending to financial management, program budgeting, 'value for money' budgeting, or performance evaluation—topics which later became commonplace and, arguably, central to the department's role. Yet, departmental records indicate some wide ranging debates occurred inside the department as to the nature of the roles Finance should perform, and some officers actively promoted 'radical' changes to existing roles and budget processes. Encouraged especially by Castles, these debates remained internal and few were publicly aired.[4]

By contrast, despite their tough rhetoric, Coalition ministers with responsibility for the budget formulation process did not push for major budget reforms or show great foresight in expenditure management. The Treasurer and initial Finance minister, Phillip Lynch, and his successor as Treasurer, John Howard (1977–83), were both principally preoccupied with containing aggregate expenditure and fiscal rectitude rather than internal reforms to the budget process. The subsequent two Finance ministers, Eric Rob-

---

4 Peter Walsh, Finance Minister from 1984 to 1990 and the last minister Ian Castles served under as secretary, remembered that the department had developed a culture of internal 'technical' debates and that being briefed by Castles was often akin 'to attending an ANU lecture' (Walsh Interview 1997).

inson (Dec 1977—Nov 1980) and his successor Dame Margaret Guilfoyle (Nov 1980—Mar 1983)—a Victorian Liberal and former Social Security minister—largely saw their role in conventional terms as guardian gatekeepers of the public purse. Their prime objective was again one of expenditure restraint. Indeed, Guilfoyle recalled that by the time she assumed the portfolio 'we had really been labelled very firmly as a government that was trying to control expenditure' (Guilfoyle Interview 1996). Along with the Prime Minister, who shared similar views, these budgetary ministers aimed to *restrain the rate of growth of public expenditure and where possible, freeze or reduce outlays*. This philosophy of aggregate restraint endured over six of the Fraser government's seven budgets from 1976–77 to 1981–82; the last Coalition budget of 1982–83 departed dramatically from this pattern for the reasons that are examined in more detail below.

INTENSIFIED PRESSURE TO LIVE WITHIN BUDGETS

The expansion in public spending under both the McMahon and Whitlam governments contributed to a significant rise in Commonwealth outlays to GDP over five years (from 23.1 % in 1969–70 to 28.6% in 1975–76, although contemporary figures placed the peak at 30.1% in 1975–76) (DoF 1980b:3). While many argue that such levels of spending were long overdue and necessary, others highlight the suddenness of the increases, the lack of consideration to long-term implications and 'complete chaos' through which many significant expenditure decisions were taken (Visbord Interview 1997). Commonwealth net debt levels rose from −1% of GDP in 1974–75 to 1% in 1975–76 and to 4% of GDP in 1977–78. In retrospect, the early 1970s provide strong empirical evidence that sound fiscal management is hard to create, hard to maintain, easy to lose and even harder to regain. The Whitlam years in particular indicate that governments can ratchet up expenditures relatively quickly, but the task of reducing expenditures (even when governments are committed to this end) is a protracted and difficult process.

Faced with burgeoning outlays, the Fraser government was concerned to bring down actual spending so the Commonwealth could live within its means (B. Fraser 1977). Government rhetoric suggested that the Coalition was prepared to withdraw from certain areas of government activity and reduce the size of the public sector. Certainly, a number of important initiatives of the Fraser government were directed at these ends. Initially, public spending was reduced (by around 2% of GDP between 1975–76 and 1979–80), but over its seven years in office there is little evidence that aggregate expenditure decreased or that the government withdrew from significant areas of activity—notwithstanding the efforts of the infamous 'Razor Gang' in the early 1980s (see below).

More pragmatically the Fraser government was determined not to overspend. It acknowledged its frustration at being confronted with 'uncontrolled' big-ticket expenditure items (mostly inherited) that often involved long-term and unpredictable commitments. These areas of expenditure in 1975–76 included social security and welfare, health, tertiary education, transport and communication, housing and urban development. The proportion of outlays spent on these functions had generally increased significantly since 1969–70. For instance, social security rose from 17.3% of Commonwealth outlays in 1969–70 to 23.2% in 1975–76, health rose from 6.3% to 13.5%, education increased as the Commonwealth accepted responsibility for universities from 3.3% to 8.4%, and housing and urban development rose from 2.8% to 4.5%. Of the major areas of expenditure only three decreased significantly—defence from 14.2% to 8.5%, transport 7.7% to 6.1% and primary industry assistance from 4.8% to 0.8%. Payments to the states also declined as a proportion of Commonwealth outlays from 23.9% to 20.3% (see Appendix C).

The method used by Fraser was to approach the annual budget process with toughened political resolve in an attempt to 'rein-in the growth of the public sector', reduce expenditure and restore some discretion over the types and magnitude of expenditures (1980b:3). At this stage relatively few modifications to the budgetary processes were contemplated and even fewer introduced.

One of the first ways the Fraser government attempted to rein-in future expenditures was to make the estimates for projected expenditure more accurate and rigorous. Indeed, by the end of the government's second term officials in Finance argued in a paper entitled *Controlling Public Expenditure* (1980b:6–7) that:

> Formal forward estimates have been collected from departments for a number of years but had not been much used until more recent years. Since the mid 1970s these estimates have been progressively integrated into the Government's budgetary decision framework, providing as they do an initial assessment of likely funding

> requirements . . . Since 1976–77, the Budget estimates for the year ahead have been complemented by a formal system for the *regulation and control of a range of commitments*; this replaced a number of embryonic measures directed to commitment control which for the most part lacked any firm authority.

This 'out-year' control was particularly important in relation to decisions that established on-going expenditure through statute or formal agreement. A larger proportion of Commonwealth outlays had become *non-discretionary* in that they were legal entitlements (for pensions, social security) or pre-committed though intergovernmental agreements.[5] By the mid 1970s the government estimated that over two-thirds of total expenditure was non-discretionary (and rising due to the automatic indexation of pensions and transfers, public service salaries, joint programs with the states, and the interest payments on the public debt). The remaining third was directed to the Commonwealth's own 'discretionary' functions, from defence to economic services and its own administration. With so much of the budget pre-committed, the government's capacity to control expenditures was therefore constrained. They could lower or restrict future entitlements (but this was politically difficult); they could increase revenue to balance the projected budget (again politically difficult); they could attempt to reduce formula funding to authorities or levels of government by cutting grants to the states and local governments (possible, but highly contentious); or they could focus on controlling their own discretionary spending (an available option, but one which would undermine the Commonwealth's own policy ambitions). Governments in this situation find themselves squeezing the margins.

The Coalition's determination to trim future commitments was accordingly augmented with 'in-year' expenditure controls over discretionary spending. From their first Budget in 1976–77 an annual round of savings were achieved by 'across the board percentage cuts after estimates had been virtually settled in normal processes' (DoF 1980b:7). These across-the-board cuts were expedient

---

5 The government argued it was difficult to wind back the size of the public sector because of the reduced flexibility in expenditure allocations 'arising from the increasing extent to which various outlays tend to be committed for years ahead'. This was compounded by the automatic indexation of welfare payments, and wages and salaries, and by the cost-sharing and tax-sharing agreements with the states together with the rising interest on public debt (*Controlling Public Expenditure* DoF 1980b:3).

and politically palatable, but irrational in that priority areas were cut at the same rate as areas which were of less priority to the government. Departments were expected to absorb cost increases within their allocations and it was made more difficult (although not impossible) for departments to mount a case for additional funding during a year for existing activities or new initiatives. Additional requests from spending departments were expected to be partly 'offset' against savings within the department's existing budget.

Besides the arbitrary across-the-board cuts, a laborious system of 'in-year' regulation was refined consisting mainly of top-down mechanisms to 'cap' expenditure. Two instruments were relied on particularly to discipline the spending patterns of departments (or to curtail their unrestrained demands). First, centrally imposed ceilings were often placed on departmental staffing levels below the 'establishment' numbers allocated by the PSB. This meant that agencies were restricted in the number and often categories of employees permitted at certain census times (reporting in July). Staff ceilings had been intermittently used since the 1960s, but from 1975 were 'applied in a continuous fashion' as a way of cutting the number of public servants (and other employees covered by the 'ceilings'). Second, Finance and PM&C imposed annual cash limits on departmental spending as a rationing mechanism to prevent over-spending. These cash limits were introduced in 1975 and were intended to hold spending departments on a relatively tight cash leash. Cash limits were applied to 'in-year' departmental spending and extended to budget allocations for the year ahead.[6] Intended limits were approved *within* the overall budget estimates for the department (i.e. were less than the budget allocation).

Although these top-down limits on cash and staff were relatively crude devices, the government signalled its intention to seek more detailed controls on expenditure and that these would be exercised and tightly controlled by the relevant central agencies (Finance, PM&C, and the PSB). In the late 1970s, for example,

6 Cash limits restricted the amount of funds an agency could consume within the year—usually a budget figure which meant agencies were often operating with fewer full-time employees than the staff ceiling levels permitted. One of the reasons for the imposition of dollar cash limits was that the methods of accounting for staff levels was notoriously difficult and rubbery. The net result of the PSB, PM&C and Finance each regulating agency resources was a high degree of micro-management in the day-to-day affairs of line agencies.

the 'real' departmental staff ceiling numbers were imposed by the Prime Minister on advice from his staff and Treasury, rather than by the Board which approved nominal establishment levels. Even under such politically driven parameters, determined line departments could find ways of evading the Prime Minister's staff controls. Once such controls were introduced their success was inevitably mixed,[7] but (perhaps in the absence of other effective tools) the Coalition continued to believe in their effectiveness and tended to tighten the limits whenever the opportunity arose.

The latitude for spending departments to shift their costs to future years similarly became more restricted. Finance (1980b) imposed limits on 'undischarged commitments outstanding at the end of the financial year [and] payable in future years' that departments had previously expected to be payed in the following year from consolidated revenue (perhaps as unexpected items or one-off supplements). This was seen as a measure to prevent agencies double dipping into consolidated revenue to pay for their liabilities. The government also embraced the notion of 'sunset legislation' involving an end to resourcing for particular purposes once the stipulated time had expired, and they began to adopt a 'user pays' approach for 'marketable-type services'.

In terms of results, some control of aggregate expenditure levels was achieved by the Fraser government—especially if it were assumed that without explicit constraint expenditure outlays would have continued to trend upwards. The strategy of limiting commitments and containing current outlays so that government lived within its budget met with some initial success in reducing expenditure increases. The effectiveness of these measures was always likely to be short-term because they remained exclusively *ex ante* and *ex post* controls imposed from central agencies. The problem was that central agencies could not control the expenditure decision-making within agencies that could create unforeseen expenditure blow-outs. Moreover, when forced to operate under such external controls year after year, spending agencies gradually invented

7 Ed Visbord (deputy secretary in PM&C) argued the system of staff controls was a 'bloody chaotic system. Fraser believed that the only way to keep in his pocket an effective cut was to reduce the numbers and you had three ways of reducing numbers [establishment levels, staff ceilings and cash limits] . . . I remember that the accounting for these was a very farcical exercise. But I guess you have to say that in the end Fraser achieved some of what he wanted by controlling public service numbers' (Interview 1997).

creative ways of circumventing these limits to secure additional staff and resources beyond those permitted.

Nevertheless, a Finance briefing paper *Budgeting and Expenditure Control* (1982a:8) expressed succinctly the government's effectiveness in limiting expenditure increases:

> For five years the Commonwealth Budget actual outcome has been held very close to the original Budget estimates (the 1976–77 outcome was 0.8% below the original estimates; for 1977–78 to 1980–81 the outcome exceeded original estimates by 0.5%, 0.6%, less than 0.1% and 0.7% respectively.

The department (1982a:9) went on to say:

> It is, of course, unlawful to spend amounts for any purpose in excess of those appropriated for that purpose by the Parliament. Apart from rare inadvertence, departments have generally been punctilious in this regard, and controls recently incorporated in the Department of Finance centralised computer system now ensure that departments cannot 'overspend' even through clerical error. At the same time, departments are well aware that there are means of supplementing appropriations (the 'additional estimates or further appropriation process' . . . and a limited amount—the Advance to the Minister for Finance—appropriation for allocation by the Minister for Finance to meet urgent and unforeseen requirements). Their willingness to contain expenditure can thus depend in part on awareness that recourse to these means will not be readily available, and that they will therefore need to apply sufficient prudence and foresight to avoid situations where some likely contingency could exhaust an appropriation.

The following table indicates the pattern of budget stringency imposed by the Fraser government throughout the latter 1970s—the restraint that was abandoned in 1982–83.

THE 'RAZOR GANG': REVIEW OF COMMONWEALTH FUNCTIONS (1980–81)

In late 1980 Fraser created a ministerial committee to conduct a comprehensive Review of Commonwealth Functions (RCF—immediately dubbed the 'Razor Gang'). The committee reported directly to cabinet and was headed by the trusted Phillip Lynch, the Minister for Industry and Commerce (and former Treasurer).

Table 6.1 Commonwealth Outlays 1975–1983

Year	Total Com. Outlays $ Billion	Com. 'Own Purpose' Outlays % of GDP	Total Com Outlays as % of GDP	% Real Growth in Budget Outlays
1975–76	21.94	16.5	28.6	4.9
1976–77	24.23	17.7	27.6	-0.7
1977–78	26.86	17.8	28.4	2.6
1978–79	29.20	16.9	27.2	1.7
1979–80	31.75	16.8	26.3	-0.7
1980–81	36.31	17.0	26.4	3.2
1981–82	41.52	17.9	26.8	2.6
1982–83	49.39	19.3	28.9	7.4
1983–84	57.29	20.1	29.6	8.5

Source: DoF 1982a; Budget Paper No 1, 1993–94:5.6.

Other ministers appointed to the review were the Treasurer John Howard,[8] Peter Nixon, Margaret Guilfoyle and Ian Viner (Weller 1989:245). The review was meant to be 'much more than an expenditure review exercise' (RCF 1981:40) in that it would attempt to reduce the size of the Commonwealth government sector. After five years in office the Coalition had managed to reduce the *growth* in expenditure but real outlays were still increasing by 1% per annum.[9] The 'Razor Gang' was briefed to examine Commonwealth functions and establish which could be better performed by other levels of government (states or local governments) or by the private sector. The stated intention of the government was to 'streamline and fine down Commonwealth operations' either by 'withdrawing from functions more appropriately handled by the States or private enterprise' or 'by rationalising

8 The Treasurer Phillip Lynch resigned during the 1977 election campaign over his alleged misuse of public office in relation to property dealings in Victoria. Fraser selected John Howard (a former lawyer and Minister for Business and Consumer Affairs) as Treasurer over other more senior contenders.

9 In presenting the report of the review to Parliament Malcolm Fraser stressed that he sought a 'turnaround' in the level of expenditure and for the size of the Commonwealth government to be reduced. He indicated frustration that the government had up to that point merely slowed the rate of growth rather than achieved a reduction. He stated 'In the three years before 1972–75 there was a real growth of 4.5% in Commonwealth outlays. In the next three years there was an enormous 10 per cent real growth per annum. In the five years since then, this government has brought the growth down to only about 1 per cent per annum' (RCF 1981:5).

the functions which properly belong to the Commonwealth' (Ministerial Statement—RCF No 96/1981:1).

The final recommendations of the 'Razor Gang' were reported to Parliament through the Prime Minister on the 30th April 1981. Although many 'big-ticket' functions had been discussed in the committee's deliberations—such as the sale of the two airlines, the Commonwealth Bank and the abandonment of the new Parliament house (Weller 1989:246–51), the eventual recommendations of the review were a mixture of the serious, the trivial and the bizarre. Cabinet agreed to sell certain assets, reduce regulation, restructure some administrative functions and extend contracting out.

The assets proposed for sale were minor. They included the ordinance factory at Bendigo, the Mugga quarry and hotmix plant, a clothing factory at Coburg, the Belconnen Mall, the Wool Testing Authority and some surplus Commonwealth land. Australia Post's courier services were abolished and other public providers (such as Telecom, the Government Printer and the Mint) were ordered to allow the private sector greater access to their business. Some specific administrative functions were to be transferred to other governments (such as the Sacred Sites Protection Authority to the Northern Territory, and school and curriculum functions back to the states), or abolished (e.g. the Council for Aboriginal Development, the Assisted Passage Scheme for migrants). Specific items of administrative expenditure (furniture, maintenance, fitting out, property) were to be reduced by 3% in real terms over the 1981–82 budget year. Fees for second and higher degrees at universities were advocated (but not fees for first degrees—which had been discussed by the RCF but not recommended). The entitlement of public servants to paid study leave was restricted to essential cases, and remuneration for members of government advisory boards was withdrawn. Measures recommended for contracting out included the manufacture of artificial limbs, the development of computer software, coinage blanks for the Mint, some government printing, and the cleaning and security of Commonwealth properties. In retrospect, these relatively slight measures served as the precursor of things to come—as subsequent governments undertook more ambitious targets for privatisation, for contracting out and to apply user-charging provisions.

The government also announced that a 'freeze' would be imposed on capital works—and that no funding would be committed in the current budget year for a list of intended projects (most were actually deferred not terminated). Major projects deferred included: the Canberra law courts, ASIO and Federal Police headquarters, and regional Commonwealth offices. Funds were withdrawn for the electrification of the Sydney-Melbourne railway, but Fraser vetoed any proposal to stop the new Parliament building. The Commonwealth's provision of industry assistance would be reduced, but other recommendations were simply matters of redefinition: Aboriginal housing grants were to be incorporated (but still earmarked) in the general Housing Agreement with the states, and the control of nuclear activities was to be implemented by the states but coordinated by the Commonwealth.

The Prime Minister claimed that the 'estimated overall effect of these measures will be an eventual on-going saving in Budget outlays of the order of $560 million' and asset sales and reductions in industry assistance would raise a further $130 million (RCF 1981:41). But given the main aim of the 'Razor Gang' was to reduce the size of the government, the list of public functions to be discarded was minimal (most expenditure items were simply transferred or deferred). Some largely marginal functions were offered as sacrificial lambs while the major targets escaped the net. As with many government reviews, the original political intention went awry. Even a group of hard-nosed, senior ministers ideologically committed to public sector reduction could not deliver on the harder decisions. As an internal audit of Commonwealth functions the review team and their advisers often found convincing reasons to retain if not expand existing operations.

Although the government subsequently attempted to quantify the results of the 'Razor Gang' exercise (and claimed in October 1981 that 74% of the decisions were achieved or progressing—Weller 1989:250), this review did not achieve much in the way of smaller government or expenditure savings. Actual achievements were minimal and many recommendations were frustrated by the Senate's capacity to block legislative amendments (eg. fees for second degrees) or by a reluctance among the private sector or state governments to assume the nominated Commonwealth functions (e.g. assets were difficult to sell even at 'give away prices'). The RCF did not manage to reduce outlays, in fact Commonwealth spending continued to grow from 26.3% of GDP in 1979–80 to 28.9% in 1982–83 (Budget Paper No1, 1987–88:406)—although it could be claimed that this growth may have been higher without the cuts.

In many respects the 'Razor Gang' became a 'victim of its own high expectations' that resulted in some embarrassment to the

government (Weller 1989:251). It attracted much negative publicity and came to characterise the 'uncaring' attitude of the government among interest groups and the community. Instead of being seen as a bold attempt to reduce government, as the Coalition hoped, the 'Razor Gang' episode was a damp squib symbolising that government was ruthless and heartless yet unable to achieve its desired ends. Official assessments were more coy if not generous, with Finance claiming the exercise was useful in enabling the executive to look across the whole sector of Commonwealth activity 'in a context where Commonwealth withdrawal from a function was the focus of attention' (DoF 1982a:13). The department conveniently evaded the question of how much actual 'withdrawal' had actually occurred.

BUDGET INNOVATIONS UNDER GUILFOYLE: BI-LATERALS, PORTFOLIO PROGRAMS, CONSIDERATION OF PROGRAM APPROPRIATIONS

After Margaret Guilfoyle became Finance Minister in November 1980, she allowed Finance to exercise its reform ambitions. Although generally approaching the job with a conscientious accountant's mentality (her prior occupation), Guilfoyle encouraged those in her department who were advocating other possible ways to achieve better expenditure control. Even though she was only the minister for just over two years, she supported some important innovations to the budget process and was not averse to her officials exploring alternative principles of budget preparation. She enjoyed a reputation among her colleagues and staff as a minister who cared about the job of Finance minister. She was regarded as a tough negotiator with other departments, and contemporary officials still speak highly of her performance in the portfolio.

In December 1981 Guilfoyle won cabinet approval to introduce a refinement to the process of annual negotiations between Finance and the other spending departments. The revised system of 'bi-laterals' involved separate negotiations between Finance and the individual spending departments to discuss and agree portfolio expenditures *within the context of cabinet's fiscal targets and priorities* (see Weller 1989:252).[10] Bi-lateral negotiations were promoted as a means to reduce the workload of ministers, but more importantly they were intended to enable Finance to impose greater discipline over expenditure by improving its relative bargaining strength. Such 'bi-laterals' were heralded at the time as a major step forward in controlling expenditure because cabinet and the central budgetary agencies could hold down expenditure claims from individual departments and yet maintain confidentiality about any concessions granted.

A further dimension of the bi-laterals process, promoted by Guilfoyle, was the attempt to gain firm undertakings from spending departments that they would remain within budget limits. Her rationale was that more control over discretionary expenditure could be extracted if spending ministers and senior departmental officials were prepared to accept more responsibility for managing their own expenditure within the budget year. She attempted to get her counterparts to agree to stay within limits and not agitate for additional top-ups. This more facilitative orientation toward relations with other departments was perhaps a consequence of her background as an ex-spending minister who came to the Finance portfolio from Social Security.

Such bargaining-centred adaptations to the budgetary process still indicated that Finance remained focused on agency-level budget limits and top-down expenditure control techniques. The central budget agency was yet to embark upon the more systematic approach to budget control using financial and managerial

10 In the 1960s spending ministers had to front up to the Treasurer and Treasury in the annual budget round, but these negotiations were not part of an overall cabinet process of expenditure limits and portfolio targets.

techniques. It is also apparent that each proposed reform gradually increased Finance's interest in 'value for money' management which seemed to provide a better means of fiscal restraint than crude expenditure limits.

A second area of innovation under Guilfoyle's tenure involved Finance officials investigating various extensions to the logic of program-based budgeting—to emphasise portfolio structures and examine parliamentary appropriations by program. To that point, functional-based *information* was included in the Budget Papers, but Parliament continued to appropriate funds on a detailed line-item basis. The government had included information on the functional classification of budget outlays since 1973–74 (Castles 1983).[11] This data was mainly produced for reporting purposes although it was used by cabinet in conjunction with forward estimates in determining adjustments to resource allocations. Increasingly, program-based presentations of the budget were used by Parliament in the scrutiny of estimates—and this occasionally required special up-dates in program allocations to reflect administrative changes. Guilfoyle also pushed for greater reconciliation between program information and portfolio responsibilities. In August 1981 and again in August 1982 she presented a ministerial statement to the Parliament in which Finance had allocated all program outlays back to the portfolios that were responsible for their implementation (see *Functional Classification of Outlays—Departmental Estimates 1981–82*, PP 184/1981 and *1982–83*, PP 215/1982). Such portfolio calculations of program-based information under Guilfoyle remained essentially a reporting exercise, but this reconciliation of program funds and portfolios was an embryonic step toward the adoption of full portfolio budgeting that would later characterise Australian budgeting in the mid-late 1980s.

Other political players also offered suggestions on further innovations to program-related budgeting. For instance, the House of Representatives Standing Committee on Expenditure had raised the issue of program appropriations and recommended in 1979 that 'the government provide Parliament with a paper that outlines the advantages and disadvantages of changing the annual Appropriation Bills from their present form to one which records the estimates in a program format'. The committee was really asking the executive

---

11 See Appendix C of this volume for a historical survey of Commonwealth outlays by function from 1975–76 to the estimated outlays of 2003–04.

to consider whether parliamentary appropriations by program classification was a feasible reform to adopt. The committee's recommendation was seriously investigated by senior Finance officials (notably Ian Castles) who prepared a position paper for the Minister in late 1982. The paper entitled *Program Appropriations*[12] reported on the Constitutional provisions relating to financial control, and on the current arrangements for appropriation (annual appropriation acts constituting around one-third of outlays, and special or 'on-going' appropriations included in particular acts). The paper then contrasted the existing 'input' format appropriation organised into departmental categories with various 'program formats' for appropriation. Arguments for and against program appropriation were organised under three headings: usefulness for parliamentary scrutiny and expenditure control; usefulness for debate on the proposed allocation of resources; and the impact on efficiency. The advantages of program appropriations were that more emphasis would be placed on the purposes and priorities of expenditure, and that in turn, this would lead to greater concern with results and the effectiveness of program spending. The position paper noted that some managerial efficiencies could be expected to occur as a result of resource flexibilities *within* programs under program appropriations. However, the arguments against program appropriations included that Parliament would lose the detailed information necessary for its examination of expenditure; verification and accountability would become more difficult (for parliament and auditors); that ministers and central coordinating bodies would risk having to trade off control for flexibility; and that strict program-based appropriations 'could restrict management more closely than is now the case' (1982:10)—which would lead departments to seek higher aggregations of appropriations and thus less transparency.

No firm recommendations were advanced in the position paper on whether to adopt program appropriations. The conclusion stated:

> the best format of appropriation will depend upon the relative importance which the Parliament attaches to the purposes which may

12 Senator Dame Margaret Guilfoyle, Minister for Finance, Program Appropriations—Response to Recommendation 8 of the Report of the House of Representatives Standing Committee on Expenditure Entitled 'Parliament and Public Expenditure', Presented Paper No 49 (not ordered to be printed), Senate, 11th November 1982.

> be served by appropriations, and in particular upon the form of financial control considered to be most desirable—control over inputs or control over performance in relation to objectives—and upon a judgement about the related question of the balance to be allowed between central control and managerial flexibility (1982:15).

The authors of the paper were careful to make a clear distinction between better *program-related information* and *program appropriation*; arguing that additional budget information in program form (and relating to portfolios) could be added to the existing input information.

Tabling the paper *Program Appropriations* on 11 November 1982, Guilfoyle presented her response to the proposal in a ministerial statement, arguing it:

> will become evident to those who consider the paper . . . that the appropriation acts are not suitable as the basic means of presenting expenditures on a program basis. Statement 3 of Budget Paper No 1 comes much closer to presenting expenditures in that way, but cannot be easily related by readers to the relevant appropriations. With these considerations in mind, my Department is now working to produce a presentation of the existing appropriation items which will show them on what will as closely as practicable be a program basis. Such a document would be of assistance to those interested in program information and should provide a basis for more complete presentation of cost information on programs (Senate 11.11.1982).

Her reasoning owed much to Castles' view that the appropriation process was not the most appropriate way of introducing program management, and that in some areas it would 'raise difficulties for departments' (Castles 1983:7). Guilfoyle indicated in the statement that a full program based document could be produced for the next budget (for 1983–84) 'sufficiently quickly after that Budget is introduced to assist the Parliament in debate on the Budget'—but her commitment was overtaken by events, namely the demise of the Coalition government after an early election in March 1983.

BACK TO BUSINESS: THE REID COMMITTEE'S REVIEW OF COMMONWEALTH ADMINISTRATION (1982–83)

After seven years in office the Fraser government was uncertain how to proceed in its desire to reform the public sector. Isolated problems were being addressed incrementally by isolated measures. For instance, at the end of 1982 the cabinet was preparing to consider further revisions to budgetary procedures for the consolidation of individual line items of administrative expenditure. An emerging debate had begun inside government over both the need to improve management and budgetary systems and the relative merits of particular reforms. In this context, the government launched a wide-scale public review of Commonwealth administration, called because there 'was a real feeling that the administration wasn't managing and somehow that was linked to the government's inability to govern . . . [and that this had created] a real sense of frustration that the frameworks of administration were actually holding back what could happen' (Nicholls Interview 1996). Fraser and his key advisers believed the Commonwealth public sector needed to improve management by embracing private sector practices. Fraser was not particularly interested in the findings of the 1975 Coombs' Report commissioned by the Whitlam government, but he accepted aspects of the reform agenda arguing that 'there has been a breakdown in Public Service administration over recent years' (Fraser 1982:1).

The Review of Commonwealth Administration (RCA), chaired by John Reid, was established in September 1982 as a short, sharp investigation into 'the constraints which face public sector managers, and the challenges that they will have to confront in the future' (RCA 1983:134).[13] Given the tight timeframe for the review (Fraser was disdainful of lengthy reviews and set a four month deadline), the Reid team undertook intensive discussions with departments, gleaning ideas and endorsing commendable practices. The committee acted as a vacuum cleaner for innovations to improve management. As one observer said: 'a lot of these committees don't add anything they just summarise where you are and I think that's fundamentally what [the Reid Committee] did. I remember them wandering around the place and going from department to department' (Visbord Interview 1997).

The Reid Committee quickly recognised the need for financial management reforms to allow departments to use resources more

13 The RCA team included: John Reid, John Rose and Ronald Elliott. As chief executive officer, Bruce MacDonald was seconded from the PSB. Ted Mathews was seconded to the review team from DoF—and he played an important role in integrating Finance's financial management reform proposals into the text of the report.

flexibly. The review team met with Finance officials from October 1982 through to January 1983. Most discussions were conducted informally but then translated into draft proposals for further discussion. The review team also wrote to departments with formal requests for input. To assist in its review of budgetary processes, Reid wrote to Castles on many occasions asking for papers, information and specific proposals for reform, and shortly after for comments on the committee's draft findings. At the outset of the review Castles sent Reid two papers: one on the role of the DoF in providing financial advice and the services it provided to other departments; and the other on career histories of senior officers in DoF which showed that 'the great majority of them have spent a significant proportion of their careers in other departments or organisations' (DoF 1982b). The first paper stated that the:

> prime functions of the Department of Finance are to act as the central coordinating body for the Commonwealth financial administration and to provide accounting services for the government (DoF 1982b:1)

The department then argued it had two main roles: first a 'vertical' role—giving advice to the ministry and discharging its formal responsibilities under the principal statutes (e.g. the *Audit Act*); and second a 'horizontal' role—giving 'financial advice and counsel to client departments'. The paper went on to discuss budget policy coordination, accounting operations and payments of monies into and out of the Commonwealth Public Account. It indicated what financial management techniques the department was implementing before calling for an investigation into the merits of adopting financial statements for Commonwealth undertakings (drawing on the work of committees of both Houses of Parliament, the Auditor-General, and a joint working party from Finance and the Auditor-General's office). Finance argued that at this particular juncture, the main sticking point in improving expenditure management was the apparent ill-fit between the present system of detailed 'manpower' controls versus an emerging framework of management based on the financial management of resources.[14]

14 Finance argued that the old system of manpower controls placed strains on the budget formulation process—in particular they raised the difficult issue of who sets annual staff ceilings, by what process or criteria were they set and how could these determinations be included in forward estimates for resource allocation.

From its perspective as the central budget agency, multiple types of 'controls' in practice created difficulties in imposing control and in assessing future resource requirements.

When the Reid report was released on 26 January 1983 two major themes formed the basis of its recommendations: the need for improvements in the 'quality and experience' of senior management, and the need for changes in the relationships between the central agencies and operational departments (RCA 1983:xvi). Picking up ideas from the UK, the report proposed the introduction of a 'financial management improvement program' (FMIP) to address both these issues and recommended: 'if the financial management improvement program proposed . . . is to be successful, the Department of Finance will need to adopt a high profile in a positive and constructive, rather than regulatory, role' (RCA 1983:59). Although the PSB and Finance were given joint carriage of the proposed FMIP reforms, in retrospect, this finding signalled the demise of the PSB (see Chapter 8).

In relation to the financial management reforms, the Reid report proposed two key innovations, which would substantially alter the regulatory role of the central budget agency. First, it recommended the truncation of administrative (running costs) appropriations into one or two lines (rather than the existing twenty or thirty separate lines). This recommendation aimed to reduce the level of detailed (and presumably redundant) budget control imposed by Finance to facilitate a more efficient use of public funds. Second, to complement this new flexibility, the RCA encouraged Finance to further develop its capacity to advise and assist senior departmental managers on financial management. The latter proposal reflected underlying scepticism concerning the 'let the managers manage' philosophy (promoted by the Glassco Commission in Canada). The RCA doubted that managers knew *how to manage*, especially in relation to financial matters. It is clear from the language of the report that these recommendations were seen as a significant shift of orientation for the budget agency which also opened up new opportunities, leading the authors to predict that increased financial flexibilities would enable Finance 'energetically to pursue enhanced advisory and consultancy work' within the APS (RCA 1983:59).

Budgetary reform was central to the implementation of the Reid agenda. But while the report argued for Finance to be more active and dynamic in financial management, it rejected the department's proposal that it should take over staffing controls or authority over pay and conditions from the PSB.[15] Instead, the report envisaged the PSB would remain the primary agency in many of its areas of responsibility, and warned of the 'possible dangers if financial aspects were to dominate totally the thinking on staffing needs' (RCA 1983:56–57). This finding meant that two institutions (PSB and Finance) had overlapping responsibilities and were effectively serving one policy objective (resource management). The PSB's role was largely preserved due to the influence of Bruce MacDonald, the Chief Executive Officer of the Reid committee seconded from the Department of Administrative Services. At this stage, it is also unlikely that the government was prepared to relinquish detailed staffing controls imposed through the PSB (especially Fraser who according to one source still 'wanted staff ceilings' and establishment controls retained—Visbord Interview 1997). Reid appears to have deferred to Fraser's wishes in this regard. However, increasing concern was shown at the financial inflexibility caused by centrally-authorised staffing levels. On this point, the Reid report recommended improved coordination between the budgetary and staffing functions, arguing the PSB and Finance should develop a close working relationship.

In relation to expenditure management within departments, Reid picked up the theme of 'intensified pressure to live within budgets' including this as one of the final recommendations of the report. In meetings with Finance the review team floated the idea of compelling department managers to 'live within budget appropriations'—a proposition that could easily be stated, but not necessarily enforced.[16] Furthermore, the Reid report favoured 'the

---

15 Finance had been shown a penultimate draft of the report in early January 1983. Castles replied to Reid (12.1.1983, RCA file 82/042) that he had read the report with 'great interest' and found it 'succeeds admirably in 'providing signposts and practical proposals to meet the perceived problems of public administration'. He was more sceptical about the 'somewhat half-hearted' support for the retention of staff ceilings, arguing that 'the proposed retention of centralised staff ceiling controls, in addition to establishment controls and overall financial controls, seems to be at odds with the overall thrust of the Report towards providing departmental managers with greater flexibility, authority and responsibility'.

16 The CEO of the committee Bruce MacDonald wrote a note to file recording that the Deputy Secretary (DoF) 'Dr Keating referred to the suggestion that managers should live within the simplified appropriations and said that Finance agree provided this can in fact be done. I asked whether they would have some positive suggestions on how it can be done and Dr Keating said that they would'. But no specific details were provided.

progressive development of systems for the provision of financial information on a program basis'. The report was less enthusiastic in respect of program appropriation. It pointed to difficulties highlighted in the paper presented to Parliament by Guilfoyle in November 1982, and concluded 'that the wholesale introduction of program appropriations would be likely to add to management difficulties in the Commonwealth administration rather than reduce them' (RCA 1983:63).

In January 1983 Fraser asked for Finance's evaluation of two recommendations contained in the Reid report: the consolidation of expenditure items into 'one line' budgets and the FMIP. Finance was in agreement with both, but with qualifications. It would only support 'one-line' budgets provided that fixed cash limits were placed on these budgets and that a price factor be included to avoid further supplementation. Castles advised that 'some savings achieved under present procedures [such as fortuitous savings returned to Finance] will not be realised under the recommended procedures', but added that Finance 'supports the introduction of the proposed trial arrangements commencing in 1983–84 if complementary procedures to fix cash limits in respect of non-salary administrative appropriations are introduced' (Castles in DoF Minute 3.2.1983). On the recommendation to introduce a FMIP the department simply stated 'agreed'. Castles further noted that preliminary discussions at an official level had already taken place with the PSB over a FMIP to begin to define the program and work out a *modus operandi*. These discussions took place in January 1983.

From the eleven chapters of the Reid report a total of 32 major recommendations were made, many of which were broken into multiple parts (totalling 88 components). Of these component recommendations Finance agreed with 73, although some included qualifications. They made no comment on 11 (largely because they did not fall within their responsibilities) and disagreed with only one. Three recommendations were to be reconsidered later because they were dependent on other changes being made. The one item Finance disagreed with was the recommendation to maintain staff ceilings. But considerations on how to implement the Reid report were cut short by the Prime Minister's sudden announcement of an election on 3rd February—called in the hope of beating Bill Hayden as Labor leader, but lost to the charismatic Bob Hawke who displaced Hayden at the outset of the campaign.

THE 1982–83 BUDGET: WHEN POLITICS AGAIN TRIUMPHED OVER THE BUDGET PROCESS

While the government was engaged in exploring managerial agendas, its control over the annual budget process came unstuck in 1982. In late December 1981 the government began to sense it faced a looming budget deficit for the current year, but it was unsure of the size of the figure. The economic recession, falling tax receipts, prolonged drought and rising unemployment had undermined the government's fiscal position. Although Treasury was unmoved, the Prime Minister responded to the 1982 economic recession with conventional expansionary fiscal policies. The 1982–83 Budget was used to pump-prime the economy while adding to the ballooning fiscal deficit in the process—a fiscal reversal of major proportions.

So, paradoxically, after six years of austerity, elaborate controls on expenditure and some (ultimately vain) attempts to reduce the size of government, the Fraser government reversed its belt-tightening in its budget of 1982–83. Both features—the relaxation of expenditure control and the fact it became the final budget before the election—were not planned and caught the government largely by surprise. The cabinet initially appeared to be following convention in formulating the budget: premising the budget on fiscal restraint, imposing top-down cuts on expenditure, and extracting 'agreed' savings of around $650 million from bilaterals between the Finance minister and departments (from March to May 1982).[17] Budgetary processes appeared to be operating as usual and there was little hint of a major reversal of strategy. Moreover, the 1982–83 budget fell mid-way through the political cycle and was not intended as an electoral 'give-away' budget. It was only the second budget in the government's third term, but it became the Coalition's last after the March 1983 election loss.

The reversal over public spending did not eventuate according to a planned course of action. The painstaking preparation of previous budgets was jettisoned as the government made a series of decisions on the run in the midst of a deepening political crisis (Weller 1989:251). For a government that had fought to earn the

17 Initially cabinet had set the figure of $606 million as a savings target in early March, but increased the figure to $650 on March 22nd. Guilfoyle and her departmental officers then began negotiating the detail of departmental spending with individual ministers.

reputation for fiscal stringency and tight expenditure discipline the sudden relaxation of expenditure controls appeared out of character—and once unveiled the budget was immediately castigated by media commentators as fiscally irresponsible. So what occurred with this budget and what explains the government's sudden change of tune? Five related factors caused the government's internal decision-making processes to lapse into a shambles: unclear deficit projections; a lack of reliable information on which to budget; difficulties in extracting cuts; political infighting; and arguments over the appropriate fiscal strategies.

During the first few months of 1982 the government was confronted with multiple and escalating projections of the size of the expected deficit for the current year. As the recession began to impact on economic indicators, various budgetary forecasts were presented to senior ministers between December 1981 to February 1982 (see Weller 1989:252–266). Before Christmas, Fraser's economic advisers Cliff Walsh and John Rose had predicted a deficit for 1981–82 of $612 million (up from the projected $146 million), but by early January the Treasury estimated the deficit at $700 million. Within six days DoF had estimated the deficit to be $1045 million, which was matched by a PM&C estimate. Treasury again revised its estimate on 10th February to a deficit of $1300 million. These escalating figures made the task of framing the 1982–83 budget extremely difficult (especially gaining agreement on appropriate expenditure allocations).

The lack of reliable information and the variety of sources from which projections were generated compounded the problem for the cabinet. Fraser distrusted Treasury advice and was suspicious of their estimates of revenue, expenditure, the money supply and interest rates. His criticisms were mainly devoted to the lack of accurate and timely information. In 1982 Fraser was confident only of the imprecision of the most important information to the budget:

> You could be pretty sure about expenditure, but it was on the revenue side that Treasury were so often wrong . . . Tax and inflation figures are two of the most important [pieces of budget information]. A small movement in either of them can make a very big difference. The most variable figure on the expenditure side was unemployment benefits—in view of the sudden fall-out in employment—but for a lot of expenditure figures, as long as your administration is tight, you can be very, very accurate. You've got your figure and that's what you are going to spend. In 1982 people

> forget that we budgeted for a surplus in that term [ie, by the 1983–84 fiscal year], certainly a domestic surplus and I think an overall budget deficit [for 1982–83] of about five hundred million—infinitesimal in the order of things. In six weeks we knew that these figures were totally and absolutely wrong; in six weeks we had figures which said that the country's going into a great bloody hole. Why wasn't Treasury aware of that two months earlier? (Fraser Interview 1997).

The third factor compounding the government's difficulties was the failure to extract the $650 million in cuts—a figure agreed by cabinet in early December. Cabinet's decision on required savings legitimated Finance's increased demands for expenditure restraint, but achieving the target proved harder under the bilateral process.[18] Guilfoyle recalled that she was able to base her arguments in the bilateral negotiations on the fact that she was 'bound by the cabinet decision' (Interview 1996). But after two months of intense negotiations over April and May Finance had managed to extract only around half of the intended cuts ($353 million) and even some of these 'agreed' cuts were later overturned by Fraser. The political will to impose such cuts was by this stage fast evaporating. After a July budget-lunch for senior business leaders, which encouraged the government to budget for a deficit of over $2 billion, Fraser performed a sudden U-turn and began to promote expenditure increases. Demands for cuts were replaced with requests for additional spending bids.[19] In the final budget outlays were projected to rise by 13.9 per cent.

The atmosphere surrounding the 1982–83 Budget had become charged with political uncertainty. Infighting within the Fraser ministry had arisen over two issues: between rival camps in the Liberal party over the leadership and between senior economic ministers over the question of stimulating the economy in the throes of a recession. Andrew Peacock had challenged Fraser only

18 Cabinet decided on 3rd December 1981 that the Finance minister would attempt to extract the required savings ($650 million) from spending departments though 'bilateral discussions'.

19 Treasury mounted two later rear-guard actions to attempt to limit expenditure growth. In July they encouraged Fraser and then cabinet to impose 3% cuts across the board, then in August just days before the budget was due they again tried to reduce expenditure and increase taxes. The Treasurer John Howard was told the deficit for 1982–83 was expected to be $1824 million and for 1983–84 it was projected to be $4204 million (Weller 1989:264).

four months out from the Budget in March 1982. Surviving but wounded, Fraser wished to appear active in addressing economic problems and injecting growth into the economy. He also wanted to placate his spending ministers on whose support his prime ministership rested. The tense political situation made it more difficult to impose cuts in outlays or refuse demands for increased spending.

Policy disagreements also brought tensions to a head within the senior ranks of the cabinet and between central agencies over proposed fiscal settings. In particular, PM&C and Treasury disagreed over the severity of the economic recession and over the economic approaches to adopt. The former favoured a mild fiscal stimulation through an expansionary budget (with a projected budget deficit of up to $2.5 billion), while Treasury continued to insist on the need to aim for a surplus of $1.2 billion to contain growing inflationary pressures. Treasury also considered the government should defer or cancel promised tax cuts as a way of maintaining the revenue base, but Fraser's advisers opposed this fearing an electoral backlash over broken promises. By June/July relations between the Prime Minister and his Treasurer, John Howard, had soured over the government's contradictory priorities and over Fraser's insistence to increase outlays and exacerbate the deficit. Howard considered resigning from cabinet over the issue but was dissuaded by close colleagues. He also met with Fraser a number of times and with the assistance of Treasury officials managed to persuade cabinet to re-evaluate the fiscal strategy. This move was too late to have much effect.

Significantly, while Fraser managed to antagonise both Treasury and the Treasurer, he retained the support of his National Party deputy Doug Anthony and Industry Minister Phillip Lynch. With these senior ministers, Fraser effectively insisted that political expediency and economic imperatives triumph over the rigours of the formal budgetary processes. The 1982–83 budget clearly illustrates the limitations of budgetary processes, however stringent, when confronted with the determination of a Prime Minister to get his way (Weller 1989:251–266).

THE PARADOX OF THE FRASER YEARS

The Coalition struggled to control public expenditure through their seven years in office under Fraser, yet in the final year they undermined their own agenda of restraint. Concerned over the size of the public sector, the government sought to restrain spending and implement reforms designed to keep departments within their budgets. The government made genuinely large strides, along with their bureaucrats, to put in place detailed processes to ensure increased control of the public purse. But after six years of austerity the government found it politically opportune to ignore these same control processes.

Initially, the Coalition exercised top-down restraint within the framework of traditional line item budgeting. This was based largely on inherited base budgets, consistent with a non-radical and incrementalist approach to public expenditure allocation. Toward the end of their period their attention turned to improving the management of expenditure and the adoption of some private sector practices in resource management. The immediate response of the Fraser cabinet to the recommendations of the Reid committee indicates the Coalition government was beginning to pursue a managerialist agenda focusing more on financial management than on *ex ante* cash limits or crude staffing controls. After 1983 this emerging agenda was to be inherited, further refined and implemented by the Hawke Labor government. From the watershed of the Reid review of 1982–83, a convergence developed between both major political parties with regard to expenditure management and the consolidation of administrative items. Managerial and financial reform within government now enjoyed bipartisan support—even if the particular expression of the reforms would ultimately be implemented by Labor throughout the remainder of the 1980s.

7 Unfinished business: budget reform under Hawke

LABOR RETURNED TO government in March 1983. In their early years in office they were motivated as much by fear of failure as by what they hoped to achieve. In particular, they needed to avoid being seen as a re-run of the Whitlam Labor government, generally viewed as accident-prone and marred by poor fiscal and budgetary management (Walsh P 1995:103; Oakes 1976; Mills 1993). Labor still felt tarred with the brush of fiscal irresponsibility and incompetence. Even former ministers in the Whitlam government considered that a 'cavalier indifference to economic disciplines' had been a major characteristic of the period (Hayden 1996:218). The new Hawke ministry, by contrast, was determined to win business and especially financial market support for its performance in managing the economy and the public purse. Hawke's ministers kept reminding themselves they were in government for 'the long haul' and were not about to be subjected to a pre-emptive ousting from office by their opponents.

To prepare for office Labor had access to a series of reformist manifestos that urged budgetary reform. The incoming Hawke government was arguably more responsive to change in the public service than their immediate Coalition predecessors. While ideas for reform were already in the air and generally welcome within the APS, Labor believed it had to win over the 'old style' public service still perceived by some to have been antagonistic to the previous Labor government. Reforms also received a positive reception from senior Labor ministers—especially the powerful 'Troika' of the Prime Minister, Treasurer and Finance ministers. But the encouragement of reformist thinking did not necessarily translate into a coherent plan or a strong sense of purpose. During its first term (March 1983 to December 1984) Labor produced a number of influential, though divergent, plans for administrative change. From the outset, therefore, the Hawke government was prepared to encourage selected reforms, but had no overall strategy for *public sector management.* It will be argued in the following chapter that the centrepiece of the Hawke government's administrative reforms in the mid-to-late–1980s (the Financial Management Improvement Program—FMIP) was piecemeal and only gradually emerged as a multi-faceted financial management system. While the government gradually embraced reform proposals throughout the 1980s, it is evident that budgetary and financial management became the cornerstone of the Hawke government's strategy for public sector management almost by default.

Neither did the government articulate a clear program of reform for *budgetary management.* Ministers were simply relieved to be in a position to get their hands on the budget, or were initially preoccupied with other 'big issues' such as the National Economic Summit, financial deregulation and macro-economic policy. Fiscal rectitude and financial responsibility became guiding philosophies providing a semblance of coherence in the absence of an overall strategy. Gradually senior ministers accepted that improved budgetary systems were needed and that budget reform should become an item on the government's agenda. Under tight fiscal constraints, improved techniques of budgeting were increasingly regarded as the key to the government's capacity to resource its own policy preferences. As the final section of this chapter shows, Labor's budgetary reform agenda was experimental and many initiatives were advanced to achieve limited or short-term ends—they were kept or extended only if they demonstrated an immediate effectiveness.

Even before Hawke had finalised his first ministry, reality bit hard. The Prime Minister was confronted with the news that the incoming government was faced with a much larger deficit than expected. If this projection from Treasury was intended to scare Labor it certainly underscored the imperative of fiscal discipline on the new government.

COMPETING MANIFESTOS: COOMBS, REID AND *LABOR & QUALITY OF GOVERNMENT*

In Opposition Labor's attitude to the public sector had undergone considerable revision. Key spokespeople on the front bench were no longer prepared to adopt blind ideological commitment to the virtues of public sector growth and government interventionism. They considered the public sector had been pilloried during the Fraser years, but not substantially changed. Now, Labor's front bench believed they could be better *managers* in government than the Coalition and that there was much scope for improvement. Though the practicalities of such a task were daunting, Labor was prepared to sketch out some general principles and approaches.

Underpinning its otherwise pragmatic approach, Labor had three sources of ideas on which to base its reform programs—the Coombs Report (1976), the Reid Report (1983) and Labor's own 1983 electoral statement on its plans for government administration. An issue for the new government was that the three reports contained important contradictions. Many features of the Coombs Report were still regarded as germane and some among the new government felt there remained much still to be implemented. Officials at the time were conscious of the importance of the inquiry to Labor's immediate reforms. For example, a Finance officer in the mid–1980s, volunteered that 'to be honest . . . [Labor's reforms] stem all the way back to RCAGA—the Coombs Commission. A lot of what was implemented in 1983 and 1984 was straight unfinished business from Coombs' (Bartos Interview 1996). The Reid Report had also been favourably mentioned by Labor in the election as indicative that far-reaching public sector reforms were still needed. Although Labor described the Reid review as 'short and simple' its findings nevertheless promoted a range of contemporary management ideas.[1] Finally, with the assistance of Peter Wilenski, there was Labor's own manifesto for public sector reform, *Labor and Quality of Government* (ALP 1983).

Labor and Quality of Government (*LQG*) was released two weeks after the Reid Report appeared and one week into the 1983 federal election campaign. The *LQG* document originated from the work of two sequential pre-election Labor task force inquiries into the APS. The first was prepared for the 1980 federal election and the second in 1982 in anticipation of the 1983 election.[2] The second

---

1 Finance's response to Reid Inquiry recommendations was extraordinarily positive. This is perhaps less surprising given that the Reid Committee relied heavily on the submissions and supporting documentation supplied by Finance. The Reid Report largely endorsed the reform directions Finance was following.

2 The authors of the first version of 1980 were: Brian Howe, John Button,

version of *LQG* drew on the work of the Reid Review to support many of its arguments. It was the culmination of a series of internal reviews into relations between the executive and legislative arms of government and between the ministerial and administrative arms of the executive. The *LQG* manifesto was not a detailed plan, but constituted an outline of the approach to be adopted if Labor won office. Wilenski was included as an expert consultant on the second paper—a significant development given his earlier report on reforming the NSW public service and then subsequent appointment as PSB Chairman (1983 to 1987). Although accepting the Reid Report contained 'some useful analysis of shortcomings and constructive recommendations for their correction', *LQG* criticised the quality of the RCA arguing it was 'weak, superficial, erratic and eccentric in many respects' (ALP 1983:3).[3]

Nonetheless, both *LQG* and the Reid committee supported greater devolution of decision-making power over resources. Significantly, both documents only gave partial support to the introduction of *program budgeting*. The Labor paper argued program budgeting should be 'progressively implemented', but initially only in statutory authorities (ALP 1983:22). They were more cautious about its introduction in government departments and committed Labor simply to 'study reform of the budgetary system' through a task force under strong ministerial direction. The task force was charged with examining 'whether and in what form program budgeting should be introduced' (ALP 1983:19). Both the Reid team and the ALP front bench were cognisant of state government progress in this area, especially the determination of the Victorian and NSW governments to implement program budgeting (the latter advised by the Budget Task Force of the Wilenski review of NSW government administration), and by attempts to implement program

---

Arthur Gietzelt, Gareth Evans, Neal Blewett, Moss Cass and Patrick Weller. The revised 1982 draft (finalised on 8 February and released on the 9th) was undertaken by a caucus team that included Gareth Evans (chair), Bill Hayden, Ros Kelly, Neal Blewett, Susan Ryan, Arthur Gietzelt, Bill Morrison, Moss Cass and John Coates with assistance from co-opted members such as Peter Wilenski, Patrick Weller and Ken Fry. In the election campaign Evans, Blewett, Button and Michael Costello advised the Opposition leader on public sector issues (namely, Hayden in the lead up to the campaign and Hawke once the campaign started).

3 The *LQG* document accepted Reid's recommendations concerning greater devolution of managerial authority.

budgeting in the early 1980s under the Tonkin and Bannon governments in South Australia (Pugh 1984).[4]

On the other hand, there were a number of important issues upon which the two documents disagreed. In contrast to Reid, the *LQG* proposal crucially urged that staff controls and budgeting for personnel be transferred from the PSB to Finance—to enhance resource flexibilities and reduce the unnecessary delays in approving staff positions. The PSB had arguably built its power and influence precisely on its elaborate 'manpower controls' across the public sector. Labor's *LQG* (1983:17) argued that the Board's main role was to ensure a neutral career public service, but that this had gradually been extended to cover

> control over staff numbers through the Board's establishment and position classification function. Labor believes that this [role] . . . is pre-eminently a political one, appropriately subject to both political direction and direct ministerial accountability to Parliament, and that it ought to be transferred to an appropriate department of state, preferably the Finance Department.

Labor was not calling for the abolition of the PSB. Rather they were beginning to sense that the PSB was holding on to 'old' controls that were increasingly acting as an impediment to good management. Moreover, some of the authors such as Wilenski were of the view that despite the PSB's extensive array of bureaucratic controls, they were not in fact effective in controlling staffing. Agencies had found creative ways to avoid or circumvent the central controls. For example, the PSB establishment controls looked only at *positions* and not actual *staff*, so departments had developed ways of ensuring they had an excess of positions, and therefore maintaining broad flexibility in their actual *staffing*. Also, many departments would manipulate the annual 30 June headcount in various ways: by declaring staff on long-service leave 'inoperative', and by contractors 'losing' their job for the one day of the headcount.

The *LQG* document, therefore, began an implicit attack on

---

4 SA (1979), Tasmania and Victoria (1981) and NSW (1982) had each taken policy decisions to adopt various forms of program reporting, accounting and budgeting. WA followed in mid–1983, while Queensland and the NT were well off the pace in program-related public service reforms. The Commonwealth produced a review of the progress of 'Program Budgeting in the Australian States' (DoF 1983).

the standing and role of the PSB using the arguments of operational management as the immediate terrain. Of course, many of the PSB controls on staffing and classifications had long been criticised within the public service for being unnecessary, overly procedural, time-consuming and ineffective. By 1983 these criticisms had gained political support in both the new ministry and among some key central agencies. The Labor ministry, therefore, was not short of ideas for reform: competing manifestos existed and technocratic agendas were emerging. If the government was initially unsure in which direction to go, they were faced with situations that demanded immediate decision and action rather than debate. Arguably, this recognised need to demonstrate financial rectitude allowed them to avoid either procrastination or ideological disputes that could have hindered their ability to function as executive government.

LABOR'S WAKE-UP: INHERITING A PROJECTED $9.6 BILLION DEFICIT

Labor's general policy commitments and intentions to improve government administration have to be interpreted in terms of the financial situation they found themselves in on taking office. In the 1983 campaign Labor had made electoral commitments (of around $1.5 billion) believing the Coalition would leave a small deficit to the incoming government of no more than $4 billion. They believed this situation would impose no great burden on public sector resources or divert them from their intentions. However, Hawke had warned that if the deficit Labor inherited was large then they may be forced to forego intended tax cuts. Upon winning the election Hawke asked Treasury to review the deficit projections for 1982–83 as some preliminary figures indicated it could rise as high as $5 billion. On 6 March, before the ministry was sworn in, the Secretary to the Treasury, John Stone, handed a letter to Hawke advising of a projected deficit of $9.6 billion for 1983–84—with the implication that this was left to them by the outgoing Coalition government. This figure was more than twice the expected deficit for the budget year and almost four times the projected deficit ($2 billion) shown in the 1982–83 Budget handed down only 7 months earlier in August 1982.

Treasury's calculations assumed no change in government policy. They also estimated the impact of the continuing economic recession, the rural drought and massive bushfires in SA and Victoria. With reduced revenue and increasing outlays the deficit was expected to rise from under 1% of GDP to 6% in two years. Government net debt was again rising (to around 5% of GDP up from –1% in 1974–75). Treasury's brief painted a bleak picture and, on the assumption that neither the economy nor the rural sector would rebound quickly, provided Labor with little scope to spend on its own policy agendas. Treasury estimated that if its projections were accurate and Labor also went ahead with its spending and tax cut plans, then the deficit may blow out to more than $11 billion (see *Australian* 9.3.1983:1).

Fraser claimed subsequently that Treasury's 'famous document' suggesting the Commonwealth had a $9.6 billion deficit for 1983–84 was a despicable act manufactured for political advantage or done to serve Treasury's own ends. Fraser (Interview 1997) considered Treasury's advice 'a very political and in my view totally dishonest piece of paper because . . . it was based on a continuation of existing policies'. Australia, he argued, was

> experiencing a very major drought so the policy was based on the view that it wasn't going to rain through 1983. Now when you get to March or April that's the time when a lot of Australia expects to get some rain and in fact it did, so you knew your drought expenditures were going to fall off dramatically. And to provide the Treasurer or the Opposition with a bit of paper which implies that there's not going to be any change in the weather . . . is hardly an honest document. And, you know this might be a bit of self-justification, but in the [Coalition's] budget papers in 1982–83 . . . there were a couple of paragraphs that said that the shortfall in revenue and the blow-out in expenditure were almost entirely due to the recession under which the government was falling—so increased unemployment benefits and reduced revenue. Treasury, if it was good, should have been able to see this coming at least by the end of July the previous year [ie 1982].

Clearly Fraser's view of Treasury had not improved since his period in office. Following the disclosure of the projected deficit, the former Treasurer John Howard demanded Hawke publish more details and questioned the validity of the figures. He suggested that 'projections made at this time of the year for the likely budget deficit are not a reliable guide to the final outcome' (*Australian* 10.3.1983:2). But Howard later acknowledged he had been told before the election the projected figure could exceed $9 billion and had chosen not to disclose the figure publicly (*Australian* 11.3.1983:7). In the media, the deficit projection was widely cited and regarded as credible. One commentator suggested that the Coalition had shown a 'reckless desire for power' and that the 'political instincts of the former prime minister, Mr Malcolm Fraser, smothered his desire for careful and cautious economic management' (*Weekend Australian* 12–13.3.1983:4).

The actual deficit for 1983–84 was $7.987 billion, with outlays up by 8.5% (to 29.4% of GDP) and revenues down by 0.8% of GDP. The figure was large (representing 4.1% of GDP) being the second highest deficit since the early 1950s (second to the year 1975–76 when the deficit in nominal terms reached 4.7% in GDP terms). The 1983–84 figure was somewhat less than the inflated $9.6 billion projected by Treasury in March. Nevertheless, the larger estimate was significant because it suggested a deteriorating fiscal position and caused the incoming Labor government to focus immediately on expenditure restraint. It also spurred experimentation with administrative reform agendas aimed toward resource management. The inherited deficit developed into a 'deficit fetish', where the comparative size of the annual deficit emerged as the main criterion by which to judge the success of a budget. Against this measure, the annual deficit was progressively reduced until the Treasurer, Paul Keating, delivered a budget surplus in 1987–88.

INSTALLING THE 'TROIKA'

One of the most striking features of the Hawke cabinet was the gradual rise to prominence of a small group of key economic ministers who were simultaneously guardians of the public purse and active reformers. Their power was enhanced through a smaller cabinet structure. Unlike the Whitlam government that operated with the full ministry in cabinet, Hawke won caucus approval to divide the 27-member ministry into a 13-member inner cabinet with the remainder in the outer ministry. The intention was to make cabinet more workable and able to provide coherence to the government's decisions. It was also the case that even though Labor had been out of office for only 7 years, almost all the new cabinet was relatively inexperienced in the ways of executive government.[5]

---

5 Hawke had been in Parliament for just three years, and few of his ministers had previous cabinet experience. Among Hawke's first cabinet only three had

In this context the three senior economic ministers (the PM, Treasurer and Finance Minister) emerged as a powerful 'Troika' overseeing resource decisions. Peter Walsh, Labor's second Finance minister, began as a *de facto* fourth member of the 'Troika' and was particularly influential in expenditure restraint even though he then administered the Resources and Energy portfolio.[6] These ministers together with their personal staff and senior departmental officers became the centrepiece of the Hawke government's budgetary decision-making.

The 'Troika' grew in importance because it complemented Bob Hawke's personal style of management. It operated as a budget sub-committee at the epicentre of cabinet through which Hawke was able to agree common positions and lock in other senior cabinet ministers. Hawke as a former ACTU president and was a skilled political negotiator with a reputation for consensus-building and dispute resolution. A pragmatist, he was an effective chair of cabinet, ran meetings well and facilitated debate. Reputedly he often cared less about which way a particular decision went than that an agreed decision should be taken (Weller 1986). To make decisions he typically relied on a process of building a consensus of views among his senior ministers. On budgetary and resource matters the 'Troika' began to impose their authority, though to accomplish this they initially had to 'doggedly persist and wear down the other side' (Dawkins Interview 2000). Labor's decision to set up a formal expenditure review process—by re-establishing cabinet's Expenditure Review Committee (ERC)—provided a forum through which the 'Troika' could both extend and exercise its power.

The second member of the ERC's 'Troika' was the Treasurer, Paul Keating. Although an economic novice, Keating had been appointed Treasurer in March 1983 as a result of a factional deal providing support for Hawke's leadership bid in January-February 1983.[7] A political scrapper from the NSW Right faction, Keating

---

previous experience in the Whitlam ministries: his deputy leader Lionel Bowen had served as Special Minister of State/Postmaster-General and Industry minister (1972–75), Bill Hayden had been both Minister for Social Security from 1972 and then Treasurer from June to November 1975, and Paul Keating served briefly as Minister for the Northern Territory in the last month of the Whitlam government. Tom Uren, also a former Whitlam minister, was included in Hawke's outer ministry.

6 It may have been serendipitous that Walsh's first ministry was a policy and regulatory department rather than a big spender.

would become what many regarded as the high priest of economic rationalism throughout the 1980s—reorienting federal Labor to a more market-oriented philosophy. Together with Hawke he initiated the decision to fully float the dollar and deregulate the financial sector. While his department coordinated the annual budget, Keating (like Hawke) was not particularly interested in the housekeeping details but, more importantly, used his political standing to contain aggregate spending. He was an effective spokesperson for Treasury and also became a master salesman for the economic and budgetary achievements of the government. In cabinet he generally entered budget debates to put Treasury's position. He was not often an active participant beyond this, allowing others to fight the battle to find savings or contain outlays.

The third and arguably most significant member of the 'Troika' with direct responsibility for expenditure was the Finance minister. Two senior ministers occupied this position during the 1980s, John Dawkins (1983–84) and Senator Peter Walsh (1984–90). In different ways the emphases these two ministers brought to the role shaped the government's strategy and reform agendas throughout the decade.

JOHN DAWKINS AS FINANCE MINISTER, WITH RESPONSIBILITY FOR THE PUBLIC SERVICE

Hawke appointed John Dawkins as his first Minister of Finance.[8] In Opposition Dawkins had been spokesman on education and briefly for industry during the 1983 campaign. In the factional realignment following Hawke's ascendancy (Kelly 1984; Weller 1999:151) Dawkins was given the option of being Industry or Finance minister. He chose Finance—then a much less high-profile

7 Under Hayden, Labor's economic spokesman in Opposition was Ralph Willis, but he was ousted from the Treasury portfolio immediately prior to Hawke's ascendancy. In March 1983 Willis remained in the inner cabinet and became Minister for Employment and Industrial Relations—he subsequently became Finance minister (1990–93) and Treasurer (1993–96) in the Keating governments.

8 Dawkins, a little-known Western Australian, had been a union secretary before entering the House of Representatives as the member for Fremantle. He first won a lower house seat in 1974, was defeated in 1975, returning to Canberra at the 1977 election. He held degrees in economics and agricultural science and as a centre-left faction member was a strong Hayden supporter in caucus.

ministry, but one he believed would be a crucial portfolio to the government's long-term agenda.

Nevertheless, a mix-up resulted in Dawkins not being included in the cabinet of 13 ministers. Fate played a major part in two episodes that both enhanced the ministerial career of Dawkins and also shaped the way the management of public expenditure would unfold under the Hawke government. When the first Hawke cabinet was being put together Dawkins accepted the job of Finance minister and was initially included in cabinet. But Hawke had forgotten to include the Defence minister Gordon Scholes in cabinet. Hawke regarded it as imperative to include the Defence minister and rather than merely increase the size of cabinet, chose to place Dawkins in the outer ministry. Yet Dawkins was invited to attend cabinet and received all the cabinet papers, demonstrating that cabinet cannot work effectively without the input of the Finance minister across a vast array of decisions likely to impact on the public purse.

Secondly, the Tax Office had been attached to Finance briefly in the immediate aftermath of Labor's election, but was quickly returned to Treasury at the insistence of Keating on 30 June 1983. The separation of tax policy (Treasury) from tax administration (Finance and the Tax Office) was undertaken to better align revenue with expenditure and allow for greater scrutiny of tax expenditures. The move highlighted that Treasury had no effective ability in taxation policy without the ATO. Keating and Stone wanted the ATO back.[9] They suggested that with the government beginning to think about tax reform, the separation left the Treasurer short of policy advice. Hawke agreed and Dawkins had to relinquish the Tax Office. He insisted on a deal as compensation and persuaded Hawke to transfer the additional responsibilities of Minister Assisting the Prime Minister for Public Service Matters (moved from Industrial Relations and effective from 1 July 1983 (Dawkins 1983). Dawkins was also formally 're-included' in cabinet on 14 July 1983 (in a minor reshuffle following the standing down of Mick Young as Special Minister of State over the Combe-Ivanov affair) (see *Parliamentary Handbook* 1996:492).

The appointment of Dawkins as minister in charge of Finance and the public service provided the keystone in Labor's unfurling

9 It is interesting to contrast Treasury's determination to regain the ATO in 1983 with their apparent lack of interest in reclaiming Finance after the split of 1976.

reform agenda. The decision to combine these responsibilities appeared almost serendipitous; but the implications of combining expenditure control with the management of the public service were momentous. While other ministers may have been less concerned with internal reform of the public service, Dawkins saw the two sets of responsibilities as inherently complementary and used them as an opportunity. The dual role allowed him wide scope for a reform agenda that arguably would have been more difficult to claim from the Finance portfolio alone. And they also gave Dawkins ministerial oversight of the main institutional protagonists—Finance and the PSB. The coupling of these roles, which occurred as an afterthought but nevertheless lasted for the government's first two terms, became significant since it allowed Dawkins an authoritative platform from which to promote his ideas. The ministerial integration of these two resource functions (financial and human resources) would subsequently shape the trajectory of public sector reform throughout the remainder of the 1980s. Significantly, Walsh, his successor, also retained these dual roles.

THE GUARDIAN OF THE GUARDIANS: PETER WALSH AND THE CRUSADE AGAINST 'MIDDLE-CLASS WELFARE'

While the Hawke government became noted for its economic responsibility, Peter Walsh stands out in the area of expenditure management as a tough, and uncompromising Finance minister (1984–90) who almost obsessively ran a tight fiscal policy. Considered an 'Australian iconoclast' he described his personal philosophy as 'always opposed [to] wasting taxpayers money on what I judged to be unworthy causes' (Walsh 1990:329–330). In particular, Walsh was an avowed crusader against what he believed to be 'middle-class welfare'. His main achievement was the delivery of four consecutive years of budget surpluses from 1987–88. Other achievements included overseeing many technical budgetary reforms, introducing a series of top-down cuts to portfolios, and ruthlessly pursuing savings in program spending and transfer payments. He claimed that his enjoyment at being Finance minister was due to the fact that 'you have a licence to meddle in just about everything' because 'almost everything governments do entails spending money' (Walsh P 1995:124). He liked being close to the centre of decision-making and revelled in the fights over tough fiscal or policy decisions. Yet he was disappointed and frustrated by his colleagues and by what he regarded as wasteful public policy approaches (especially in welfare). For this reason he perhaps somewhat disingenuously entitled his memoirs *Confessions of a Failed Finance Minister* (1995).

As Labor's second Finance minister, Walsh was not particularly interested in the budgetary reforms proposed by his department. He argued that these were the 'technical aspects' that did not really concern him as minister. When interviewed about the reforms he presided over, he ventured that 'politicians are really less well equipped to get involved in those sorts of arguments than bureaucrats are'. He also believed the FMIP (introduced from 1983) was more of a 'gimmick', saying,

> I didn't regard it as truly important . . . Dawkins had a lot of good ideas but he also had a capacity for stunting . . . I picked up a lot of these things and, I guess, I regarded them in the stunting category . . . Dawkins was, I think, often attracted to change for change's sake rather than having any coherent idea of how change would lead to improvement.

Walsh nevertheless maintained a close relationship with his departmental officials. There was a high degree of mutual respect. He held their expertise in high regard and backed their reforms. He would take up the fight in cabinet relying on his instincts and departmental briefings and options papers. His officials felt they could rely on Walsh who as a minister was not only 'across the issues' but who also had a keen interest in restricting public expenditure. Within the 'Troika' Walsh became a forceful adversary with an uncompromising attitude to fiscal restraint and to whom both Keating and Hawke increasingly deferred on expenditure items.

CABINET'S EXPENDITURE REVIEW COMMITTEE—REVIEWING EXISTING EXPENDITURES

To impose their own priorities and to cope with budgetary stress, Labor restored the Expenditure Review Committee as a standing ministerial sub-committee of cabinet from March 1983. The rapid re-establishment of ERC was recognition that Labor was anxious to demonstrate it was prepared to take budget rectitude and management seriously. Labor was prepared to institutionalise and extend the practice of restraining resource bids by referring them to special purpose expenditure committees of cabinet.

While the ERC gradually became an integral feature of the Australian budgetary system after 1975, interpretations of its role have differed. Broadly there are two interpretations of the early role performed by ERC. First, some regard the ERC as an authoritative institution—a high-powered *political committee* charged with overall budget strategy and direction. Key ministers sat on the ERC and 'ran' the government's political and ideological agenda. Alternatively, others have viewed the ERC more as the central hub of the budget process—an integrative process providing a single-point of budget coordination through which decisions were made or ratified. An important question is how much in conflict these two approaches were within the single committee. In practice, the ERC operated as an 'inner-budget process' of consultation and deliberation with stakeholders, and a major function was to operate a 'scorecard' of resource decisions so that the government would always know where it stood in expenditure terms. These interpretations are not necessarily inconsistent or contradictory, but over a number of years and with regard to particular decisions, the relative emphasis within the ERC tended to fluctuate.

There were five original members of ERC who served during the first three Labor terms (1983–1990): Hawke, Keating, Willis, Dawkins and Walsh. Other ministers joined ERC later, such as Bowen, Button and then Howe and Evans. While ERC was initially an inner-cabinet committee of five ministers (and up to nine or ten between 1987–91), the 'Troika' of guardian ministers tended to pre-empt many of the important fiscal and expenditure decisions.[10] Generally Hawke chaired the ERC and shaped its agenda and processes. Even during 1987, when Treasurer Keating took the chair, Hawke's influence remained—overseeing the imposition of $2.6 billion in expenditure cuts including $1 billion cut to state grants (*Australian* 14.5.1987). A small number of senior officials also attended ERC and these were particularly important in preparing options and clearing the path for decisions.

To a large extent the Labor governments success in constraining public expenditure and in delivering four consecutive annual budget surpluses over the late 1980s can be attributed to the

10 The dominance of ERC by the Troika was something that continued throughout the Hawke-Keating governments, see Blewett 1999.

powerful role and mechanisms of ERC. As Mills (1993:93) has argued, the ERC became the 'cabinet engine room' under the Hawke years. Walsh certainly regarded it as the 'key committee in the Hawke government's early years' (1995:101). Ministers not on ERC also tended to see the ERC as the cabinet's nucleus of power (Weller 1999; Blewett 1999). The main power attributed to the ERC was that it both set overall expenditure limits (and was prepared to make significant aggregate cuts) and acted as a judicial board determining the appropriateness of restraint strategies developed by the respective line agencies (Kelly 2000).

One way the ERC expanded its influence over budget decision-making was to extend its role beyond the examination of new initiatives in the annual budget round to an expenditure review of existing allocations and programs. This allowed the ERC to call for evaluations into how existing funds were being implemented and to consider where cuts could be imposed. In an address to the National Press Club Dawkins (1984b) recognised the limitations of a once a year formal review of government expenditures through the budget process. He argued that 'it was quite possible during the course of the year for "spending" ministers to create a drift away from original budget objectives, without intentionally trying to do so'. The alternative, he argued, was to use ERC to force more decisions involving expenditure into the formal budget process (as a way of limiting them) while extending the review process throughout the entire budget year. By 1984 the ERC had 'been given the responsibility of continual oversight and review' and was intended to stop spending ministers 'drifting away' from original tight budget parameters.

According to Dawkins (1984b:8–9), the early ERC was given a wide charter to review:

> one with another the larger initiatives advanced by Ministers which relate to the priorities and interests of the Government as a whole. It thus helps to reduce substantially the workload of the 'Budget Cabinet'—that is cabinet convened to consider the final terms of the budget. The Committee also provides an opportunity for Ministers with coordinating responsibility to reconcile that margin of unresolved expenditure proposals—new and continuing—which I have not personally been able to settle in my portfolio round of discussions with each spending Minister . . . The ERC is also to play a pivotal role in the review of programs, quite outside the budget process where time constraints make it difficult to examine in detail

> more than a handful of the more complex of the Commonwealth programs. There is very much a need for a facility in government to pick up and examine on a continuing basis existing programs to see whether they are still valid, cost effective, meeting the Government's objectives, and so forth. Past attempts to do this at the officials' level have tended to run out of steam. I believe that a Cabinet level committee at the centre of such a process should be more effective.

The effectiveness of the ERC was assisted by the fact that the spirit of restraint was generally accepted across the ministry. At the time Dawkins (1984b:9) praised spending ministers for being prepared to agree to reduced budgets and portfolio targets. He maintained that,

> in the 1983–84 Budget, the portfolio round of discussions where I met with ministers individually in an attempt to resolve as many outstanding issues as practicable, managed to resolve 70% of the budget issues which required ministerial attention.

In short, political will in cabinet and a commitment to restraint from spending ministers were both vital ingredients within the existing institutional framework as Labor attempted to control expenditures. Yet, as we shall see, while Labor's course of expenditure restraint occurred concurrently with measures to reform the budget process, the two tended to remain separate exercises.

SETTING THE BUDGET PARAMETERS: AGGREGATE LIMITS AND SAVINGS TARGETS

By the mid–1980s, Labor's main means of expenditure control was achieved through the setting and enforcement of budgetary parameters for aggregate expenditure levels. ERC and budget cabinet were central to the process of determining spending levels and delivering specified savings to the budget. One of the key components of this 'expenditure-limiting system' was the regular public announcement of expenditure limits and 'savings targets' as a form of discipline on the ministry (Treasurer 1985).[11]

---

11 Expenditure cuts were either announced in the lead-up to the annual budget negotiations or in specific 'savings statements'. In both 1985 and 1987 savings statements were announced in May cutting $1.26 billion and $2.6 billion respectively from programs and forward estimates.

It was always a politically difficult task to set and impose the aggregate targets, particularly when they involved a substantial decrease in intended outlays or cuts to certain portfolios. Although the departments of PM&C, Treasury and Finance provided input and options to senior ministers, the setting of targets remained essentially a political decision. While discussions with relevant officials in these departments often pre-agreed parameters, the final figures were generally politically decided. Ministers also made decisions on new policy initiatives—such as how and when they would be considered and what expenditure ceilings would apply to these items.

Annual outlays were politically constrained through ERC by a system of tight budget parameters. Aggregate and portfolio outlays were set annually through a cascading series of cabinet specified limits designed to impose discipline on expenditure across the whole of government. ERC's intention was to rely on a hierarchy of top-down parameters in order to control the scope for subsequent expenditure decisions further down the budget chain. At each institutional level (from the entire budget, to portfolios, individual departments, agencies and then activities within them), existing budgets would be constrained by earlier decisions taken above and then locked in by reduced forward estimates in the out-years. In this process, controls on spending were typically focused on aggregate limits while 'savings targets' were imposed on portfolios, particular agencies or large policy/program activities (Barrett 1988). Savings targets were so-called because portfolio ministers would be given a specific figure of expenditure cuts to their areas and then expected to deliver savings to meet the specified targets. The use of the word 'savings' was intended to convey the message that these enforced cuts constituted savings to the budget bottom line—the government 'saved'. ERC was then able to determine the latitude for new policy initiatives available to cabinet. With the annual budget presented to Parliament in August, the schedule for these decisions on the budgetary parameters was as follows.

During the 1984 election the government also made the famous 'Trilogy' commitments.[12] In a radio interview the Prime Minister

12 The 1984 'Trilogy' commitments were: not to increase either taxes or expenditure as a proportion of GDP over the life of the Parliament and to reduce the budget deficit as a proportion of GDP over three years (subject to some important 'let-out' clauses). Some senior ministers were dismissive of the importance of the Trilogy (see Walsh 1995:126).

Table 7.1 Annual Budget Parameters used to Limit Expenditure

Timing and Sequence of the Decisions	Determining Fiscal and Budgetary Limits	Who is Involved in Making the Decision
February	Discussion of 'approximate savings targets'	Cabinet on briefing from Finance minister and PM
Early March	Budget and fiscal strategy and restraint options/intentions	ERC and/or Troika of PM, Treasurer and Finance minister
Mid/late March —forward estimates tabled in Parliament (March)	Agree overall budgetary parameters on a 'no policy change' basis	Troika, ERC and DoF—generally endorsed by cabinet
April–May —savings targets often tabled in Parliament (May)	Specific savings targets and/or fixed limits to resources available for new policy initiatives; but could be adjusted right up to the finalisation of the budget	Troika and ERC, while Treasurer tables any savings targets or forward estimates
April	Portfolio limits/guidelines issued with draft portfolio estimates	Finance, ERC and budget cabinet
May–July	Portfolio round of discussions to finalise portfolio limits; program limits/targets within portfolio	Finance minister and respective portfolio ministers; finalised in budget cabinet
August	Budget tabled in Parliament	Treasurer

gave an off-the-cuff commitment, effectively to freeze the level of outlays and revenues relative to GDP for the entire term of the next government (1984–87). His commitment was personal and apparently given without consultation with officials but it included a let-out for exceptional circumstances. Among the media the Trilogy became a benchmark for the second Hawke government. Financial markets and the Opposition in particular monitored government finances against this target—expecting the government to fail or fall short of its commitment. The OECD also regarded the Trilogy as the centrepiece of Hawke's management of fiscal policy and the public sector at large. Many officials in both central agencies and spending departments tended to regard Hawke's commitment as a rash electoral gimmick motivated by expediency.

Cabinet, however, tended to regard the commitment as a serious proposition and an accountability constraint which forced them to impose fiscal discipline. Hawke's While the Trilogy was perhaps unplanned when it was announced, it did heighten political resolve to curtail expenditures.

The process of setting annual expenditure targets was also a 'rubbery exercise' on occasions (Kelly 2000; Walsh P 1995). For instance, Walsh (Interview 1996) recalled that in the 1985 budget negotiations the ERC's 'Troika' of Hawke, Keating and himself were involved in setting aggregate targets for the forward estimates. Finance had urged Walsh to push for savings of $600–800 million in their green brief. However, the ministers were interested in presenting an attractive figure to the markets and Hawke suggested that they announce $1 billion in future savings to the bottom line. According to Walsh, Keating then said no one would believe them if they announced a round-figure of a 'billion dollar saving', and that instead they ought to invent one that looked precise. So Keating deliberately said they would make the figure $1.2 billion which had more prospect of being taken seriously. This latter figure was agreed, and Finance then had to go back through the detailed savings in the forward estimates and carve out further 'savings' to produce the new figure. Walsh (1995:155) subsequently claimed Keating may have 'disdained argument about what he once called the "nickels and dimes", believing it to be unworthy of the maestro painting on the grand canvas—especially if I would do it anyway, and absorb the antipathy it sometimes provoked from colleagues'.

Labor typically claimed credit for clawing these saving from the budget and their style of 'savings brinkmanship' impressed the financial markets, some economic commentators and the press gallery. But in the 1985–86 Budget round a further $1.5 billion expenditure was added—a figure greater than the savings projected (including $716 million in new Commonwealth programs and $810 million in transfers to the states). Hence, budgetary decisions remained compartmentalised and different dynamics were played out as political contingencies changed. In addition, ministerial commitment to restraint ebbed and flowed. For instance, in 1987 when the government announced its largest cuts, it was the Prime Minister's office that took the initiative, while other key players had by then lost interest in ERC (such as Keating and Treasury) or were focused on less ambitious cuts (such as Walsh and Finance).

A related 'savings' initiative of the mid-1980s was the establishment of the Efficiency Scrutiny Unit (ESU) headed by a private sector businessman David Block. After witnessing similar initiatives in the UK (the 'Rayner scrutinies'), Hawke announced the formation of the unit to assist the achievement of greater efficiencies and savings of outlays and staff. Formed in July 1986, the unit was attached to PM&C, and reported directly to Hawke and to ERC.[13] The ESU adopted an interventionist style described at the time as a 'crash through or crash approach' (Shand 1987). It conducted a series of confidential 'razor gang-style' reviews. Block's main *modus operandi* was to investigate and review public service behaviour to eliminate waste, rationalise processes and streamline administration. The ESU particularly focused on financial administration and risk management (advocating the management of risk, rather than the avoidance of risk at considerable cost in terms of administrative processes). The scrutiny reports remained the property of the respective departments for the purposes of implementing the recommendations, but the ERC could make overarching decisions imposing efficiencies. Its final and most noted report was into the abolition of the PSB and the successor arrangements (ESU 1987).[14] The ESU's report urged greater devolution of operational personnel matters to departments (including responsibility for equity, industrial democracy and management improvement), while retaining a smaller Public Service Commission. The report recommended allocating responsibility for pay and conditions be given to the Department of Employment and Industrial Relations—it did not support centralising or merging 'employer' functions with budget functions in Finance.[15] The ESU was disbanded in late 1987 to be replaced by an Administrative Reform unit in PM&C.

BUDGETARY REFORM UNDER LABOR

From early 1983 Labor began seriously to explore the possibilities of reform in the public service. Armed with Labor's *LQG* electoral

---

13 Halligan and Power (1992:99) argue that the establishment of the ESU gave PM&C added influence as the reform process began to assume a new emphasis.

14 The government had announced in May 1987 that the PSB would be 'restructured' (or abolished) largely as a cost saving measure and that its core personnel functions would be retained, but with more emphasis on rationalisation.

15 The abolition of the PSB was a controversial move that attracted much debate and criticism: see the discussion under the *nom de plume* SR Kelleher (1987).

platform and the findings of the Reid inquiry, Dawkins and Hawke persuaded cabinet to establish a Public Service Task Force to show 'our determination to implement the pre-election commitments' and provide a reform schedule (Dawkins 1984c).[16] As Minister for Finance, Dawkins requested his department to provide him with options for expenditure analysis and continuous expenditure review as a means of injecting rigour into the deliberations of the Public Service Task Force. His department seemed uncertain as to its own role in relation to the task force and about what the government intended. In particular, senior officers wondered whether they should provide input to the task force, comment on its draft papers, or analyse its final reports.

The apparent contradictions in the various pre-election manifestos now began to play their role. In July 1983 Finance advised Dawkins that consideration of the Reid Report 'should not occur prior to some resolution of the issues contained in the *Labor and Quality of Government* paper' in relation to public sector management (Beale Minute to Minister 20.7.1983). The department asked him how he wanted to respond to the recommendations contained in the *LQG* as 'it would seem more appropriate' to 'take note of those *LQG* recommendations . . . rather than responding now to Reid'. Dawkins agreed, preferring to articulate the new government's own

16 The members of the Public Service Task Force were: Ros Kelly, Peter Wilenski and John Monaghan.

agenda, while taking note of Reid's main message, that management was a vital but neglected function of government. The department also queried what would be the new relations between Finance, PSB and PM&C and whether the task force would clarify these relations.

The task force began 'a fundamental overhaul of Commonwealth administration' with the 'prime focus being efficiency and effectiveness or, in other words, to get better value for money' (Dawkins 1984d). It provided the impetus for a series of subsequent reform statements. Dawkins identified three separate but inter-related projects of reform each publicly released over 1983–84. These were:

- a major statement encapsulating the government's main principles of reform which culminated in the policy paper *Reforming the Australian Public Service* (December 1983);
- a subsequent policy paper on reform to financial administration eventually produced as *Budget Reform* (April 1984); and,
- a green paper on organisational and managerial reform in statutory authorities (1983) which prefigured the *Policy Guidelines for Commonwealth Statutory Authorities and Government Business Enterprises* (1987).

During 1983 and 1984 Dawkins made a number of key speeches linking these three projects. In April 1984 in a speech at the ANU, Dawkins outlined his views and his preference for a pragmatic approach. He described this approach as pursuing public sector reforms that were 'realistic, sensible, desirable and most importantly have waited long enough for their time' (Dawkins 1984c). The extant manifestos, conflicting though they may have been, gave him the opportunity to make such statements. He noted that Labor's announced reforms had 'prompted considerable comment and discussion' that was 'overwhelmingly favourable' and 'satisfyingly constructive' (Dawkins 1984c). Labor's enthusiasm for reform enjoyed considerable goodwill in both the press and bureaucracy.

In terms of budgetary and financial reform, Labor adopted a technocratic approach relying heavily on advice and some public debate. As one of the main technocratic reformers, Dawkins stressed four key agendas for the immediate period. The first involved the need to reorient the public service away from its input-oriented focus to a greater emphasis on outputs and outcomes. The second was the need for better-informed decision-making at all levels in the public service with appropriate devolution of authority and responsibility. Third, Dawkins stressed that reforms had to facilitate public and parliamentary scrutiny of the public sector at large. Finally, he called for further improvements in public sector management skills; rationalising processes while enhancing skills, experience and training. These agendas were not simply considered internal restructurings, they were crucially linked to the wider economy and Australia's economic performance (Dawkins 1984d).

To improve budget and resource management he advocated the 'integration of staffing and financial decision-making' within the context of the total resources available to government (Dawkins 1984a:9). He was scornful toward the previous system of PSB staffing controls because it was centralised, did not allow for the participation of ministers, produced 'quite arbitrary decisions' and was 'not adequately coordinated with budget decision-making'. And in addition, he concluded that 'experience has shown how difficult it is to estimate salary votes—the actual numbers are only one element, with such issues as leave and vacancy rates, making accurate estimating difficult'. A 'logical' and more preferable system was to control staffing 'through the financial allocating process' alone. He believed further,

> that financial and staffing decisions would be better integrated if overall management was under the control of one body. In the policy paper [*Reforming the Australian Public Service*] the government announced its intention to transfer the responsibility for advising on and administering staff numbers and profile controls from the PSB to the Department of Finance. We are also aiming to ensure that there should be a much closer involvement of ministers in decisions about the level, mix and distribution of resources (Dawkins 1984a:10).

The importance of this change is too frequently underestimated. In essence, the situation that prevailed was to be reversed. Previously, staffing levels had been a determinant of budget outlays; now budget limits were, in conception at least, to be the determinants of staffing. This can be argued to change the dynamics of public service growth and to make reductions in employees far more feasible. It knelled the end of 'permanency' in the APS at all levels of appointment.

In *Budget Reform* (1984:1) the government committed itself to reform the machinery of government and improve the 'processes of decision-making on budget priorities'. Four aims were articulated. The government sought to 'develop better means of identifying and setting budgetary priorities'; to 'focus attention more clearly on the goals and objectives of particular programs'; to develop techniques 'aimed at improved performance and more efficient resource use; and to 'set up machinery to ensure that the effectiveness and efficiency of programs are reviewed regularly' (1984:1–2). The paper committed the government to an annual meeting of ministers for a strategy review to address long-term budget issues. The Economic Planning Advisory Council was incorporated into the budget deliberation process and the role of the ERC was acknowledged. The policy paper also confirmed that the annual 'portfolio round of discussions is an important element of the budget process' and 'has now been established as a basic process in budget formulation'. It confirmed that the 'usefulness of the portfolio round of discussions is borne out by experience in the preparation of the 1983–84 Budget' which 'resulted in the redirection of significant resources from then existing to new programs' (*Budget Reform* 1984:7).

After acknowledging the decision to publish forward estimates on a regular basis both to enhance parliamentary scrutiny and to impose a discipline on the government itself, the paper discussed the advantages of moving toward program budgeting. Improved information, better ongoing cost projections and better management efficiencies were all promoted as attributes of a program-based budgeting system. While ministers made many new policy decisions on a program basis, the departmental base budgets were not based on programs and the existing budgetary framework still operated for appropriations on an administrative input basis. A pilot study was announced consisting of a small number of departments coordinated by Finance 'in consultation with the PSB'.

By 1984 the pace of budget reform was increasing markedly. Finance had effectively taken over responsibility for 'staff budgeting', linking resource needs with an emerging notion of corporate planning (DoF 1984a:4–6). *Budget Reform* (1984:9) had indicated the government's intention of 'integrating staffing and financial decision making' and had entrusted DoF with responsibility for the integrated framework. The paper suggested that future resource needs (both financial estimates and staffing levels) should be determined by 'joint, step-by-step' interaction between the Finance minister and portfolio minister. However, formal staffing establishment numbers would no longer be centrally set. No central agency would henceforth set general staffing numbers for operational agencies (with the exception of senior executive numbers that were restricted by Finance until 1997–98).[17]

Finance as the central budget agency was also 'examining its activities' and reviewing its resource management framework. It intended to become the lead agency in public sector reform by using the budget process as the principal instrument of reform.[18] By contrast, the PSB was half-heartedly promoting corporate planning as the catalyst of reform. Although it was cognisant of the importance of connecting the budgeting system with the objectives and corporate goals of organisations, the PSB did not have a clear idea of how budgetary reform should proceed.[19] They were also wary of relaxing resource controls too freely. Eventually, the traditional controls exercised by the PSB were regarded as redundant (if not counter-productive) and the PSB was abolished in 1987.

With hindsight, it is apparent that the years 1983–84 formed a watershed of technical reforms to the budget process with an intense amount of behind-the-scenes activity and many possibilities for reform open for discussion (see Barrett *et al.* 1995). Still, the agenda for change was not yet extensive and remained focused on procedural flexibilities within a given set of public sector responsibilities. Labor operated from a limited agenda in the early Hawke years. They were inexperienced in office and this made them simultaneously cautious while prepared to experiment. New budgetary models were initially imprecise—perhaps appropriately leaving the details and technicalities of particular instruments to be filled in later as the system evolved. They sought to transfer some authorities within the system and relax some controls to give flexibility, but they had little sense or vision of what they intended

17 Even after the SES notional item was removed in April 1997, agencies still had to report amounts paid to the SES under the heading 'remuneration of executive' (DoF Estimates Memo 1997/29).

18 This was a period of flux when many potential champions of reform could have emerged. The PSB was officially supportive of reform; Treasury and PM&C were promoting economic reform; and some line agencies were pushing ahead with program and corporate management reforms internally. Finance had not previously undertaken the role as a driver of reform; but in the mid–1980s the department became the Hawke government's principal reform agency for public sector change (see Barrett 1988; Halligan and Power 1992:98; Zifcak 1994; Wanna, Kelly and Forster 1997).

19 For instance, Commissioner J. Monaghan (1984) argued that it would be 'difficult to appreciate the relevance and importance' of departmental plans 'unless there is some connection with, or relationship to, the budgeting system'. Yet Monaghan provided no details as to how this could be achieved.

the new system to look like. The government was iconoclastic rather than prescriptive.

Moreover, the germinating ideas behind the budgetary reforms were almost all borrowed from elsewhere. Even as early as 1984 Finance officers were claiming there was 'very little in [the] model which is original' in that the reforms drew on 'experience/practice/proposals for reform in Australia (notably RCAGA), Canada (mixed experience with envelopes covering more than one spending department) and the UK (the Public Expenditure Survey Committee System)' (DoF 1984e). Labor's pragmatic agenda was driven by concerns of technical efficiency and organisational performance; a *technocratic approach* rather than a desire to realign government toward a neo-liberal philosophy.

PORTFOLIO BUDGETING

The gradual introduction of *portfolio budgeting* emerged as a major budgetary innovation for parameter-setting. The adoption was piecemeal and extended Guilfoyle's attempts to use program information and portfolio presentations in the budget reporting. Nevertheless, while portfolio budgeting came to be internationally recognised as one of the distinguishing features of Australia's system of expenditure control (OECD 1997), the government never explicitly set out to implement a budgeting system based on portfolio allocations. Rather, the government drifted into portfolio budgeting, principally because the portfolio unit was a convenient basis for allocating resources and the system seemed to work (Barrett 1988, cf. Keating and Holmes 1990).

The process followed meant that portfolio budgets were decided after the overall size of the aggregate expenditure budget was indicated. Between 1983 and 1985 there were around 28 separate portfolios. By 1987 the government had reorganised every area of public sector activity so that it came under a portfolio represented by one of the 14 cabinet ministers at the cabinet table (these 'super-portfolios' could have multiple ministers, departments, agencies and/or major programs within them). Consequently, all areas of government were now represented in cabinet and the proposed budget could be allocated or divided across the 14 portfolios (16 in 1990 and 17 in 1993), or conversely the sum of the portfolio allocations should equal the aggregate budget. Portfolio rationalisation and the establishment of 'mega-departments' was a crucial part of portfolio budgeting because it reduced the number of key players in the formulation of budgets.[20]

Once portfolio limits had been agreed, however, the relevant minister was provided with a single resource allocation which could be deployed according to portfolio priorities. Portfolio budgeting was essentially a form of 'one line' budgeting using the consolidation of activities under the one portfolio as the unit of budget allocation. The advantage of portfolio budgeting was that cabinet and ERC was not called upon to become involved in the micro-managing of line budgets within departments. Similarly, where the ERC was looking for expenditure reduction, savings could be extracted from individual portfolios with the respective minister able to determine where the impact of the savings would fall (and generally had sufficient resources within the portfolio to deliver the savings). This provided sufficient operating scope to allow for expenditures to be recast and priorities readdressed.

Portfolio budgeting had clear political advantages as well as budgetary ones. The adoption of the portfolio unit as a convenient 'envelope' for resource allocation reduced the need for political conflicts over resources within cabinet. Once portfolio limits had been set by ERC, ministers were at liberty to decide the particular composition of resource allocations within their respective areas of responsibility. The main politics associated with any budget round about who would emerge as winners or losers were buried within the portfolio rather than fought out between cabinet ministers. This factor may provide some explanation for the survival of portfolio budgeting throughout subsequent governments. Cabinet saw portfolio budgeting as offering 'win-win' situations in that the guardians in cabinet achieved budget discipline while the individual portfolio minister had discretion to allocate resources within the portfolio. This was preferable to either zero-sum games fought out at cabinet level or a ministerial stalemate where no side would concede.

Where disagreements arose between ERC and spending ministers over limits or cuts, then mostly the process was resolved through a bilateral process of negotiation involving the Finance Minister. Walsh (Interview 1996) claimed that if conflicts over spending levels could not be settled between officials from Finance and the relevant department, then 'the two ministers, or sometimes

---

20 Two issues of the *Canberra Bulletin of Public Administration* (No 52 October 1987 and No 54 May 1988) discussed the 1987 machinery of government changes and the establishment of 'mega-departments'.

there would be more than two ministers, would get together and cut a rough sort of deal based on no scientific grounds . . . I'm not sure you can be too scientific about anything like that'.

ERC's role was to put together the resource jigsaw when the aggregate expenditure levels had been set. They often did this by extracting cuts from forward estimates and ensuring that the portfolio budget estimates could be adjusted to equal the amount sought. More tricky was the process of allowing scope for new policy and particular political commitments that the government wanted to prioritise. Generally, tight upper limits were placed on the resources available for new policy.

THE ENTICEMENT OF *PROGRAM* BUDGETING

Arguably, the Hawke government resorted to *portfolio* allocations while intending to implement *program management and budgeting* (PMB). From early 1983 the government had articulated the presumed benefits of program budgeting and given commitments of their intention to adopt a version. For instance, Dawkins (1984a) claimed that program budgeting was 'not yet a reality in the Australian financial system' but that it was a clear 'trend'. He defined program budgeting as involving the 'drawing together of all resources involved in the implementation of a program and constant monitoring against the policy objectives laid down by the government of the efficiency and effectiveness of the delivery of that program'.[21] Such thinking led to a catch-cry from the central policy agencies for line departments to 'manage their programs against clearly defined goals and objectives'.

Around 15 years after Treasury had first proposed the introduction of program budgeting (Treasury Minute 68/946), a pilot-study was eventually commissioned over 1984–85 and involving a number of departments linked with the FMIP diagnostic study

21 Dawkins remained realistic as to the difficulties involved in implementing program budgeting across the Commonwealth. In the government's first term, Dawkins (1984b:16) stated 'let me make it quite clear, however, we are not about to switch over to a program budgeting basis of operation, headlong, overnight. The administrative task of doing so would be too complex, too large; it could not be achieved quickly without incurring high costs and causing considerable short-term dislocation. Apart from anything else, it will take time and effort to develop the necessary skills amongst officials and the systems they will need to manage under the new order'.

(see next chapter). The initial task in establishing program budgeting was to convince agencies to identify their 'program structures' (i.e. combining loosely related activities and administrative components under program labels). This in itself was a major undertaking. The issue was *how* to combine *which* activities into *what* programs. Some agencies were enthusiastic while others were recalcitrant and obstructionist (with some central agencies pretending the new framework did not apply to 'policy departments'). Many proposals were prepared within government discussing preferred program formats and canvassing issues on how to identify programs. Finance's preferred format consisted of amassing all activities within a given portfolio within one or more programs, under which sub-programs and components/activities were assembled. For the purists, every activity and administrative function had to be incorporated into program structures. This produced a hierarchic pyramid for each program which were intended to be 'broadly defined' and total no more than 'between 150 and 200 programs government wide' (DoF 1984c:5).

Program structures were, therefore, required from departments. These 'structures' were defined as 'a systematic presentation of government activities which, as far as possible, permits performance towards state objectives to be related to the resources used and, ultimately, to the results obtained' (DoF 1984c:5). Program structures would 'be used *only* for monitoring and estimates discussion purposes' when presented to central agencies. However, it was also intended that program information would be 'brought forward to ministers and co-ordinating agencies for resource allocation purposes; presented to Parliament and the public for scrutiny and information purposes; and collated for departmental resource management and manager appraisal purposes' (DoF 1984c:7).

By dint of repetition, the government convinced itself it was implementing program budgeting, and by the end of the 1980s began boasting of having implemented PMB (DoF 1990a:16) even though problems were still raised (*APS Reformed* 1992:250–252). Certainly, program 'structures' were created and continually revised throughout the APS, and some operational areas were managed through program formats and reported by program. There was never a serious suggestion that the government would *budget by programs*—meaning that resources would be decided and then appropriated on a program basis. Although some officials in central agencies toyed with the idea of program appropriations, the general consensus was either that the idea was impractical or that Parliament would not agree to this change and so any reform proposals in this direction were stillborn. Budgeting under the guise of program budgeting remained principally driven by the institutional units arranged into portfolio amalgamations.

Nevertheless, by 1986 the term *program budgeting* had been officially adopted as 'a budgetary framework for systematically reviewing the achievement of programs against their objectives as part of the funding process, and to establish accountability of departmental management for the end result of the expenditure of funds' (DoF 1986b:16). These sentiments tended to be expressed by the central agencies. Progress in implementing PMB on the ground was slow during the 1980s. Halligan and Power (1992:101) pointed to a good deal of rhetoric surrounding the reforms, but found governments often 'unwilling' to adopt program budgeting; and even though departments had adopted program structures its 'significance was less clear' at the end of the 1980s.[22] Clearly, program management and program budgeting implied a public service based less upon administrative structures and more on program based expenditures. Such a major change would necessarily cut across traditional lines of administrative control and perhaps render public service jobs less secure (jobs tied to programs might be more ephemeral than jobs in departments). Consequently, the potential for public service turf wars was immense. It is not surprising that the budgeting component was never capable of being implemented and the emphasis then fell on program management entirely within departments. As Wallace (Interview 1996) argued:

> One of the difficulties we had in embracing program budgeting as a whole was the apparent clash between the devolution of control over inputs and a stricter program structure. The way we appropriated money through running costs was intended to give managers flexibility to manage their inputs . . . as they saw necessary to effectively or efficiently deliver their programs. As soon as you started to appropriate money on a program basis, the extreme version would be to allocate running costs to programs. Now under the sort of legislative structures that we've got, that would mean you couldn't

---

22 Indeed, Halligan *et al.* (1996) later reported scepticism from among departmental secretaries they interviewed in relation to the worth of program budgeting. One secretary claimed program budgeting 'fell into a heap and they still haven't got program budgeting' (p.16).

> transfer money laterally between programs or at least not very readily . . . So we tended to argue against going down program appropriation lines . . . because on balance the notion of devolution was more important than an appropriation structure which perfectly matched the program structure . . . The alternative was to elevate appropriations to such a [high] level—for example, a department having only one program and then trying to overcome [problems] the best way, but I think the view was always that there would be great resistance from the Parliament to such a move.

Perhaps a more accurate presentation of the enticement of program budgeting was offered by two senior managerialists, Keating and Holmes (1990:169), who argued that it merely provided a 'program framework which facilitates devolution of authority to managers for the pursuit of cost-effectiveness . . . and provides a basis for a "new accountability" by setting out government objectives for program activities and by reporting performance alongside full program costs'. The key to the program-orientation was operational flexibility with resources and reporting of performance according to objectives. By the early–1990s the term program budgeting was quietly dropped from the government's lexicon.

TOUGHENING UP THE FORWARD ESTIMATES PROCESS

Meanwhile, attention returned to the use of forward estimates to add rigour to the budget process and control spending desires.[23] A subsequent evaluation by the Task Force on Management Improvement (*APS Reformed* 1992) depicted the accuracy of the forward estimates as one of the most successful budget reforms of the 1980s. Officials writing the draft report under the chairmanship of Vic Rogers had been explicit about the need to separate politicians who they saw as principally interested in resource maximisation from overall budgetary decision-making. The draft argued:

> Expenditure restraint largely relates to sustained political will; but it was difficult to sustain the interest and enthusiasm of politicians in restraint. If greater discipline was required, one solution was to take decisions away from the politicians and (insofar as possible) lock them into prescribed limits. Making forward estimates rigorous and reliable

23 The evolution of the forward estimates process in Australia is traced in Appendix B of this volume.

> would in theory remove the temptation from politicians to each expand their own area of responsibility. Toughening the forward estimates process was part of a process of keeping politicians away from the detailed incrementalism of budget creep (*Not Rhetoric Alone* 1992:s.9).

Essentially the message was: expenditure restraint can be achieved if only the politicians would 'butt out'. In the final version of the report far more moderate and ambiguous wording was used to convey the same sentiment.[24] The evaluation team was convinced that in the 1980s control over the public purse rested largely on the control of out-year commitments through a tough forward estimates process. They called the new tougher forward estimates the 'linchpin' of the Hawke government's budgetary system—an assessment echoed by a former economic adviser to Malcolm Fraser, Cliff Walsh (1990), who believed that the process of setting and sticking to the new forward estimates was the main ingredient of control and a spur to devolution.

Improved forward estimates became the preferred system of outlay control. In the mid–1980s some important changes were made to the process of setting forward estimates which were designed to make the figures accurate, reliable and predictable. First, in the 1983–84 budget round the forward estimates for the next three budget years were published for the first time, and from then on routinely released. The importance of the publication of the forward estimates is not necessarily tied to disclosure of the information; disclosure helps prevent governments from changing things at will. Rather, the rolling of forward estimates into the budget estimates became important because it embedded certainty into budget formulation.

Second, departments were required to translate their institutional activities and line budgets for administrative items into program structures. A select number of trial departments and

---

24 The final version of the *APS Reformed* report did not include the derogatory references to politicians nor to the notion of taking decisions away from them. Rather, the report argued (1992:16) that 'although expenditure restraint largely relates to political judgement, the capacity of government to manage expenditure has been aided by the new expenditure control framework based on three-year forward estimates . . . Ministers have been encouraged by the system to address deliberately the 'out year' consequences of any spending decision. There has been a decline in what was seen as the creeping incrementalism of earlier years'.

agencies were chosen for implementation and these had to translate their forward estimates into programs by January 1986—if they intended to use 'program budgeting' in 1986–87. Portfolio program structures had to be lodged with Finance prior to the commencement of each budget cycle. Spending departments were required to submit forward and draft estimates and new policy proposals, approved by their minister. Finance then prepared estimates for these programs for the next budget year and conducted discussions with departments (usually at the sub-program or component level) over the estimates for the two years ahead. *Portfolio Program Estimates* were then also published as part of the Budget Papers in 1985.

Third, Finance began preparing and imposing its own calculations as the basis for establishing the published forward estimates. In November 1985, Finance Minister Peter Walsh announced that components of the next forward estimates had been set by his department. Walsh noted that Finance had used 'its own estimates for administrative costs and staffing growth for 1985–86 and beyond, and these estimates are generally lower than those which were estimated by departments' (Press Release Minister for Finance 11/1985). He went on to give examples. Finance's estimate of administrative costs was $450 million less than the figure from departments and on staffing growth it was 0.3% compared to the figure submitted by departments which totalled 1.7%. The figures from line departments were simply 'disagreed' and so disregarded from the estimates in out years.

Forward estimates were 'firmed up' between 1985–87 and became the reliable basis for the budget estimates. Forward estimates which had once been padded 'wish lists' and best guess predictions suddenly became 'hard' figures. Effectively the estimates were set unilaterally by Finance after consultation with respective department officials. In practice, estimates were calculated by Finance as the minimum cost of continuing all ongoing existing policies and programs (then aggregated into portfolios). Once such estimates were set they then could become the basis for guaranteed funding between Finance and the department. As Bartos (Interview 1996) argued:

> if government decided to make absolutely no policy changes, then the budget could still be produced and it would just be a print out of the forward estimates, and it would still be a completely workable budget. That's a really big plus for [the system of] forward estimates.

So in becoming *fixed* the estimates process then locked in both central agencies and spending departments in terms of future expenditure commitments. Henceforth, forward estimates provided agencies with firm commitments they could expect without a great deal of re-justification. The strength of the new estimates process would later become a weakness.

Throughout the late 1980s the 'accuracy of the forward estimates' had become of paramount importance to both the key political and administrative players (Keating Interview 1996). By the use of the term 'accuracy', the government meant the degree to which any variation occurred between the published estimates and their translation into base portfolio budgets. Any variation in the budget allocations implied a certain inaccuracy in the estimates setting process. In December 1986, Finance reported that:

> More emphasis has been placed in compiling this year's forward estimates on the function they serve as the first stage in the subsequent updating and refinement of the estimates that will provide the basis for next year's budget. Unlike those in past Reports, these estimates represent the level of resources that have been agreed as necessary to maintain existing policy over the next three years. As such, any further variations of the estimates will reflect government decisions or agreed changes in economic or program specific parameters. This change is expected to improve significantly the efficiency of the budget process (DoF 1986c:2).

The 1987–88 Budget was the first to use forward estimates as firm budget estimate figures. The Finance Minister reported that:

> the forward estimates for 1987–88 published in December 1986, varied for decisions and parameter changes, were carried through the Budget process into the 1987–88 Budget estimates. By providing a consistent and continuing basis for budget deliberations, and minimising unproductive contention over base line estimates, these new procedures improved outlays control and enhanced the Government's capacity to focus on substantive issues in the budget context (DoF 1987a:2).

By the end of the 1980s Finance officials were beginning to pride themselves on their unilaterally imposed forward estimates. They considered the estimates not only a rigorous tool of expenditure control, they were also a source of much greater predictability to line managers who then had the capacity to better plan and manage resources (Keating 1990; *APS Reformed* 1992:225–230).

PARSIMONY AND THE PUBLIC PURSE

As the Hawke government settled into successive terms in office, the fear of echoing the Whitlam government's cavalier attitude to public expenditure receded. The Labor government of the 1980s was from the start a different animal to the one ejected from office the decade previous. Hawke's ministry gravitated toward economic rationalism and was prepared to liberalise financial and economic policy. If expenditure as a proportion of GDP was not reduced, neither was it allowed to grow. Total outlays remained constant for much of the 1980s. Program expenditure became more targeted to align with the government's priorities and areas of social need. In almost nine years in office, Hawke showed that a Labor government could also be fiscally conservative.

Budgetary management was a key feature of Labor's years in office. The government adopted a resource-oriented approach to public sector reform; with budgetary reform central to its intention to managerialise Commonwealth administration (Barrett *et al.* 1995). The PSB was first sidelined and then abolished under this regime as resourcing decisions became *the* system of control across the public sector. Finance emerged as the leading managerialist agency, determined to hold agencies to their budgets and far less interested in overseeing staffing, training and human resources issues. The limited agenda for budget reform beginning with great trepidation in 1983 was gradually extended throughout the Hawke years. Pragmatism and cost-effectiveness were principal drivers of the process, and adaptations on adaptations became the norm. While the government believed it was heading in the direction of program budgeting, the key characteristic of expenditure control became portfolio budgeting rationed by a powerful ERC. This system of imposing resource constraints was backed by a political commitment in cabinet to hold public expenditure in check and by a tightening of some technical budget instruments (such as unilaterally decreed forward estimates).

Between 1983–84 and 1986–7 the government progressively reduced the annual deficit inherited from its predecessors; and from 1987–88 until 1990–91 the government achieved four consecutive years of budget surpluses, with a surplus of over $5 billion in 1988–89. Against their own criteria this was certainly a measure of success in budget management. Such results rested largely on the political commitment of the senior ministers in cabinet, and on the strengthening economy throughout the mid–1980s. The

Commonwealth was also tight with its funding to the states, making substantial cuts in 1987. Yet, the immense difficulties experienced in controlling the amount of public funds was not itself the end of the matter. The more operative point was to ensure that the funds committed were well spent and managed. It is to this latter dimension that we now turn.

8 From control to management: the FMIP and beyond

MANAGERIAL REFORM IN the public sector was introduced progressively by Labor during the mid–1980s. Traditional bureaucracy was seen as problematic—especially its command-oriented, hierarchical structures and preoccupation with due process rather than results. Devolution of decision-making authority, management by objectives and managerial flexibility evolved as Labor's chosen solutions, and were quickly designated 'managerialism' by both opponents and supporters alike (Considine and Painter 1997). In contrast to the Fraser government, the motivation behind managerialism did not stem from a desire to reduce levels of public expenditure. Instead, it aimed at delivering a greater efficiency and effectiveness driven by financial and budget reform—arguably the distinguishing feature of public sector reform in the 1980s. The theoretical underpinnings of this movement required that public service managers be given far greater financial responsibilities than ever before. But the eventual changes would become far more significant than the designated precepts of financial management. They would change the nature of Australia's bureaucracy irrevocably.

While the Hawke government publicly stressed the need for *budget reform* to control expenditures, behind the scenes they increasingly accepted the need for complementary *financial management reform*.[1] They were conscious that *budget control* and the

1 Financial management in the public service was defined as consisting of three parts: 'the basic accounting processes relating to the receipt of moneys, the payment of accounts, ledger keeping and the preparation of annual financial statements; the preparation of estimates and the control of receipts and

management of financial resources were discrete phenomena. In early 1984 the Secretary of Finance advised that 'financial management is distinct from budgeting. It is primarily concerned with decisions taken at a detailed level, and usually in a different way to budgeting decisions' (Castles to Wilenski 23.2.1984). Australian policy-makers were further counselled in May 1984 by a US budgeting expert, Professor Allen Schick, that financial management and budget reform 'are not usually linked. They are usually provoked by different cycles or circumstances—but they are not incompatible' (Schick 1984). For most of the 1980s the Hawke government worked independently at these 'not incompatible' agendas.

Although the main impetus for financial management reform appeared rationalist and technocratic, at each stage the proposals had to overcome not only ideological opposition, but also the practical doubts and wariness of senior executives. Consequently, the development and philosophical refinement of financial reforms were incremental and evolutionary. As government reformers began to think in terms of 'resource frameworks' and 'management systems' they experimented with ways to replace detailed 'line-item' appropriations. Dissatisfaction with traditional line-item controls was longstanding; the problem was to find something better. Experimentation meant that reforms were introduced by administrative direction and not by legislation, with complex and far-reaching reforms being implemented incrementally over a long timeframe. Reforms were continually amended and extended as additional possibilities or new topics of concern emerged. Parliament was regularly informed of the changes but did not drive the process. Hence, in contrast to New Zealand,[2] it would be mistaken to assume that financial management arrived as a 'big-bang', mandated by legislation. Instead, components were added over time as temerity and timidity alternated, and the experience of implementation refined the initiatives. Where initiatives proved unsuccessful or of dubious worth they were dropped without fanfare, often portrayed as interim measures when overtaken by subsequent initiatives.

---

expenditure within those estimates; and the use of management accounting techniques by, or in support of, line managers' (DoF/PSB *Proposed Financial Management Improvement Program* 25.11.1982).

2 In New Zealand the *Public Finance Act 1988* imposed financial devolution on agency heads and made them responsible for the delivery of specific outputs. It also introduced accrual accounting and capital charges on agencies.

This chapter discusses three initiatives aimed at improving resource management each emerging in the 1980s. One was a top-down, service-wide Financial Management Improvement Program (FMIP), intended to provide better management performance through an integrated resource framework. The second involved a series of bottom-up, technical refinements to administrative budgets—producing consolidated appropriations for 'running costs arrangements'. The third initiative involved the use of program evaluation and completed the package by asking whether governments received value for money. These initiatives shared common ground in their endorsement of operational discretion, but emerged from different concerns and involved different champions. The development of a top-down management plan attracted many advocates across both central agencies and spending departments (but was principally promoted by the PSB and Finance).[3] The bottom-up consolidation of administrative budgets was a largely technical exercise crafted by budget and supply officers in Finance. These two initiatives would eventually be combined, but not before they had excited some institutional rivalry between central agencies over the principal direction and orientation of the reform agenda. The push for evaluation came from both line and central agencies—but attempts to impose a strenuous evaluation regime linking the results back into budget formulation were driven by Finance officials.

The emergence of Finance as the lead-agency in introducing financial and managerial reform across the public sector cannot be over-emphasised, given that the main push for reform came from within the bureaucracy and not government. Over the 1980s Finance developed a reform momentum, increased its influence in the preparation of the annual budget, and adopted a 'central catalytic role' in devising a resource management framework (Keating 1990).[4] This was a period of rapid change, where innovation and reform were encouraged. Finance's role as the secretariat and advisory agency to the ERC strengthened their guardian role in budget formulation, but Finance was not yet the natural *management board* of the public service. However, it performed a 'catalytic role'

---

3 Treasury under John Stone and Bernie Fraser generally absented itself from the managerialist reform process, and became largely irrelevant to this agenda.

4 Evidenced by the proliferation of substantial documents over 1983–87 on public sector reform, budget reform, the components of FMIP, and GBE reform (see Keating 1990; Wanna, Kelly and Forster 1997).

as it developed new resource frameworks. In doing so it gradually displaced the PSB in the management board role. The key to this was the replacement of the traditional system of staffing establishments for departments, which precisely determined numbers of staff at all levels within the hierarchy for any given department. Establishment figures, mainly the domain of the PSB and the source of much of its power, partly determined budget levels instead of the reverse. Despite strong debate within Finance, senior budgetary officials pushed ahead with a variety of pragmatic agendas preferring to control agencies through tighter financial controls rather than through centralised staffing or administrative line controls (Shand 1988; *APS Reformed* 1992:214).

So, as much by default and evolution as by deliberate purpose, Finance became the prime mover of managerialism by following the path of *controlling the dollar.* This conformed with the government's technocratic bias, but also influenced their orientation towards the managerialist agenda. Finance's administrative skill was shown in its ability to initiate, evolve and integrate resource initiatives into an ambitious agenda for public sector reform entertained by successive Hawke governments.

INTRODUCING THE FMIP: MANAGERIALISM, FINANCE AND THE PSB

The FMIP was conceived and developed in 1982–83 and progressively introduced from 1983–84. In many ways the FMIP began as a peripheral initiative half-heartedly proposed by a variety of actors with different motivations. But later it came to be regarded as the centrepiece of the Hawke government's expenditure management across the public sector (*APS Reformed* 1992). Contrary to some claims, the FMIP did not 'emerge in response to a report [by Reid] on the efficiency and effectiveness of the civil service' (Zifcak 1994:92). Rather, considerable work and many of the early ideas for an Australian 'special management improvement program' (following the British Financial Management Initiative of 1982) were well underway when the Reid team began its investigations in late 1982. Moreover, there was already much inter-agency correspondence between the PSB and Finance negotiating the aims such a program would encompass.

The PSB and DoF had been communicating about the need for financial management training since 1979. Both were aware departments tended to see resource management as marginal to their activities. For example, they argued in 1979 that 'one of the basic problems of financial management (in the Service) may be that many senior managers and policy advisers regard resource control and management as being a support activity at best, limited in scope, negative in outlook and not an integral part of their managerial responsibilities'.[5] In November 1982 a joint memo issued by DoF and the PSB suggested a 'Proposed Financial Management Improvement Program' would focus on *education* and the development of middle to senior management with respect to 'training, systems and procedures, working arrangements, organisation and classification and performance standards. Particular attention would be paid to senior and line managers' perspectives of, and their direct involvement and responsibilities in respect of, financial management'. In these early documents the FMIP was conceived of principally as a staff training initiative 'analogous to the Personnel Management Scheme'. In its submission to the Reid inquiry the PSB admitted the need for additional training in financial management, but stressed 'it would be necessary to build on the considerable training activity which exists and to present this in a more coherent manner to a large number of officers'.[6]

Reid supported these initiatives and his endorsement spurred implementation, but it was not clear at this time precisely what the FMIP would entail. The main aims of the FMIP were unclear from the outset and the features of the initial program were, therefore, ambivalent. Significantly, official representations of the aims of the FMIP were only clarified retrospectively (see *Not Dollars Alone* 1990:7–8; *APS Reformed* 1992:214).

Finance and the PSB jointly worked on the FMIP proposal over 1982. The head of the PSB, Bill Cole, even suggested to Finance in February 1983 that preparatory steps could be taken while the election campaign was on but that they ought not be perceived as pre-empting the government. After the change of government and the establishment of the Public Service Task Force, a *provisional joint FMIP initiative* was proposed by the PSB in June 1983 and announced publicly in the *PSB Bulletin* in July. At this stage the aims of the FMIP were to 'improve financial management practices . . . to achieve more *effective* management'. The an-

5 William Cole, Chairman of PSB: letter to Ian Castles Secretary of Finance.

6 Quoted in Summary in DoF Minute 22.8.1983.

nouncement gave few details, but spoke of the need to create a 'heightened perception of the resource implications of policies' and mentioned 'that one element of the program will be an examination of the role of those units in departments which are responsible for coordinating resource plans, estimates and budgets' (PSB 1983:1).

Differences emerged between the PSB and Finance about the aims of a management improvement program. The PSB intended the FMIP to be a collaborative venture between itself and Finance, and continually referred to the scheme as a 'joint project'. The Board intended its financial management program to be a limited, nuts and bolts, training exercise for the financial branches of departments across-the-service, perhaps partnering other initiatives DoF was pursuing. Finance was less committed to a joint program because they held different views as to the purpose of the FMIP. They were far more ambitious, believing the FMIP should be directed toward the policy-makers and senior managers whom they felt ought to become better informed about the resource implications of decisions and the administration of programs.[7] Whereas the PSB envisaged a service-wide training program, Finance's initial preference was to run a pilot financial management scheme with a small number of pro-active departments. A number of agencies had already expressed interest in redesigning financial systems to assist administrative efficiency and by 1983 some departments were experimenting with different resource management strategies attached to corporate management.

As the central budget agency, Finance began to insist on carriage of FMIP; and in this endeavour it was largely successful, at the expense of the PSB. The latter's attempt to get up a *broader* management training program to partner the FMIP failed because of a lack of a clear service-wide commitment and focus. Instead, the PSB proposed that a diagnostic study should be undertaken to 'marshal views across the service' and 'test ideas on how the

7 Finance was also not very specific at this stage about what they intended but felt they had a clearer idea of the problems. Its submission to the Reid review stated that: 'financial management in the public service is presented with particular difficulties since, often, the nature of the results sought by programs allows only imprecise assessment of the effectiveness of the different approaches to program management. Despite the difficulties, there is an over-riding need to develop a capacity for a fully informed perception of resource implications of policies, and for encouraging an attitude of mind that constantly relates the development and operation of individual programs to broader budgetary and other objectives' (DoF Summary in Minute 22.8.1983).

program should proceed'.[8] Finance was worried that this would delay or possibly obstruct the introduction of the FMIP. The PSB also floated other ideas in financial management though were unable to push them through. One such idea proposed by the PSB in 1984 suggested that a 'productivity investment fund' be established from which departments could borrow to fund future efficiencies and then repay 'savings' back to the fund. Presaging later 'resource agreements', the proposal was not well received at this stage. Finance strenuously opposed this idea, not only on the grounds that it was outside existing policy, but because it would require all administrative appropriations be consolidated and tightly controlled in order for savings to be meaningful. They remained cautious about removing all line item controls and allowing agencies full discretion to deploy resources as they chose.

Following the announcement of the FMIP, the PSB was successful in having a Diagnostic Study commissioned in mid–1983; the study team commenced its work in September intending to finish by mid-December.[9] The terms of reference for the Diagnostic Study included a review of financial management practices within the APS. The study was asked to examine the level of financial skills of senior managers, whether resource considerations were integrated into policy formulation, the capabilities of central agencies responsible for coordinating resources, estimates and budgets, and whether organisational arrangements, financial management tools and techniques contributed to greater program efficiency. The report of the Diagnostic Study (finalised in February 1984) endorsed the direction of the FMIP It recommended (PSB/DoF 1984a):

- a shift to performance-oriented management;
- clearer definitions of goals and objectives;
- a greater focus on outputs and outcomes;
- the development of performance indicators and reporting of ongoing performance against stated objectives;

---

8 Letter from Cole to Castles 23.2.1983.

9 The diagnostic study was undertaken by management consultants W.D.Scott. The joint steering committee included: chair J. Monaghan (PSB), deputy chair J. Carroll (DoF), with other members: D. McAlister (Defence), J. Rowland (Aviation), F. Pryor (PSB consultant) and, as an observer, C.Monaghan (Auditor-General's Office). Finance's other deputy secretary, M. Keating, had initially been nominated for the steering committee but was replaced by Carroll, following Caroll's appointment as Secretary, Department of Employment and Industrial Relations.

- greater flexibility in resource deployment;
- upgrading of management information systems; and
- the need to relate policy development with resource considerations.

The report also endorsed the adoption of many elements of program budgeting and highlighted the need for program evaluation. It recommended: 'where evaluations of the overall status and value of programs/projects are undertaken, these evaluations be, where possible, joint line/central agency reviews conducted as a special exercise', which would then 'be of value to Government in making choices between ongoing and new programs within the Budget context'.[10] The recommendations were not new or surprising and many were already underway in departments (Beale 1985). Indeed, some assessments of the study's usefulness and impact were at the time less than positive. The Secretary to the Treasury, John Stone, argued the report suffered a 'failure to come to grips adequately with the question of how the Government's overall objectives and priorities' can be coordinated in the budget process (Stone 1984). Other critics regarded the study as redundant and largely a waste of time and money (Keating Interview 1997). Nevertheless, it did reinforce a cultural shift toward managerialism within the APS. Its positive tone also helped the government to back the reforms.

THE EMERGENT AIMS OF THE FMIP

Labor's first Finance Minister, John Dawkins, made a number of increasingly firm commitments toward the FMIP after the findings of the Diagnostic Study were released, indicating that the government would proceed to implement FMIP in April 1984. He declared 'we intend both to create an environment in which managers can manage better and more freely, as well as to improve the skills and quality of the managers themselves' (Dawkins 1984b:17). He then told senior executives that the FMIP was concerned with management performance in which 'departments will be encouraged to improve their management capacities to take full advantage of this increased financial flexibility'. The FMIP would 'heighten awareness of the resource implications' of activities

10 Minister for Finance, Press Release, 6.2.1984:2.

and, while 'designed to address flows in financial control procedures', would also address 'the wider matter of managing the total resources made available by government for the purpose of implementing its policies and programs' (Dawkins 1984a: 7–9).

Once the 1984–85 annual budget preparation round was finalised, the government followed this with details of the pilot implementation of the FMIP initiative. On 20 July 1984 the PSB and Finance issued a joint circular *FMIP Implementation* to all departments and authorities staffed under the *Public Service Act*. This circular included both the key concepts and goals of the FMIP as well as the implementation plans. The FMIP was described as assisting the 'application of systematic approaches to the management of resources', which would produce benefits to government:

- improved advice . . . on the resource implications of meeting government objectives;
- greater ability to identify programs which are not meeting the objectives of government;
- enhanced capacity to determine priorities between programs as a basis for resource allocation; and
- increased ability of agencies to change the direction and emphasis of programs and activities in line with change in the government's priorities.[11]

The emerging aims, therefore, were largely concerned with responsiveness to changing priorities and improved resource usage. They focused specifically on priority-identification and resourcing; performance oriented approaches; encouraging managers 'to explore alternative ways of meeting objectives so as to improve effectiveness and efficiency'; controlling 'resource use against approved objectives and within appropriation; and allowing managers to 'respond to changes in the operating environment during the financial year stemming from shifts in government priorities or market place factors' (PSB/DoF 1984b:2). The broader aims did not particularly emphasise efficiency or intended reductions in expenditure or resource allocations.

Indeed, there was perhaps an understandable reluctance to be too specific in defining the intentions—with one official describing the vagaries of progress as 'feeling our way'.[12] Officials promoting

11 Extracts from PSB/DoF *FMIP Implementation* 1984b:2.

12 Notes on FMIP Group Implementation Meeting 27.9.1984.

the FMIP were content for the program to be considered an evolving framework focusing on the management of resources within agencies. Castles initially claimed the program 'would aim to develop the capacity for a fully informed perception of the resource implications of policies and relate the development and operations of individual programs to broader budgetary and other objectives'.[13] Other officials associated with planning groups or committees were anxious not to become too specific or prescriptive. Finance even toyed with the notion of renaming the FMIP as the Resource Management Improvement Program in 1984.[14]

Nevertheless, official descriptions began to define the FMIP as a 'comprehensive package' or 'aggregate control framework' which offered an 'integrated results oriented approach to management in agencies'. The FMIP was seen as a way of *integrating resources and program planning*. By late 1984 one of the key agency-level objectives had now become the *devolution of management authority within agencies* to allow maximum degrees of flexibility. Line departments also saw a further role for the FMIP in 'emphasising the drawing together of resources into program budgeting structures'.[15] The FMIP began to be seen as all things to all people—perhaps to avoid creating enemies. Finance began to consider the program's main role was to 'encourage a greater emphasis to be given to the outcomes sought by Government from its expenditure programs'. By December 1984 the FMIP was now seen as having three elements that focused attention on:

- the objectives of programs;
- performance indicators, which assist in assessing the extent to which objectives are being met; and
- evaluation and review of programs, elements central to the successful implementation of both FMIP and program budgeting (DoF 1984b:1).

The inclusion of 'evaluation' as one of the 'central' elements was a belated addition.[16] Thereafter, these three principles were repeated in public documents as the most important components of the FMIP. The aims were now more coherent but remained at a high

---

13 Minute from Castles to Prime Minister 3.2.1983.

14 Not using the term 'Resource Management Improvement Program' was a point of later regret, as acknowledged in the *APS Reformed* (1992:207).

15 M. Keating in DEIR Resources Management Strategic Plan 1984–85.

16 For example, John Dawkins gave many speeches in 1984 and generally included only the first two criteria, failing to mention the third criterion of evaluation.

level of generality. Soon the term *managing for results* was coined to describe the program. In 1986 the FMIP was presented as an 'initiative to achieve effective and efficient management of programs and resources' that:

- shifts management focus from 'compliance' and inputs to a focus on performance and outcomes;
- has a strong focus on results, achievement of government priorities/objectives [and] related resource requirements;
- creates a flexible structure so managers can manage better and a climate which encourages and rewards them (1986b:16).

Such depictions of the FMIP stressed its real focus was on *efficiency*. The aims were becoming sharper with the underlying message being to encourage government agencies to make more efficient and effective use of the resources available to them. Finance now began to see program budgeting as concerned with the broader policy aspects of resource allocation, and the FMIP as primarily concerned with the narrower operational aspects of efficient resource management. Thus, in July 1985 an advisory committee was already discussing redrafting the objectives of the FMIP to emphasise the *achievement* of efficiency and effective management of programs. This was only a matter of 15 months after the introduction of the program! Within another two years the FMIP initiative was again being presented as a component of program budgeting (DoF 1987b; Zifcak 1994:96–97) following a pilot study into program budgeting (DoF 1985). Major changes of emphasis so shortly after the program was launched raised questions about the credibility of the program among those implementing it in line agencies. Their problem was that the FMIP had from the start never been conceived simply as a 'good housekeeping program'.

These sometimes contradictory statements suggest that the FMIP was a flexible instrument whose main purposes could be changed relatively easily. It evolved over the first three years (1984–87) to mean different things to different people—arguably both a strength and a weakness. But by the late 1980s the FMIP had gradually acquired a consistent set of features—a briefing to the OECD in September 1989 presented the main features as:

- increasing flexibility for managers in the use of financial and personnel resources over the medium-term;
- the implementation of program management and budgeting designed to focus on efficiency and effectiveness; and

- the promotion of more efficient resource use and control of administrative expenditure (incorporating administrative clawbacks).

The FMIP had become code for resource efficiency.

IMPLEMENTING THE FMIP

If defining its objectives was difficult, so was implementing and managing the FMIP. The program was overseen by a select steering committee established in June 1983 and composed of a chair plus other senior officials from line departments and a representative from the Auditor-General's Office.[17] Finance provided secretarial services to the steering committee and often sent observers. At some meetings up to four observers were sent from Finance, and these 'observers' not only outnumbered the non-Finance members of the committee, but from the recorded minutes did most of the talking. The steering committee initially was active and met 10 times by the end of 1984, but thereafter its activity began to slow.

A further FMIP Interdepartmental Advisory and Development Committee (IADC) was established in May 1984 to provide input and to allow recipients of the program to voice their concerns and criticisms. The members of the IADC included: Finance, the PSB, Transport, and the ABS, and the four pilot FMIP departments plus the three pilot program budgeting departments.[18] Other departments were able to attend as observers. Finance acted as the convenor of the advisory committee and provided the secretarial support, but did not occupy the chair position, which went to one of the line representatives.[19] This committee met on a bi-monthly

17 The departments included: Finance, Defence and Transport (with the PSB and Audit Office represented along with an executive from the private sector). Initially the steering committee was chaired by PSB Commissioner John Monaghan, but shortly after, Finance took the chair providing first Roger Beale and then Pat Barrett as chair.

18 The four departments selected to be part of a pilot implementation study were: Communications; Defence; Health; and Immigration and Ethnic Affairs. Three departments were included in a program budgeting pilot study: Education and Youth Affairs; Employment and Industrial Relations; and Industry and Commerce.

19 The advisory committee chair was initially Frank Pryor—a special consultant to the PSB(and former department secretary)—and then Lionel Woodward from Immigration and Ethnic Affairs (formerly of PSB).

basis and tended to discuss proposed workplans, as well as implementation problems and difficulties that were usually transmitted to the steering committee. The ninth meeting of the IADC in July 1985 discussed the item of redrafting the goals and objectives of the FMIP.[20] There was also a series of 'practitioner forums' held in Canberra at the commencement of the program and 'FMIP support units' were established in departments to facilitate its introduction. Education modules were prepared for wider dissemination and distribution, each covering a particular topic (eg. program management, evaluation, information systems).

Because agencies would be responsible for ongoing implementation themselves (rather than the central agencies), it was decided 'that overall success of the program would be facilitated by concentrating initially on a small number of agencies which have developed, or were already embarked on, resource management improvement processes' (PSB/DoF 1984b:1). Discussions between Finance and line departments emphasised the setting of objectives, program costing, introducing reliable information systems and training requirements. These pilot departments began to report progress between August and October 1984, some indicating confusion over the implied relationship between FMIP and program budgeting but others seeing the exercise as basically similar. Departments questioned whether these initiatives were separate or integrated—a debate also doing the rounds in central agencies. There was recognition of the advantages of having undertaken some corporate planning or 'management by objectives' exercise, but also much discussion of the difficulties of imposing program structures on diverse organisational entities. One department was critical of the lack of direction and guidance, stating that 'people in Finance were not sure on what was planned or how quickly things were going to happen'.[21] Another department noted that agencies would develop more enthusiasm for the FMIP if it delivered more resources, but not if it did not. Another department acknowledged Finance had been a 'catalyst for starting' resource management but spoke of 'having to confront' them about program identification. Conversely, an official from Industry and Commerce recounted

20 In November 1984 the sixth IADC discussed a draft paper prepared by Finance on the preparation of new policy proposals by departments, specifying objectives and performance indicators and restricting the process of initiating new policy bids.

21 Note on FMIP Group Implementation Meeting 27.9.1984.

that 'Finance telling them what their program should be, had made it easier to reach internal agreement'.[22]

EVALUATING THE FMIP

Not all agencies welcomed the FMIP.[23] While accepting the need for limited financial management reform (some truncation of 'purely administrative items'), Treasury argued that the government's overall objectives could not be coordinated adequately through the budget process. It felt that individual ministers 'can and do from time to time have objectives which do not coincide with those of the Government' and that devolution would exacerbate this feature. Treasury Secretary, John Stone, criticised the FMIP for delegating too much authority to departments, with little appreciation of how the difficulties would be overcome. He urged the need for strong central control pointing to the results of the Diagnostic Study showing departments exaggerated bids and manipulated the system. He felt the philosophy of the FMIP did not apply to Treasury because it did not administer spending programs. Seeking exemption from the need to set objectives and be measured against them, Stone countered by insisting Treasury should retain its unchallenged monopoly status. He suggested Treasury's 'main function lies in providing economic advice to the Government and it would doubtless be widely agreed that there would be extreme difficulty in measuring success against this objective!'[24]

There were a variety of internal mechanisms for monitoring progress of the FMIP and suggesting further modifications or agenda topics. An FMIP Evaluation Task Force had been convened in 1984 and from its early assessments recommended that too much prescription should be avoided (citing also as evidence the Canadian experience where over-elaboration of financial systems were seen as a problem). The task force recommended in 1985 that the role of *evaluation* be extended into program management and budgeting

---

22 PSB/DoF (1984b) Minutes Program Budgeting Pilot Study, October.

23 Defence as a major department stood out as a non-adopter. The central budget agency could devise management improvement practices, yet they could only encourage them on departments, not impose.

24 Letter from Treasury to PSB 28.2.1984. Stone also advised that it was 'one matter to speak of [the] collective objectives of government in the abstract, and another to consider those objectives in light of [the] consequences' (DoF Minute, Treasury Response to FMIP 6.3.1984).

(PMB). Cabinet agreed and stipulated that all new policy proposals had to be accompanied by evaluation strategies and departments be required to report on evaluation plans for next couple of years—a decision not entirely honoured by ministers. An initiative proposed in 1985 was for all specified programs to be jointly evaluated by a team of officials from both Finance and the respective line department. The idea of joint evaluation was regularly floated over the late 1980s and early 1990s but never compulsorily imposed.

Incentives and Disincentives

In March 1988 the newly established Management Advisory Board (MAB) called for a formal evaluation of the FMIP. Finance prepared a briefing paper *Management Incentives in the Budgetary Process* (DoF 1988). This document outlined what they regarded as 'incentives and disincentives' for good management and proposed 'priority actions directed at improving incentives'. The 'incentives' were divided into three levels each requiring managers to accept greater control over resources (incentives were not personal rewards).

Disincentives or reservations about the scheme were acknowledged. For instance, Finance questioned whether the present system of accountability to the Auditor General was sufficiently timely to have a substantial impact on managers. Another disincentive under the FMIP framework was that 'there is evidence that managers exhibit considerable reluctance to undertake evaluations of program performance because they fear loss of resources and some reflection on personal assessment' (DoF 1988). The briefing concluded by raising potential disincentives such as: 'will a risk management approach backfire on managers?' and 'are personnel conditions (e.g. the ability to hire and fire) still far too restrictive?' Finance then floated the possibility of coercion, making evaluation a 'pre-requisite for getting *any* resources'. They finally proposed their future agendas: to clarify the arrangements for some areas of revenue retention (eg asset sales); encourage department secretaries to give high priority to devolving the full range of flexibilities; give greater recognition to the positive role of evaluation in achieving value for money; and review the current 'very weak' penalties for poor management.

The IADC's Concerns

In 1988 the IADC was re-constituted with generous representation of program managers from operating departments.[25] In August 1988

Chart 8.1 FMIP Incentives and Instruments to Make Managers Manage

Levels or Requirements	Incentives	Instruments
1. 'let the managers manage'—allowing greater control over resources in line agencies	Involves devolution of authority from central agencies to departments and sometimes to program managers; the use of portfolio targets to allow managers to meet priorities.	Medium-term planning of operating budgets; allows carryover of unspent funds, relaxation of staff budgeting controls, and the delegation of forward obligation controls.
2. 'encourage the managers to manage'—encouraging greater control over resources in line agencies	Provides greater autonomy for budget-dependent agencies and authorities; measures aimed at providing rewards for the agency for good performance.	Revenue retention and profit sharing once receipt targets are met; the use of user-charging shifting purchase from supplier to consumer; systematic program performance monitoring; efficiency scrutinies and efficiency bonuses to agencies.
3. 'make the managers manage'—forcing greater control over resources in line agencies	Forces managers to make the best use of resources; live within their budgets; and achieve specific goals; the incentives in this set are primarily punitive (of the 'stick' variety) and include penalties for poor performance.	Clawbacks, cash limits, and over-spending hurt poor performers; other flexibilities can be withdrawn if resources are not managed well; poor services may lead to program termination; program performance indicators presented to parliament are incentives to improve performance; agencies are accountable to the Auditor-General for performance.

25 The revised FMIP-IADC had 13 members, with only one from Finance (David Shand). The chair was Tony Harris from Immigration—but who had previously served in Finance between 1983–85).

major concerns were expressed over the implementation of the FMIP. Members considered there was still a long way to go in terms of providing greater resource flexibilities and demonstrating real benefits; there was 'concern that in some quarters, FMIP was seen to be running out of steam, particularly after the PSB's demise'. The committee found information flows in the APS were 'not good' and the 'thrust' of the program was 'not filtering down to lower levels'. The meeting (IADC 1988:2) went on to note that:

> considerable discussion ensued regarding the incentive (or lack thereof) for departmental managers to embrace the logic of FMIP, when they may have little control over savings achieved from better management and little personal reward for improved performance. Several members commented that current arrangements seemed to reward non-performers and that there needed to be more easing out of staff who were contributing little, so that better value for salary dollars could be obtained.

There was criticism of the lack of attention to the cost effective use of resources. Too much attention was given by departmental managers in central office to policy issues at the expense of resource effectiveness and efficiency. Agencies did not have realistic targets to drive effectiveness and suffered from inadequate outcome-oriented objectives. Despite line departments having responsibility for implementation, Finance was accused of taking a 'hands-off' and largely theoretical approach to management. Managers did not accept that the proposal to allow agencies (termed 'Commonwealth monopolies') to charge other agencies for services would make them efficient. Faced with such negative assessments, the IADC was conscious of the need to present some positive images of success, perhaps identifying some 'heroes of the Service' to provide role models. Finally, one of the Finance officials, Malcolm Holmes, questioned how far the original aims of the FMIP 'were illusory' and whether a new strategy was now needed. He flagged that 'resource agreements' should be pursued between Finance and line agencies to address some of the structural problems with the FMIP. At this stage little detail was provided on what resource agreements would entail, although it was apparent that such agreements were conceived as 'performance contracts' with agencies.

The IADC's assessments were transmitted to the FMIP steering committee in September 1988.[26] This committee reiterated that the 'thrust is not filtering down to lower levels', and that the lack of incentives for managers was a 'big issue' (FMIP/SC 1988:1–2). Problems were still being experienced with the process of aligning organisational structures and program structures. They advised that too much prescription was to be avoided in evaluation, and that departments should report for two years on their evaluation plans. New policy proposals ought to have evaluation strategies included as part of the bid. Seemingly making the best of a bad job, the steering committee concluded that 'evaluation activity should be tied to Program Management and Budgeting, as the logical last element of FMIP's management thrusts'. The premise presumably was that if only they could move on to the next stage of reforms, the problems of the previous ones would be solved.[27]

Public Evaluations 1986–1992

Public evaluations of the FMIP were more sanguine. Four major reviews were publicly released—some after intense redrafting of the findings.[28] The first report in 1986 provided an outline of the FMIP and indicated that agencies were producing approved program structures. A second FMIP Report in 1988 reported positively on progress in the first two years of implementation. Even so, it provided little detail on the intended aims of the FMIP. The second report provided progress reports from the larger and pro-active departments as a form of proselytisation. A third, more substantial assessment entitled *Not Dollars Alone*, was undertaken by a parliamentary committee, which found the FMIP an 'appropriate' initiative providing greater autonomy and flexibility, but 'weaknesses in execution and implementation' remained (1990:xiii). Improvements had been made in a number of areas of management (e.g. streamlining of budget processes, program structures, simplified rules, less restrictions on managers, enhancing ministerial awareness of priorities and providing a rational framework for government spending decisions). However, it was not convinced that major improvements had been made in the provision of information for accountability purposes or that government was

---

26 There was also a resolution taken was to have joint annual meetings of the IADC and steering committee, so that 'all members of the respective committees could get a feel for the others' views' (FMIP/SC 5.9.1988:2).

27 The *1988 FMIP Report* also stressed the link between the FMIP initiatives and PMB and organisational design to enhance strategic decision-making.

28 These were: the *1986 FMIP Report*; *1988 FMIP Report*; *Not Dollars Alone* 1990; and the *APS Reformed* 1992.

more directly focused on the purposes of programs. The committee called for better integration of financial management with other areas of public sector reform and for improved training of staff (1990:121–122). It reiterated that savings from the program were difficult to quantify, and urged a further review be undertaken in 1992 to focus closely on a 'quantification of the savings' produced by the program.

The fourth report (*APS Reformed* 1992) was a major evaluation of the public sector reforms within which the financial management reforms were prominent. This report commissioned by MAB focused on the degree to which resource flexibilities had been devolved to operational areas and on identifying the benefits attributable to the changes. The report cited favourable responses from agencies (1992:217–224) and from senior executives and staff. Executives were highly receptive in their perceptions towards the financial management reforms, though a sizeable minority of lower staff felt that the quality of services had suffered. The report did reiterate that achieving precision in assessing the reforms was problematic. It did not attempt to quantify the savings from the FMIP reforms as recommended by Parliament, but argued that 'a widely shared view is that the reforms to budgetary and financial management have yielded the greatest improvement in effectiveness and efficiency to date' (1992:267).

Despite the intense glare of attention the FMIP received in the mid–1980s, by the early 1990s the financial management changes introduced were regarded as *passe*. It was both regarded as having served its purpose and overtaken by other reform agendas. The FMIP steering committee was disbanded in 1989 and the IADC was replaced with the Management Improvement Advisory Council (MIAC). Indeed, the department most responsible for its development, Finance, did not even directly mention the FMIP in its 1993–94 *Annual Report*

TOWARD ONE LINE BUDGETS—THE RUNNING COSTS ARRANGEMENTS 1987–88+

In 1982–84 as the FMIP was being constructed, Finance in conjunction with the PSB began to investigate 'truncating' staffing and administrative expenditure items into consolidated amounts. Truncation involves the amalgamation of budget line items intended for similar administrative purposes.[29] Initially, Finance explored consolidation of line items for such purposes as telephones and postage, stationery and minor equipment and some personnel lines (such as part-time and casual staff items). These limited proposals eventually led to simpler operating budgets to cover all administrative running costs. In 1983 Finance amalgamated administrative appropriations for the year 1983–84 into two categories: (i) salaries, allowances, overtime and related expenses; and (ii) other administrative expenses (including travel, stationary, equipment and small consultancies). Administrative costs considered beyond a department's immediate control (such as legal and property costs) were excluded and remained centrally dispensed.

Such a simple but fundamental change in classifying line appropriations allowed other management features to be questioned. For instance, the truncation of expenditure items covering staff into a single appropriation made central control of staff numbers impracticable—a point keenly felt by line departments. Contrary to views expressed by Dawkins at the time, many central agency officials remained convinced of the imperative of tight staffing controls over departments. But gradually the view developed that financial controls on administrative spending could provide a better instrument of real control than offered by centrally-imposed staffing restrictions. As financial control arguments proved the more influential over time, the Hawke government responded by stripping the PSB of pay and staffing responsibilities. Responsibility for staff budgeting had been transferred to Finance in 1984, and the Department of Industrial Relations was given responsibility for pay and conditions in 1987.[30] Staff budgeting was thereafter controlled purely through annual cash limits within a single appropriation (except on numbers of senior executive positions). Many sceptics remained unsure that reliance on tighter financial frameworks would work and at the same time encourage

29 A more limited truncation of salary and administrative items had already been put in place for Commonwealth budget-financed statutory authorities such as the Australian Broadcasting Corporation, National Library, and National Capital Development Commission.

30 Ian Castles warned Peter Wilenski (chair of the PSB) that the transfer of functions to Finance should occur with the 'minimum of disruption' adding 'it would be regrettable if any caution were to be incorrectly interpreted as an attempt to slow down (or obstruct) implementation of the Government's proposals' (Letter from Castles to Wilenski 13.1.1984). A history of staff budgeting was included in the *Running Costs Arrangements Handbook* (DoF 1994d:26).

increased devolution of resource decision-making. There was also concern over whether line departments had the skills and expertise to manage their resources effectively if given greater latitude (Carroll Interview 1996).

These moves were extended when the Prime Minister announced to Parliament in September 1986 that a series of measures, the *Running Costs Arrangements* (RCAs), were to be introduced in the budget year 1987–88. While implementation of some of the measures preceded the announcement (e.g. the truncation of salary items and the ability to carry forward unspent administrative funds to the next year), the RCAs packaged them with some new initiatives as a more rational, resource management system. The RCAs were intended to provide agencies with a single, consolidated cash appropriation to cover most administrative costs—applying to around 10% of total Commonwealth outlays. Consolidation implied greater simplicity and assisted the government's 'thrust to devolution' by increasing the freedom to manage funds (Forster and Wanna 1995). Items funded included recurrent costs (operating expenses, salaries, equipment etc) and minor capital works up to $250,000. Agencies were permitted to carryover up to 2% of operational funds provided they were able to specify an intended use (i.e. the carryover was not meant as a 'bank').

The RCAs were never totally 'one-line budgets' for not *all* running costs were included (e.g. property, legal expenses, long-service leave and superannuation costs). They were agency specific and cash limited, but were *not divided according to program* (agencies had the ability to move funds internally between programs and activities). Given these flexibilities, agencies were expected to make efficiencies and return a productivity 'dividend' to government (see below). Many refinements to the running costs provisions were made in quick succession and further features added (MAB/MIAC 1991). Agencies were given the ability to retain revenue in 1988–89 subject to a sharing formula agreed with Finance and property operating expenses were added to the RCAs in 1992–93.

Carryover provisions were introduced in 1986–87, the year before the RCAs, allowing departments to save administrative funds not needed in a particular year (other than salaries) for use in the following year.[31] The purpose of the provision was to 'give

31 The carryover was officially defined as 'an underspend of an appropriation in the current year that is carried forward and added to the relevant appropriation in the following year' (Estimates memo 1997/46).

departments the scope for between year flexibility to either carry forward unspent funds or to borrow against future year appropriations' (DoF 1989:6). The carryover limit was initially 4% of non-salary administrative funds. In 1988–89 the limit was reduced to 2% when agencies were allowed to include salaries as part of the total running costs carryover. Unsure of the consequences of the change, Finance was cautious in setting the limits. Borrowings (or 'negative carryover provisions') of up to 2% against future running costs were also introduced in 1987–88. A higher carryover and borrowing limit of 3% was introduced in 1990 and Finance was examining proposals to increase the carryover provision to 5% in early 1990 (Minute 24.1.1990).

Agencies took to the carryover provisions with gusto, with many carrying over the maximum year after year. In 1986–87 departments carried over $19 million unspent into the next budget year; in 1987–88 (the first year of the RCAs) the amount carried over had risen to $29 million. The next year 1988–89 approximately $41 million was carried forward and in 1989–90 carryovers totalled over $58 million. Thus, in the first three years of the RCAs, agencies collectively carried forward under 1% of their running costs budgets (MAB/MIAC 1991:2). To provide greater flexibility carryover provisions were subsequently increased to 6 % in 1992 and then to 10% of running costs in 1995. By 1993–94 most agencies (numbering 79 or 64%) under the running costs program were carrying forward unspent funds constituting $203 million. Multiple year carryovers were also permitted in 1995 allowing agencies to hold funds over at least two years subject to the agreement of the Finance. These multiple year carryovers also attracted commercial rates of interest paid to the line department on the amount saved, while single year carryovers did not, even if successive carryovers were achieved. Borrowing limits were lifted to 6 % in 1992 but not increased thereafter. Borrowing requirements were of a far lower magnitude, with agencies borrowing in total only $12 million over the first three years (1987–88 to 1989–90). The ability to carryover reduced the need to borrow, but borrowings were made for 'one-off' projects, voluntary redundancy payments, or unusual payments (MAB/MIAC 1991:2). Multiple year borrowings were subject to interest charges with a default rate of 8% in 1994–95.

In 1988–89 agencies were encouraged to extend user-charging, with the incentive of revenue retention—they could keep some or all of the money they could earn from selling services (*Not Dollars*

Alone 1990:41–56). Income sources could include sale of non-property assets, rental of staff housing, user-charging, sub-leasing, and minor sales receipts. Revenues were retained by agencies mainly as 'net annotated appropriations'—implying that amounts received were deemed to be appropriated by Parliament and then reported in the next year's budget (under section 35 of the *Audit Act*). In 1988–89 revenue retention was zero, but agencies retained $70 million in 1989–90, $140 million in 1990–91, $220 million in 1991–92, $250 million in 1992–93 and $320 million in 1993–94 (DoF 1994c:9).[32] Agencies became innovative in finding new ways to supplement their budgets, but DoF also kept track of these amounts and routinely took into consideration the revenues raised when determining budget estimates.

RCAs gave agencies a greater degree of certainty over the resource baseline for their running costs (projected forward in 'hard' three year estimates), assisting them to plan and 'manage within their budgets'. A significant aspect of the initiative was that it embodied 'a medium term planning approach, which gives managers funding certainly based on estimates for future spending rather than the previous year's outcome' (DoF 1994c:1). Central scrutiny of detailed administrative expenditure was avoided, managers could move funds freely within single line appropriations, and agencies could 'save' or 'borrow' funds for administrative purposes beyond a budget year. Simplified operating budgets allowed managers to decide how to spend their resources to best achieve their objectives. According to the Secretary of Finance 'aggregate running costs for each agency [were] essentially set for a 3 year period'; and 'as a result, Finance officers no longer spend significant time examining the detailed components of administrative expenses such as postage and telephones, travel and stores, or in monitoring the detail of how the funds are spent' (Keating 1990:6–7).

Nevertheless, total running costs continued to rise (but in real terms less rapidly than earlier—with Finance (1990a:49) claiming an increase of 3%—over 1987–89 half the previous rate of growth). Spending departments could augment their running costs budgets

---

32 In 1989–90 Finance imposed an upper limit on the amount an agency could retain under the revenue retention policy. The limit in the first year was 0.5% of the agency's running costs unless 'special arrangements' had been made with Finance (the ABS and CSIRO had both made special arrangements for increased revenue retention). Thereafter there was no 'a priori limit on the maximum amount which may be retained' (*Not Dollars Alone* 1990:44).

if their workload increased or when cabinet supported new policy proposals which included running cost allocations. The first year under the RCAs there was no restriction placed on the lower levels of running expenses included in new policy proposals. But in 1988–89 a 'threshold' was introduced which required agencies to absorb minor running costs of new proposals and seek additional running costs only for major items. For Finance 'the major area of concern [was] the continuing practice of agencies seeking extremely minor additional resources in post-budget new policy proposals, when threshold arrangements require departments to meet minor variations from budget resources, and so preserve the cash limits and budget estimates' (DoF 1989:6). Running costs grew in real terms—by nearly 20% in terms of average staffing levels in the first five years of operation (HRSCBFPA 1994:S358). Over the two years 1988–90 the running costs budget increased by 2% per annum, the following year by 7%, by 5% in 1991–92 and by 2.5% in 1992–93. While total RCAs rose (a subject of some criticism by parliamentary committees) many agencies saw only minimal growth while others faced reduction. To government, running cost increases were not evidence of failure. Increases were reflective of 'the ability of the arrangements to allocate resources to areas of high priority and approved workload increases within an overall tight budget' (DoF 1989:8). Moreover, carryover provisions had not curtailed end-of-year spending surges. The ability to save unspent funds had 'done little to moderate the rate of end-of-year spending' (DoF 1989:6; MAB/MIAC 1991:4; Rothman and Thornton 1990:98). In late 1980s end of year spending was 160% pro rata for the last two months of each budget year and this rate did not decline when carryovers were introduced.

By the late 1980s budget consolidation for operating expenses was largely achieved but it never produced pure 'one line' budgets for total administrative costs within portfolios or agencies. Agencies did have more flexibility and discretion in that a range of different operational costs (staffing, equipment, travel, and other administrative expenses) could be charged to a single appropriation and, in theory, deployed efficiently. Under the evolving arrangements only certain 'recurrent' administrative costs were provided as a single allocation and even these were divided into 'notional items' (sub-amounts which could be tracked for accountability purposes—such as senior executive salaries, non-executive salaries, legal services, property expenses and minor acquisitions). In addition, other administrative-related expenses were never included (such as the value of fixed assets, depreciation and long-term liabilities which were later included under accrual appropriations) or only included at a later date (e.g. property and legal expenses included in 1992–93).

ANNUAL CLAWBACKS—IMPOSING EFFICIENCY ON RUNNING COSTS

An 'efficiency dividend' (ED) was introduced in 1987 as part of the RCAs to effect a clawback from administrative budgets. The clawback applied to agencies on their total running costs allocation (Defence and the ABC were initially exempt). It was a uniform percentage cut applied each year and taken from portfolios *before* their budgets were released.[33] Hence, the ED was retained centrally rather than given to departments and recouped—allowing no chance for it to be spent. Cabinet intended an annual clawback would operate continuously, gradually squeezing the administrative budgets in portfolios. It applied irrespective of agency size or demonstrated efficiency. Consequently, it was a blunt instrument that relegated to the portfolio how to respond.

The annual clawback proposal emerged when Mike Keating assumed the secretaryship of Finance in 1986—and he is often credited with proposing the measure. Hawke also knew the measure was supported by David Block of the Efficiency Scrutiny Unit. The rationale for the ED was 'to capture a proportion of productivity gains' made by operational managers and return the funds back to government (hence the misleading title 'dividend' back to government). It was a 'dynamic concept' forcing managers continually to seek new ways to improve efficiency and save resources. Cabinet endorsed the ED because it offered two important benefits; it assisted in controlling aggregate expenditure and gave the ERC an amount of extracted 'savings' available for reallocation. In many ways, however, the ED was a re-run of the annual percentage cuts arbitrarily imposed on departments by the Fraser cabinet, except that the process was routinised and the rate consistent. Finance generally emphasised that the combination of the RCAs and the

---

33 Cabinet Minute No.7524 of 1.5.1986. The initial decision was to be 1% per annum over three years—but with flexibility on the timing of delivery—so agencies could have put off the 3% cut to the third year. This decision was amended before the ED was implemented for the budget year 1987–88.

ED avoided the need both for 'arbitrary or *ad hoc* cuts in resources' (DoF 1989:1) and 'for DoF to identify . . . detailed savings resulting from efficiency improvements' (DoF 1994c:6). As well, because the ED was set at a low level it allowed operational managers to retain the benefits of any additional efficiencies. 'Equally importantly, it also allow[ed] ministers collectively the discretion to redirect a proportion of the productivity gains to priority uses, including for new expenditure' (Minute DoF 1991).

The clawback did not change for six years. Initially the rate was set at an average of 1% per annum over three years (1987–88 to 1989–90), but cabinet increased the annual rate to a flat 1.25% prior to the budget in 1987. In 1990 cabinet agreed to retain rate at 1.25% for a further three years, promising a review in 1993–94. The continuation of the ED also indicated cabinet's preparedness to live with this measure seeing it as a relatively de-politicised means of achieving administrative reductions (everyone suffered the same rate). Initially, some exemptions (full or partial) from the clawback were allowed on the grounds of either the unacceptable service reductions that would result or where 'recent comprehensive formal review' had shown agencies to be efficient (DoF 1989:4). Exemptions included: bodies with guaranteed funding (Defence, universities); agencies jointly funded with other governments (Anglo-Australian Telescope); commercial agencies operating trust accounts; or agencies where the government was concerned to improve the quality of services.

Nevertheless, the ED regularly came in for criticism from ministers, agencies and government backbenchers; a sensitive issue precisely because it was a visible, annual cut to portfolio budgets. Within the first twelve months the FMIP Steering Committee noted that 'Finance would have to look at the future of the efficiency dividend on running costs and consider possible alternative arrangements, for example, resource agreements which could be entered into for varying timeframes'. Other agencies believed the ED did not provide incentives to improve efficiency. It is evident 'some departments regarded themselves as relatively more efficient and therefore penalised by an efficiency dividend' while 'many departments perceive the efficiency dividend as a burden' (FMIP/SC 5.9.1988:4). Finance at this stage was determined to retain the ED, but offered a review during 1988–89 with any changes to apply after 1989–90.

After cabinet's decision to extend the ED in 1990, opposition intensified from line departments (DEET, HHCS, DPIE) as well as other central agencies (PM&C, DFAT, Attorney-General's). Some departments opposed the extension in principle; others quibbled over the rate set or sought exemptions. One argument was that many agencies had small operating budgets and so could not show productivity gains without sacking staff or reducing services. Some worried that new initiatives like blood screening (after the AIDS outbreak) would be detrimentally affected. Others like Social Security or the ATC argued they were hurt because they had proportionally large administrative budgets. The ATO considered that despite labelling the clawback an 'efficiency' return, ERC and DoF were only interested in expenditure *reductions*. The ATO argued,

> The efficiency dividend would achieve efficiency if inputs were cut while outputs remained constant or increased. The fact that the Department of Finance does nothing to measure outputs suggests that it is not really interested in efficiency *per se* only budget cuts. The Department does not explain why it believes inputs can be cut indefinitely, especially through a period of low staff wastage generating salary costs which are not within agencies' ability to control (*APS Reformed* 1992:244).

Indeed, a survey by the Task Force on Management Improvement found that over 65% SES staff did not consider the ED an effective device to realise efficiency and productivity gains (*APS Reformed* 1992:246).

So, did the annual ED work? The clawback 'saved' $72.6 million per year over the first seven years—from $53.9 million in 1987–88 to $81.7 in 1993–94. In cumulative terms the ED had clawed back some $508 million to 1993–94 or around 9% of running costs. However, annual running costs budgets increased as new policy proposals augmented the running costs allocations to agencies by a greater amount than the ED took. For instance, in 1988–89 over $110 million in new policy related running costs were added while the ED clawed back only $67.2 million. Over the late 1980s the amount available for reallocation was almost equal to the amount returned by the ED. In other words, cabinet would have had fewer resources to reallocate in the absence of the ED. The ED therefore represented an across-the-board form of 'offsets' on running costs, but one which also increased the scope for 'gaming' around new policy proposals. It encouraged agencies to invent ways to recover the amounts lost to the ED through new policy measures or even capture a greater share of the pool of clawed-back resources.

Another problem was that the ED only applied to the administrative costs of the Commonwealth's own programs and many areas of public finance escaped the discipline. Cabinet investigated ways to extend the ED principle to program areas administered by non-Commonwealth agencies (including specific purpose grants to the states). In July 1991 the cabinet's ERC asked Finance (in consultation with other central and line agencies) to prepare a memorandum providing options and recommendations on whether the ED should be extended to non-Commonwealth agencies (Cabinet Minute 15357). The proposal would mean that the administrative clawback would be applied to areas funded by the Commonwealth, but not administered by them. The type of areas or bodies affected included: inter-governmental programs, many social policy programs with combined federal/state funding, legal aid commissions, hospitals and special health services (e.g. blood transfusion services), universities and other tertiary education institutions. Finance was strongly of the view that the ED should be extended to these areas to deliver efficiencies and provide consistency with the other departments already included under the scheme. There were political sensitivities involved and cabinet did not want to buy a fight unnecessarily with the states. So, three categories with different applications were devised into which all programs or agencies in receipt of Commonwealth funding could be allocated. They were: programs/agencies to which the ED should apply; programs/agencies on the border—which ministers may wish to encourage; and programs/agencies to which the ED should not apply. Cabinet agreed to this framework with an incremental phase-in rate of 0.5% in 1991–92, becoming a flat 1% for 1992–93 and 2% for 1993–94.

Conscious of the criticisms, Labor's third Minister for Finance, Ralph Willis, wrote to the House of Representatives Standing Committee on Banking, Finance and Public Administration in 1993, asking them to conduct a public investigation into the scheme. The minister wanted further details about how the ED was applied within and across agencies; and in particular hear the experiences of small agencies. Willis opted for an 'independent and open' parliamentary inquiry 'instead of an in-house bureaucratic review' (Treasurer 1.9.1993). The review was to assist in developing options for future arrangements, but Willis announced that receipts, donations and charges generated by cultural, sporting and recreational agencies would be exempt from the ED. The committee's report, *Stand and Deliver* (1994), (delivered when Willis was Treasurer) recommended the ED be retained, but that the government consider both reducing the rate and increasing the number of exemptions for small agencies (with running costs under $10 million). Following the ED review by the parliamentary committee, cabinet reduced the rate to 1% from July 1994 (including property costs but subject to a property resource agreement). By mid–1994 the number of exempted agencies had grown to 46.

RESOURCE AGREEMENTS—AN ALTERNATIVE TO CLAWBACKS?

One reason the ED could be relaxed was that other efficiency and performance contracts were beginning to supplement the ED from the late 1980s (DoF 1987b). From 1987 a small number of agency-specific efficiency agreements had been negotiated between the central budget agency and line agencies (such as the ATO, DPIE, and DIR). Agreements needed to be signed by both the Minister for Finance and the portfolio minister (or their respective delegates—such as the head of an agency). These bilateral resourcing agreements were multi-year performance 'contracts' relating not just to efficiencies in input costs (running cost efficiencies), but to improvements in levels of outputs. Generally, resource agreements involved additional funding to enable agencies to achieve later projected savings. Agencies could also suspend or set aside the annual ED clawback provided that greater dividends were produced in future.

Resource agreements began addressing the special needs of a few agencies. They expanded until by the early 1990s almost all agencies had various forms of resource agreements in place. The original resource agreements were relatively limited to funding major organisational changes over three to four years to reduce operating costs in the longer-term. However, agreements were quickly extended to cover a range of issues from new IT and data processing equipment, to workload variations, redundancy packages, to cost recovery and special receipts retention (some of which were unlimited in time). By November 1990 a total of 45 resource agreements had been established (MAB/MIAC 1991:12–16) and by mid–1993 a total of 49 agreements were in operation—covering large and small agencies and selected programs involving the states

(DoF 1993). In 1993 property resource agreements were introduced and virtually made compulsory by the cabinet decision in early 1994 to reduce the ED rate for those with property resource agreements. In 1995 resource agreements totalled around 300, consisting mainly of six types of bilateral performance contracts: receipts retention; multiple year carryovers; carryovers of greater than 10% or borrowings of greater than 6%; workload adjustment formulas; property resource agreements; and workplace bargaining agreements (DoF 1995c:8). Around this time, demand-driven or workload adjustment agreements were segregated from the other resource agreements and a list of specific criteria was devised that agencies had to satisfy before they could enter a workload agreement.

Resource agreements provided a temporary relief from the annual ED, and many agencies even achieved increased running costs budgets over the shorter-term. Multi-year performance agreements proved popular with agencies and the rapid growth in the number was largely due to their demands to enter such contracts. Agencies could propose to enter agreements themselves or the portfolio department could offer to negotiate agreements for agencies under their responsibility. Nevertheless, the eventual clawback would be more substantial even if some years into the future.

PROGRAM EVALUATION TO FIND 'SAVINGS'—ASKING VALUE FOR MONEY

The introduction of program evaluation was intended to 'close the loop' by completing the 'management cycle' from planning to budgeting, implementation and monitoring and, finally, evaluation. Once objectives had been devised and program management introduced the government's interest switched to program evaluation and performance measurement in both GBEs and budget sector agencies. Public enterprises were targets of performance evaluation principally because of their economic importance (valued at $25 billion in the late 1980s with around 40% of Commonwealth employment). With government less interested in the detailed day-to-day operations and more in bottom line performance, the GBEs were given greater commercial and managerial freedoms. They were held accountable and disciplined through performance agreements based on financial targets and specified annual dividends paid to the government. Financial targets were set after advice from

Finance and calculated on an earnings ratio to assets or turnover. GBEs also had to pay the taxes applying to the private sector and were expected to perform community service obligations determined by ministers.

A more formal approach to evaluation was promulgated for budget sector agencies in 1986–87.[34] Finance and the PSB produced a comprehensive introduction to program evaluation for agencies that was both internally-focused and non-prescriptive. The primary aim of these evaluation techniques was to 'assist managers and other decision-makers' assess the relevance and priority of a program; test whether stated outcomes were achieved; ascertain whether better ways to achieve the outcomes existed; and decide whether the required 'resources for the program should continue at current levels, be increased, reduced or discontinued' (DoF/PSB 1987:3). The handbook was essentially produced as a form of 'good practice' advice to agencies; evaluation was presented normatively as a 'good thing' that all agencies should adopt.

Cabinet extended these initiatives by endorsing a service-wide evaluation regime in December 1988. Holmes (1991:163) maintained that program evaluation strategies linked three elements of the Hawke government's budgetary approach: controlling aggregate expenditure; improving program effectiveness and efficient resource use; and improving accountability. The emphasis on performance was intended to deliver 'systematic evaluation of all government programs on a regular basis' which would 'contribute to judgements on how well programs have achieved their objectives and how well they have been managed' (DoF 1990a:126). Indeed, it is apparent that program evaluation was conceived primarily as a central financial instrument—delivering information on value-for-money back to the executive. In Finance's words, evaluation contributed towards enhanced accountability through the

> better identification of program costs and linking these to outputs and outcomes. Portfolios are required to explain total expenditure, actual and proposed, in the context of what was achieved by the program and what the proposed expenditure will achieve. This

---

34 Earlier joint management program evaluations had existed prior to the mid–1980s (and were often chaired by PM&C) but these reviews were not routinely integrated into the budget review process. The policy paper Reforming the Australian Public Service (1983) had foreshadowed the development of an evaluation process that was linked to the budgetary process—see also Barrett *et al.* (1995:61–65).

> enables judgements about cost-effectiveness to be made on a well-informed basis (DoF 1990a:126).

Under program evaluation, the determination and implementation of evaluation strategies was devolved to individual portfolios and agencies. It was compulsory to produce 'planing for and reporting on evaluations' to cabinet, but it was left to the discretion of the portfolio minister when and how they were done and whether support was to be sought from others (DoF 1994f:13). All portfolios were required to submit evaluation plans to Finance listing the evaluations proposed over the next 3–5 years. Finance vetted these plans, suggesting amendments and, if desired, becoming involved in the proposed evaluation activities. By 1990 Finance had been involved with 10 agencies in 21 evaluations (either participating in the working group or on the steering committee)—the most being in Defence (5), DEET (4) and DPIE (3)).

The emphasis on evaluation proved to be the 'most controversial element' of the government's reforms (DoF 1990a:55). In part this was because evaluation was not only intended to report performance. It was also to provide evidence of where program expenditures could be reduced. Evaluation was centrally driven with savings options uppermost in the minds of central agencies. Although evaluation was sometimes sold as a methodology to assist managers, it was made clear that the 'primary use for program evaluation will generally be to assist decision making on priorities between competing needs'—which for established programs often meant skimming from them to reallocate elsewhere (DoF/PSB 1987:9). Later Finance would collect data showing the 'influence of evaluation on savings options' in terms of millions saved to Commonwealth outlays in each budget cycle (DoF 1994b).

Three problems quickly emerged with the government's evaluation strategy. First, evaluation was not sufficiently connected to the budget formulation process.[35] As Bartos has since argued, 'significant gaps' existed in the budgeting-performance nexus, and 'despite the views of the most senior advisory body on public management [MAB/MIAC], little progress was made' in incorporating performance information into budget deliberations (Bartos

35 Though one former DoF official has argued it was considerably more so than in Canada, the 'home of evaluation', where there was practically no connection to the budget process—a constant source of 'amazement' to Australian officials (Barrett Interview 1996).

2000). In fact, 'systematic barriers' existed that reduced the effectiveness of the evaluation regime. Appropriations were not closely linked to objectives, and governments did not allocate resources or set base budgets according to the partial pieces of information submitted by agencies in the name of evaluation.[36] Performance 'promises' were not directly related to actual reported performance. Program definition and redefinition (and reporting responsibility) was in the hands of departments with little oversight from the executive or legislature (Bartos 2000). Hence, although compulsory, agencies themselves had control over the process and they could work it to their advantage. They could evade evaluations or avoid evaluating their more problematic programs. ERC could 'review' specific programs although in such cases it was likely the programs were already coming under political scrutiny.

Second, the approach chosen by the government did not particularly focus on the quality of evaluation—it merely stipulated that rolling 3–5 year plans for evaluation had to be produced. Finance (1994e), in offering to assist the process, became worried about the ballooning list of 'excuses' agencies were able to proffer as to why they were unable (or unwilling) to conduct evaluations (including such reasons as inadequate skills, too soon, too time-consuming, extenuating circumstances, already efficient and optimal). External critics also highlighted the narrowness and instrumental nature of program evaluation methodologies (Ryan 1992). The effectiveness of the exercise was even questioned by senior officials who had championed its adoption. For instance, Barrett questioned how far evaluation assisted operational managers or was linked to the coalface level. He concluded that there was a need to 'improve the linkages between evaluation and program management' (Barrett 1992). Holmes (1991:168) also acknowledged perceptions of 'hidden agendas' (cost cutting) had made departments defensive in their evaluation strategies.

Third, the involvement of Finance in the program evaluations of spending agencies raised a new dilemma. According to Finance its involvement did not imply it could not otherwise 'pursue greater cost-effectiveness in program performance'. Yet, some agencies believed that with Finance participating in overseeing the evaluation,

---

36 One deputy secretary of Finance argued that the government had not sufficiently succeeded in moving resources from old priorities to new priorities. Early argued (Interview 1996) that evaluating 'old policy' was far more problematic than estimating the costs of new policy.

the budget of the program would automatically be safe where the evaluation was favourable. The dilemma for Finance in pursuing 'value for money' on a program basis was that if it chose not to become involved in evaluations, the departments ran them controlling the information and quality of the evaluation. If Finance did become involved, some agencies felt that they then had met the approval of Finance, and the budget agency should not then come back and suggest other cuts. The relational and logistical difficulties in conducting evaluations to achieve savings proved a fatal flaw in the review of programs. In response, the Keating government (1991–96) began to widen the scope of evaluation, conducting policy evaluations and policy management reviews with broader and often external representation on the reviews.

WATCHING THE 'WATCHER': EVALUATING THE PERFORMANCE OF FINANCE

With Finance pushing for the evaluation of line departments, its turn to be evaluated soon came. The Joint Parliamentary Committee of Public Accounts (chaired by Robert Tickner) announced in October 1989 its intention of conducting an inquiry into Finance. The inquiry was motivated by two developments—the committee was interested in evaluating the role of Finance after the devolution of financial responsibilities to departments, and the review was a second in a series following a successful inquiry into the role of the Auditor-General (*Ally of the People*, Report No 296). The terms of reference of the inquiry were to investigate the effectiveness of the department, its controls over other departments, its coordination and resource allocation functions, and its role in providing advice to other departments in the performance of management functions (JCPA 1989). Essentially, the committee was interested in gauging the performance of Finance as a resource manager in the context of devolution. With intentionally wide terms of reference, the committee was concerned to discover whether the role and practices of the central budget agency had changed, and whether Finance's activities assisted other agencies in improving performance.

Finance did not welcome being the subject of a special review (Keating Interview 1996) but complied with the investigation after attempting to clarify or limit the terms of reference (DoF 1990a:7). It produced a 170 page submission divided into five chapters explaining and justifying their role—articulating perhaps the clearest overview of Finance's managerialist phase ever assembled. It insisted that the 'counterpart to devolution—and indispensable to it—has been firm control over aggregate resources which are subject to managerial discretion' (1990a:9). Their central budget role was exercised primarily for the benefit of ministers and, as the advice was confidential, 'the value of that advice is best assessed by those ministers' (1990a:10). Finance admitted that it was a 'challenge' to 'achieve a balance between the "questioning" role and "letting the managers manage" which is a central element of the reforms' (1990a:15). The bulk of the submission provided an extensive overview of the functions of the department, the budget process and resource management framework, the interaction with other departments, the 'enhanced accountability framework', and the department's own internal management.

Submissions from 'client' spending agencies were sought assessing the contribution and effectiveness of the central budget agency. Only 20 were received and almost all were overwhelmingly positive.[37] Treasury referred to Finance's very significant contribution as the 'keeper of the public purse', suggesting it was the 'watcher' looking over the 'watched'. Other departments referred to 'substantial improvements', and the benefits of greater devolution, and of 'cordial and cooperative relations' with Finance. Other submissions were more self-serving. The Defence portfolio made a lengthy submission outlining its own resource management processes and arguing its case to be treated differently in budgetary matters. Immigration wanted to keep more of its own revenues without affecting its outlays. Administrative Services felt the controls on the number and level of senior executives ought not to apply to itself. Only a couple of criticisms were made in two of the 20 submissions: the ABC resented the secrecy involved in budget-setting and in finding out its actual budget only 'on budget night', while the ATO considered that program budgeting had become 'somewhat stalled'. There is anecdotal evidence that cabinet did not want a full and frank evaluation of Finance, especially just prior to an election, and that some senior officials 'lent on' other heads of department not to become involved or not be too critical. Also, there are clearly powerful reasons why agencies that had to deal

---

37 Submissions are contained in Joint Parliamentary Committee of Public Accounts Inquiry into the Department of Finance, Volume 1 (submissions from other agencies), Volume 2 (submission from DoF), Australian Archives, Canberra.

with Finance regularly would not want to put criticisms on the public record. Whatever caused the evaluation to be stymied, the committee never reported or produced any findings. An election interrupted the process, subsequently leading to Tickner's elevation to the ministry, and the new Public Accounts Committee decided to abort the inquiry.

Other reviews were more forthright in commenting on how well Finance had managed to adapt to the new environment of devolved management. Parliament's review into the FMIP commented on Finance's schizoid internal culture and roles. Departments had drawn attention to conflicting roles in the new central budget agency 'as to whether it should act as the watchdog of the public purse to the detriment of assisting departments implement government policy' (HRSCFPA 1990:65). More substantially the initial draft of the Rogers' report to MAB said:

> The dual role for Finance—'consultant' and 'controller', involves a tension common in public service agencies. But the question of balance, in adhering to the spirit of the devolved environment, is important. While there remained individual officers who had retained a 'traditional' outlook, the common view found, especially among heads of agencies, was that Finance had indeed successfully changed its 'culture' (however some, especially on the basis of reports in recent academic work, are not as accepting of this at this stage) (*Not Rhetoric Alone* 1992:S9).

The final version of *The Australian Public Service Reformed* (1992) reported the findings from line agencies on how well DoF had implemented budgetary and managerial reforms. Of the agencies sampled, 13 were positive, four were 'mixed' and five were negative (1992:93). Among the agencies there was no support for a re-centralisation of authority or going back to the former era of detailed central controls. Agencies felt there were internal differences within Finance over the reform agenda, different messages coming from the different divisions, and that conflicts over its role remained unresolved. Finance was also criticised for inadequate consultation and for making 'major financial and policy decisions about [line] departmental matters without taking account of the relevant information' (1992:95). Most senior executives in line agencies felt that Finance should not continue to play a 'controlling' role over finances, but assist them in managing in a devolved environment.

Hence, by the early 1990s, many sources were beginning to

draw attention to the tensions between strict central controls and the need for flexibility to make devolution work; between older forms of command versus new managerial cultures in the public service; and between budgeting for results and the difficulties in incorporating program evaluation. Managerial reforms were falling short of achieving the aspirations of its adherents. Managerialism was reaching its limits, racked by internal dilemmas.

9 Surplus to deficit: the Keating roller-coaster

After narrowly winning the 1990 election the Labor government was riven with internal feuding. The brooding leadership struggle between Bob Hawke and Paul Keating reached its final chapter in 1991. Keating was by then the Deputy Prime Minister (assuming the position in April 1990) and Hawke's heir apparent. He had earned kudos as Labor's long-serving Treasurer[1] and was by this time actively stalking Hawke, angry the Prime Minister had reneged on a private agreement in 1988 to hand over the leadership in his fourth term (the Kirribilli pact, see Gordon 1993:84–87). There was a perception in some quarters that Hawke was tiring and had stayed too long—despite being Labor's most successful leader by delivering four electoral victories in a row. The Labor caucus was torn between loyalty to Hawke and risking all on a new but unpredictable leader. A small band of Keating supporters, including some senior ministers, actively began to undermine Hawke's position. The inevitable leadership spill became drawn out and messy, full of invective and enmity between the two protagonists—an enmity magnified throughout the Labor cabinet, the caucus and many state branches of the party.

Hawke's final months as leader were not his finest. Keating challenged Hawke at a leadership ballot in June 1991 and lost narrowly. The Hawke cabinet, after years of appearing sound economic managers and performing as a close team with clear priorities, lost its coherence and began to tear itself apart. In the

---

1 Keating became Australia's second longest serving Treasurer—surviving eight years and three months from March 1983 to June 1991.

process the Hawke cabinet looked amateurish and incompetent. Keating resigned as Treasurer after the June challenge to sit on the backbench, preparing a second challenge. Hawke had to sack John Kerin his new Treasurer in early December 1991 after the former chook-farmer, agricultural economist and Minister for Primary Industries and Energy had looked out of his depth and incompetent in the job. At one stage Kerin confessed candidly to journalists he had little idea of where key economic indicators were likely to trend—something that Treasurers are not supposed to admit, even if true. Hawke then appointed Ralph Willis to the Treasury portfolio on 9 December. This was just ten days before he was himself defeated in the Labor caucus. Instability played into Keating's hand.

The turmoil abated once Keating wrested the leadership from Hawke at his second attempt, in December 1991. His victory was based on convincing a bare majority in caucus of his policy credentials and political instincts—promoting also his reputation as the 'driving force' behind many of the Hawke government's reforms. Whilst claiming it was his turn, Keating also questioned Hawke's ability to win the next election. Having grasped the 'hollow crown', and becoming Australia's 24th Prime Minister, Keating had to deliver on his promises. Staring almost certain electoral defeat in the face, Keating shifted the policy focus toward what he would later term the 'big picture'. After years of tight expenditure restraint and surpluses, he now began to spend during the 'recession Australia had to have'.

Keating's term as Prime Minister heralded in a period of expansionary fiscal policy and substantial increases in standing appropriations. Outlays rose substantially in each year of his prime ministership (1991–96). This was not simply a blow out of the budget. Rather, the Keating cabinet consolidated Australia's tight expenditure management system in the light of the government's chosen expansionary policies. The government was confronted with the problem of how to manage public expenditure when running a moderate counter-cyclical fiscal policy. As such, the Keating years illustrate the difficulties of addressing conflicting priorities through the budget process. Labor under Keating provides a good case study of how two apparently contradictory aspects of public expenditure management—expansionary fiscal policy and expenditure discipline—can co-exist. Eventually, however the contradiction contributed to the defeat of the Keating government in March 1996, but not before it had unexpectedly won a further term in

1993. Although Keating's successors were able to highlight his shortcomings, they were nevertheless able to return Australia to a budget surplus without really changing the expenditure management system—an important point to retain when one reviews the Keating record.

KEATING'S BIG SPENDING GAMBLE

When Keating seized the leadership, the government had around 16 months left before an election. Labor was so unpopular in the polls that re-election seemed impossible (Edwards 1996). An invigorated opposition led by John Hewson had released a substantial policy blue-print entitled *Fightback!*, prepared by external consultants for the Liberal leadership and advocating in great detail a new GST and smaller government. Hewson had campaigned well in 1990 as the Coalition's shadow treasurer, and was challenging Keating to call an early election. Journalists began to convince themselves that Hewson was about to fight the 'unlosable election'. Moreover, Australia was pitching headlong into a severe recession largely brought about by high interest rates, collapses in business confidence and the financial fall-out after the corporate excesses of the 1980s.

Directly on assuming office Keating formulated a new-look ministry—largely rewarding his own supporters who had pushed for him in the leadership tussle. He appointed his close friend and confidant, John Dawkins, as Treasurer on 27 December 1991, moving Ralph Willis back to the Finance ministry.[2] He also brought many former advisers and senior officials from Treasury and Finance into his private office. His immediate priority was to prepare a major economic statement to be released in early 1992—and his advisers were given the job of assembling ideas and

---

2 Keating's first ministry lasting one week was formed from the existing Hawke ministers. Ralph Willis's first stint as Finance minister was under Hawke (from April 1990 to 9 December 1991) and his second term under Keating (from 27 December 1991 to 23 December 1993). Willis also served two terms as Treasurer, briefly from 9 to 27 December 1991 in the last days of Hawke, and then becoming Keating's second Treasurer replacing John Dawkins on 23 December 1993 and remaining in the position until March 1996. Kim Beazley was appointed as Finance minister in the last days of Hawke's tenure, and again between December 1993 to March 1996. Both Willis and Beazley enjoyed reputations as competent Finance ministers.

suggestions. They began a brainstorming and barnstorming exercise, premised on a major re-injection of funds into transport infrastructure (expanding and upgrading national rail corridors for the new national rail corporation). Officials such as the new PM&C head Mike Keating went round the country seeking input from business, the states and other interest groups. As the process of compiling the statement was compressed into two months, the Prime Minister's advisers began dredging up all sorts of possible policy and de-regulatory suggestions to be included into the statement. This was despite Treasury admitting to ERC in early 1992 that they had underestimated the deficit by approximately $2 billion—a miscalculation the new Treasurer reputedly tried to shrug off (Blewett 1999:119; Edwards 1996:481).

The *One Nation* statement was released in February 1992. It was intended as a top-down strategy based on a moderate fiscal stimulus and tax cuts while at the same time extending microeconomic reform—a strategy began after 1987 by the third Hawke government (Beckett 1995). But the final statement was composed largely of bottom-up spending proposals, business-related subsidies and a potpourri of separate policy initiatives. In the rush to pull initiatives together, the economic strategy receded and *One Nation* emerged as a classic example of 'garbage can' policy-making. It read as a catch-all statement, soaking up a diverse range of policy initiatives that many departments had had in their policy drawers for some time. The diversity of items included: family assistance payments of $3 per week, promised income tax cuts, deferred income tax payments for small companies, relaxed restrictions on foreign ownership of mining, and the relaxation of airline regulation including the opening up of the Australian passenger market to New Zealand. The main items remained the targeting of investment into transport infrastructure and national rail corridors (with multiplier effects stimulating the steel industry); accelerated depreciation for business investment; reductions in the cost of equity capital; loan subsidies; assistance for development and export; additional funding for the textile industry; assistance for rural adjustment; and increased funding for tourism promotion (Industries Assistance Commission 1992:296). The personal tax cuts promised in the statement were later legislated for in 1992—Keating's infamous 'L-A-W law' tax cuts. *One Nation* also assured Australians the budget would be back in surplus by 1995–96—predicting a $2 billion surplus.

Although the former Finance Minister Peter Walsh labelled the

Table 9.1 Commonwealth Revenues, Outlays and Deficit—1988–89 to 1995–96

Year	Revenue $m	% real growth	Outlays $m	% real growth	Deficit*	Deficit as % of GDP
1988–90	95 517	1.7	88 882	1.8	–6 635	–1.7
1990–91	97 705	–2.0	97 333	4.9	–372	–0.1
1991–92	92 966	–6.5	104 551	5.5	11 585	2.9
1992–93	94 448	0.1	111 484	5.0	17 036	4.0
1993–94	100 142	5.0	117 252	4.2	17 110	3.8
1994–95	109 720	9.3	122 901	4.6	13 181	2.8
1995–96	121 105	7.2	131 182	4.0	10 077	2.0

* Negative amounts indicate a surplus. Source: Budget Paper No 1, 2000–01:8.42.

statement as 'fiscal irresponsibility' (1995:247), *One Nation* achieved its purpose in two important ways. It helped stimulate the economy in the depths of a major recession and it showed the renewed Labor government under Keating to be policy-oriented and prepared to push ahead with reform. *One Nation* may not have been perfect public policy but it achieved precisely what was intended; it provided a launching pad from which Labor would seek, and win, a record fifth term.

RECORD DEFICITS

Within the space of a few years Labor's carefully established reputation as parsimonious managers of the public purse had been jettisoned in favour of substantial increases in spending programs and deficit financing. Expenditure grew at an annual rate of around 5% for six years straight—in Hawke's last year and five more years under Keating. Such spending increases compounded to almost 30% in real terms over just 6 years. In Keating's first year as Prime Minister (1991–92), real outlays increased by 5.5% and in the second year (1992–93) by a further 5%. These were the largest single year increases since 1984–85. Table 9.1 below indicates the huge jump in expenditures and the dramatic fall-off in revenues—leading to record deficit figures.

Total Commonwealth outlays rose from 25.8% of GDP in 1988–89 to 28.5% in 1992–93. Increased spending created a record $17 billion deficit in 1992–93 followed by an even larger deficit in cash terms in 1993–94 of $17.1 billion (4% and 3.8% of GDP respectively). According to Peter Walsh (1995:257) around half of the deficit was 'structural' and would not disappear once economic growth increased.

By far the largest contributor to the two large deficits over 1992–94 was increased social security spending. Outlays increased from around $25 billion per annum in 1988–89 to $35 billion in 1992–93 and to $38 billion in 1993–94 (calculated in 1989–90 prices—Budget Paper No 1, 1996–97:3.107). Over the ten year period 1986–87 to 1996–97, outlays for social security rose by over 16% in constant prices (1989–90). Health outlays rose by 5.5% over the same period and education by 3%, followed by labour and employment programs by 1%. No other functional area received any significant increase in outlays, and many actually dropped over the decade (e.g., transport and communication, housing and community amenities, and fuel and energy were all down by around 1% in constant prices). Spending on social security rose from under 29% of total outlays in 1988–89 to over 36% in 1993–94 (see Appendix C). Retrospectively, the *Coalition's* first Budget (1996–97) explained these remarkable increases by stating that social security and welfare outlays

> have significantly increased reflecting both policy decisions and the economic cycle. The major contributors to this growth have been assistance to the unemployed and sick, assistance to families with children, assistance to the aged, assistance to people with disabilities and aboriginal advancement programs. The majority of growth has occurred in the last five years (Budget Paper No 1, 1996–97:3.32).

Others were less forgiving. Alan Wood argued in hindsight that Keating's legacy was a $69 billion deficit accumulated over the five year period from 1991–92 to 1995–96 (*Australian* 21.8.1996:1). However, it would be fallacious to suggest the increased deficit figure indicated government expenditure was 'out of control', because the decisions to increase public expenditure (and therefore the deficit) were *explicitly made* by the Keating cabinet. Increased benefits to families, the unemployed and the aged represented both a consequence of the economic downturn and a policy response to ameliorate living standards for the disadvantaged. Discretionary expenditure increased on the basis of *intentional* cabinet decisions (and revised parameter estimates); not because of departmental spending 'blow-outs' or unforeseen expenditure commitments. Whether or not the decisions to increase spending were appropriate will depend on one's judgements and assumptions of the role of

Figure 9.1 The Keating Roller Coaster: Real Growth in Outlays 1980–81 to 2000–01

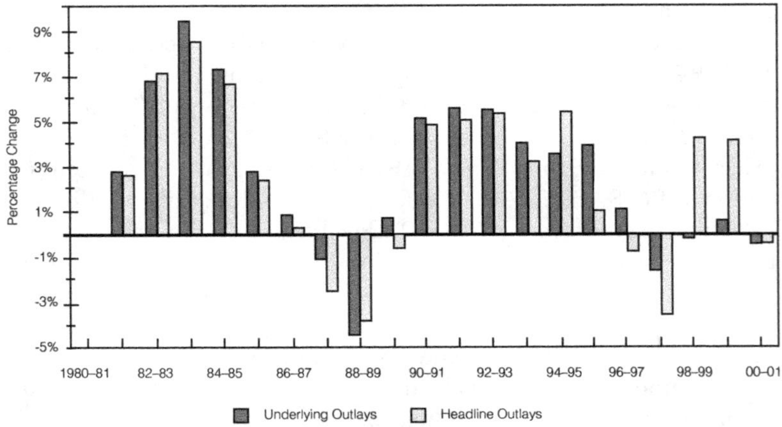

Percentage Change
9%
7%
5%
3%
1%
-1%
-3%
-5%
1980–81 82–83 84–85 86–87 88–89 90–91 92–93 94–95 96–97 98–99 00–01
Underlying Outlays Headline Outlays

Source: Budget Paper No.1, 1997–98:4.3.

government and level of appropriate involvement. Keating's decisions to operate an expansionary fiscal policy are of a different order to the more detailed field of management and control of public expenditure. While expansionary pressures clearly materialised for Keating, there was also increased attention aimed at imposing restraint and discipline within budget parameters.

The point remains that government spending under Keating did take on a roller coaster pattern; rising high in the mid–1980s, then plummeting by the late–1980s only to rise again sharply in the early/mid–1990s. Figure 9.1 below indicates rates of annual growth of outlays in the 1980s of greater than 7%, falling to negative growth (real reductions of 4% in 1988–89, with three further years of high real growth over 1990–91 to 1992–93. It is somewhat ironic that one of the chief architects of the reduction in spending in the 1980s and the achiever of four budget surpluses was the same person to pump up spending in the early 1990s. Such is life, as Ned Kelly was reputed to have said as he mounted the gallows.

DAWKINS' DEBACLE—THE BUDGET OF 1993–94

The first Keating budget after the unexpected victory in March 1993 became one of the more notorious in memory. To match

Hewson's personal tax reductions in *Fightback!*, Labor promised to reduce tax rates without resorting to a GST. During the 1993 election campaign, Keating had consistently maintained that, if returned, he would implement the 'L-A-W law' cuts in full. But after the election Treasury was increasingly worried about the deficit, and eventually convinced both Dawkins and Keating that the tax cuts were too generous and could not be afforded. The reasoning behind the advice was sound and consistent with Treasury's approach to fiscal policy—but the commitments had been made politically and backed by legislation. At the first opportunity, the government looked to find a way to escape their electoral commitments.

The 1993–94 Budget provided that opportunity. Traditionally, governments attempt tough budgets in their first year—getting the bad news out of the way early to allow scope for munificence closer to the election. The strategy behind the 1993–94 Budget was to commence 'the process of withdrawing the stimulus and cutting the deficit' (Dawkins 1993). Although Dawkins announced that the first instalment of the tax cuts would be brought forward to November 1993, he insisted that the second instalment (already legislated for) was to 'be deferred from 1996 until a time when fiscal conditions permit, probably in 1998'. He cut existing outlays by $2 billion, proposed large increases in excise rates on petrol and tobacco, and sought to increase wholesale sales tax rates over two years. Wine tax was increased from 20% to 31% and taxes were increased on lump sum superannuation payments. The fringe benefit tax was extended to social club membership included in salary packages and the repayments of the higher education contribution by university students were increased and brought forward. And the Medicare scheme was not extended to dental care as promised in the election (and the proposal on Budget night was for Medicare benefits to be removed from eye tests). The deficit would be reduced by $9 billion over four years. Dawkins' Budget Speech was a litany of 'bad news' inflicting pain across the board, with few redeeming 'good points' to promote (Dawkins 1993:1–15).

The Budget met with howls of outrage—not least by unions, community groups, business groups and taxpayers associations. Most concern was over the appearance of broken promises and the perception of the Budget's 'socially regressive character' (Weller and Young 2000). The opposition announced it would use its numbers in the Senate to block all taxation measures, effectively

giving the Democrats, Greens and an independent senator the right of veto over the Budget measures. Dawkins initially refused to deal with the minor parties, but was forced to reconsider by both the political realities and growing unrest among unions over the budget strategy. A second set of budget revenue measures was produced at the end of August (Budget Mark II) giving some concessions to the demands of the minor parties.

The passage of the budget through the Senate was tortuous—particularly the passage of the sales tax bills (see Young 1997). A total of 148 motions to amend the Budget were made in the Senate, mainly by the Coalition parties but with significant influence from the minor parties and the Independent. The government was forced to negotiate with the various holders of the balance-of-power, often clause by clause in the tax bills, to enable their budget measures to be passed. The final piece of budget legislation was passed on 26 October 1993 with the Democrats and especially the Greens extracting many concessions from the government, although as Young (1997) has argued it is easy to over-emphasise their obstructionist intent. From the government's perspective the 1993–94 Budget was a debacle, fought through deal-by-deal with Senators who commanded a relatively tiny electoral base but who exploited their strategic position to unpick or modify the government's budget measures. In the process the government also agreed to keep the minor parties more informed over economic forecasts in the budget formulation stages from then on (a commitment that has not been continuously honoured).

Bruised by the encounter John Dawkins suddenly resigned from politics. He had been the one-time 'campaign manager' for Keating in cabinet and served just two years as Treasurer—a post he had personally sought. He cited family reasons and the arduous travel commitments imposed on Western Australian ministers as the reasons for his departure. But, the debacle of the 1993–94 Budget and the torturous reception he had received as Treasurer could not be discounted as factors.

WE'VE CUT OUTLAYS BY MORE THAN ANYONE

Keating's response to criticism over the magnitude of the deficit was to take the offensive. Political opponents and commentators were all fair game—and abuse was used to much effect in discrediting their views. Rebutting criticism in the budget debates Keating told the House of Representatives in August 1993 that 'we have cut outlays by more than any cabinet in the Western world in the last 10 or 11 years. We have more experience with budgets and cutting outlays than any group of people in this country'. He supported his claim by arguing,

> In the 1980s we took government outlays in this country from 30.5 per cent of GDP to 23.5 per cent . . . We now have the smallest revenue share in the OECD and a set of outlays to go with it. Anybody who is arguing that one can have a sophisticated, industrial economy like this, with all sorts of public services—be it in the areas of health, hospitals, roads, telecommunications, air services or anything else—and deliver them by cutting further into outlays is an extremist, or malicious or a fool . . . Let me make it quite clear: we are not cutting outlays any further (Keating in House of Representatives *Debates*, 18 August 1993, quoted in Adams 1997:15).

Nonetheless, behind the scenes 'savings' were still extracted from existing outlays. Over the three year period 1991–92 to 1993–94 the value of saving options clawed back from budget estimates in the annual budget round increased from $1.3 billion to $1.4 billion to $1.8 billion. This imposed further efficiencies or policy rationalisation on spending departments. Yet, in Keating's first year as prime minister, new policy proposals ($2.4 billion) by far outweighed the amounts recouped in savings ($1.4 billion). Only in 1993–94 did savings options exceed new policy proposals (by around $600 million) in the budget round. And with an election approaching saving options fell away in 1994–95 to a low $700 million compared to $3 billion put forward as proposals for new policy. But, according to a survey of Finance staff, 'evaluation findings were used much more extensively in 1994–95 than for each of the preceding four budgets' in assisting cabinet to decide on new policy proposals (DoF 1994b). In other words, the Keating government attempted to impose discipline on existing outlays *via* increased attention to policy and program evaluation, thereby freeing resources for re-allocation (Mackay 1996).

Program evaluation was extended in two directions. First, in-house portfolio plans were expanded into higher-level policy reviews and policy management reviews (Weller and Stevens 1998). These generally embraced more agencies and attempted to consider policy effectiveness within a whole-of-government context. The main focus of such reviews was the appropriateness of policy, not necessarily the cost-effectiveness of particular programs. Second, by the early/mid–1990s evaluation efforts also expanded to include joint evaluations between departments and Finance (or with Finance providing limited consultancy services to assist evaluations—DoF 1994e; Mackay 1996:5). The benefits of such joint approaches were greater rigour and less partisanship, but the danger for Finance was that its participation in such evaluations could compromise their capacity to subsequently provide 'devil's advocate' advice in budget negotiations. An independent review of such joint policy review practices by John Uhr (1995) praised DoF's contribution in enhancing greater accountability, but also established that such evaluations risked over-extending the department's role and specific areas of expertise. He found that budget officials increasingly saw themselves as promoters of 'best practice policy' rather than expenditure review. Uhr urged a more cautious approach, 'a retreat from the highlands of evaluation to the lowlands of assessment' (1995:3). Uhr noted that although Finance could assist 'other agencies with specialist advice on policy development and implementation', it ought instead to focus on its 'distinctive speciality: its capacity to evaluate and advice on "value for money" in government programs' (1995:1). Finance was warned to stick to what it did best—evaluate and advise on expenditure policy and expenditure management practice (Uhr 1996). However, already the evaluation tide was turning and new forms of assessing value for money based on market-testing and contestability were being promoted.

Although Labor's regime of evaluation was extensive, the

rigorousness of performance information became a growing concern. Finance initiated a major performance information review in 1996 to isolate the weaknesses and provide a more reliable base for decision-making. The aim was to make performance reporting more consistent and enforceable. Among the more substantial weaknesses was not only the constancy of change, but also the flimsiness and variability of performance indicators and the difficulties government had in holding agencies to account for their performance. With hindsight, budget officials have declared that little progress was made in obtaining reliable performance information and that there 'was no clear relationship between the budgeted performance promises and the actual performance reported in annual reports' (Bartos 2000).

KEEPING THE SCORE WITH OFFSETS

While the Keating government deliberately allowed higher budget deficits, they were also mindful of the need for fiscal targeting and the direction of funds to those most in need or to meet political priorities. Keating in particular was determined to ensure that policy expanded within an expenditure management system that remained disciplined. So although prepared to see budget aggregates rise and increase levels of debt (to 18.9% of GDP by 1995–96—up from around 4% in 1989–90) Keating insisted those increases remained within predefined fiscal parameters. While much of the enthusiasm for further public sector reform and innovative financial management had dissipated by the early 1990s, the fifth Labor government continued to maintain a close eye on aggregate expenditure and discretionary spending. Even with Keating's major policy statements, such as *One Nation* (1992) *Working Nation* (1994) and *Creative Nation* (1994), not only were pre-determined expenditure limits imposed, but the available resources were mostly targeted with a high degree of precision. Often these national policy statements simply packaged a range of related initiatives that were already in the budget or were identified for capped funding.

Keating continued to employ the 'Troika'-driven budget processes which facilitated macro-level control of aggregate expenditures by the guardians. Throughout the mid–1990s aggregate expenditure targets continued to be used by ERC and cabinet to control spending in all portfolios and to frame budget negotiations. ERC capped the total funds available to each portfolio for new policy proposals before detailed negotiations began in the budget round. One senior officer in Finance volunteered that

> We were very tough in terms of saying we would not accept [portfolio budget] submissions which did not meet the targets. If people brought in submissions that didn't meet the targets, they were sent away again and told to . . . meet them.

Hence, fiscal limits continued to be decided by ERC *before* policy decisions were made. Policy-makers had to cut their coats to suit the cloth. A preliminary round of ministerial talks replaced the first round of ERC meetings. Once cabinet set portfolio spending and savings targets, further trilateral negotiations occurred with a small sub-committee consisting of the Treasurer, Finance Minister and relevant line minister. These trilateral negotiations established the resource framework within which that minister's submission must comply and 'discussed the sort of things that are reasonable and whether the minister is broadly on track to meet their targets (McRae 1996:2). Line ministers then revised the policy content of their submissions on the basis of these trilateral discussions. Often many of the portfolio submissions had been tentatively agreed before the ERC considered the final shape of the budget.

To quell the demands of line ministers yet further, the ERC and DoF imposed a strict policy that required existing resources to be offset against any new policy bids for resources (although for political reasons there were numerous exceptions allowed). Generally, before spending departments could bring forward new policy proposals in the budget round, they had to find savings in their existing estimates and offset these against any new claims for resources. This imposed a tight resource grid on departments, and one premised on attaching 'costs' to departments when proposing to submit new policy bids requiring resources. Departments increasingly found it difficult to 'win' additional resources with new policy bids as they had done with some success in the late 1980s. They now had to find most of, if not all, the resources required from their own allocations before they could entertain new policy development. From 1992–93 the government made offsets almost obligatory—and DoF began systematically using offsets to limit aggregate expenditure requirements and extract savings from spending departments.

Not only did the government insist on a disciplined approach to the bid system within portfolio submissions, they also regularly monitored compliance and the accuracy of their internal estimates process. In June 1992 the government produced an evaluation of budget and forward estimates entitled 'Keeping the Score' (DoF 1992b) which reported specifically on the accuracy, robustness, timeliness and consistency of the estimates and the impact of new policy on running costs. The evaluation of the estimates showed that over the previous five years budget estimates had been relatively accurate—finding 'the average absolute difference between the budget estimate of total outlays and the final outcome has been less than 1%' (DoF 1992b:2). Indeed, the accuracy of budget estimates became a leitmotif of Australian central agencies in the early 1990s. The report was less definitive about the other dimensions it investigated—perhaps because these other dimensions involved more qualitative judgements about performance than quantitative.

Two parliamentary reviews were undertaken of the Commonwealth's resource management framework. In September 1993 following a reference from the Finance minister—the House of Representatives Standing Committee on Banking, Finance and Public Administration (HRSCBFPA 1994) investigated the impact of the efficiency dividend on government administration. The committee received around 40 submissions most of which generally supported the government's desire to enforce efficiencies throughout the public service. Departmental submissions generally commented that the rate set was arbitrary and made no allowance for size or levels of efficiency operating in organisations. A number of agencies (small and large) argued they should be exempted for multifarious reasons. The committee's report, *Stand and Deliver*, urged the retention of the efficiency dividend and its extension to property expenses, but recommended cabinet reduce the annual rate to 1 % and allow more exemptions for small agencies (those with running costs under $10 million). It justified its recommendation by arguing that while the ED was a blunt instrument it kept the pressure on agencies and 'yields results'. The government agreed with this recommendation and from July 1994 reduced the rate from 1.25% to 1% (although agencies had to negotiate a property resource agreement, and property costs were included in the running costs arrangements).

The second review was broader in conception, investigating the entire operation of the running costs arrangements in budget-dependent agencies. The main concerns of the committee were the efficiency and effectiveness of the *devolution* of responsibility for resource management in the APS, and whether actual improvements had occurred in service delivery. The committee's report entitled *Keeping the Customer Satisfied* (HRSCBFPA 1995) endorsed the system of resource flexibilities under one-line administrative budgets. But while it applauded the system-wide devolution, it found limited devolution taking place within individual portfolios or large departments. The report argued that progress in introducing devolution in agencies was uneven, and that there was considerable room for improvement in devolving responsibilities to reduce costs and improve client services was disappointing. In other words, spending ministers and their senior management enjoyed the benefits associated with devolved responsibility, but were not themselves passing on such devolution to the operational managers within their departments. So, although some service delivery benefits had occurred, the full benefit to 'customers' had not yet materialised. The House Standing Committee urged departments to devolve greater responsibilities to the coalface.

THE INTRODUCTION OF MULTI-YEAR EXPENDITURE PLANNING

To avert further political criticism and a backlash from financial markets, the Keating ministry articulated a multi-year spending plan in the 1993–94 Budget. During the 1993 election Keating had promised to reduce the budget deficit to 1% of GDP by 1996–97, yet the measures introduced in the *One Nation* statement and more recent election commitments still threatened such a target. The medium-term expenditure plan (not yet a full fiscal and economic framework) was designed to impose a fiscal constraint on government, showing how they would achieve their deficit objectives. Keating was forced into this measure by criticism of what appeared to be arbitrary annual fiscal stimuluses—reaffirming the point that financial reforms are often a reaction to bad practice. Instead of simply announcing figures for annual total spending, the medium term plan detailed a schedule to impose fiscal discipline in the future. It also allowed observers to judge the annual budget figures in the context of a wider set of indicative fiscal plans.

The 1993–94 plan indicated the government's intended containment of budget aggregates over the medium-term. The plan set out 'item-by-item' exactly how the government intended to cut the deficit by $10.2 billion in order to reduce the deficit to around $5 billion by 1996–97. The plan included a detailed schedule for expenditure cuts over the next four years and presented clear expenditure targets on both an aggregate and portfolio basis. Keating also ruled out any changes to fiscal policy over the next four years, promising not to entertain spending increases or resort to major tax increases (Burton and Dodson 1993:1). Such specific commitments were meant to show Keating was serious in his endeavour to wipe out the deficit—but their rigidity over the medium-term was unprecedented in Australia. Keating's multi-year expenditure plan locked the government into a disciplined budgetary regime for the rest of the term of the government (Burton 1993:12). It was a far more specific set of constraints than Hawke's Trilogy commitment of 1984–87.

But, in practice, the fiscal discipline implied in the multi-year plan did not align with Keating's short-term policy objectives. His attempts to initiate 'big picture' policies in selected policy areas resulted in additional demands for spending. Keating's desire to show 'leadership' by announcing a series of major community and client group statements for business, the unemployed, the cultural sector, research and scientific communities, may have won plaudits from the client groups affected, but damaged the government in other ways by prevented the government from delivering on its plans to rein-in spending. The Prime Minister was becoming increasingly open to attack for unsound financial management.

A few years later the noted US expert on budgeting, Allen Schick (1996:59), argued that budgetary systems were deficient where nations produced annual budgets without the discipline imposed by a multi-year fiscal plan; by inference that the Australian system was so flawed. However, contrary to Schick's assessment, Australia had begun to take seriously the need for multi-year expenditure planning—if not to enhance accountability then to shore up the credibility of government. Unlike New Zealand, Australia's multi-year budgetary plan was incorporated in the budget documents themselves—not published separately several months before the annual budget is brought down. Hence, Labor's initial attempt at constructing a fiscal framework included in budget documents was one of the more important budgetary developments to emerge from the early 1990s. Yet subsequent experience under Keating also demonstrates the problematic nature of such forecasts and their lack of 'authoritative power' actually to constrain governments. No matter how earnestly governments commit themselves to future expenditure plans, they remain subject to change, amendable to suit changing circumstances and, perhaps most noticeably, dependent on different political styles and perceptions of expediency.

A parallel process of financial accountability and audit reform occurred through the legislature, with the aim to improve the accountability of executive government for its use of public money. In the late 1980s the Australian Parliament began a process of revising the main financial and audit acts operating within the Commonwealth. The Joint Committee of Public Accounts (1989) produced a major report entitled *The Auditor-General—Ally of the People and Parliament* (Report 296) which advocated a complete rewrite of the audit act to improve the effectiveness of accountability for the use of public funds (see Taylor 1990). An incremental process was undertaken to update the *Audit Act 1901* and other financial directions or guidelines used by government. Three separate bills were drafted and presented to Parliament in June 1994; the Financial Management and Accountability Bill, the Auditor-General Bill and the Commonwealth Authorities and Companies Bill. Alongside the parliamentary input, these bills had been in preparation for over a decade and the subject of considerable debate within the executive. However, although formally presented, the bills remained on the table of Parliament at the end of the Keating government's tenure (ie, they were not regarded as of immediate priority by the government). They were eventually re-presented to the succeeding Parliament and passed in 1997—with the legislation coming into effect from 1 January 1999.[3]

In the final months of the Keating administration a substantial process of renewal was begun in the Department of Finance—influenced by ideas of public service agencies becoming 'learning organisations' (Sedgwick 1996). The central budget agency considered that it should redefine its role and organisational philosophies away from its former centralised command orientation (the 'jackboots' approach), toward a more interactive and cooperative set of relations with line agencies. The process of re-engineering was commenced in mid–1995, and was known as 'the Future of Finance' project; the intention being to implement a complete reconfiguration of the department by 2001. This project enjoyed top-level support and was run from a small secretariat within the department. Commencing from a view that major organisational and cultural changes were required, the project team proposed a

3 See Joint Committee of Public Accounts and Audit (2000).

new mission for the department 'good public policy—well delivered' (DoF 1996b.4). To achieve this they believed that DoF had to 'encourage diversity, creativity, innovation', find 'new ways of working' with departments and 'build trust with those with whom we deal' (DoF 1996b:6–8). They also recommended that the department be restructured to three main functional groupings (Budget Development and Financial Accountability; Program and Policy Analysis; and Corporate and Business Services) which better reflected government priorities and the integrated nature of what the department did. Such a consolidated organisational format represented a break from the inherited structures of the old Treasury.[4] The 'Future of Finance' project now recommended DoF adopt a structure based on the *types of advice* the department gave (emphasising in particular where it could *add value* to government decision-making). The review sought to invest the department's future (and its importance or comparative advantage to government) in a more activist policy analysis role. There was serious discussion of 'forging a new culture building on the strengths within the department' and aiming to become 'world's best practice' (Early 1998:62; and Interview 1996).

Following the change of government in March 1996 the Coalition appeared to have less interest in pursuing this approach. With the replacement of Steve Sedgwick as departmental secretary by Peter Boxall in December 1996 (with Boxall commencing in January 1997), the 'Future of Finance' was quietly disbanded in early 1997. However, some of the re-organisational design promoted by the project group was incorporated into the department's new structure (adopted in July 1997) based on three outcomes and the outputs delivered by the department rather than different client types. Seven departmental groups are organised to deliver sustainable government finances; improved and more efficient government operations; and an efficiently functioning Parliament.[5]

---

4 DoF had been organised around its principal client departments (the supply areas) at the time of separation in 1976 and its internal divisions had not changed greatly in the meantime. A few cross-divisional or whole of government functions were gradually added (such as resource management and asset sales) but most divisions up to 1996 still reflected the departmental supply functions inherited from Treasury.

5 DoF was renamed the Department of Finance and Administration (DoFA) in October 1997 through its amalgamation with the former Department of Administrative Services. The seven groups of DoFA are: Budget; Property and Contract Management; Resource Management Framework; Business Services;

PLAYING HIDE AND SEEK WITH THE DEFICIT

Attempting to balance the competing pressures of political expediency and economic management, Keating had become even more interventionist in his last year as Prime Minister. In the 1995–96 budget process ERC decisions were often pre-determined by Keating in negotiation with his most trusted advisers and with Willis and Beazley (the main guardian ministers). With an election looming the Budget of 1995–96 would be an important political document—serving perhaps as the last chance for the presentation of a set of fiscal and economic figures. Accordingly, the budget 'numbers' were too important to leave to the routine processes of budget deliberation. Instead, he centralised budgetary decision-making to his own office.

The existence of the deficit had not featured large in the 1993 election—both sides had other more pressing agendas and the business community tended to be reconciled to the rationale for the increased spending. Three years later it was a different story. In the lead-up to the 1996 election the deficit suddenly loomed as one of the major issues of the campaign. This was in spite of the fact that the deficit was now only around one-third of its former size. But Keating had promised it would virtually be gone by 1995–96, and subsequently promised to reduce the deficit to 1% of GDP by 1996–97 (around $5 billion). He had then attempted to forecast that the budget would be in surplus by June 1996. Such claims became increasingly unconvincing and the government's credibility was on the line. By mid–1995 it was clear to many that the actual deficit was unlikely to disappear, and that the figure would remain significantly large.

So, from the government's point of view, the deficit had to be hidden—at least until after the next election. Political pressures prompted the Prime Minister to manipulate the budget estimates (particularly economic growth estimates) to show the budget moving into surplus. It was 'psychologically important' to make the deficit 'disappear'. Key assumptions and indicators informing the determination of budgetary parameters were picked-over by his

---

Ministerial and Parliamentary Services; Corporate; and Financial Management—the latter two being essentially responsible for DoFA's own operations and financial reporting. It is worth noting that Budget Group now encompasses virtually all of the business functions of the previous Finance department (except the corporate area).

inner-most staff. Decisions made to present the economic assumptions and fiscal balance in the best possible light. Funds from the second round of privatisation of the Commonwealth Bank were included as additional revenues in the 1995 budget round—helping to achieve a balance between income and outlays. The 1995–96 Budget predicted a surplus of $718 million over the budget year, with outlays projected to decrease by 2.5% and revenue predicted to rise by 8.9%. Each of these projections would turn out to be wrong—with each shown to be far optimistic in the government's favour.

Keating did his best to obscure the deficit in 1995 and early 1996. Yet, claims the 1995–96 Budget would be in surplus were met with scepticism by experienced commentators. One trenchant critic of Labor during its final terms, Alan Wood, the economics editor of *The Australian* argued,

> This budget is not in surplus. Measured on the basis the federal Treasury says provides 'a more accurate picture of the underlying position of the Budget' it shows a deficit of over $8 billion' (Wood 1995:1).

History was to prove Wood right.

10 The new business of budgeting: expenditure management under Howard

AFTER 13 YEARS in opposition, John Howard led the Liberal and National parties to government on 3 March 1996. The Coalition government assumed office with no ownership or necessary investment in the budgetary reforms of its predecessor—thus allowing exploration of the extent to which the framework and techniques of expenditure management change with incumbency. While the main direction of Labor's reformist approach was accepted, some elements were rejected by the new government or overtaken by new accounting techniques. Operating from a very different philosophy of the role of government, the Coalition pushed the agenda for budgetary reform further and even more aggressively. The managerialist orientation of Labor gave way to a more neo-liberal business-oriented approach under the conservatives. Government activities were regarded as contestable markets, budgeting came to reflect business practices, and performance was increasingly assessed according to balance sheet results and the 'bottom line'.

This chapter traces the administrative and political processes through which the Coalition translated its election promises into the 1996–97 Budget. We then review important changes to the budget processes and the decentralisation of the estimates process. Significant changes were made in the Coalition's second term with the introduction of an accrual-outcomes budgetary framework utilising appropriations by 'outcome purposes' and price reviews of output costings. Other reforms aimed to make the government's fiscal policies and financial performance more transparent, with legislative requirements stipulated in the *Charter of Budget Honesty 1998*.

Despite the neutral-sounding language associated with business and accounting, the events reviewed in this chapter illustrate again the highly political nature of budgetary allocation and resource management in the public sector. They demonstrate that budgetary systems and processes are more than merely accounting functions that present clear choices and rational courses of action. Rather, budgetary systems require politicians to frame the terms of the debate and to persuade different constituencies of the validity of their proposed strategies and fiscal objectives. Like their Labor predecessors, the Coalition soon found that their commitments to 'sound financial management' became harder to maintain once they settled into office.

THE COALITION'S 1996 ELECTION COMMITMENTS

The 1996 election campaign simulated a 'sham auction' with both sides bidding new expenditure programs across a range of policy areas. The commitments were based on optimistic projections showing a $3.6 billion surplus in 1996–97 and increasing surpluses in the following two out-years to 1998–99. The temptation to spend these surpluses proved too much for politicians, and headlines such as 'roll-up, roll up, for poll giveaways' and 'on the trail, money to burn' became a feature of election commentary.

The Coalition's expenditure commitments were set out in three documents, promising a range of new spending proposals in most program areas, the largest of which were a $1 billion tax rebate with their *Families Scheme* and $450 million in rebates for private health insurance.[1] Together the three documents tied the Coalition into $6.8 billion in new spending programs. Not only did they propose new programs, they also excluded large portions of existing expenditure from the spectre of budget cuts. Included in this promise were the big spending areas of tertiary education, Aboriginal affairs and the ABC. In addition, they proposed to guarantee state governments a fixed percentage share of total Commonwealth taxation revenue (Howard 1996:9). Partially to offset the increases in spending the Coalition promised to reduce the running costs of all agencies, except Defence, by two per cent from 1996–97 onward—an aggregate reduction of $500 million over three years.

---

1 Howard's 'Policy Launch Statement' of 18 February 1996; Costello's *Meeting our Commitments* on 15 February 1996; and Howard's *Fair Australia*, speech delivered to ACOSS on 13 October 1995.

On the revenue side, Howard promised not to 'impose new taxes or increase existing ones'. In fact, tax reduction was a major feature in their platform and numerous rebates were proposed for individuals and business. To complete their commitments the Coalition promised the 1997–98 budget would be in surplus. Taken together these commitments were regarded at the time as a 'straightjacket' by commentators (Burton 1996:4).

Pressure mounted during the campaign for both parties to cost their growing list of election promises. Commentators suggested that the substantial budget surpluses predicted by Treasury ($3.6 billion for 1996–97) would be insufficient to meet the proposals of either party. This raised the prospect of significant spending cuts in a post-election budget to pay for new policy initiatives. Some demanded to know which programs would receive cuts and which recipients would be affected. Others in the financial press pointed out the budget was still actually in deficit and that additional commitments raised the prospect of continuing and increasing budget deficits. They argued that if governments could not achieve budget surpluses during one of the most prosperous periods of economic performance, then the country faced spiralling levels of public debt (which for the Commonwealth alone had risen to almost $100 billion or 18.9 % of GDP in 1995–96).

Pressure intensified when the ABS suggested economic growth had slowed well below the rate of 3.5% used in budget projections. As a consequence, expenditures would increase as statutory outlays on individual benefits rose, and revenue decrease due to declining taxation receipts from individuals and companies. Such re-estimations removed the likelihood of budget surpluses in any of the budget out-years, the basis on which both parties had premised their electoral strategies. The Treasurer Ralph Willis was repeatedly urged to produce updated budget estimates.

The Treasurer's refusal to revise and release these figures only served to fan perceptions of concealment (*Australian* 4.3.1996:17). The government was accused of putting short-term political expediency ahead of budget honesty. The adamant withholding of information on the financial position also fuelled speculation over the size of the likely budget deficit. The Business Council of Australia estimated that 'in 1996–97, the deficit could still be about $6 billion' (*Age* 6.2.1996:A10). The Liberal Premier of Victoria, Jeff Kennett, surpassed most with an extreme estimate of a deficit of $15 billion. However, his comments undercut the electoral strategy of his federal colleagues (based on the Coalition's stated assumption of a budget surplus of $3.6 billion). Senior Liberals, including John Howard and Peter Costello, chastised him for making gross exaggerations, forcing Kennett to recant (*Age* 10.2.1996 and 13.2.1996).

John Howard called for updated budget figures to be released. Either way he could not lose. If Labor refused to release updated figures the Coalition could continue to assume a budget surplus was available for its spending plans; if Labor agreed to release figures showing a deteriorating budget position, then political mileage could be gained highlighting Labor's failure as economic managers. In the end, Labor's refusal to update the figures played into the Coalition's hands; they did not have to adjust their own spending promises in the campaign, and were able to continue characterising Keating as arrogant and deceitful for not 'opening up the books'. Despite criticism of his own record as Treasurer (leaving Labor with a deficit in 1983), Howard won the electoral fight over fiscal honesty. To reinforce the point, he promised legislation requiring complete fiscal disclosure before any future election.

SETTING A NEW BUDGET AGENDA: FINDING AN $8 BILLION 'BLACK HOLE'

The Coalition assumed government on 11 March 1996 facing the challenge of transforming their promises into budget reality. The new Treasurer, Peter Costello, released Treasury's revised forward estimates on 13 March 1996. Expenditure estimates were revised to include any additional spending arising from new policy decisions taken by Labor after its May 1995 Budget. Costello argued these new figures showed a massive deterioration of $7.6 billion in the budget bottom line (or 1.55% of GDP) (Treasurer 1996a). Economic growth forecasts were revised downward from 3.5 to 3.25%, with negative implications for the budget. Lower than expected economic growth necessitated a readjustment of the unemployment figures, causing expenditure estimates to be revised upward. Revenue estimates were revised downward due to the weaker demand in the economy. Treasury itself warned against reading too much into their projected figures stating 'revenue estimates for the out-years are typically subject to substantial revision and should be treated with caution'. Labor's latest policy decisions had only a minor impact on the budgetary position, with new spending programs adding $0.5 billion to the budget estimates for each of the four years from 1995–96 to 1998–99. Revisions to the economic parameters were far more significant, adding from $2 to $10 billion per annum over the same period.

Unlike their predecessors, the Coalition emphasised the budget's *underlying* position (in place of *headline*) allowing Costello to claim the deficit had increased significantly. A headline balance includes government revenues and expenditure plus net advances from asset sales and net debt repayments by the states. The underlying budget balance figure excludes any payments from asset sales—from privatisation for example—or the debt repayments of state governments. By focusing on the worst possible deficit figure in the new estimates the Coalition produced a $7.6 billion deficit for 1995–96, which they quickly dubbed the '$8 billion black hole' even though this was later recalculated to be $10.3 billion (Treasurer 1996c).

The black hole was a political god-send to the new government seeking to dismantle many of Labor's programs and re-prioritise outlays to accord with their own platform. By changing economic assumptions underscoring the budget figuring and switching focus to the underlying budget balance, the government was able to manufacture a sense of fiscal crisis. With support from market analysts, the urgent need for large cuts was now premised on this impression of an impending fiscal blow-out. Costello moved quickly to lay responsibility for the crisis squarely on Labor's shoulders, accusing former Finance Minister, Kim Beazley—now the leader of the Opposition—of deliberately misleading the public. He suggested the 'figures give you a good idea of why Labor was so strident in its refusal to release updated Budget data during the election campaign . . . He [Beazley] failed and failed dismally. He was the weakest Financial Minister this nation has ever had' (in Burton and Ellis 1996:1,6).

How real or significant the deficit was remains a question of judgement. In both historical and international terms, the deficit was low and had declined from 4.2% of GDP in 1992–93 to 2.1% in 1995–96, even on the Coalition's figures. During the same four years the proportion of revenue to GDP had increased and outlays gradually decreased. Commonwealth net debt was higher than in previous years, although was still low at 19.5% of GDP (Budget Paper No 1, 1998–99:7.27–30). The deficit was real, but the 'problem' was a matter of perception.

Reaction to Costello's discovery was mixed, but the popular impression of a black hole resonated. A survey of economists by the *Financial Review* found they considered Treasury's predicted growth figure of 3.25% to be overly optimistic, implying a worse deficit could be expected. Quiggin (1996) introduced a measure of academic scepticism arguing that it was 'difficult to avoid the conclusion' that the government had searched 'for the set of parameters that would generate the largest possible projected deficit while remaining superficially plausible'. The eventual size of the deficit could be considered a combination of political decision and changed budget parameters. It did not necessarily indicate expenditure was 'out of control' or that departmental spending had somehow 'blown-out'.

In March Costello set out the government's medium-term strategy designed to reverse the deteriorating fiscal position. First, he reaffirmed the Coalition's commitment to fiscal targets and taxation guidelines set down during the election: there would not be any new or increased taxes and the budget would be returned to an underlying balance in 1997–98. Second, he confirmed the government's intention to meet its election promises entirely. Still, the revised budget position forced him to implement severe remedial action to 'fill Labor's $8 billion black hole' and return the budget to an *underlying surplus*. This would be achieved by cutting $4 billion from spending in both of the next two budget years (1996–97 and 1997–98). Finally, Costello announced two initiatives aimed to address the longer-term problem of government spending—the establishment of a National Commission of Audit (NCA) and the government's intention to introduce legislation to provide a Charter of Budget Honesty.

Most commentators provided a relatively positive assessment of the government's intended budget strategy. They also warned Howard persistently about the likely political fallout of cutting the budget, with some arguing the task was inherently difficult for democratic government (Short 1996; Milne 1996). Mitchell (1996) argued that 'cutting the Budget deficit by $8 billion over two years without raising taxes is a huge political task. You wonder whether, after 13 years in Opposition, John Howard remembers how big a political task it is'. Another political analyst (Burton 1996:4) summed up the government's problem thus:

> The real problem for Costello remains the straightjacket the Coalition put on itself in its ruthless campaign for election. With a promise to not increase taxes or introduce any new taxes, Costello will be left to scratch around the bottom of the revenue barrel to find any

> significant measures to help him balance the Budget. And on the outlay side he is similarly retarded after the Coalition made numerous pledges to guarantee funding, ranging from the States to the ABC to the massive Defence budget. The obvious answer is to push as many of Canberra's programs back to the States as possible.

Nevertheless, he went on to argue, 'in a $125 billion Budget, if a new government can't find what amounts to just over a 3% cut to 13 years worth of Labor programs it is not trying' (1996:4). Similar opinions were expressed in an editorial in the *Financial Review* (1996:16) that argued, the 'Finance department, with Mr John Fahey as its Minister, will be judged a failure if it can't identify programs which are wasteful, untargeted and so ripe for cutting'. Political expectations were being managed; Australians were being told by the media to expect a 'horror budget' on 20 August 1996.

SYMBOLIC POLITICS: THE 1996 NATIONAL COMMISSION OF AUDIT

The sense of fiscal crisis was further enhanced by the findings of the NCA. Established in accordance with the Coalition's election promises, the Commonwealth's audit commission followed an emerging pattern of newly-elected Liberal state governments that had each undertaken commissions of audit (Walsh C 1995). The ostensible rationale for conducting these audits was that governments needed an independent source of advice on the financial position of the government. Politically, the audits provided the government with ammunition for attack on the financial mismanagement of their predecessors. To the extent that audit commissions 'dug up dirt' they were valuable, but to the extent they suggested remedies they complicated things.

The government carefully selected four audit commissioners to undertake the task supported by staff of both Finance and Treasury. The chairman, Professor Robert Officer (Melbourne Business School), was assisted by three other members selected from business: Elizabeth Alexander (Price Waterhouse), John Fraser (SBC Brinson), and Maurice Newman (Bain & Co). Geoff Carmody, Director of Access Economics (and responsible for costing the Coalition's electoral promises) became the executive officer, and a secretariat was established consisting of nine senior Finance officers, and one Treasury officer. The Commission's terms of reference focussed directly on major aspects of public expenditure management. They were directed to report on the actual state of Commonwealth finances; the publication of a balance sheet and advice on government reporting techniques; the impact of demographic changes and how pressures could be provisioned; the adequacy of infrastructure; a methodology for implementing financial performance targets; and the effectiveness and efficiency of current service delivery arrangements with the states (Treasurer 1996a:8). The commissioners were essentially given a wide brief to consider fundamental questions about the nature of public expenditure and the government's role in the economy.

The NCA was able to determine the scope of its study and frame the issues to be addressed. It began with a neo-liberal ideological framework, choosing to analyse government activity largely according to financial accounting criteria. The Commission also adopted a purchaser-provider model for their investigation into whether governments should deliver services, what services and how. Not surprisingly, the Commission stressed the importance of constructing comprehensive financial information, tackling problems of asset valuation, accrual accounting, and the imbalance in the Commonwealth's high out-goings (on transfers) and its low asset base. The limitations of conventional accounting assumptions arose when future capacity to tax was not defined as an asset, yet future spending was defined as a liability. And in declaring a neo-liberal philosophical preference at the outset, the Commission posed a series of minimalist options for assessing the

Commonwealth's roles and responsibilities. The NCA also adopted the principle of subsidiarity (devolving responsibilities for managing policy areas and providing services to lower levels of government), that if accepted could severely undermine the Commonwealth's policy capacities.

The Commission reported in June 1996 finding a deficit of expenses on revenues of $10.6 billion for 1994–95 and a deficit of liabilities over assets of $73.4 billion with a further $176.8 billion in contingent liabilities (NCA 1996). The Treasurer was quick to point out that these figures did not indicate insolvency or unsustainability (Treasurer 1996b). The Commission also found many deficiencies in financial practices. It recommended whole of government financial statements and endorsed the proposal for a Charter of Budget Honesty. It urged a greater focus on cost savings and efficiency in payments to the states, and highlighted a lack of accountability in areas of service delivery (specifically pointing to Aboriginal programs), inadequate targeting of programs and program overlap, and lack of oversight and accountability in the way some authorities spent public funds (e.g. the ABC's pay TV debacle).

More controversially, the Commission recommended the transfer of selected Commonwealth policy responsibilities to the states. Examining Australia's pattern of intergovernmental fiscal relations the NCA identified areas of 'service delivery interface' between the two levels of government. Included in this list were the politically sensitive areas of education ($7.2 billion); health and health related services ($5.7 billion); housing ($1 billion); transport ($0.9 billion) and Aboriginal affairs, regional development, the environment, workers compensation and industrial relations. The NCA recommended that implementation of these programs be transferred entirely to the states, with continued funding from the Commonwealth as untied grants. In handing over responsibility, no more than 90% of current funding should be transferred, reflecting scope for rationalisation and savings by the states in reduced administration. States should also be required to provide output and outcome data to the Commonwealth. If national policy bodies were to be retained, they 'should limit their activities to joint work on national co-ordination and strategic directions and the development of standards, benchmarks and performance measures. They should not be involved in service delivery or approval of projects' (NCA 1996:32). The recommendations were potentially explosive.

When the findings were announced, the government responded by watering down many of the findings saying these were only 'for consideration by the government and the community' and that many of the recommendations relate to 'longer term objectives and will require detailed work'. It was accepted that recommendations to transfer policy areas to the states would not only represent a substantial shift in federal-state relations—it would also cut the Commonwealth out of many areas where it had specific interests. Costello made it clear the NCA was 'not a report by the government but a report to the government'. NCA preferences were not automatically embraced as government policy.

WIELDING THE AXE: RETAINING THE ERC TO IMPOSE BUDGET DISCIPLINE

To review program expenditures, rank priorities and identify areas for substantial cuts, Howard chose to reinstate the ERC early in the government's term, adopting a budget process and timetable similar to that of previous Labor governments. Membership of the ERC was announced within the first month of assuming office. Prime Minister John Howard assumed the chair and Treasurer Peter Costello became deputy chair. Other members were: the Minister for Finance, John Fahey, the deputy National leader and Minister for Primary Industries and Energy, John Anderson, the Health

Minister Michael Wooldridge, and Assistant Treasurer Senator Jim Short. The membership had reverted to the tighter structure of the early Hawke years, dominated by guardians on a ratio of four to two. Similar arrangements were retained in the second Howard government with Senator Rod Kemp replacing Jim Short as Minister Assisting the Treasurer, and Mark Vaile (Minister for Trade) replacing John Anderson (who, upon becoming leader of the National party in 1999, joined the senior ministers' review—replacing Tim Fischer).

Decision-making in Howard's budget cabinet operated in three stages. First, the ERC initially considered a series of expenditure reviews identifying the possible areas and scope for expenditure reduction. Finance assembled and presented to ERC its list of 'recommended' expenditure cuts across all departments. These were used along with Treasury's economic estimates to determine an initial fiscal strategy and aggregate level of expenditure. The Coalition's 'Troika' (Howard, Costello and Fahey) determined the aggregate level of savings required, and distributed these between ministerial portfolios.[2] Second, portfolio ministers were directed to target 'housing, labour market, welfare, health, education and industry programs' to find $4 billion in cuts (Dodson 1996), but responsibility for the detailed review of expenditure programs was devolved to portfolios. Finance continued its own simultaneous reviews to find savings. Third, final decisions about which programs should be cut were made by the ERC in considering each department's detailed reviews and deciding on actual expenditure reductions.

The context within which the Coalition's first Budget was prepared was marked by Howard's professed determination to meet election promises for new expenditure. Howard was convinced that

---

2 The Coalition's three main guardian ministers were all Liberals: Howard was the leading Liberal 'dry' with over five years experience as Treasurer; Costello was often regarded as an ideological zealot favouring smaller government (or at least the appearance of) and a less regulated economy. Meanwhile, John Fahey (a former NSW Premier) was initially a reluctant guardian who told journalists he had sought a spending ministry, arguing that no one wanted to be Finance minister because it was a thankless task (but he successfully clung to the position when challenged by Senator Nick Minchin at the start of the Coalition's second term in late 1998). Later, as Deputy Prime Minister and leader of the National party, John Anderson became effectively the fourth member of the 'tetrad' of senior Coalition ministers—but he operated far more as an advocate for his constituency than as a guardian of the purse.

the demise of the Fraser government was largely due to the cynical way in which it broke its election promises to deliver a 'fistful of dollars' in tax cuts immediately after the 1980 election. Keating was also perceived to have reneged on his 'L-A-W' Law tax cuts in the post-election 1993 Budget. Howard appeared determined not to fall into the same trap. The difficulty for ERC was in culling $8 billion from the budget without raising damaging perceptions they were renouncing their 'core promises' and still 'meeting their commitments'.

The Coalition Troika's main challenge was to distribute cuts across portfolio and department areas, bearing in mind the exemptions announced. As the likely targets or size of cuts were leaked to the press, some intense political battles ensued. The government received criticism for threatening to cut trade and export incentives for business (including the $230 million Export Market Development Grants Scheme), for curtailing overseas development projects, and especially for leaking proposed cuts to funding for the universities and the ABC, or projected rises in the higher education contribution payments for tertiary students. Whilst these debates appeared to hamper the government's budget process, they enabled it to gauge public opinion on the various cutting options being considered by the portfolio ministers. In this respect the process provided useful information to the ERC in coming to its final decisions. The slow drip of announcements also prepared the electorate for budget cuts, the severity of which was in some instances overplayed so the eventual decisions appeared to be an easing of government policy. This was intended to minimise the 'political pain' expected with the August budget.

While the ERC process enabled reduction in a range of portfolio areas, funding to the states was also one of the first areas examined by the Howard's budget cutting team. Despite guaranteeing general funding to the states would not be cut, the Prime Minister announced prior to the Premiers' Conference of 13 June that overall funding would be cut (*Weekend Australian* 8–9.6.1996). The Treasurer also attempted to impose sales tax on state government purchasing (raising up to $1.2 billion) and freeze housing funding and replace housing grants to the states with income support payments directly to public housing tenants. The states vehemently opposed additional tax levies or budget cuts to their payments. They argued the Commonwealth was merely using them as an expedient source of savings. After some intense tactics by state and territory leaders (7 out of 8 were Coalition colleagues),

Costello backed down on the main parts of his agenda. While the level of financial assistance grants (FAGS) to the states was maintained in real terms, other funds were trimmed and the premiers were forced to accept a 'state fiscal contribution' to assist the Commonwealth's deficit reduction strategy (estimated at $1.4 billion over two years—see *AFR* 14.6.1996 and Chapter 11 in this volume). Nevertheless, the bruising received at the Premiers' Conference provided the Howard government with an early lesson in fiscal federalism and the difficulties in getting state leaders to agree to trim their resource demands.

In subsequent years, the Coalition has held senior ministers' reviews (usually around late November or early December) with only the 'tetrad' or four most senior ERC ministers present (PM, Treasurer and Finance Minister and the Deputy PM representing the Nationals). The senior ministers' review sets the major priorities for ministerial submissions and provides guidelines for the later deliberations of ERC. Portfolio ministers are advised in writing of the results of the senior minister's review by the Prime Minister. In late 1998 Howard insisted that ERC would only consider submissions for new initiatives that had been explicitly promised in the election. Also new initiatives almost always had to be accompanied by 'offsets' from within the portfolio equal to the resources sought by a new submission. In 1999 and 2000 ERC relaxed this budgetary stringency for new programs aimed at rural and regional communities—spending an additional $330 million in the budget year and $2 billion over four years (Budget Paper No 1, 2000–01:1.30–32).

SELLING THE 'HORROR BUDGET' OF 1996–97

The Coalition's first Budget of 1996–97 was introduced amid an air of apprehension. Already tagged a 'horror budget' by sections of the media months before it was finalised, most of the major cuts were known well before the formal Budget Speech. Significantly, many supporters had rallied to the government's defence. The financial and economic press not only endorsed attempts to reduce government spending, they urged Howard to exceed the $4 billion target for cuts. Des Moore, an economic writer and former Treasury official, argued, for example, that the government should make a more substantial contribution to saving by wielding the axe to deliver 'even larger expenditure reductions so as to move the

Budget into underlying surplus' (1996:19). On the eve of the budget, the Governor of the Reserve Bank, Bernie Fraser, gave the government some unexpected support by denying that the proposed expenditure cuts were 'draconian'.

Costello's Budget Speech emphasised that while the government believed it needed to make severe cuts, it had maintained its 'core promises to individuals'.[3] The Treasurer announced substantial savings measures designed to 'reduce the underlying deficit by around $4 billion this year and $7.2 billion over two years', and overall the Budget showed outlays increasing by only 0.1% of GDP in 1996–97. As part of the Budget Papers, the Treasurer produced a document entitled *Meeting our Commitments* (1996) which argued that 'the overriding priority of fiscal repair has been met without compromising . . . our election commitments' and without the resort to new tax measures (1996:1). Although the document listed pages of new measures aimed at 'families and those in need' and small business, it produced a net budget impact of $1 billion in savings.

In total $4.45 billion was cut from existing outlays (a cut of 3.9% of total outlays and 5.5% over two years). The net impact to the budget was predicted to be $2.93 billion once new spending measures were incorporated. The main items cut were state fiscal contributions ($619 million in 1996–97 and $1.6 billion over three years); labour market programs ($575 million and $1.7 billion respectively). Other significant cuts over three years were to running costs ($565 million); roads funding ($408 million), and the imposition of a two-year waiting period for welfare payments to migrants ($356 million).[4] Export grants were capped (at $150 million), though not abolished, and HECS payments were increased and structured into three bands (saving $1 billion over three years). An efficiency dividend was also imposed on special purpose payments to the states. The Coalition also cut the budgets of the ABC (by 10% or $110 over two years), universities (by 4.9%), ATSIC

---

3 The government made a distinction between 'core' and 'non-core' promises made in the 1996 election. Core promises were those they intended to keep—non-core were those they chose to break or perhaps attend to at a later date.

4 Len Early, Deputy Secretary of Finance at the time, argued that 'there were some big movements in running costs in both directions' with some 'substantial new running costs being provided for'—implying that cuts in one areas were reallocated (Early Interview 1996).

(by $90 million but exempting health, housing and employment projects). Foreign aid fell to 0.29% of GDP after it was cut by 10% (to $1.4 billion). Defence was largely immune from further cuts although its budget was reduced by $50 million in line with reduced base funding inherited from Labor. The government announced reduced tax concessions for R&D, increased taxes for high-income earners (superannuation surcharge and increases in the Medicare levy) and childcare rebates were reduced for higher earners. To boost rates of child immunisation, the government announced a campaign directed straight at the hip pocket: don't immunise, don't get child support money. And, as agreed with the states (following a shooting tragedy at Port Arthur, Tasmania), a new gun buy-back levy was introduced to raise $500 million over one year though an additional 0.2% increase in the Medicare levy.

TOWARD BUDGET HONESTY—UTOPIANISM V REALISM

Following the 1996 election the government confirmed it would introduce legislation for a 'Charter of Budget Honesty' in time for the next federal election. It argued the Charter would increase the transparency and accountability of government finances and ensure more honesty in electoral promises. The move was not merely triggered by recent electoral experience (or even by echoes of the Coalition's lack of disclosure in 1983). It was also triggered by money markets needing reliable financial information on the state of public finances and by the need to have more disciplined and timely financial reporting as governments proceeded down the path of accrual budgeting. The charter (reflecting the NZ *Fiscal Responsibility Act 1994*)[5] was intended to make governments publish a prudent fiscal strategy and provide regular economic and budgetary updates with a full disclosure of the government's fiscal position before every election. It also accompanied a parallel trend in which Australian governments had been seeking to make their budget information more comparable and consistent across jurisdictions with agreed accounting standards. The Australian Loan Council of Commonwealth and state treasurers was proposing a uniform framework for the presentation of budget and financial information. An earlier agreement had been made at the 1991 Premier's Con-

5 The NZ *Fiscal Responsibility Act* was about disclosure and avoided any commitment on fiscal discipline.

ference to standardise reporting in annual budgets on an ABS-GFS basis[6]. Agreement was reached in 1997 requiring each jurisdiction to publish a set of standardised forward projections and a mid-year fiscal report from 1998–99. As a consequence, all Australian governments now publish three year forward estimates twice yearly for the general government sector, including estimates of Loan Council allocations for borrowing requirements (Budget Paper No 1, 1998–99:7.5).

Parliament passed the *Charter of Budget Honesty Act* in April 1998 to 'provide a framework for the conduct of government fiscal policy' (s.1). The Commonwealth's budgetary processes became 'enshrined within' a 'legislative requirement to observe the principles of sound fiscal management and facilitate public scrutiny of fiscal policy and performance' (DoFA 2000:3). The Charter stipulates a list of requirements to be met by federal governments in disclosing their financial position and fiscal strategy. The act stipulates that fiscal strategies have to be set within a sustainable medium-term framework, the principles of which (DoFA 2000) include to:

- manage financial risks faced by the Commonwealth prudently, having regard to economic circumstances, including by maintaining Commonwealth general government debt at prudent levels;
- ensure that its fiscal policy contributes to achieving adequate national saving and to moderating cyclical fluctuations in economic activity;
- pursue spending and taxing policies that are consistent with a reasonable degree of stability and predictability in the level of the tax burden;
- maintain the integrity of the tax system; and
- ensure that policy decisions have regard to their financial effects on future generations.

The act also requires the heads of the two budget agencies (Treasury and Finance and Administration) to produce a pre-election economic and fiscal outlook within 10 days of the issue of the writ for an election. Also upon the request of either the leader of the government or opposition, the agencies are required

---

6 Australian Bureau of Statistics and Government Finance Statistics to produce consistent data—called the uniform presentation framework agreed by Commonwealth and state governments.

to undertake costings of election commitments made by the political parties during the campaign.

When first introduced into Parliament in 1996, the non-government majority in the Senate blocked the legislation. The Senate twice voted down the bill proposing the Budget Honesty charter, objecting to the requirement that the parties must have their electoral platform costed by Treasury and Finance in the context of a federal election. The opposition and minor parties considered this provision unfair, and possibly open to executive abuse given that the departments were still under executive direction and the heads of the agencies were, under different legislation, dismissable at a minute's notice. In order for the bill to pass before the Parliament was dissolved, the government agreed to a series of amendments which made electoral costing optional.

Five more substantive points are worth mentioning in relation to the current *Charter of Budget Honesty*. First, it does not require a balanced budget or a surplus. Second, it is an ongoing statute that any future government can change or amend (although if they simply sought to repeal the act they may face a credibility problem). Third, it is not clear what the consequences are for non-compliance—that is, if a government (for whatever pressing or expedient reason) were to avoid the provisions entirely. Fourth, the legislation contains many 'let-out' clauses and statements that are open to political interpretation. And, fifth, the heads of Treasury and Finance are themselves part of executive government—a more independent approach would have required the Auditor-General to endorse the financial statements.

In line with the philosophy of the Charter, but before it was passed, the government issued its first 'mid-year budget outlook' on 27 January 1997. In many respects, the Mid-Year Economic and Fiscal Outlook (MYEFO) was not a radical budgetary change, as previous governments had produced updated budget information in one form or another since the mid–1980s. The MYEFO suggested a $2.9 billion deficit blow-out on the government's own estimates for the 1996–97 budget. Of this amount, $1 billion was linked to policy decisions taken by the government since the budget, $1.4 billion arose from a revenue shortfall due to lower than expected company tax collections, while $0.5 billion was incurred in additional expenditure (due to benefits paid as a result of unemployment increasing.[7] Yet, within a month a 'Treasury corrigendum' advised the underlying budget position for 1996–97 had been underestimated again by $1.2 billion and had thereby blown-out to a figure of $9.3 billion. The new deficit figure resulted entirely from 'an upward revision in government sector outlays outside the Budget sector' (*Australian* 27.2.1997:6). It was also revealed that the shortfall in their budget revenue estimates announced in January 1997 had been noticed as early as one month after the August budget statement. In contrast to the MYEFO figures, however, little publicity was given the new forecasts or revelations.

The Howard government quickly became aware of the tensions between budgetary utopianism and political realism. In its defence, the government admitted making a 'major error' in the MYEFO estimates and blamed Treasury and the ATO for overestimating company tax (*Australian* 27.2.1997:6). Treasury also reported to a Senate estimates hearing that 170 errors had occurred in 'spreadsheets' and that the Department of Finance was to blame—who had in turn relied on estimates from line agencies. While the central agencies ducked for cover, the revisions to the first MYEFO highlighted some of the problems of imposing a rational framework onto an essentially political process and that the new discipline of regular official budgetary updates had attendant risks. This included the potential to throw into conflict the bureaucrats professional duty of care with that of the immediate political interests of their ministerial masters. Also, in the first two instances where Treasury updated the budget assumptions (in March 1996 and then in February 1997), the figures were the subject of partisan political debate. In the first instance they fuelled the '$8 billion black hole' controversy and in the second they were used to suggest the need for harsher budget cuts by the media and opposition. While this may not be surprising in the climate of fiscal conservatism, such 'politicisation' may reduce the credibility or usefulness of producing budget updates. Rather than remaining a relatively accepted budget instrument used to improve the planning and transparency of decision-making, updates have the potential to become the subject of political manipulation. Equally, Treasury's revenue forecasts are susceptible to the same pressures, and may in the future become more opaque and difficult to interpret. If governments find themselves attacked for fiscal incompetence every time they publish updated budget figures, then they will respond in many ways,

7 Unemployment increased by the comparatively small margin of 0.25% from 8.25% to 8.5%.

perhaps making data harder to compare, or even disguising sensitive figures in the ways the data is published.

AND NOW FOR MORE SPENDING

The main parameters of the Coalition's second budget delivered in May 1997 were framed by the first. The 1997–98 Budget maintained an austere line on spending, predicting outlays would be reduced by –1.4% (the actual reduction was –1.6%). The estimated deficit was predicted to be $3.9 billion (with a projected small surplus of $1.6 billion in 1998–99). The government's priorities remained 'primarily on outlays restraint' which would provide for 'a decline in underlying outlays from 27% of GDP in 1995–96 to just under 23% of GDP in 2000–01' (Budget Paper No 1, 1997–98:1.4). New spending was virtually avoided (with only $550 million committed to new measures) and a further $780 million was reported as additional cuts ('savings') since the 1996–97 budget. Education outlays were reduced along with primary industries and transport and regional development. Modest increases in outlays were made to the portfolios of immigration, environment, health and industry. Areas cut in the previous budget were not targeted for further savings in the 1997–98 budget. In addition, the final 50.4% of the Commonwealth Bank was sold by public float between July 1996 and November 1997 (raising in total $8 billion) and the first third of Telstra was sold in late 1997 followed by the second tranche of 16% in 1999 (together contributing $30 billion).

Despite the severity inflicted in the Coalition's first two years, their third budget was introduced only five months before an election, in May 1998. It was not an 'election budget' in the sense that the government ran straight to the polls, though with an election due at the latest by early 1999 this was the last realistic opportunity to indicate the government's spending priorities. So after two abstemious years the government returned to the pattern of increasing expenditures even in the context of strong economic growth. Although real outlays were predicted to rise by 0.6% they actually increased by 4% over the year. Nevertheless, in the government's last cash-based budget, a surplus of $2.7 billion was predicted over 1998–99 rising to $4.7 billion in 1999–2000. The budget continued to question 'public sector involvement in non-core activities' (Budget Paper No 1, 1998–99:1.16), but emphasised the commitment to a social safety net for those 'most in need'. The government remained motivated to reduce public debt and improve national savings (and passed legislation prior to the 1998 election committing them to sell up to 49% of Telstra).

Adopting an accrual budgeting format, the Coalition's fourth budget increased real outlays by around 8% (although the Budget Papers went to considerable effort not to disclose increases in outlays)[8]. A surplus of $5.4 billion was predicted by June 2000 rising to $7.2 billion in 2000–01. The strategy of the budget was premised on 'expenses restraint' and specific increases in outlays were to 'targeted new policy spending' (including non-governmental schools, a national illicit drug strategy, health and medical research and the expansion of work for the dole scheme). Significantly the government's fourth budget continued to insist cash outlays would fall from around 25% of GDP (in the mid–1990s) to 19.7% by 2002–03 (a wildly optimistic target).

Costello's fifth budget saw revenues and outlays rise to around $173 billion—an estimated increase of 7 %. At Treasury's insistence the expected $25 billion in revenue from the GST was not included in the presented budget figures—which claimed to show net revenues as only $153 billion). The government also shied away from repeating its previous bravado over medium-term targets for the reduction of outlays to GDP, preferring instead to talk of 'sustainable' finances and the merits of tax reform. In a number of places the government made reference to treating figures with 'some caution' and that 'a fiscal policy response may not always be appropriate to changing economic circumstances' (Budget Paper No 1, 2000–01:1.27–29). In this budget the government's main priorities were to fund additional provisions for rural and regional Australia (committing an additional $327 million in the budget year and $1828 million over four years to 2003–04).

The main issue in the 2000–01 Budget was the sudden erosion of the large surpluses. Instead of the $7.2 billion surplus projected the year before, the new budget scaled back the surplus to only $2.8 billion (in part due to Australia's commitment to East Timor and the package of measures surrendered by the government to get the GST through the Senate—e.g. exempting basic food). However, even this modest surplus was premised on the future sale

---

8 A Pre-Election Economic and Fiscal Outlook (PEFO) was subsequently produced, which updated and reduced the forecasted surplus.

of licences for air space covering an additional digital spectrum (used for several purposes, including mobile phones). Spectrum sales had occurred in previous budgets although their value had been lower. The amount incorporated into the budget for the sale of this asset from 'thin air' was $2.6 billion—this figure was not shown in the formal Budget Papers. Rather the estimated sale figure was only shown on a press release available at a budget briefing (the media lock-up), but according to some journalists it was not widely available and only produced by officials when specifically asked. The precise figure incorporated for the expected returns from the communications spectrum was admitted only after intense media pressure—it was certainly not an example of budget disclosure in keeping with the spirit of the *Charter of Budget Honesty*. Moreover, without the unexpected windfall many analysts considered the budget was technically in the red, and likely to end with a small deficit by June 2001—especially if economic conditions trended downwards during the financial year.

MAKING BUDGETS MORE BUSINESS-LIKE: ACCRUAL-BASED 'OUTPUT-PRICE' BUDGETING

Despite the topsy-turvy nature of their outlays, budget reform under the Coalition proceeded apace, guided by a philosophy that dictated government practices needed to be closer to 'best practice' in the private sector. Reforms were implemented to allow governments to use purchaser-provider disciplines in budget formulation, questioning at the same time whether public service provision was either the most cost-effective or most preferred form of delivery (NCA 1996; Boxall 2000). Labor's managerialist agenda of the 1980s was quietly superseded, and in place of Labor's emphasis on program objectives and managerial reform within public service delivery (Considine and Painter 1997), the Coalition consciously shifted their agenda to promote financial accounting and business-like principles in resource management. Government was conceived as a set of business units not necessarily producing goods for markets, but producing identifiable products that could be priced in competition and through contestability. They sought a greater focus on cost efficiency, competitive tendering and contracting-out, and purchaser-provider delivery models (Boxall 1999). Budgetary reform remained a prominent feature for the Coalition—but it did not drive the reform agenda as it had for Labor. Instead, broader practices borrowed from the private sector together with a marked preference for financial accountancy analysis became the more pronounced aspects of the reforms. As part of this agenda, Australia became the third nation in the world to introduce accrual budgeting (behind New Zealand and Iceland).

The Coalition's fourth Budget (1999–2000) was the first entirely produced using an accrual budgeting methodology with agencies funded directly for their longer-term liabilities.[9] The government's intention was to replace the traditional cash-based budget with a more strategic and business-like approach to the management of resources. Essential to the project was an emphasis on both the bottom line and the financial performance of individual budget units. As part of this business-like reform, Labor's notion of the 'portfolio budget' was quietly dropped and individual agencies now received separate budgets. The 45 major agencies (now called 'material agencies' and comprising around 99% of the Commonwealth's finances in terms of revenue, expenses, assets or liabilities) were regarded as business units and each provided with accrual-based budgets (complete with depreciation allowances, capital injections, estimates of long-term liabilities, and capital charging for assets set at 6%). Smaller agencies (totalling around 180) were 'considered together' for allocative budgeting purposes, though funded discretely within their portfolio. Agencies were not expected/permitted to run in the red (showing losses) without the approval of the Finance Minister (transgressions may result in an unsympathetic review of the agency's budget). Some agencies received approval for 'losses' in 2000, mainly as a result accounting requirements in translating cash carryovers from the previous running costs arrangements.

Perhaps more importantly, the 1999–2000 Budget was also the first based on an explicit purchaser-provider model involving an *outcomes and outputs framework* where the full costs of 'deliverables' over time were shown and funded using accrual accounting practices. Not only was the annual budget transformed into an accruals format, the internal logic and allocative processes were organically changed, reflecting a results-based philosophy. These were simultaneous reforms which, it was claimed, would alter the basis of budget decision-making and involve tighter results-based

9 Australian governments had earlier presented their annual financial statements in accrual form—using end of year adjustments and accrual accounting techniques.

reporting and monitoring of performance. Instead of government funding agencies simply on the basis of approximate historical costs (input-driven funding), agencies were funded according to the purchases the government wished to buy from them (output-driven funding). In short, agencies received funds for their 'departmental items' (expenses incurred in delivering outputs) consisting of agreed 'prices' for their products which were increasingly open to contestable pricing or market testing. Although the changes this produces to departmental bids and in terms of actual costs of government will only really become noticeable over time, the importance of output-price funding is the shift in mind-set it signifies, and the new philosophical disposition toward relations between central and line agencies and the business of government.

According to the Commonwealth, outcomes were defined as key results the government sought to achieve (e.g. efficient industry and competitive markets, or the protection and promotion of the health of Australians). Outputs were the goods and services 'purchased' by government (from agencies or non-government suppliers) in order to achieve those outcomes.[10] Responsibility for determining both the outcomes and outputs was devolved to the portfolio level and operating agencies. Once appropriate outputs had been defined, a set of 'prices' or costings for given quantities of outputs (collated as 'departmental items' or expenses) were agreed with Finance. According to DoFA (2000:3) the new budget framework put

> outcomes and outputs at the centre of how agencies plan, budget, manage and report . . . Under accruals, agencies are resourced for the price of their outputs—what they produce to contribute to outcomes. The agency output price will include full costs, such as depreciation and employee leave entitlements. An agency's output price will also include an appropriate return on equity provided by Government.

Agencies were allowed to define their own outputs—while contributing to the achievement of outcomes (negotiated with the relevant minister). Initially the government hoped to build ownership of outputs by agencies so that they reflected what they

10 Australia has generally followed New Zealand in the adoption of the distinction between outcomes and outputs, except that Australia does not make quite the same formal separation making ministers solely responsible for outcomes and agencies/managers responsible for outputs.

actually did. And, if agencies could not show that outputs contributed to an outcome, then the implication was that government would get out of supplying those services—by not purchasing the outputs. One initial consequence of such flexibility was that outputs and outcomes were conceived in different ways between portfolios, making cross-comparison difficult. In theory, the budget process operated to provide government with the opportunity to review their outputs, and commit to 'buy' certain quantities of outputs from agencies according to current priorities. Such output prices would increasingly constitute 'purchase contracts' between ERC and the relevant agencies—against which their subsequent performance could be judged and any price movements monitored.

The former centralised system of estimates-setting (used to determine the baseline for budget expenditures) was re-engineered to incorporate accrual information and provide accurate measures of full costs (to set 'prices'). In a further substantial change to the budget process, responsibility for estimates production was devolved to departments. From 1999 line departments directly input the estimates data into a central financial computer system. The Accrual Information Management System—AIMS (replaced the previous Budget Management System)—became the IT system used as the primary basis for recording and determining expenditure estimates to both departmental and the government as a whole. Rolling forward estimates were retained and were still considered a crucial component of the expenditure management framework. The Adjustment Tracking Module (ATM), a module within AIMS, incorporated information on pressures so as to recognise likely changes in the established expenditure base by tracking the effect of cabinet decisions and economic parameter or price adjustments.[11] Financial officers in line departments, rather than DoFA, were given the responsibility for entering data into AIMS; although DoFA scrutinised the estimates and were responsible for 'quality assurance'. To ensure data quality in 1999, private accounting firms were engaged to conduct pre-focused spot-checks designed to ensure consistency between new and old financial data, and between agencies.

Departments were largely prevented from padding the estimates because they were transposed from the previous year (and controlled

11 This replaced CERCIS—the cabinet expenditure review committee information system.

centrally) and because Finance insisted on verification of accrual estimate pricings through both investigative methodologies and comparative benchmarking. Clearly such circumstantial advantages were temporary, and DoFA's withdrawal from the estimates setting process had the potential not only to reduce their relevant knowledge and expertise, but also to reduce its role and importance to executive government in the process of budget formulation. Some DoFA officials have argued the reverse; that the process of devolution got DoFA out of tedious estimates creation and gave the department more analytical capacity. Yet, even if agencies retain responsibility for the preliminary inputting of estimates data, it is argued here that some central expertise in rationalising estimates is a functional precondition for an effective central budget agency.

Devolution of the estimates indicated a fundamental shift in the processes of budget formulation—reflecting an intention to move away from bureaucratically determined estimates of departmental expenses to one based on contestable and market testing of the estimates. Within aggregate parameters, budget setting was to be organised according to a calculation of the lowest costs required to achieve the government's desired policy outcomes. In theory, evaluations of the competitiveness of estimates (and the efficiency with which an agency achieved desired results) now provided criteria for determining the appropriateness of budgetary allocations. Under this system detailed bottom-up estimates became far less important in budget determination to be replaced by top-down market pricing. Budget statements still produce forward estimates of intended expenditure, but these now serve three related purposes—they provide a base framework for accrual adjustment calculations, for calculating *long-term resource commitments* and to assist decision-making in managing cost structures in *program-management.*

The adoption of more business-like budgetary practices did not merely change the executive's internal operations or decision-making processes. Parliamentary appropriations were also redefined to constitute 'prices' paid to departments for outputs relating to the broader outcomes the government wished to achieve (GAO 2000:20). In 1998 Parliament accepted that the 'purposes' of Commonwealth appropriations were to achieve outcomes by purchasing outputs. The wording of the appropriation bills under the accrual-output framework requested 'prices' be 'paid' to departments for the declared outputs the government wished to purchase. Departmental appropriations were appropriated as single, non-lapsing amounts covering operating costs, long-term costs and asset depreciation. Crucially it was now expected under an accruals format that not all appropriated authorisations would be required in the budget year (i.e. depreciation and long-term staffing liabilities)—hence departmental appropriations no longer lapsed at the end of the financial year and in effect agencies enjoyed ongoing carryovers and the ability to transfer resources over budget years. Agencies could also be granted equity or capital injections according to government priorities. By contrast, the budget estimates for administered appropriations (funds administered or transferred onto others) were limited by criteria not amount, implying that any non-required component of the budget estimates would lapse constituting a 'saving' to the budget.

Other supporting information showing the planned allocation of these budgetary amounts within agencies was also provided to enable parliamentary scrutiny of intentions/results and assist agencies in terms of planned performance, but is not required for appropriation purposes. Such supporting documentation reinforced the emphasis on 'output prices' and 'results-based' budgeting.[12] Portfolio Budget Statements included in *Budget Paper No. 1* articulated the relationships between organisational structure, strategic priorities, portfolio outcomes and structure, and agency outputs. These documents divided appropriations on an outcome basis between administered expenses, total operational expenses (the cost of producing departmental outputs), and a separate line of appropriations for *new* asset expenses. The latter does *not* include funding for asset upgrade or replacement (which must be covered by each agency) and signify a separate and specific decision by cabinet. By linking 'prices' to outcomes, rather than funding inputs, the new system is designed to extend the managerial flexibility previously available under the running cost arrangements.[13] The change deliberately makes *planned outcomes* and the government's policy objectives the *foundation* of budget appropriations (i.e., they are built in, and do not just exist separately to the budget process) and provides a more accurate basis for the market testing of services. Previously, while governments may have identified strategic objectives they were usually not connected directly to the budget process.

12 These include Budget Speech; *Budget Paper No1, 1999–2000*; and *Guide to the Commonwealth Budget Papers 1999–2000.*

13 A subsidiary goal is to reduce the 'end of year surge'.

Furthermore, to assess the accuracy or cost-effectiveness of output prices, a new system of 'pricing reviews' was promulgated. ERC asked DoFA to conduct reviews in conjunction with several agencies to test the veracity of output prices. Eight major 'pricing reviews' were trialed in the budget year 1999–2000 with the intention of establishing 'independent' prices for outputs and in the long-term determining some forms of pricing benchmarks for the lowest cost of supplying given outputs. The pricing of outputs occurred in two stages: first an accurate costing of outputs was undertaken, followed by an evaluating of the costs through comparisons with other providers. The initial 'pricing reviews' were conducted by both line agencies and central agencies, on various outputs including the costs of policy advice, generic functions (e.g. corporate services) as well as on specific deliverables in agencies. There was no standard costing methodology imposed. Agencies were able to adopt costing regimes appropriate to their circumstances, provided it produced 'robust and reliable' information. In the first round, these reviews remained confidential, but the government intended subsequently to release details of these reviews to give them bite and serve as an instrument of public accountability. By looking to competitive 'output prices' (and taking into account comparable prices in private markets or prices registered through tendering processes) the government hoped to minimise problems of locking in large proportions of the discretionary budget into standard public service provision. Instead, cabinet decided in 1999 that competitive tendering and out-sourcing were to be increasingly used to determine 'prices' and market-test internal pricing structures. This decision expanded the role of the central budgetary agency from compiling budget estimates to serving as an adviser on 'contestable prices' and as 'strategic investor' advising government on best purchases (Andrews *et al.* 1998).

However, the introduction of the accrual budget of 1999–2000 was marked by conflicts between the two guardian budget agencies and by logistical and methodological problems (Kelly and Wanna 2000b). Major disagreements occurred between Treasury and DoFA about the nature of the annual budget and the integrity of the accruals project. Success was tarnished by the emergence of technical and political difficulties in the process of creating and using the accruals information. Budget analysts in both central and line agencies lacked the practical accounting skills necessary to bring together the accrual budget and instead had to rely heavily on private accounting consultants. Within DoFA, the lack of internal capacity revealed itself in the final months before Budget day when the department was forced to call in accountants from KPMG to complete the budget—although another version of events would suggest the department was just outsourcing, in line with government expectations. Nonetheless, relief in having delivered the Budget on time was tempered with a mood of despondency about being found wanting. Further, many line agencies felt that DoFA's homogeneous implementation design placed too much emphasis on accounting purity, while ignoring the demands of government budgeting and fundamental differences between departments and their activities.

In the wake of the 1999–2000 Budget, the secretaries of both the Treasury and Finance and Administration sought an independent review of the budget process under the accrual format, and especially the arrangements for the production of budget estimates. A former head of the Tasmanian and Victorian Treasuries, Dr Michael Vertigan (assisted by a small team from Treasury and DoFA) was selected to undertake the review which was completed in July 1999 (Vertigan Report 1999). The main objective of the review was to investigate the problems associated with the implementation of the first accrual budget—especially the roles and performance of the guardian agencies. Vertigan's report emphasised the enormity of the changeover to a full 'accrual-based, outcomes and output framework' and gave the Commonwealth a pat on the back arguing the new system 'constitutes international best practice' (1999:4). However, the review found that agencies had underestimated the magnitude of change and that the practical difficulties turned out to be far greater than had been foreseen. Such problems were exacerbated by the relatively compressed timeframe for the changeover. Vertigan was specifically critical of the inadequate preparation made before the change and of the overlapping and blurred responsibilities between Treasury and DoFA in producing budget estimates. He also criticised (1999:7–8) the preoccupation with accrual financial data at the expense of data produced for fiscal (cash) purposes and implicitly chastised DoFA for presenting accounting information in the budget process that could not 'be readily interpreted by non-specialist users' (i.e. ERC and other ministers).

Vertigan recommended the establishment of a budget coordination committee to oversee the budget process each year (comprised of officials from DoFA, PM&C and Treasury), and the development of a 'project plan' to cover the entire budget process from a whole of government perspective. The report also recommended a clearer ascription of roles and responsibilities, with tasks and deadlines codified in a series of protocols to ensure a smooth functioning of the process. Memoranda of understanding were urged between Finance and line agencies 'to explicitly acknowledge that agencies are accountable for meeting the deadlines specified'. Treasury and DoFA were counselled to 'agree a protocol that sets out the working arrangements between the two departments' (1999:16). The essence of the report was that the government's internal processes needed considerable refinement to ensure an effective budgetary system under the accruals framework. Receiving the report, the government announced it would implement Vertigan's recommendations. Responsibilities were clarified and protocols signed, and the 2000–01 budget process operated much more smoothly and over the final months of formulation in early 2000 both Treasury and DoFA were well ahead of schedule.

CONCLUSION

The Howard government accepted and extended many of the budget reforms of their Labor predecessors. But the direction taken by the Coalition was guided by a prevailing neo-liberal mindset and a desire to reduce government responsibilities. Senior Liberal ministers, in particular, insisted government operations become more business-like and cost-effective. While Labor sought to squeeze more performance out of the public service, the Coalition now sought to squeeze government responsibilities and reduce the size of government. The lessons drawn from this chapter suggest that while the objectives of the Coalition differed from previous governments, the inherited budgetary systems and institutions tended to be more influential and lasting. When measured by movements in real budgetary outlays the Coalition was spectacularly unsuccessful in its endeavour to curb government growth. Resource demands were far more stubborn than ideology suggested.

Initially, expenditure cuts were trumpeted as a necessary corrective, but within two years substantial growth in expenditure was resumed. A government ostensibly committed to smaller government proved unable to trim the size of government in the midst of counter-pressures to spend. They entered office with a political will to defeat the deficit—and after extensive cuts achieved this goal. But once the deficit was gone, their commitment to impose stringency on the budget soon dissipated and was replaced by a begrudging acceptance of the need to satisfy various client groups (rural and regional sectors, defence, immigration, aged care, labour market assistance and family support). Other crises such as the Asian financial crisis and East Timor crisis of 1999–2000 also placed burden's on the government's resources. The government found itself unable to meet its target of reducing outlays as a proportion of GDP to 23% by 2000–01—and, indeed, Commonwealth outlays remained around 28% of GDP in 2000–01 (using GFS figures and including the GST), a proportion not dissimilar from the level of outlays in the mid–1980s. This is a long way from the government's other target of outlays to GDP of 19.7% by 2002–03. To give the appearance of Commonwealth outlays declining, the government tried to exclude a major source of revenue (the GST) and the associated transfer payments from its own reporting (excising some $25 billion from its outlays by means of classification). A new fictional size of government was preferred to one based on budget honesty.

Two major budgetary reforms undertaken by the Coalition will have long-term impacts on Australia's system of budgeting and the management and accountability for resources. The Commonwealth's accrual budgeting reform in 1999–2000 was crunched through over a restricted timeframe. Agencies are now funded in cash for the full costs of delivering public goods and services, but many aspects of the accrual package remain provisional and subject to modification. Accrual budgeting rests far more on assumptions and adjustments than cash-based budgets, and this implies the scope for politics is greater and the rules and accountabilities will inevitably become a contested terrain. Moreover, the adoption of an output-price budgetary system has extended the broader agenda of public sector reform. The rationales behind the purchasing of outputs suggests a transformation of the budgetary system from one in which government was positioned as the main price-taker to one where it has considerable say in determining prices, as well as the quantities and qualities purchased. Nevertheless, the output-price system remains embryonic, and the eventual consequences of this change on the quality of advice and the patterns of public provision are yet to be seen.

11 Cutting expenditures, avoiding deficits and managing surpluses

ATTEMPTS OF SUCCESSIVE Australian governments to cut expenditure cannot be viewed in isolation from international trends. Perhaps one of the most important ways in which public expenditure management has changed during recent decades has been the way in which innovations are monitored, disseminated and diffused, especially among the advanced economies. Promoted by international agencies such as the OECD, IMF, World Bank, and Asian Development Bank, there is arguably a rapid convergence of budgetary agendas and practices (or even fashions) between countries. One instance of this convergence over the past decade or so is that governments have felt constrained to eliminate deficits by attempting to balance their revenues and expenditures; or, more strikingly, creating budget surpluses to reduce public debt. These efforts have concentrated upon the containment or cutting of expenditures, rather than the raising of new revenues; thus forcing governments to reconsider expenditure commitments. Arguably, the cutting of expenditure has emerged as a new orthodoxy among democratic governments around the world—and deficit elimination and debt reduction is now trumpeted as one of the major achievements of international public financial management and budgeting.

Principal reasons for cutting expenditure are that it enables the re-allocation of resources, it is arguably the most effective way of avoiding deficits and reducing debt, and it has the potential to reduce the size of government. Fairness to future generations (intergenerational equity) is also a strong motive for attempting to maintain, on average, a balanced budget. However, the post-war expansionist and interventionist state used deficits to stabilise the economy in the short-term. More recently, such behaviour has been supplanted by the notion of governments paying their way (i.e. avoiding borrowing from the private sector to finance activities). Governments are changing the methods they employ to deal with the perennial problems of governance. The Howard government, for instance, has declared the primary objective of its medium-term fiscal strategy is to 'ensure that, over time, the Commonwealth budget makes no overall call on private sector saving and therefore does not detract from national saving' (Budget Paper No.1, 1996–97:1.9). This view has been consistently applied up to the government's most recent Budget Papers (Budget Paper No.1, 2000–01:1.23–25). This appears an acceptance of the 'crowding-out' doctrine—that public expenditure is at the expense of private investment rather than private consumption (Rosen 1999). In practice it has meant avoiding deficits and reducing overall levels of public debt, thereby reducing government's need to spend on debt interest. Given Australia's relatively low level of public debt by international comparison, this policy could return Australia to a position of being net debt free by 2003—a situation not witnessed since the early 1970s.[1] But why have governments changed their orientation to the use of public spending and borrowing?

BUDGETARY ASYMMETRIES AND THE CUTTING OF EXPENDITURE

In the post-war decades Keynesian policies relied on public expenditure for demand-management adjustments. According to the theory, if the economy was experiencing a downturn, aggregate public expenditure was *increased* to stimulate the economy. The purposes to which that expenditure was put, and the efficiency with which it was used, were largely immaterial for short-term

1 See for example Chart 4;1.15 of Budget Paper No 1, 1997–98. This chart shows a net public debt in the early 1970s and then records a cyclical pattern of net debt increase/decrease to the present, but with an underlying trend of increasing net debt until the mid–1990s. It also shows government intentions to lower net public debt into the new century. Implicitly this chart also indicates that caution is always required in using any such figures as these are largely estimates and have been subject to past revisions (see Footnote to Chart 4). There is little doubt that further revisions will occur in the future. The Howard government in the 1997–8 budget foresaw net debt reduced to 10.5% of GDP by 1999–2000, compared to nearly 20% in the mid–1990s (Budget Paper No 1, 1997–98:1.15).

demand management purposes. And, conversely, according to the theory, if the economy overheated then governments could also *reduce* expenditure to restrain aggregate demand.

Attempts to implement such policies had three important consequences for public expenditure. First, there was a distortionary impact. Projects favoured were those with large and significant macroeconomic impacts, rather than those that were best for long-term viability and cost-effective infrastructural development. Second, there was a long period of boom from the 1950s to the 1970s, which meant that the need for regular boosts to the economy was lessened (though government spending continued to grow). Fiscal policy based on expenditure increases risked adding to inflation, rather than leading to real increases in employment and output. As a consequence, government expenditures aimed at stability tended to substitute the public economy for the private economy. Third, public expenditure management *within* government was nowhere near the concern it has become, and large inefficiencies crept into the system. All three impacts converged to create and sustain an inefficient allocation and utilisation of public expenditures.

The implied Keynesian symmetry between expansions and reductions in government expenditures proved difficult to implement. A ratchet effect or 'lock-in' phenomenon was apparent in public expenditure: expenditures moved upwards in times of economic downturn, but were hardly ever cut or reduced once the economy recovered. This asymmetry began to appear as if it was an inexorable rule of the social and administrative sciences, that applied irrespective of country or the political persuasion of governments (Wildavsky 1964; 1985). As a result, some public choice scholars such as Niskanen (1971; 1975) created general models showing permanently rising public expenditure, with no role given to expenditure cutting, far less aggregate falls in public expenditures.[2] The point was that, in empirical terms, government budgets were not automatically flexible in both directions—they were upwardly incremental, but downwardly 'sticky'. If occasional expenditure cuts were difficult, the record suggested systematic

---

2 There have been numerous critiques and applications of the Niskanen model but the basic tenets have proved resilient: see Breton and Wintrobe (1975); Miller and Moe (1983); Eavey and Miller (1984); Bendor, Taylor and Van Gaalen (1985); Banks (1989); Horn (1995); Dunleavy (1991); Blais and Dion (1991).

multiple-year cutting exercises were virtually impossible. The record of the Thatcher government in the UK is often cited as an example of neo-liberal austerity. Yet, despite a pronounced bias against the public sector, the proportion of public spending to GDP *remained virtually unchanged* (Thain and Wright 1995).

Various reasons are often posited for this apparently inexorable law of expenditure growth. Some reasons highlight changing social and economic needs, or the appetites of politicians chasing votes in electoral markets. Other contributing factors include displacement effects caused by war, crises or major disturbances that stimulate public spending—after which there is no return to previous levels. Alternatively, the power of spending agencies is frequently viewed as greater than the guardians, with respect to their capacities to request, justify and win additional resources. Once resource amounts are agreed for one year, they can become incorporated into that agency's 'base', and it often becomes virtually impossible to re-evaluate them, or revise them downwards in subsequent years. In addition, spending agencies are adept at expanding their resource-base from year to year, hoarding small amounts of savings while resisting cuts. Furthermore, while new spending initiatives or current priorities consume discretionary funds, they are often dear to the hearts of governments. Once 'in place' these new expenditures frequently become non-discretionary, especially when they relate to individual entitlements. A government's most recent initiatives are always difficult to cut within the life of that government, precisely because they wanted them. At the same time it is difficult to assess the worth of long established programs and activities, often disguised within agencies as the essential base of their budgetary-setting. Such asymmetry reflects a mixture of administrative imperatives, the practice and theory of economics, of politics and human nature.

Experience appears to confirm the budgetary asymmetry affecting government spending—expenditure remains relatively easy to increase, but notoriously difficult to wind back. Moreover, this asymmetry has operated even when politicians were adamant they had the political will to make significant cuts to have an impact on deficits (Savoie 1990; Schick 1990). There is no easy way to de-politicise budgetary processes to enable a purely clinical analysis of policy—and many would argue we should not attempt to de-politicise them as they are political and not innately technical exercises. Budgeting is in part an arbitrary political process contingent on many factors, which change from year to year and even within years. Spending increases are pleasant; line ministers enjoy spending, new programs can be announced, more staff employed. Cutting and pruning calls for 'hard decisions'—they are painful and unpleasant as well as draining on ministers and officials. Cuts generate conflict: in parliament, in cabinet, in the party room, within the bureaucracy itself and among affected clients. Staff may have to be retrenched. Reduced numbers on budget sheets mean not only that organisations suffer the consequences of reductions in funding, but so too do their members or employees, their families, their clients and others who do not fulfil any new criteria for government spending.

Yet Australia, almost alone outside the rapidly expanding Asian economies, managed to achieve government surpluses for a period in the 1980s and again—this time joined by many other OECD countries—since 1997–98. Building on its general record of fiscal rectitude over the post-war period, Australia has been at the forefront of the international currents in eliminating deficits and debt. Buoyant global economic conditions over the past decade, especially pumped by the strong growth in the US economy, have contributed increased revenues and delivered small budget surpluses. During the last few years, governments such as those of the USA, Canada, Sweden and the UK have also been able to eliminate deficits over several budgets. While these surpluses were created in an economic upturn and remain comparatively small, they may not survive a downturn unless expenditures are cut (and any rise in unemployment will make this difficult). Governments have suddenly achieved surpluses, but to maintain them they face tough choices in the future and may opt to side-step them in favour of renewed deficit financing. There is also the related problem (addressed toward the end of this chapter) of, having created and maintained consecutive surpluses, what does government do with them?

Therefore, there is something of an emerging discordance between the historical record which suggests budgets are asymmetrical and cuts to expenditure are inordinately difficult to achieve, and more recent experience which indicates governments around the world *can* make major cuts and deliver surpluses. This chapter goes some way towards resolving this discordance. Instead of merely assuming ideal budget 'flexibility', rather, resolution is attempted by trying to understand and describe budget expenditure asymmetries, and the contradiction between past and current experience.

THE ROLE OF EXPENDITURE CUTS AND THE DIFFICULTIES OF CUTTING BUDGETS

As needs and government priorities change, existing patterns of expenditure allocation are no longer considered essential or productive. It is open to government to tighten programs, make selected culls or withdraw from activities entirely.[3] As such, there are social and political benefits from an ongoing expenditure cutting process. Cuts reduce committed expenditure and free up resources. Government then have more choices. They can create and implement new policy, without (if they prefer) either having to raise new revenues or increase the size of government. Australian governments have tended to do precisely this—skim off existing activities to enable new spending in areas of priority. Expenditure cuts also allow government the possibility of *reducing* taxes. Or cuts can help generate surpluses to reduce government debt, improve intergenerational equity and reduce debt service interest payments. Moreover, governments can improve operational efficiencies via selective cutting and re-allocation of resources. Eliminating or reducing existing activities and their expenditures is vital both to efficient and effective government.

Whatever rationale lies behind individual cuts, without the *ability* to make them, government expenditure would seem condemned to perpetual growth. Not surprisingly, both governments and senior ministers boast of their ability to take the *hard* decisions associated with making cuts (even while using euphemisms like 'efficiency', 'savings' or 'reducing waste'). Paul Keating told the House of Representatives in 1985, for example, that

> The Prime Minister (Mr Hawke) and I have emphasised a number of times that in this year's Budget [1985–86] we will cut the deficit in money terms. I can assure honourable members tonight that that cut will be significant. This Government wishes to ensure that companies borrowing to increase their levels of activity and investment will not be impeded by sustained public sector competition for borrowed funds. Deficit reductions are also required to slow the growth of

---

3 A recent example was the demise of the Commonwealth's agency (with 5,000 staff) responsible for organising services and procuring provisions across government—the Department of Administrative Services. The commercial functions of the department were largely transferred to the private sector, while its remaining legislative and control responsibilities were added to the Department of Finance in 1997 (to become DoFA).

> public debt. It is clearly not appropriate, now that we are achieving strong growth, to continue adding to our debt at the rate of recent years. Taxpayers of the future would certainly not thank us for the interest burden (Treasurer 1985:2314).

Given such claims, it might be expected that any savings would be announced with fanfare—especially in the budget statements where the reductions should become a matter of public record. Yet, when we look for the records of cuts we do not easily find them; they are not always displayed and their impacts are often downplayed.

There are several reasons for this shyness on the part of politicians of all persuasions. Two are most apparent. The first is a desire to minimise electoral risk—governments risk political damage by alienating specific groups with an interest in the areas to be cut. The second is the wish to avoid technical risk or being seen to have erred. A mistake may not have direct electoral repercussions but may undermine the credibility of the minister responsible, and provide parliamentary mileage to the opposition. Thus, although cuts are essential, they suffer from the logic of collective action: a small or isolated cut is only a slight benefit to the whole, but to the specific groups affected by the cut the impact is immediate, identifiable and disadvantageous. Consequently, cuts are frequently hidden or obscured unless there is some overriding political gain to be derived from an announcement.

A government's budget is arguably its primarily strategic and operational statement, considerably more than a mere record of revenues and expenditures. Yet, even when governments produce what they themselves proclaim are strategically 'austere' or 'tough' budgets it is often more expedient to emphasise the 'good news'—new programs and priorities—than dwell upon the demise of the old. New priorities and programs are usually banners for a government's strategy. Even when they do not require much expenditure new initiatives still appear in accompanying budget statements with their virtues extolled. Often, cuts are made with much more difficulty and wrangling behind the scenes, and are frequently 'hidden' despite their relevance to determining the shape of budgets. New priorities are 'selling points', while discussion of the demise of former priorities incites criticism or hostility from those most affected. Nevertheless, it is the cuts a government is prepared to make that provides a better indicator of its resolve and vision than its expansion into new areas of expenditure.

In short, the reasons for expenditure cuts are legion. All the same, there are enormous practical difficulties in making and implementing a decision to cut. Expenditure cuts are frequently politically dangerous and administratively difficult to achieve. This is one of the major contradictions of public expenditure management that was little acknowledged in the Keynesian model: it is essential and rational to make periodic cuts yet remarkably difficult to achieve them.

PARTY INCUMBENCY AND EXPENDITURE CUTS: DO IDEOLOGICAL DIFFERENCES MATTER?

If there is a rational basis for expenditure cutting, the adversarial nature of politics is often cited as an impediment to rational expenditure management. Vote-bidding between competing political parties (aiming to 'buy' the median vote) tends to ratchet-up expenditures. And in a majoritarian 'all-or-nothing' political system, if one side threatens to make cuts, the other can promise the opposite and agree to restore deleted programs. The prospect of being thrown out of office may also deter governments from embarking on serious cutting exercises. Even so, there is evidence to suggest a plausible counter-argument to this conventional view.

Compared to consensus-style or coalition-based political systems, adversarial systems of government provide more opportunities to impose brakes upon expenditure. The combination of competition between separate and exclusive political entities and the prospect of regular changes of government replaces an entire team of incumbents with another. The 'winner takes all' nature of the electoral outcome allows new personalities with new agendas to assume control of the public purse. Changes in incumbency (and the continual threat of being ousted by one's opponents) are likely to have two types of impact. First, there is some evidence that within overall levels of expenditure, *certain* policy areas are promoted and others downgraded according to the ideological disposition of incumbents (Castles 1982). At the margins, conservative governments will reduce the proportion of outlays to employment programs while favouring defence spending; social democrats traditionally favoured the reverse, spending more on training and further education. Second, governments in office for long periods of time are unlikely to be advocates of continuing expenditure cuts. With the passing of years it is harder to cut one's own programs than it was to cut those of ones opponents (but not impossible—as the case of Canada's Alberta province under the Klein government in the 1990s demonstrates—see Bruce *et al.*1997; Forster 1997).

Within adversarial systems it is accepted practice for governments to make cuts on purely party-political grounds. The Howard government, for example, quickly culled an entire set of labour market programs inherited from its predecessor, while specific bodies such as the Industrial Relations Commission and the Human Rights and Equal Opportunities Commission were targeted for cutting. Much of this cutting is symbolic, although the consequences are no less severe on the individuals and groups that lose their influence or livelihoods. In one sense only politicians can make such cuts—they are ideologically driven and politicians are held accountable. In Australia, cabinet or its ERC will hold the final say over cuts or can veto proposals for cuts from within the bureaucracy. Usually when cuts to programs are foreshadowed, central agencies like Treasury and Finance are quick to emphasise that it is cabinet, not central agencies, that determines budget parameters and makes the final decisions about where pain is inflicted.

Elections and changes in incumbency, therefore, may help explain *when* cuts are likely to occur and also the *patterns* and *targeting* of cuts. One way this can be gauged is in the growth in outlays in the years immediately following elections and especially changes of government (Gruen 1985). The three lowest rates of growth in outlays under the Fraser government were in their first, fourth and sixth budgets (2% in 1976–77, 1.8% in 1979–80 and 2.1% in 1981–82). These budgets were handed down respectively in its first year in office (immediately after the Whitlam Labor government), in the second budget after it had been returned for a second term in December 1977, and in the first budget after re-election for a third term in October 1980.

The pattern of outlay growth under the Hawke government—coming to office during a recession—is noticeably different. Labor's major cuts to outlays in real terms occurred in their 5th and 6th budgets (reducing outlays by –1.5% in 1987–88 and –4.2% in 1988–89). Overall Labor recorded five consecutive years of low or negative outlay growth from 1985–86 to 1989–90 (their 3rd to 7th budgets inclusive), after which spending increased substantially.

The Howard government made major cuts in its first two budgets (containing outlays to a 1% growth in 1996–97 and achieving a −1.6% reduction in 1997–98), but again began increasing outlays in its next three budgets. In short, post-election budgets are prime occasions for cuts, while longevity tends to reduce the likelihood and attractiveness of cuts (the last two Hawke government budgets and the four Keating government budgets increased outlays by around 5% per annum). The third budget of the Howard government increased outlays by 4% in 1998–99 while the fourth and fifth (using accrual budgeting) increased outlays by 8% and 7% respectively over 1999–00 and 2000–01 (using GFS figures allowing for the GST). As Machiavelli (1911:68) pronounced, it is often far better for a ruler to inflict injuries 'all at one time, so that, being tasted less, they offend less; benefits ought to be given little by little, so that the flavour of them may last longer'.

Trends in the *growth* in real outlays from 1969 to 1999 indicate only a slight variation between parties. Commonwealth real outlays increased in all but three years (1987–88, 1988–89 and 1997–98) with the highest rate of increase in 1974–75 (of 15.5%). Coalition governments increased outlays on average by 3.46% per annum, but with comparatively little deviation or variability from year to year. Labor, by contrast, increased outlays by 4.84%, but with slightly more variability from year to year. The rate of change in outlays under Labor ranged from 15.5% to −4.2%, whereas for the Coalition the range was more compressed (from 10.2% to −1.6%).[4] While these figures allow for incumbency and inflation, they do not allow for the economic cycle. Without exception the larger increases in outlays (and higher deficits) occur in periods of economic recession—irrespective of which party is in power.

When Australian governments of different persuasions are compared, how can differences in expenditure priorities be identified? If ideological differences mean that governments do target different areas for cuts, this should show up in the larger policy areas such as defence, education and social welfare. Yet, upon inspection of functional classifications of outlays over time there appears to be minimal difference on partisan lines. Defence and/or social security are potentially useful in the sense that neither set of expenditures

4 Source: Budget Paper No 1, 2000–01:8.42. This result is still not statistically significant (using a T Test statistical measure). A longer historical timeframe using an alternate set of data indicated far less annual variability between the two parties in outlay growth. From 1953–1993 Coalition outlays across 26 budgets increased by 4.46% per annum while Labor over 14 budgets increased by 4.34%.

performs a direct economic function and, therefore, pits those who emphasise upholding the state (pro-defence) as opposed to those who champion the disadvantaged within society (pro-social security). Analysis of the data for Australia since the mid–1970s shows both sides have increased social security as a proportion of total outlays over time—with substantial increases occurring during the Fraser years (jumping from around 23% in 1975–76 to 29% in 1982–83). Social security again increased under Labor to 36% in 1993–94 and again rose under the Coalition to 37% by 2000–01. In defence, the Fraser government increased spending from 8.5% in 1975–76 to 9.6% in 1982–83; while Labor gradually reduced spending back down to the former level by the mid–1990s.[5] Successive annual cuts to defence under Labor reduced spending from 8.8% of outlays in 1990–91, to 8.3% of outlays in 1993–94, and 8.36% in 1997–98. But the Coalition reversed the decline by increasing spending to 10.2% relative to total expenses in 2000–01 (with some increases attributable to the East Timor crisis).[6]

Further evidence of difficulties in detecting ideology as the driving force behind expenditure cut-backs can be found from the US. Schick (1990), in a case study of the Reagan administration, portrayed expenditure cuts in the American system as an institutional struggle between Congress and the President, where parties played little role. Schick holds the conventional view that although programs were cut by Reagan, the 'characteristics of contemporary budgeting' were responsible for driving 'expenditures upward even when programs have been retrenched' (1990:85). Although Schick predicted some system change, he argued it was more likely to be through expediency than real change. Subsequently, with improved economic performance the US political system has shown itself capable of controlling expenditures, creating and maintaining surpluses and even, perhaps, achieving real cuts.

RECORDING AND MEASURING EXPENDITURE CUTS

In Australia, no systematic longitudinal study measuring expenditure cuts exists for periods longer than a few years. Part of the

---

5 Even the Whitlam period (1972–75) is not one of pronounced defence cuts, especially if one allows for the impact of ending the Vietnam engagement.

6 Budget Paper No 1, 1997–98:4.25; Budget Paper No 1, 1998–99: 4.27; Budget Paper No 1, 2000–01:6.26–27, and Defence Portfolio Budget Statement 2000–01:11.

reason for this is that annual budget statements are notoriously inconsistent from one to the next, and unreliable with respect to reporting any cuts.[7] Tables in various budget statements record the intended revenues and expenditures for appropriation purposes rather than disclose any adjustments or reductions. The final numbers represent a net figure and do not usually indicate the amount of any 'savings measures'. In the statements where cuts are labelled they may be illusory or real, and their magnitude over time is difficult to discover. For instance, in the 1983–84 budget more than $2 billion was cut from existing activities yet overall Commonwealth expenditure increased by 9.9% or $7.9 billion (almost all this increased expenditure was deficit funded). Again in the 1985 May economic statement $1.26 billion was cut from the forward estimates and transfers to the states yet real outlays rose by 3.3% or $6.2 billion. Hence, expenditure cuts may not become visible when one year is viewed in relation to the expenditure of the previous year, unless there are specific reasons for wishing to make the cuts known. This is certainly so in the two cases we examine in this chapter, the sixth Keating budget of the late 1980s and the first Costello budget of 1996. It is precisely because of the absence of longitudinal data that the case study approach has been employed here.

Year-to-year comparisons are fraught with methodological and measurement problems. The types of problems that can occur include changes in accounting systems, especially the major change from cash to accrual, changes in definitions of activities as well as changes in departmental location. Inflation rates, fluctuations in GDP and changes to the definition of general government sector will influence the relative size of outlay changes, as well as a host of other minor complications such as allowing for carryovers from previous years. As a general rule: the further apart the measurements, the greater the chance of error.

This does not mean that we have no data on cuts. Specific measures can produce longer-term reductions in outlays for which we have evidence. Relative budget cuts to the Defence portfolio already mentioned indicate that its share fell from around 10% to

7 Governments are also prone to recalculate previous governments' figures after making adjustments to criteria or reworking data. Given that governments are keen to put the best spin on the figures in any one year, there is always a degree of cosmetic presentation in budget data.

8% of total outlays—representing a 'lost increase' of around $3 billion assuming relativities had been maintained over the mid–1990s. Defence outlays declined after the decision in the 1993–94 Budget round 'to apply year-on-year reductions to the Defence outlays base' for four consecutive years. The Coalition government then decided that estimates for 1997–98 onwards would 'reflect zero real growth in Defence base outlays' (Budget Paper No 1, 1997–98: 4.25). Within the Defence portfolio cuts were felt mostly in personnel and the defence support industry. In later budgets the Coalition gradually increased Defence outlays back to over 10% to total outlays.

Another example where data exists is the imposition of an 'efficiency dividend' on departmental running costs (see Chapter 8). The cumulative effect of the clawback on administrative activities during 1987–99 was of the order of 15–20%, depending upon the measurement base used. Relating to expected improvements in labour productivity, the government believed the bureaucracy would be able to take advantage of increased productivity, but would not voluntarily return those savings to consolidated revenues. The clawback imposed a compulsory levy. Nevertheless, a measurement problem for the size of the cuts remains. While the government regularly produced figures showing how many millions the efficiency dividend cumulatively 'saved', this does not mean that administrative expenditures were reduced by up to 20% over that period (again the problems of measurement surface when both base years for calculation and the impacts of inflation can alter both the real and nominal levels off cuts). Rather, new administrative expenses were incurred as programs changed and new initiatives were funded. In practical terms funds were often recycled rather than reduced.

More information is needed on how bureaucracies cope with cuts to provide some guide to how they can better manage the process. This may be a crucial lacuna in our knowledge if governments resort to substantial across-the-board or *ad hoc* cuts, especially if ministers do not clearly identify the areas for excision.[8] One practice is to internalise 'savings measures' often through 'crimping' and 'narrowing the margins' in place of real savings initiatives (deciding which activities to terminate or significantly reduce).

---

8 See Hood and Wright (1979) for an early examination of the way bureaucracies in the UK coped with the first wave of restraint in the 1970s.

Bureaucratic organisations will often adopt evasive or disguising tactics such as delaying appointments and purchasing orders, retiring senior staff, leaving positions vacant, or just reducing travel. Marginal pruning is not necessarily the best option. This raises another fundamental problem. It is difficult for public bureaucracies to have an internal resource re-allocation mechanism independent of executive government or parliament, without impinging upon their prerogatives. Yet financial devolution allowing 'managers to manage' implies such operational freedom.[9] So to the extent managers can make cuts they are likely to be constrained merely to place emphasis on efficiency and effectiveness rather than the worth of programs or whether continued government involvement is even warranted.

Finally, governments frequently attempt to re-create fiscal histories of themselves and their predecessors—usually to their advantage and sometimes inventively so. Examples have already been given, such as the deficit forecast re-calculated by Treasury as the Hawke government entered office. The Keating and Howard governments differed on their preferred measures for the deficit and debt, each constructing a different impression of the financial position of the government.[10] In successive budgets these governments produced different sets of historical figures of the Commonwealth's outlays, revenues and budget balance. The advent of accrual accounting and the change from cash accounting in the 1999–2000 Budget allowed another set of recalculations to occur. Notwithstanding the Howard government's *Charter of Budget Honesty*, the necessary adjustments to cash budgets succeeded in making before and after comparisons extraordinarily difficult. In the 2000–01 Budget, the

9 Previously line-item budgets denied even this ability by stipulating specific amounts for, say, postage or telephones. Managers could not even attempt to be micro-efficient by cutting back expenditure on one item (postage) if they found that another (telephone) could do the job more effectively but where the individual budget line-item was insufficient.

10 See Budget Paper No. 1, 1997–98, Chart 1, 1.11. The distinction is made between the 'underlying budget balance' and the 'headline budget balance'. Similarly Chart 5, 1–15 shows different projections of government net debt using 'with consolidation' and 'without consolidation'. The Howard government chooses to use the former figure when it also states 'The Government's fiscal strategy will see net debt reduced to around 10 1/2 per cent of GDP in 2000–01' (1–15). Using 'Without Consolidation' figures would produce a net debt figure of around 17–18 per cent, showing the fiscal strategy in a less flattering light.

Howard government steadfastly refused to incorporate GST revenue giving a false impression of the size of Commonwealth outlays to GDP. The argument is not the facile one that politicians are inherently dishonest, but that they have distinct preferences on what type of information is generated, the ways it is defined, collated, and presented. If systematic measures of cuts do not exist, our understanding of expenditure cutting and its imperatives has to be based upon case analyses. Consequently, it is to two case studies that we now turn.

SELLING AUSTERITY TO THE PUBLIC: A STUDY OF TWO BUDGETS

Two approaches to controlling and cutting expenditures in different budgets are examined below. These are selected from two governments at different points in the electoral cycle. The first case concerns the sixth Budget of the Hawke Labor government brought down in 1988–89 by Treasurer Paul Keating after a number of years of fiscal austerity. The second examines the 1996–97 Budget of the Howard government delivered by Peter Costello—the first Coalition budget since coming back into government after 13 years in opposition. Both cases involved explicit self-congratulation by the government on its fiscal prowess and rectitude. In both cases there was an attempt to avoid a deficit, if not create a surplus, and both governments were anxious to take credit for making savings, while still going to some lengths to hide where cuts had been made. In the case of the Labor budget, real outlays *decreased* by more than any other year in the post-war period. The Coalition's budget announced a series of cuts over two years that saw real outlays *decrease* by 1.6% in 1997–98. It will be shown how both cases highlight different approaches to cutting expenditure and the roles played by individuals and institutional arrangements.

The Sixth Keating Budget 1988–89: 'Bringing Home the Bacon'

When Labor brought down its sixth budget in 1988 it had already won three consecutive federal elections and was used to holding the reins of power. Importantly, from a methodological viewpoint this budget does not have to be seen as tentative or reactive to policies and budgets of other parties that had recently been in office. In addition, the main actors were familiar with the budgetary processes. These included the procedural use of the ERC as a gatekeeper, the use of savings targets set by the 'Troika', and the resort to Savings Statements indicating where cuts would be made. In many ways this Budget was the apogee of that process—though it still showed a $2.8 billion increase in outlays[11]—with Keating famously declaring in his Budget speech to the House, 'This is the one that brings home the bacon'. However, the surplus produced in this Budget (intended to be $2.2 billion but the final figure actually came in at $6.1 billion) was not solely due to expenditure cuts but to revenue increases accruing from economic growth, new imposts (such as capital gains tax), or bracket creep affecting income tax payments. In a sense, the revenues that helped this budget were a result of 'windfall' gains from economic growth and other impacts unscripted in the budget. The Minister for Finance (Walsh P 1995:152) remembered:

> The ERC was concentrating on the outlays side of the Budget. There was not then, or at any later time, an explicit decision to take the Budget into surplus. The surplus which ultimately peaked at 2.2 per cent of GDP was a residual, the fallout from continuing expenditure restraint and revenue boosted by economic growth.

Arguably the 1988–89 Budget was the high-water mark of Labor's expenditure control processes, although Peter Walsh (1995:169–198) has since argued such processes were then already in decline.

The cuts in the 1988–89 Budget were concentrated in the areas of defence, roads, pharmaceuticals, fertiliser subsidies, transfers to the states and territories, and to a lesser extent, to local government (see Budget Paper No. 1, 1988–89:73–76 for detailed outlines of cutting measures).[12] By far the greatest of these cuts were those imposed by Canberra on the states. Table 11.1 below shows the major cuts and totals of the 1988–89 budget.

The three columns show the immediate impacts of the government's decisions across major functional areas in the budget year. What is clear is that despite this budget aiming to provide a surplus of $2.2 billion there were policy decisions leading to a net decrease of expenditure within the budget year of only $784 million

11 Budget Paper No. 1, 1988–89: 69.

12 Hidden within each of these is a set of generic cost-cutting measures such as the 1.25% efficiency dividend applied to running costs within the budget sector of the Commonwealth.

Table 11.1 Major Policy Increases and Decreases ($m) in the 1988–89 Budget

Function	Increase	Decrease	Net
Defence	20	142	–122
Education	318	135	183
Health	223	118	105
Social Sec.	232	269	–37
Housing	33	98	–65
Culture	134	–8	141
Econ. Services	149	393	–244
Public Services	175	20	155
Govt. Transfers	–	900	–900
TOTAL	1283	2068	–784

Source: Budget Paper No. 1, 1988–89:69, 'Reconciliation of Forward and Budget Outlays Estimates 1988–89, By Function ($ million)'.

dollars. This is certainly consistent with Walsh's view. Also consistent is the fact that expenditure cuts tapered off in following years (and indeed outlays again began to rise). Conversely, while some of the net outcomes are trivial, such as the overall impacts on social security, the gross figure for the cuts was relatively large. This indicates an active process of re-allocation at work rather than a process of cutting to produce surpluses. Labor was also *targeting* outlays so as not to be seen to be hurting less fortunate members of society. In the case of both the cumulative effects and immediate effects of policy, however, one item stands above all others—the cuts in transfers to other levels of government. The $900 million cut to the states contributed virtually the entire net reduction figure. These are the easiest cuts for Commonwealth governments to make for they inflict the pain upon a different constituency to their own. The Commonwealth did not inflict net cuts on its own budget, but essentially re-cycled funds for its own purposes. Four Commonwealth policy areas received net cuts but these were nowhere near the almost $1 billion in cuts inflicted on the states.

These figures are consistent with Walsh's contention that the surplus was largely accidental and that the political will to cut the Commonwealth's own outlays was disappearing. However, the processes of fiscal rectitude may operate for a while even when a political will has disappeared—for how long is a vital question when we examine the creation and management of surpluses later.

The First Costello Budget 1996–97: 'Something to Prove'

Dilemmas faced by governments over cutting expenditures are exemplified by the situation the Howard government created for itself during and immediately after the 1996 election. By focussing on a supposedly enormous deficit left hidden by Labor, the Coalition made the existence and elimination of the presumed deficit a cornerstone of a successful election strategy. It also gave commitments to balance the budget and create surpluses within a relatively short time. Ironically, the deficit referred to as the '$8 billion black hole', was actually lower in 1996 than at the time of the 1993 election, when the deficit issue received nowhere near the same attention. To compound its problems, the Coalition promised not to make cuts in several key areas, including health and education. Once in government Howard and Costello found they had to make unpalatable choices between what they had promised to do and their fundamental promise to eliminate the deficit.

Their decision to give priority to the deficit elimination program meant that significant cuts were made, while promises of 'no cuts' in several important areas had to be broken to a significant degree. The Coalition did not attempt to conceal these significant cuts. On the contrary, it made a virtue out of its preparedness to 'meet their commitments'. The ways in which these cuts are described and presented in the Budget papers are crucial. An aggregate statement of cuts made in the 1996–97 Budget is provided below in Table 11.2. Note the rather different format in which these cuts are presented to those in the 1988–89 Budget. This indicates the fundamental difficulties of measurement and comparison alluded to already.

The cuts are listed in this format to reflect the government's electoral promises. A more precise statement of the cuts is presented in a special budget paper, *Meeting Our Commitments*, issued by Treasurer on 20 August 1996. Such visible statements demonstrate the importance placed by the Coalition in managing perceptions. Believing its promise to cut the deficit was popular, it also realised specific cuts would incite opposition and make enemies of those affected. Consequently, a careful use of language was employed that described cuts in terms of affecting as few voter interests as possible. Making the cuts was, in Costello's terms, necessary to 'meet our commitments'. The phraseology employed in the budget documents repeatedly describes cuts in terms of election promises kept and mutual contributions to the 'savings'.

Just as it was suggested Labor under Hawke was frightened of

Table 11.2 Major Savings Measures ($m) in the 1996–97 Budget

Saving Items	1996–97	1997–98	1998–99	1999–00
Running costs (2% reduction)	–187	–188	–190	–194
Migrant two-year wait for Social Security	–28	–140	–188	–194
State fiscal contributions	–619	–640	–300	–
AUSTUDY eligibility	–56	–123	–136	–143
HECS differential course costs	–133	–373	–569	–694
Labour market program savings	–575	–956	–130	–175
Abolish Development Import Finance	–94	–126	–130	–134
Export Scheme capping	–	–77	–122	–145
Reform Aged/Community Care	–6	–141	–190	–231
Diagnostic Imaging & Pathology reform	–62	–127	–174	–223
Tighter childcare targeting	–17	–147	–170	–170
DFRS efficiency savings	–56	–113	–116	–120
Tighten JSA/NSA activity test admin.	–39	–105	–110	–115
Reduce national highway funding	–113	–138	–157	–214
Other (includes lower national debt interest)	–2464	–3829	–4354	–5260
Total Savings	–4449	–7223	–7036	–8012
Total Savings (after new spending)	–2929	–5197	–4847	–6065

Source: Budget Paper No. 1, 1996–97:1.18 (Table 4).

failure in its early days, so the Coalition portrayed an early uncertainty. In *Meeting Our Commitments* the less threatening terms 'increase efficiency', 'reduce funding', 'achieve portfolio savings', 'disband', 'rationalise' and 'abolition of . . .' or 'abandon planned . . .' all appear where some form of expenditure cuts were applied. Cuts to the Administrative Services department shown in Table 11.3 referred to 'reduce running costs' and even more euphemistically to 'increase returns' from its business units or requirements to 'better manage' its property holdings so as to produce 'savings' to the budget. Although $25 million was cut from operating costs over three years, by far the largest contribution to the cuts came from departmental returns and cost-recovery initiatives.

In the Attorney-General's portfolio $11 million was taken from running costs, while 'increased efficiencies' (user-charging) accounted for $17 million raised by the legal practice, a further $6 million from efficiencies from both the Family Court and National Crime Authority, $6 million from the 'abolition of the Industrial

Table 11.3 Cuts in Administrative Services 1996–97 Budget ($m)

Department of Administrative Services	1996–97	1997–98	1998–99	Total over 3 years
Reduce Running Costs	–6.0	–9.2	–9.4	–24.6
Increase Returns from Business Units	–377.3	51.8	9.3	–316.2
Better Manage Commonwealth Property	–64.0	–413.3	83.9	–393.4
Totals	–447.3	–370.7	83.8	–734.2

Source: Meeting Our Commitments (August 1996:9, Table 3).

Relations Commission, and $3 million from reduced funding to the Human Rights and Equal Opportunities Commission. Total cuts imposed on the portfolio came to $53 million but net cuts equalled $38 million, as $15 million was reallocated within the portfolio to new priorities ($6 million to marriage education services and $9 million to a campaign against violence).

In making sizeable cuts the Coalition specifically intended to eliminate the deficit. This was not the only agenda item. Deficit elimination was becoming a means and not just an end to which the government would strive. It allowed the government to explain cuts as necessary unless there was to be recourse to increased taxation. Surreptitiously, it enabled them to reallocate funds to implement alternative policies. The government also felt the need to employ arguments about fiscal stringency to discipline its own Coalition members—especially the National party who began attempting to place budgetary demands on the new government by changing their rhetoric from 'agrarian socialism' to 'rural and regional protectionism'. Many government members held marginal electorates newly won from Labor, and many of their electorates were directly affected by individual expenditure cuts.

Labor criticised the cuts as too deep and too arbitrary, but this first budget provides the key to understanding the subsequent trajectory of public expenditure under the Howard government. Selective cuts were made, instead of across-the-board reductions. Defence escaped largely unscathed and was later bolstered. New programs and service delivery models were instituted (some like Centrelink were required to deliver $1 billion in savings over six years). It is also clear that this initial cost-cutting exercise depended upon an early fervour more than on established structures and procedures of expenditure restraint. It is worth remembering that

in 1996–97 total government outlays rose by around 1% in the budget.[13] However, in the second year the cuts would see outlays reduced by 1.6% in real terms. In summary, though the 1996–97 Budget was harsh it was not one that instituted enormous across-the-board cuts, nor was it a contractionary budget that deflated the economy.

Comparing the Two Cases

In different ways, the Keating and Costello budgets of 1988–89 and of 1996–97 were ones of expenditure cut-backs and both were openly proclaimed by their implementers to be 'restraint budgets'. In 1988–89 total government outlays were reduced by 4.2%, whereas a reduction of 0.5% was planned for the first Costello budget (with an eventual increase of 1%). They were both different in their motivations and approaches to reductions and this is a warning not to treat all cuts the same. The Costello budget was dominated by factors related to the recent election of the Coalition

13 Adjusted for inflation, total government outlays were planned to fall by –0.5%—see Budget Paper No. 1, 1996–97:3.197.

Table 11.4 The Ends and Means of Expenditure Cuts

Cuts by Type of Objective

1. *Aggregate Fiscal Targets*197targeting the size of the government sector; reducing debt and/or debt servicing payments; deficit reduction and/or elimination
2. *Political and Ideological*—size of the government sector ('crowding out' notions); deficit reduction and/or elimination and cuts to specific programs
3. *Elimination of Ineffective Programs*—withdraw from non-performing programs or re-allocation to programs with the promise of improved effectiveness
4. *Create Efficiencies*—to either force efficiencies or create incentives for efficiencies
5. *Release Resources*—for specific new programs or to reduce taxes/debt levels

Cuts by Type of Method

1. *Cuts to Input Resources*—efficiency or productivity dividends, usually to financial resources but could involve others (e.g. manpower/staffing limits, reducing 'office' locations)
2. *Top-down Aggregate Cuts*—overall imposition on portfolios/programs then flowing down to other levels of operations and service delivery
3. *Bottom-up Aggregate Cuts*—areas are nominated for cutting or reduction, then higher level decision makers (e.g. ERC) decide which suggestions to endorse
4. *Cuts in Disguise*—not indexing funding, not allowing for inflation, or known workload changes
5. *Cuts by Output*—eliminating certain outputs of government, so that costs are cut by the amount budgeted to achieving the output
6. *Cuts by Institutional Mechanisms*—as in transfer programs to states; sunset clauses on program spending mandated by legislation (including constitutional provisions in some overseas jurisdictions)

and a neo-liberal ideology of reducing government. The Labor budget was determined more by the established processes of an experienced government attempting to redirect spending. Both motivations and circumstances were different, yet without labouring the point, it must be iterated that in neither case was there a *debt or deficit problem* to match those of many other nations. And the cuts imposed were in part made easier by an established Australian tradition of fiscal conservatism, by increased revenues and by the ability to cut transfers to the states—'state fiscal contributions' in the Coalition's terminology.

These cases illustrate that expenditure cutting involves a myriad of ends and means (as outlined in Table 11.4). A single expenditure cut can serve several purposes or be achieved by several means.

Expenditure cutting is artful, especially when required as part of the standard operating practices of government.

CUTTING BACK *DEFICIT* EXPENDITURE

Deficits represent the annual difference between revenues and expenditures. But their internal make-up can be important. *Cyclical* or *non-structural* deficits are the result of increased government spending during times of economic down-turn, and are likely to disappear when the economy picks up (as less people draw unemployment benefits). By contrast, *structural* deficits represent fixed outlay commitments built into ongoing expenditure profiles (e.g. increases in recurrent administrative outlays, increases in family benefits) and are far less likely to disappear as the economic cycle improves (see Savoie 1990:320–326).

The elimination of deficits can be greatly helped by economic growth (producing an increase in state revenues and a decrease in social welfare payments in times of economic upturns)—this phenomena is known in government as 'automatic stabilisers'. But in turn, good financial management by governments helps generate growth, thus creating a virtuous cycle. This can all be for nought, though, if a tight rein is not kept on galloping expenditures through the application of cuts.

Almost all attempts to eliminate deficits in Australia have relied on *both* expenditure cuts and increases in revenues. Success in eliminating deficits has resulted from expenditure restraint with fortuitous increases in revenues above those estimated by Treasury. In examining the history of deficits in Australia it is soon apparent that governments have more often used deficit expenditure than not. From the financial year 1953–54 to 2000–01 there have only been 7 years when a budget surplus has been achieved by a Commonwealth government; yet debt has remained extraordinarily low by international standards.[14] Four of these years were in a single

14 Despite the apparent simplicity of the accounting definitions of deficits, surpluses and debt, there is always doubt as to what the figures mean in practice. In periods when the budgets are close to balance it is difficult to tell precisely if a deficit or surplus is recorded. Thus, in his budget for 1948–49, Chifley announced a planned small deficit of £17.7 million but it was later believed that a balanced budget was achieved due to greater than expected revenues. Among the states in the same period New South Wales, Victoria, South Australia, Western Australia and Tasmania all budgeted for deficits, with

period (1987–88, 1988–89, 1989–90 and 1990–91), the other three being achieved under the Howard government (1997–98, 1998–99 and 1999–2000). Put another way, in all but a very few of the last fifty years governments have chosen levels of expenditure that have necessitated borrowing—rather than face instituting comparatively more severe expenditure cuts.

A simplistic (and incorrect) interpretation of this deficit financing would be that Australian governments have been notoriously profligate. This is far from the case, especially in an OECD context. Australian governments have relied upon deficit-financed expenditure far less than other nations. The cumulative effect of these deficits (net public debt) has similarly been low in international terms. Indeed, Australian governments have actually reduced per capita levels of public debt. In 1994 Australia had a net public sector debt that was approximately 27% of GDP. The OECD average in the same year was just over 40%. Figures for other nations were just under 40% for the USA, the UK was just under 50% and even the reputedly financially conservative Germany was around 40%. The only major nation with a lower net public debt than Australia was Japan with between 7% and 8%.[15] This is a consistent story over the whole of the post-war period.

An alternative way of describing the position is to say that the *ability to service the debt created* has increased. Reduced net public sector debt levels means smaller proportions of revenues go into interest payments, thereby freeing monies for program expenditure, and in turn diminishing the proportion of expenditures that must be funded through deficit expenditures in the future. This has happened in Australia during the post-war period. The same is not true of all nations, however, and it is clear that a good many have increased their public debt at such a rate that the capacity of their economies to service the repayments on the debt has markedly declined, despite achieving lower annual deficits or even surpluses.[16]

---

only Queensland planning a surplus. In the previous financial year some states had deficits and others surpluses. The total public debt (Commonwealth and states) in 1949 was £2.8 billion with the states debt at £1 billion compared to a gross national product (GNP) of £2.25 billion. This put the total debt to GNP ratio at 125%. The Commonwealth achieved zero net debt in 1973–76 and may again arrive at this situation (projections indicate the year 2003).

15 A wide variety of sources and descriptions are available for deficit and debt figures, and each of them is rather different from the others in either definition or emphasis.

16 The achievement of sequential surpluses is not of itself a panacea for public

MANAGING SURPLUSES

During the late 1990s governments around the world recorded budget surpluses,[17] with some significantly lowering debt. In an increasing number of cases it has been suggested debt will be eliminated completely. Australia is certainly one such case. This raises questions about whether the mechanisms that helped restrict spending will remain appropriate or efficacious in an era of surplus and whether there will be tendency to return to deficit either by design or by default. It is still not clear whether the current surpluses are structural or not. And governments may be unenthusiastic about leaving a large surplus as a plaything for possible successors. In the immediate term attention has turned from cutting government deficits and debt to managing budget surpluses (Posner and Gordon 1999; OECD 1999). This is a relatively new phase in post-war budgeting.

Any relaxation in the impetus for continuing expenditure restraint is likely to shift the relationship between budget actors. Paradoxically, having now delivered surpluses the dominant position enjoyed by guardians will come under challenge and their ability to control aggregate expenditure is likely to be eroded. The existence of a surplus will tend to excite new demands for spending and spender arguments will have greater currency in budget decision-making. New priorities can now be afforded and previous stringency or rationing may be relaxed. Even relatively small policy-driven increases in spending will soon wipe out the relatively small budget surpluses recorded so far (Kelly & Wanna 2000a). However, the consequences of any relaxation have already been recognised by central budget agencies and other guardians and their arguments have quickly shifted from eliminating deficits to paying down debt.[18] The electoral advantages of this approach are that debt reduction appeals to the same groups with whom earlier

---

debt. Between 1993–94 and 1995–96, net public debt in Canada reached 70% of GDP. Although this has declined, it remained at 68.9% of GDP at the end of 1999; and public debt charges accounted for 26% of total federal government expenditure (MoF 1999).

17 For a comparison between Australia and Canada's concurrent success in achieving surpluses in the late 1990s see Kelly and Wanna (1999).

18 In some countries (e.g. Canada) no sooner were they able to eliminate deficits and produce small budget surpluses than government members began discussing ways of spending the 'fiscal dividend' as a reward for years of belt-tightening.

Table 11.5 Strategies and Options for Continuing Budget Surpluses

Strategy	Options	Potential Implications
1 Aim to accumulate the surplus—institutionalising the primacy of the guardians in setting tight aggregate limits.	1.1 Maintain as liquid reserve. 1.2 Invest or lend.	A conservative and inactive option in which surpluses are retained as an accumulated financial asset base of the government, but not otherwise utilised. Assets in the liquid reserve are credited against gross debt for calculating lower net debt. There are implicit costs of interest forgone if not utilised and potential erosion of the value of the reserve by inflation. This option is usually not considered preferable in modern economies. Surpluses can be accumulated for lending to the public or private sector. Government acts as a banker, potentially utilising the government's ability to borrow at lower rates than commercial borrowers. This option can impact on private capital markets and can be exploitative of tax payers. The financial asset base is also counted against gross debt for lower net debt. However, the asset base size and its easy liquidity can produce pressure for one-off grants to spending departments. The option is unlikely to work indefinitely. The purpose of accumulating surpluses will not necessarily be apparent. Perhaps the option is only suitable for simple economies or where governments can extract rents from a resource.
2 Aim to retire public debt—spenders constrained by the long-term strategy of the guardians.	2.1 Reduce principal debt levels.	Debt principal is progressively retired by governments paying down from each surplus. This is a conservative, financially risk-free option. Most appropriate when debt levels and interest rates are high. Can be used to reduce conflict between guardians and spenders if additional funds are released as lower interest payments are required. Surpluses can be disguised or technically avoided by calculating an amount for debt retirement within the annual budget as an expenditure item. Alternatively the surplus can be declared and debt paid down after the budget year. Available to complex economies but probably only over the medium-term and subject to the economic cycle.

Strategy	Options	Potential Implications
3 Aim to reallocate.	3.1 Tax reductions.	Tax reductions can be used as an electoral incentive or to reduce the size of government. Political/economic decisions can be made on the intended purpose, nature, extent and life-span of tax reductions. However, changes to taxation will have uncertain expansionary or contractionary macro-economic impacts depending upon reaction of corporate and consumer sectors (i.e. balance between private savings and private expenditure). There will also be greater pressure on budgets as the available surpluses decrease. Consequently not risk-free in either electoral or economic terms. Note that tax reductions can be illusory given the mix of taxes or the incidence of tax creep under conditions of inflation.
	3.2 Increase expenditures on recurrent items including transfers.	Increased expenditures can be presented as a dividend for past parsimony. Governments can re-prioritise their outlays and the promise of future expenditures may be electorally appealing (and constitute an incentive for governments deciding on current expenditure cuts). There will be immediate pressure on the size of the surplus and perhaps pressure on maintaining new recurrent allocations. Additional spending will increase the size of government. Will also have uncertain expansionary or contractionary macro-economic impacts depending upon the use of funds and market reactions. Although appearing benevolent, the option poses some electoral risks. Requires a capacity to ration requests for new expenditures on policy benefits v loss of surplus criteria, otherwise previous pattern is re-established.

Strategy	Options	Potential Implications
	3.3 Increase expenditure as strategic investment.	Guardian agencies provide incentives to enable spending and delivery agencies to 'pay their way' and reduce their dependence on general revenue (i.e. increase their future ability to make income-generating investment expenditure and/or reducing labour and other cost-cutting efficiencies). In Australia 'resource agreements' provided additional resources to reduce the long-term dependence on the budget for resources. But, spending agencies have the incentive and ability to disguise recurrent costs as investment expenditure if resource agreement monitoring is not effective.

restraint was successful; policies of debt constraint can in the short-term replace those of expenditure cutting.

Table 11.5 below categorises various options available to governments in this new environment. While renewed spending is a clear alternative to saving annual budget surpluses, expenditure itself is not one-dimensional and can be targeted toward different strategies, with implications for the government's future fiscal capacity and budgetary politics. The tabled options are not mutually exclusive and various components can be mixed. Governments are likely to prefer compromises even at the risk of sending confusing signals to electorates and markets. Following the logic of both Schick (1990) and Wildavsky (1975), the difficulties of budgeting in a new environment (here involving surpluses) will result in improvisational and *ad hoc* budgeting, or produce renewed impetus for budgetary reforms (and perhaps trigger a mixture of both). There are strong forces at work allowing surpluses to continue at least until debt levels have declined. In some nations the entire elimination of debt would take decades to achieve and almost certainly temporary surpluses would have disappeared over the economic cycle.

MAINTAINING SURPLUSES IN THE FUTURE

Compared to most OECD nations Australia has shown a remarkable capacity to make cuts and create surpluses. These have been achieved by a combination of political will, a disciplined bureaucracy and electoral acceptance. There has also been the equally important inclusion by successive governments of compensating or partially-compensating cuts in annual budgets. Arguably this fiscally responsible mindset has been adhered to by governments of all persuasions—broken only by the Whitlam government in 1974–75. This discipline requires that governments continually weigh up the costs and benefits of both old and new policies within a fiscal framework aimed at containing aggregate public spending. It is not implied that each year the weighing up was methodical or systematic—and, indeed, it was often partial and in some ways arbitrary. But such intra-governmental politics and practices have defused the 'balanced budget' arguments of the type heard in North America, allowing Australian governments greater policy freedom in defining 'sound financial management'. The emerging orthodoxy that views budget surpluses as the prime objective of government policy, as opposed to one of its outcomes, will further constrain the fiscal flexibility Australian governments have so long enjoyed and used with appropriate discretion.

It is not only by virtue of political and bureaucratic discipline that fiscal responsibility has been maintained; other structures and processes have also played a significant role. The Commonwealth's considerable taxing powers and the revenue-sharing arrangements with the states have long provided an expedient means of imposing top-down stringency on other levels of government. Cutting transfers to the states can be undertaken without great pain to Commonwealth programs or social transfers; although at the expense of distrust and deteriorating relationships with the states. These cuts, in turn, have forced state governments in the main to be frugal. Even if national governments find they have again to resort to deficit funding, they are still able to rely on fiscal federalism to help them balance subsequent budgets. The centralisation of political structures in Australian federalism considerably underscores the Commonwealth's capacity to budget. Notwithstanding the GST arrangements with the states (while initially advantaging the states, these are subject to change), the Commonwealth enjoys a structural and strategic position in Australian federalism rarely found in other federal nations.

Finally, to return to the international dimension of deficits and debt reduction. Debt removal has been promulgated as the new standard in public expenditure. If surpluses have now been achieved simultaneously by a number of advanced OECD nations, the same is not true for third world nations, with far greater economic problems and far more pressing humanitarian problems. It is likely now the developed nations that have taken the 'hard decisions' will begin to make demands for the same parsimony in nations far less able to cope. They will do this through the wide variety of international agencies and development banks they largely control and fund. The danger is that within the past few years a 'surplus orthodoxy' has been globalised. Poorer nations may suffer from this doctrine as their capacities to develop and compensate their populations will be not nearly as great as those of the advanced economies.

But, it is important to distinguish between types of indebtedness. Public debt *per se* is not a major problem for developing nations so long as it is used to promote future growth by investment in productive infrastructure and by skilling the population. However, public debt is particularly damaging to poorer economies when used to fund non-productive infrastructure or excessive current consumption (usually by local elites)—because future generations will be forced to pay the bill. Surpluses may be historically appropriate and at present popularly acceptable in many western nations, but similar arguments are not only less likely to be persuasive in developing nations, but potentially detrimental to their plight.

12 Is public expenditure better managed now?

AUSTRALIAN GOVERNMENTS HAVE embarked on a meandering journey of *budget reform* lasting over many decades. The commitment to reform may have wavered at times and the concern for budget discipline occasionally lapsed—usually during economic downturns. But the overall record has been fiscal conservatism combined with strong expenditure controls at the centre of government and a preparedness to experiment sequentially with reform initiatives. Despite the achievements of budgetary and financial reforms over the 1980s and 1990s, the process of reform is ongoing.

After all the changes in public expenditure management does government manage the public purse better today than previously? Have the reforms improved the government's management of expenditure? If improvements can be detected, are they qualitative or can benefits be demonstrated quantitatively? Have benefits been temporary or have lasting benefits occurred? And, can the real beneficiaries be identified? In order to assess Australia's management of public expenditure the first part of the chapter will summarise the evidence concerning what has changed. The second part presents explanations of why the changes were made, what differences they have made and why some but not others were effective. Finally, the chapter highlights the main arguments of the study suggesting a more comprehensive explanation of expenditure management.

WHAT HAS CHANGED? EVALUATING THE EVIDENCE

During the 1960s Australia's system of line-item budgeting was restrictive and inflexible, based on annual cash appropriations for specified items, and with minimal capacity to move resources to where they would be most efficient or effective. Although Parliament was presented with a detailed list of intended budgetary spending, in practice there was little or no management information on what or how resources were expended. The system was strong on *ex ante* controls but weak on expenditure management (Schick 1997). A complicated and labour intensive system of detailed controls was imposed on spending departments with limited effect, often structuring perverse incentives into resource demands and 'in-year' deployment. There was little emphasis on the performance of either departments or government-business enterprises. The single central budget agency—the Treasury—was preoccupied with managing post-war economic policy rather than managing the uses of public finance. And governments increasingly came to feel that budgets were unresponsive to political priorities and effectively beyond their political control.

Since that time, Australia's system of public expenditure has undergone considerable procedural and instrumental change. Together these changes have greatly expanded the potential for better decision-making, based on more transparent and reliable information. Within the context of a disciplined fiscal approach, the Australian budgetary system has emerged with the following distinctive characteristics. These are the essential attributes of the system as it stands and not a list of unqualified improvements.

Aggregate limits on spending have been imposed politically by guardians. The broad parameters for aggregate expenditure (and usually savings targets) are agreed by Treasury and Finance, and presented to a senior guardian ministers' strategic review involving the Prime Minister, Treasurer, Finance Minister and Deputy PM. DoFA advises on both savings options and where cuts can be targeted.

Budgets were allocated to organisational entities as a means of rationing overall resources. In the 1980s portfolio budgeting was devised to allow ERC to make allocative decisions between areas of government responsibility while preserving a political flexibility by allowing portfolio ministers to impose their own priorities within their total budget limits. Since 1999–2000 budgets have been allocated on an agency basis, within the accrual format, as a means of capturing their total economic events and forcing them to manage their resources more judiciously.

Central agencies developed rolling forward estimates of

expenditure assisted in both resource planning and policy decision-making. Over the 1980s tight forward estimates became the building blocks of the four-year rolling budget, where centrally determined estimates became the base budget for portfolios and agencies. Finance initially set these estimates unilaterally (after receiving some input from departments) and then placed considerable importance on the 'accuracy of the estimates' (Keating 1990b). Studies have verified the comparative accuracy of estimate forecasts to budget outcomes (*APS Reformed* 1992; Auditor-General 1998–99). More recently, the performance of DoFA has been judged according to the accuracy of the budget estimates to the operating result (within 0.5%)—an indicator also tied to the staff salary bonuses.[1] Gaining unilateral responsibility for the estimates enabled Finance to claim a more pronounced role in policy-making and enhancing its skills of policy analysis. Under the accruals format DoFA has withdrawn from the input of estimates data to scrutinising the estimates produced by departments to demonstrate quality assurance. There is less scope to 'pad' or inflate departmental estimates because both accrual accounting and sophisticated information management systems insist on consistency over time. And spending departments cannot insert higher numbers unless they have received approval or succeeded in their bids for new policy.

An additional advantage of 'hard' forward estimates is that ministers can realistically gauge the long-term costs of new policy initiatives or re-examine existing commitments. Operational managers are able to plan ahead knowing with a degree of certainty the likely resources they can expect. Increasingly, long-range 'pressures on budget' have also been modelled to accompany the agency-based estimates of expenditure.

Spending on new policy initiatives has been rationed. Governments experimented with various ways of curtailing spending departments attempting to augment their base budgets through 'bids' to secure resources for new policy. In the 1980s new policy bids were at times discouraged, then allowed only in the annual budget round (running the gauntlet of ERC). Since the early–1990s departments have had to find 'off-sets' from their existing allocations to cover new policy proposals. Moreover, the impact of the

1 Australia uses 'estimates' to indicate trend line commitments up to four years out that progressively roll into the final budget estimates. The accuracy of these forward estimates especially one year out is, thus, crucial to the management of expenditure.

senior ministers' review also narrowed the scope for new policy to those areas that encompass 'whole-of-government' core priorities.

Greater attention has been given to resource management and to more flexible procedures in financial management. Program structures and program management were introduced—essentially incorporating management by objectives into public administration and service provision. 'One line' budgets were gradually devised in which portfolios received separate 'lump sum' appropriations for their entire running costs. Within fixed parameters the running costs arrangements were progressively adapted and augmented to provide managerial flexibility. These adaptations allowed agencies successive increases in the allowable levels of carryovers or borrowings, revenue retention from the sale of goods and services was encouraged, and multi-year resource agreements enabled managers to manage their administrative resources over the medium term. Increasingly, operational managers were responsible for managing the full costs of their operations—and the adoption of accrual budgeting in 1999–2000 forced managers to manage depreciation and the cost of capital.

Devolution has coexisted with tighter central monitoring of resource usage. Relying on computerised information management systems and comprehensive ledger and register systems, DoFA can 'drill down' to examine patterns of resource use. It may withdraw or re-tighten flexibilities when agencies have mis-used the resource discretion at their disposal Generally, unless agencies depart markedly from their annual spending profile, Finance will not itself be concerned with 'in-year' expenditure controls. Rather, agencies are assessed on their operating results, cash-flows and final balance sheet. In addition, there has been a significant toughening in the requirement of financial reporting—since January 2000 agencies have been required to report publicly on a monthly basis in an accrual format.

Over the 1980s government-business enterprises were pushed entirely off-budget and the public account, and either sold off or compelled to perform on a profit basis. Their infrastructural or commercial activities became self-funding (implying no direct public funding from Consolidated Revenue) and they paid annual dividends back to governments as their stakeholders. While governments benefited in terms of the bottom line from the sale of these assets, they also removed many of the restrictions imposed on these enterprises enabling them to improve their returns, but often at the cost to the consumers. Governments simultaneously relieved themselves of any potential budget responsibility and the risks associated with continued public ownership.

From 1999 the Australian government adopted accrual budgeting and a resource monitoring framework based on an outcomes and outputs format. Parliamentary appropriations were structured around the purposes of outcomes. Amounts voted constitute the 'purchase prices' for specified outputs which include their own performance monitoring targets. Finance began to market test departmental estimates of 'output prices' through 'pricing reviews' as a method of cost containment and as a way of improving services. Agencies were also expected to show savings in the prices paid for services over time. However, agencies *set* the output definitions and are able (with the Finance minister's approval) to change or modify outputs/outcomes—making longitudinal pricing evaluations impossible. Agencies have become responsible for the costing methodology used in pricing reviews—encouraging a culture of exceptionalism and posing problems of comparability between agencies. Many outputs will remain difficult to cost precisely (or end in bureaucratic arguments), but there is growing concern that output expenses ought to be verified by a more robust method of pricing yet to be devised and agreed.

Many of these reforms *have* improved the management of public expenditure, but the contours of the present system should be viewed as the 'survivors' of a lengthy reform process. It is also instructive to consider which reforms were abandoned, either because they were deemed to have failed or had surpassed their usefulness. During the 1980s the quest to adopt program budgeting took on something of a 'holy grail' with officials treating the term as an incantation—a miraculous salvation for the ills of public finance. The 'implementation' of program budgeting remains one of the great myths of the recent era of Australian public sector management. It cannot be said that it was ever discontinued, because despite the rhetoric it was never implemented in the first place. As suggested in Chapter 7, program budgeting conflicted with existing budgetary norms, cut across the preferred allocative system to portfolios, and successive governments (and Parliament) were not prepared to appropriate running costs on a program basis. Yet this did not prevent a host of senior officials lauding the virtues of allocating by program and claiming program budgeting was actively being implemented. Yet, having exposed the myth, it is true that the *language* of program budgeting was important in enabling budget officials to reconceptualise the budget system and orient management towards the achievement of objectives.

Similarly, the fanfare with which the FMIP was announced in the early 1980s was not replicated when it was discontinued or superseded. The FMIP imploded under its own weight with too many conflicting objectives due to frequent redefinition. It was perhaps an important fillip at the time of introduction (highlighting deficiencies and preparing the way for subsequent reforms), but increasingly became outmoded and an impediment to further reform. So the FMIP was quietly shelved in 1990–91—ironically just as academics were beginning to 'discover' it as one of the essential elements of managerialism. Three major reviews failed to demonstrate any quantitative benefits attributable to the FMIP except perceptions from senior management that it was part of a broader set of improvements in resource management.

In Australia's recent experience, budgetary initiatives were quietly discontinued especially if they became problematic or had outlived their primary usefulness. Cash ceilings were imposed on departments with great relish in the 1970s but quickly abandoned when other more effective means of controlling departmental expenditure evolved. Staff budgeting was sacrificed to financial management controls throughout the mid-1980s (with some residual controls maintained on executive numbers and salaries until the early 1990s). The early production of forward estimates by spending departments was never taken seriously nor incorporated into the budget process, and the process itself was gradually enervating before central budget agencies (first Treasury and then Finance) centralised their production and aligned them to budget estimates in the out-years. Various forms of evaluation were attempted, some internal, some joint management, some external, but while these reviews may have influenced policy choices and program development, the process of evaluation was rarely an integral part of the budget process. Program evaluation reached its apogee under the Hawke and Keating governments but was dying a slow death even before it was jettisoned by the Coalition after 1996.

Why did the Changes Occur? The Explanations

When Donald Savoie (1990) evaluated the effectiveness of reforms undertaken in Canada by the Trudeau and Mulroney governments over the 1980s, he concluded that he could not tell whether the reforms and the attempts to curb expenditure growth had been successful—but added that if they had not been put in place the situation may well have been worse! Savoie reasoned that although governments had been spectacularly unsuccessful in meeting its declared goals of restraint, 'if the growth in government spending had been left unchecked. . . the main estimates for 1990–91 would be considerably higher' (1990:172). Having *some* announced targets and weak controls was perhaps better than having none. In short, he awarded a 'pass conceded' for effort.

The main argument in Savoie's account is that in Canada the spending agencies were able to maintain the upper-hand in the politics of the budget process. This explains the relatively consistent pattern of expenditure *increases* during a decade of rhetoric about restraint and of governments setting (but not achieving) regular targets to control expenditures. The clearest feature to emerge from Canada's struggle to control budgets is that the behaviour and respective powers of the principal budget actors is the principal determinant of budgetary management over time. These relationships are heavily dependent on the authority of the guardian agencies and the preparedness of the Prime Minister and/or Finance minister to both insist on parameters and then adhere to them. However, institutional authority and sheer political will are necessary components but not sufficient on their own to contain expenditures. As the Canadian record shows, guardians frequently talked tough and successive prime ministers articulated a personal determination to contain or reduce spending only to fail when confronted with political realities and economic pressures.

By contrast, Australia has won a hard-earned reputation in recent years for its capacity to manage budgets, impose aggregate spending limits on agencies, and maintain fiscal discipline over time (GAO 2000). Sound financial management and budget discipline have arisen as the main fiscal priorities of Australian governments of both persuasions over the past 20 years. Budget rationing rather than budget maximising has become the Australian creed. From the evidence assembled in this present study a plausible explanation can be presented which attributes success in budgetary management to:

- the unique political structures, tax arrangements and fiscal federalism of Australia;
- ideological and cultural norms;
- ministerial and institutional configurations; and
- the politics of the budget process.

These various levels of explanation are not discrete but invariably interrelated and interdependent.

First, the Constitution greatly empowers the Commonwealth government over the nation's purse strings, giving it considerable 'persuasive power' over the states. It is able to dictate the level of resources devoted to particular policy areas—irrespective of whether they fall directly within its specified powers. Much of the Commonwealth's power is exercised through negotiations with the states, where it is able to tie and fix limits to special purpose payments. The Commonwealth also possesses considerable budgetary leverage by controlling the principal sources of taxation, raising some 75% of total revenue. It is more able to balance its budgetary needs by either varying taxes (or non-indexing tax rates) or restraining the funds transferred to the states for their own uses.

However, unlike the states, the Commonwealth is not principally involved with the delivery of services, and in recent years has sought to withdraw further from the direct delivery of goods and services (by transferring implementation responsibilities to the states or privatising public commercial assets). Only a relatively small proportion of Commonwealth outlays—about 19% and falling—is comprised of discretionary spending on outputs delivered by Commonwealth agencies. The other 81% of outlays are in the form of standing appropriations or special appropriations (payments to the states or personal entitlements). If necessary, the criteria governing these forms of payments can be adjusted or tightened at the discretion of the Commonwealth. Arguably, because the Commonwealth controls the purse strings for activities performed by others, it is more able to contain spending pressures than if it were more heavily involved in these activities itself. The largest single item of Commonwealth spending goes to social welfare entitlements, which inevitably implies that the economic cycle remains one of the main determinants of the *level* of public expenditure (determining actual revenue receipts and the associated magnitude of benefit payments related to the level of unemployment).

Second, deep-seated ideological and cultural norms shape the 'politics of the possible' and the populist degree of acceptance for policy positions. Australian expectations of government are largely shaped by practical experience and the customary responsibilities governments have traditionally undertaken. Basic attitudes remain ambivalent: on the one hand, governments are expected to assist in times of need or market failure; on the other there is little acceptance of big government and high taxing. Policy options are cut to the cloth of available resources. Australian governments have, like many of their OECD counterparts, been forced by electoral pressures to curb spending. The past nine federal elections have each featured intense debates about tax—the types or mix of taxation, levels of tax, or commitments to reduce tax. Occasionally, limits to the levels of spending have also become political issues, causing successive governments to target their spending to best suit their priorities. While Australia does not have a large welfare state by comparison with other OECD nations, it uses means testing and program targeting to direct resources to the more needy sections of the community. Moreover, the principles of targeting public expenditure are generally understood and accepted by the community. Ideological preferences for less bureaucratic forms of government and service delivery have empowered neo-liberals and economic rationalists within government concerned to cut costs and enhance performance.

Third, governments have devised the ministerial and institutional apparatuses to restrain expenditure growth, review existing patterns of outlays and direct spending to areas of immediate priority. Institutional constraints centre on the power and behaviour of the principal budget guardian actors. A standing cabinet committee—the ERC—serves as the powerful epicentre of the budget process, rationing budgets, imposing discipline, coordinating the processes and taking budget decisions. The significance of this political committee of senior ministers cannot be over-emphasised in maintaining discipline over the public purse. Generally since the late–1970s the ERC has been dominated by ministers who have adopted an economic rationalist and market-inspired approach to the role of government, with a degree of scepticism over the value of public spending, but a commitment to achieve their policy priorities while in government. Their main task has been to impose discipline on their ministerial colleagues while controlling the spending appetites of departments (who, it must be said, have often *not* behaved as classic budget maximisers). On only a couple of occasions since 1975 have governments resorted to large spend-ups, and in both cases the governments in question had occupied office for a number of terms and were uncertain of their electoral future. If ERC was important in screening decisions and imposing political restraint, the maintenance of discipline was not solely dependent on the political will of this committee. Budget agencies were equally active, if not more so, in seeking to impose fairly strict discipline on both aggregate expenditure and departmental spending.

Australia operates with two functionally discrete budget agencies, which operate as a 'tag-team' in the annual budget process and generally maintain close working relations. Treasury advises on economic policy, overseeing tax and monetary policy. As the central budget agency, DoFA is responsible for the expenditure budget, public assets and asset sales, resource management across the public sector and accounting policies for government. After the splitting of Treasury in 1976, Finance emerged as a powerful central agency pushing experimental budgetary reform and broader managerial public sector reforms. Arguably, Finance has been the principal influence in public sector reform consistently over the past two decades—driven largely by the creativity of its senior management. Few other agencies have pushed the reform agenda in the public sector (by comparison, Treasury has been largely uninterested in public service reform, except in competition policy; and PM&C has focused on the prime minister's agenda and political issue management). Finance earned a reputation for being tough-minded and 'hard to convince' without strong supporting evidence. But also Finance gradually switched from emphasising centralised budget *control* to introducing improved resource frameworks. It has been able to focus more systematically on savings, cost reduction, value for money and the provision of counter-advice—separately or irrespective of other fiscal considerations (e.g., the business cycle or the political preferences for either contractionary or expansionary budgets). This has been the main institutional effect of the creation of a separate ministry for budgetary management (Sedgwick Interview 1996).

Fourth, reforms to the budget process enhanced the power of guardians while simultaneously allowing budget dependent agencies to improve their resource usage. Though guardian-spender relations see-saw over time, Australian budgetary practices have consolidated the power of guardian agencies and centralised the *important components* necessary to maintain budgetary control. Thus, there has been comparatively little opportunity for spending agencies to escape constraints by back-sliding or 'seepage'. Regular 'savings' exercises have cut funds from spending agencies, freeing those resources for re-allocation. Internal budget processes enabled governments to re-prioritise their commitments while adhering to budget parameters. DoFA has 'moved out of the detail' in the budget process by devolving the construction of estimates for ongoing expenditure to agencies; evaluating agencies through their financial statements, operating results and balance sheet information. Budget review traditionally focused on cost-efficiency but is increasingly moving to the measurement of performance and effectiveness. Spending agencies have tended to use their discretion *within* their limits rather than work *against* them. Although the promotion of new policy initiatives allowed spending departments at times to supplement their budget base, these avenues for 'gaming' over new policy were significantly reduced by regular changes to, and tightening of, budgetary regulations. The development of an updated medium-term fiscal plan in the mid–1990s has further sought to impose discipline on budgetary decision-making, through both the executive and Parliament.

Highlighting the Theoretical Arguments: Creating an Explanation of Expenditure Management

Budgeting represents a fundamental expression of power within government and society. The most apparent expression of this is through the particular configuration of public goods and services provided to the community including the transfers of resources across social groups. Less apparent are the means by which budgets structure social behaviour. Systems of resource allocation will significantly structure the behaviour of the recipients and establish intended or unintended internal incentive structures. How something is budgeted can be as important as what is budgeted. Australia's preference for resourcing portfolios and agencies provides a good illustration of this point. Organisational entities become privileged structures; they consolidate funds to undertake various and often competing tasks. The agency is the bargaining unit empowered to negotiate over resource issues. It has discretion over what it applies for, how it internally allocates and spends resources, and what it delivers for the money. It will also respond 'rationally' and self-interestedly to prevailing budgetary norms. So, in stating budgets are a form of power, it is worth noting they have also become one of the main internal organising principles of government.

The politics of the Australian budget process have been dominated by guardians, and this feature alone principally explains Australia's consistent record of fiscal discipline. Only when Prime Ministers (not always themselves guardians) have thrown caution to the wind has spending 'blown-out'. But this has been a relatively rare occurrence over the past 40 years. In particular, ERC 'locks-in' decisions on restraint by fixing a cascading set of budget parameters and adhering to them throughout the budget round. DoFA also enjoys a strategic position in being able to advise on policy and questions of value for money—directly to its own minister and to ERC ministers scrutinising existing expenditure and bids for new policy. But the power of guardians is not unchanging or unilaterally established. The 'devil's advocate' role remains an important part of the infrastructure of budgetary management. Periods of relative stability or reform consolidation may shift power back to the spending agencies, and procedural changes may also carry unintended risks. For example, there remains a concern that by withdrawing from the detailed setting of estimates, DoFA will lose both policy skills and its analytical expertise in being able to assure the quality of the estimates information to government. Such a loss of expertise would undermine the importance to government of the role performed by its central budget agency. Yet, envisioning subsequent changes might be a means of keeping spending agencies on their toes in the future.

Hence, political and bureaucratic will is crucial to expenditure control and management—the major dilemmas here (and empirical issues) are with questions of what engenders political/institutional will, how does it develop, how does it survive, and by what means can it remain effective over time? Many factors influence the qualities and dimensions of political will—for example, political circumstances or electoral cycles, party political persuasion, length of incumbency, the personalities of the leaders and senior managers, as well as the institutional arrangements within which actors articulate their preferences.

Australian budgetary reform has been pragmatic not programatic. Reforms have not been linear or teleological, and if some evolutionary logic can be detected it is one of disjointed evolution. Reforms have been contested, tried, abandoned, marked by many twists and turns, with central agencies sometimes changing their minds about the virtues of specific endeavours (even at times denying they attempted some changes). Many reforms were dependent on the development and increasing widespread use of information systems and computer technology. Prevailing fads and fashions may have inspired the agendas of budget reform, but to take-on ideas also had to be promoted when the system was ready to accept them.[2] At one level this could be seen as another example of 'patching up' the system or 'muddling through', but at another level it is reminiscent of emergent strategies empowered by technology and tempered by experience. Fashion may have influenced the agendas but their adoption and consolidation was subject to selection. Reforms were implemented piecemeal in the knowledge that changes were not irrevocable (Keating Interview 1996). Australia's political system and style of government makes it difficult for reform to be other than incremental following the principles of trial and error. And, over the 1980s to 1990s Australia demonstrated a propensity to experiment with budget reform.

While some reformers will argue that their reforms were consistent with a set of principles, those very principles were both multi-dimensional and have themselves changed over time, often beyond recognition. The coherence of multiple, experimental-based reform agendas is therefore problematic. It may be possible to manufacture a story of *intended coherence* over the main surviving reform initiatives, but this overlooks the often chaotic ways in which reforms emerged or were shaped by events. Indeed, one of the major reforms in Australian budgeting—the assignment of flexible budgets to portfolios—crept up almost stealthily on the reformers. It was never part of any intended strategy nor was it particularly acknowledged as a crucial part of the system until well after it had become operational. Certainly, in retrospect, Australia appears to have devised a rigorous infrastructure for maintaining budgetary discipline, similar to that recommended by Schick (1996) or Campos and Pradhan (1996).[3] But if Australia has acquired this model of control, it basically stumbled into these attributes (see Shead 2000:17–26). Many of the attributes now regarded as 'indispensable' came about as a result of expedient political reactions to immediate budgetary mismanagement.

Relative to other countries, Australian budget reforms were driven by public servants not by ministers. Mostly officials were

---

2 For example, the Public Service Board promoted an initiative to establish a 'productivity investment fund' in 1982—an idea ahead of its time and a forerunner of 'resource agreements'. The PSB's suggestion was not taken up, principally because other 'budget disciplines' were not then in place and because other central agencies were not confident that spending agencies would deliver productivity improvements without other flexibilities.

3 Campos and Pradhan (1996) undertook a major international review of budgetary institutions examining their effectiveness in imposing aggregate fiscal discipline. They concluded that three criteria were important in exercising such discipline: the adoption of a medium-term fiscal framework, the dominance of the central budget agency and the existence of enforceable constraints on spending and deficits (including sanctions against overspending).

not operating from the first principles of 'theory' nor had they read the literatures of public choice or new institutional economics. Rather, a culture developed among senior guardian officials conducive to reform-minded initiatives. Certainly, ministers gave their imprimatur or tacit acceptance, but ministers 'weren't interested' in reform (Keating Interview 1996). Although it is clear that guardian officials drove the reform agendas, it is also clear they were not always sure of where they were heading or the consequences of their actions.

The *impact* of reform also lags behind their introduction (Visbord Interview 1996). Many budgetary reforms have had lasting impact, but their impacts are not always evident at the time of implementation—rather the consequences were felt later, often years after the height of the promotion of the particular reform. Moreover, reforms suffer from declining utility, they outlive their usefulness, and frequently ought to be replaced or revised to allow guardian actors to remain on top. Paradoxically, the duration of time both creates the conditions for reform impact and the declining utility of the reform instruments—judgment is needed to gauge when the disbenefits begin to outweigh the benefits. Guardians may need to change budget rules not necessarily because existing rules are deficient but because over time spending departments will become accustomed to them and find ways of subverting them.

Australian reforms have tended to take on an overt *financial bias* (rather than a policy bias or one based on capacity building). Accordingly, one consequence of Australia's pattern of reform is that it has largely been 'path dependent' in two senses—the chosen areas of experimentation opened up new possibilities for change (but closed off other options simultaneously); and the reform 'path' chosen privileged financial agendas at the expense of more general management qualities or alternative ways of achieving objectives. Whether Australia's path of financial-driven reforms is good, bad or neutral will depend largely on cultural and ideological beliefs—what it is that one expects of government and how one views the nature and role of the public sector.

Budgeting still remains largely an incremental exercise but it is *not just* incremental. This study indicates that there is scope for more significant adjustments, for periodic re-allocation, and for strategic considerations to inform decision making.

So, can a more comprehensive explanation of expenditure management be developed? To return to the definition provided in Chapter 1, the management of public expenditure is concerned with the *planning, management, control and accountability of public financial resources from the point at which those resources enter the public domain, up to the point at which they leave.* If this is the subject matter, then a comprehensive explanation has to have both general applicability and be operational. It would need to include recognition of the *pressures and measures* impacting on budget processes, combining both immediate and long-term horizons. It would recognise the distinct and competing *cycles or trajectories governing politics and economics* (electoral cycles, honeymoons, loss of credibility, business cycles, economic growth phases). More particularly, it ought to provide explanations for *budget systems and frameworks*, patterns of *resource management, policy preferences and the strategic capacities* to pursue goals, the *performance* of management and the *outcomes* of decisions, and the forms of *accountability* for spending collective resources through government. Most importantly, it is the relationships between these various building blocks that are crucial to a comprehensive account.

A robust explanation has to avoid narrow sets of assumptions (of human nature, behaviour, power or moral extremes) or type-casting of actors and motivations. It has to encompass a rich set of institutional and political relations that negotiate and network over resources on an ongoing basis. And it has to include the structure of incentives, the nature of rules and gaming, and *budgets as institutions of power.* It should permit recognition of various actor beliefs, operating from various narratives of action and reaction. A questioning and sceptical eye is preferable especially when faced with the claims of officials or when asked to accept official versions or re-writings of events. And it should allow scope for the imperfectable, for unintended consequences or chance happenings; and for infuriation over 'stubborn facts'. This study has used these premises in progressing an explanatory framework.

Appendix A.1

PRIME MINISTERS, TREASURERS AND MINISTERS FOR FINANCE & ADMINISTRATION 1949–2000[1]

Prime Minister	Term of Office
John Howard	March 1996–present
Paul Keating	December 1991–March 1996
Bob Hawke	March 1983–December 1991
Malcom Fraser	November 1975–March 1983
Gough Whitlam	December 1972–November 1975
Bill McMahon	March 1971–December 1972
John Gorton	January 1968–March 1971
John McEwen	December 1967–January 1968
Harold Holt	January 1966–December 1967
Robert Menzies	December 1949–January 1966

Treasurer	Term of Office
Peter Costello	March 1996–present
Ralph Willis	December 1993–March 1996
John Dawkins	December 1991–December 1993
Ralph Willis	December 1991–December 1991
John Kerrin	June 1991–December 1991
Bob Hawke	3 June 1991–4 June 1991
Paul Keating	March 1983–June 1991
John Howard	November 1977–March 1983
Phillip Lynch	November 1975–November 1977
Bill Hayden	June 1975–November 1975
Jim Cairns	December 1974–June 1975
Frank Crean	December 1972–December 1974
Billy Snedden	March 1971–December 1972
Les Bury	November 1969–March 1971
Bill McMahon	January 1966–November 1969
Harold Holt	December 1958–January 1966
Arthur Fadden	December 1949–December 1958

Minister for Finance & Administration	Term of Office
John Fahey	March 1996–present
Kim Beazely	December 1993–March 1996
Ralph Willis	April 1990–December 1993
Peter Walsh	December 1984–April 1990
John Dawkins	March 1983–December 1984
Margaret Guilfoyle	November 1980–March 1983
Eric Robinson	February 1979–November 1980
John Howard	23 February 1979–27 February 1979
Eric Robinson	December 1977–February 1979
Phillip Lynch	December 1976–December 1977

1 The Minister for finance bacame the Minister for finance and Admnistration in October 1997.

Appendix A.2

SECRETARIES TO THE DEPARTMENTS OF PRIME MINISTER & CABINET, TREASURY, AND FINANCE & ADMINISTRATION 1949–2000[1]

Secretary to Prime Minister & Cabinet	Duration of Appointment
Max Moore-Wilton	May 1996–present
Mike Keating	December 1991–May 1996
Michael Codd	February 1986–December 1991
Geoffrey Yeend	April 1978–February 1986
Alan Carmody	October 1976–April 1978
John Menadue	February 1975–October 1978
John Bunting	March 1971–February 1975
Lennox Hewitt	March 1968–March 1971
John Bunting	January 1959–March 1968
Allen Brown	August 1949–December 1958

Secretary to Treasury	Duration of Appointment
Ted Evans	March 1993–present
Anthony Cole	February 1991–March 1993
Christopher Higgins	September 1989–December 1990
Bernie Fraser	September 1984–September 1989
John Stone	January 1979–September 1984
Frederick Wheeler	November 1971–January 1979
Richard Randall	October 1966–November 1971
Roland Wilson	April 1951–October 1966
G.P.N. Watt	November 1948–March 1951

1 The Department of Prime Minister and Cabinet was the Department of Prime Minister prior to 1971. The Department of Finance and Administration was the Department of Finance prior to October 1997.

Secretary to Finance & Administration	Duration of Appointment
Peter Boxall	January 1997–present
Stephen Sedgwick	February 1992–January 1997
Mike Keating	April 1986–December 1991
Ian Castles	January 1979–April 1986
William Cole	December 1976–January 1978

Appendix B

A BRIEF CHRONOLOGY OF FORWARD ESTIMATES IN AUSTRALIA 1965–2000

Date	Developments and Events
1965	A precursor to a formal system of 'forward expenditure estimates' begins. Informal 3-year trend projections of current budget items from line departments collated by the Treasury. Projections were not seen as commitments, and ministers were not involved in the process. Primarily, the data was used for macro-economic policy planning purposes and to calculate revenue and debt requirements.
March 1971	System of forward estimates for outlays introduced by then Treasurer, Les Bury. Spending departments still prepare forward estimates which were calculated on a three-year basis and presented in *constant cost* terms. They included the cost of new policy proposals ministers intended to put to Cabinet. Ministerial endorsement was sought for these estimates. The estimates were used as 'bids' for increased funding by departments but the system was not utilised in budget preparation, due to change in government.
1972	Forward estimates reports produced for internal use only by Treasury officials. They were not available to anyone outside Treasury, including the Prime Minister and the Treasurer.
1972 to 1975	Efforts made to widen access to the forward estimates by Department of Prime Minister and Cabinet and by the PM's private office. In 1974, Whitlam's economic adviser was 'allowed' to 'see' Treasury's forward estimates, but not to take the originals or a copy from the Treasury building.

Date	Developments and Events
1975	Attempt by Treasury to 'upgrade' and incorporate forward estimates into the budget process. Major focus still on current years and macroeconomic and monetary policy uses. Primary objective was the provision of information for macro-economic planning and increased flexibility in expenditure. In addition, information collected from departments ostensibly formed the starting point for budget negotiations. But departments were reluctant to 'rank' programs and give information on staffing. Despite increased usage, low regard for usefulness of forward estimates by both departments and Treasury meant they were little more than ambit bids for increased funding. There was also incompatibility between some programs and Treasury's forecasting techniques.
1976	Fraser government announces that forward estimates will be collected on a one-year rather than three-year basis. These estimates were determined on a *current costs* basis and included expenditure on policy proposals.
November 1976	Department of Finance established when the Treasury is split. Finance's primary responsibility is the control and coordination of the federal government's public expenditure. Finance assumes responsibility for the expenditure side of the budget. Budget estimates and forward expenditure estimates are included for the first time. Revenue policy (including revenue estimates) remain with the Treasury.
1978–79	After a review of forward expenditure estimates and budget procedures, the former are only produced for programs which receive Cabinet approval.
March 1983	Forward expenditure estimates published for the first time in a document entitled 'Forward Estimates on Budget Outlays'. Provided in a 'raw' form and on *current price* basis (as received by Finance from departments). Aimed to 'provide a first view of the prospective level of budget outlays estimates (by departments) to be necessary to maintain approved on-going programs'. Detailed information is provided on functional basis. Forward revenue estimates are still not published.
March 1985	Finance takes over responsibility from line departments for determination of all forward expenditure estimates apart from non-salary and administrative expenses. For 14 years DoF effectively determines forward estimates unilaterally (but still relying on some information from departments).

Date	Developments and Events
November 1985	Two major changes occur: a) forward estimates are published immediately after the budget debates (to incorporate the budgetary implications of policy changes); b) time period covered by forward estimates reduced (from 3 to 2 years). The 'Budget' becomes 'year one' of three year estimates.
March 1986	Finance takes over total responsibility for preparation of forward estimates—all provision for departmental 'bids' removed. A return to three out-years. Expenditure on 'technical new policy' is included in forward estimates to allow for the renewal of lapsed programs. This is the beginning of formal incorporation into the budget process –'forward estimates were 'upgraded' to form the basis for formulating following years' budget'. Also the beginning of the system of four-year rolling forward estimates.
November 1986	The *Report on Forward Estimates on Budget Outlays* presents forward estimates as 'an agreed upon figure for policy continuation'. From this point onward, any changes in forward estimates are deemed to indicate changes in government policy or economic parameters—'forward estimates provide a benchmark from which future changes can be measured'.
1986–88	Finance publishes regular updates of forward estimates to incorporate changes in government policy and economic parameters which form the underlying assumptions for forward estimate calculations.
August 1987	Beginning of publishing official forward estimates *in the budget papers*. Reconciliation tables published in the Budget Statement on Outlays. This links budget estimates with forward estimates and explains areas of divergence.
August 1988	Budget Statement No 3 publishes the forward estimates of expenditure for budget and first forward year.
August 1989	Three-year forward estimates included in the Budget Outlays Statement—on both an aggregate and detailed level. A separate report on forward estimates is no longer published.
1990 onward	Forward estimates calculated and updated formally 3 times a year, usually August, January and May. Process means that forward estimates published in one year's budget papers becomes the next year's budget estimates, adjusted for changes in policy and economic parameters. DoF introduces a quasi-indexation of the out-year estimates (*outturn costing*).
August 1994	Forward revenue estimates published for the first time as part of 1994–95 Budget Statement No. 4.
October 1996	DoF publishes performance information on the accuracy of its outlay estimates in its own annual report.

Date	Developments and Events
November 1997	'Carryovers' are included in the estimates for the budget each year.
1997–98	DoFA works with agencies to achieve the decentralisation of estimates construction by June 1998. Finance is to maintain a quality assurance role—memorandums of Understanding and Quality Assurance Protocols are developed by DoFA to govern construction of the estimates. DoFA initially inputs the agency-constructed data into FIRM software, which is replaced by the Accruals Information Management System (AIMS) in late 1998.
1999–2000	Agencies can enter their estimates directly into the AIMS system. Estimates continue to reflect 'outturn' prices (the prices levels expected of the relevant year of the estimate). Independent audit of budget and forward estimates covering a twenty-year period to 1996–97 finds a high degree of accuracy, although overall estimate targets were only partially achieved.

Appendix C

FUNCTIONAL ALLOCATION OF COMMONWEALTH OUTLAYS 1975–76 TO 2003–04 AS A PROPORTION OF TOTAL BUDGET OUTLAYS (%)[1]

Functional Area	1975–76	1979–80	1981–82	1988–89	1993–94	2000–01[2]	2003–04[2]
General Public Services	6.1	6.14	6.35	6.65	6.16	9.39	7.94
Defence	8.5	9.50	9.99	8.80	8.50	5.97	5.46
Public Order & Safety	0.5	0.63	0.62	0.82	0.75	0.65	0.52
Education	8.4	8.24	8.08	7.26	8.34	6.14	5.81
Health	13.5	10.[illegible]1	7.04	12.98	14.04	14.10	13.63
Social Security & Welfare	23.2	27.74	27.82	28.93	36.17	36.79	33.60
Housing, Urban & Amenities	4.5	1.52	1.45	1.46	1.10	1.15	0.78
Recreation, Arts & Culture	1.2	1.01	1.16	1.25	1.20	0.84	0.62
Mining & Fuel	–	0.05	0.14	0.57	0.51	0.50	0.33
Agriculture, Forestry & Fishing	0.8[3]	0.63	0.53	1.83	1.42	0.95	0.71
Transport & Communications	6.1	2.55	2.85	2.07	1.12	1.16	0.85
Other Economic Affairs	2.2	2.44	2.97	2.49	3.83	2.10	1.79
Other Purposes	24.7	29.45	30.93	24.82	16.80	20.18	27.88

1 Figures adapted from Budget Paper No 1, 1981–82 pp. 64, 137–160; Budget Paper No 1, 1983–84 pp. 72, 161–192, 380–387; Budget Paper No 1, 1993–94 pp. 3.281, 3.285–3.289; and Budget Paper No 1, 2000–2001 pp. 1.35, 6.81–6.83.

2 Figures for 2000–01 and 2003–04 are derived from the accrual budget estimates of functions. The figures are not directly comparable with the previous years—for example, in 2000–01 the defence portfolio spending was around $19 billion representing 10.2% of Commonwealth outlays, but the Budget Papers (2000–01: 6.81) showed only $10.6 billion attributable to the function of defence (or 5.97% of Commonwealth Expenses).

3 Agriculture, Forestry & Fishing function for 1975–76 also includes Mining and Fuel function.

Appendix D

REAL GROWTH IN COMMONWEALTH OUTLAYS 1969–70 TO 2001–02 FOR THE GENERAL GOVERNMENT SECTOR*

	Outlays		Revenue		Cash Surplus
Budget Year	Estimate $m	% real growth	Estimate $m	% real growth	Estimate $m
1969–70	6 131	2.1	7 097	8.6	966
1970–71	7 176	10.2	8 000	6.1	824
1971–72	7 987	4.5	8 827	3.6	840
1972–73	9 [illegible]20	7.0	9 414	–0.1	294
1973–74	10 829	3.8	11 890	10.4	1 061
1974–75	15 275	15.5	15 325	5.6	50
1975–76	19 876	12.1	18 316	3.0	–1 560
1976–77	22 657	2.0	21 418	4.7	–1 239
1977–78	25 439	3.3	23 491	0.7	–1 998
1978–79	27 753	2.9	25 666	3.2	–2 087
1979–80	31 041	[illegible].8	29 780	5.6	–1 261
1980–81	35 260	2.8	35 148	6.8	–112
1981–82	40 394	2.1	40 831	3.5	437
1982–83	47 907	6.4	44 675	–1.9	–3 232
1983–84	55 966	9.9	49 102	3.4	–6 864
1984–85	63 639	7.5	57 758	11.2	–5 881
1985–86	69 838	3.3	64 845	5.6	–4 993
1986–87	75 392	1.1	73 145	5.6	–2 247
1987–88	79 440	–1.5	81 217	3.8	1 777
1988–89	82 202	–4.2	88 369	0.8	6 167
1989–90	88 882	1.8	95 517	1.7	6 635
1990–91	97 333	4.9	97 705	–2.0	372
1991–92	104 551	5.5	92 966	–6.5	–11 585
1992–93	111 484	5.[illegible]	94 448	0.1	–17 036

	Outlays		Revenue		Cash Surplus
Budget Year	Estimate $m	% real growth	Estimate $m	% real growth	Estimate $m
1993–94	117 252	4.2	100 142	5.0	–17 110
1994–95	122 901	4.6	109 720	9.3	–13 181
1995–96	131 182	4.0	121 105	7.5	–10 077
1996–97	135 126	1.0	129 845	5.2	–5 281
1997–98	134 608	–1.6	135 779	3.3	1 171
1998–99	141 033	4.0	146 521	7.2	4 190
1999–00[2]	155 930	na	163 726	na	7 795
2000–01[3]	150 959	–5.8	153 803	–8.6	2 844
2001–02[4]	156 994	1.6	160 205	1.7	3 211

**Source:* adapted from Budget Paper No. 1 2000–01 p. 8.42 (Table D1).
Estimates.

Bibliography and references

INTERVIEWS WITH KEY EXPENDITURE BUDGET ACTORS

Barrett, Pat. 13.06.1996*
Bartos, Steve. 08.02.1994; 10.05.1995; 19.06.1996
Carroll, John. 24.06.1996
Carter, George. 01.10.1996
Castles, Ian. 15.09.1986†; 21.06.1996
Cole, William. 17.07.1996*
Craik, Don. 23.06.96; 15.12.1996
Davis, Steve. 15.10.1996
Dawkins, John 07.02.2000*
Early, Len. 01.09.1996
Fraser, Malcolm. 28.02.1997*
Goodwin, Paul. 15.10.1996
Guilfoyle, Margaret. 26.06.1996
Hehir, Grant. 15.10.1996
Helgeby, Stein. 06.03.1997; 30.09.1998
Henry, Keith. 09.10.1996
Keating, Mike. 21.01.1987†; 26.6.1996
Kennedy, Maurie. 15.10.1996
Khan, Abdul. 01.10.1996
Matthews, Ted. 20.06.1996
Mackay, Keith. 09.10.1996
McPhee, Ian. 15.10.1996
McRae, Ian. 16.10.1996
Moffat, Graham. 09.10.1996
Monaghan, Cyril. 04.04.2000
Monaghan, John. 22.03.2000
Nethercote, John. 21.06.1996
Nicholls, George. 24.06.1996
Olliffe, Tony. 01.10.1996
Sedgwick, Steve. 15.10.1996
Taylor, John. 11.06.1996; 18.06.1996
Venner, Mary. 15.10.1996
Visbord, Ed. 02.07.1986†; 05.02.1997
Wallace, Dean. 16.10.1996
Walsh, Cliff. 25.09.1986†
Walsh, Peter. 03.10.1996
Weller, Patrick. 10.03.1997
Wilde, Peter. 15.10.1996

* *those interviews with an asterisk were completed by telephone; all others were face-to-face (by the authors).*

† *Transcribed interviews undertaken by Patrick Weller.*

OFFICIAL REPORTS/GOVERNMENT AND PARLIAMENTARY DOCUMENTS/MINISTERIAL AND OFFICIAL SPEECHES

ALP (Australian Labor Party) (1983) *Labor and Quality of Government,* (Hawke, R. and Evans, G.) 9th February. ALP. Canberra.

APS Reformed, see Task Force on Management Improvement.

Auditor-General (1998–99) *Management of Commonwealth Budgetary Processes: Preliminary Study.* Audit Report No.38. Performance Audit. Australian National Audit Office. Canberra.

Bartos, S. (2000) 'Performance Management in the Australian Public Service', Presentation to the Business Innovation Group. 26 April. Canberra.

Boxall, P. (1999) 'How the Reforms Fit Together: An Australian Perspective.' *CBPA,* No 88. May.

Boxall, P. (2000) 'Australia's Outcomes and Outputs Framework' Presentation to the OECD's Budget Committee. 30 May.

Budget Reform Agenda (1984) Report to Joint Council, November.

Caiden, G.E. (1975) *Task Force on Efficiency Working Paper: Towards a More Efficient Government Administration.* AGPS. Canberra.

Castles, I. (1983) Minute from I. Castles to Prime Minister 03.02.1983.

Castles, I. (1984) Letter from I. Castles to P. Wilenski 13.1.1984.

Cole, W. (1983) Letter from W. Cole to I. Castles 23.2.1983.

Commonwealth of Australia (1976) *Parliamentary Debates (Hansard).* 18 November. AGPS. Canberra.

Commonwealth of Australia (1981) Functional Classification of Outlays—Departmental Estimates 1981–82. AGPS. Canberra

Commonwealth of Australia (1984) *Budget Reform.* AGPS. Canberra.

Commonwealth of Australia (1986) *Policy Guidelines for Commonwealth Statutory Authorities and Government Business Enterprises.* AGPS. Canberra.

Commonwealth of Australia (1996) *Parliamentary Handbook.* AGPS. Canberra.

Commonwealth of Australia (various) *Budget Statements, Budget Papers 1965–66—2000–01.* AGPS. Canberra.

Cooley, A. (1976) Letter from A. Cooley to M. Fraser 12.11.1976.

Cutt, J. (1975) see RCAGA Appendix 1:C.

Dawkins, J. (1983) *Reforming the Australian Public Service: a Statement of the Government's Intentions.* AGPS. Canberra.

Dawkins, J. (1984a) *'Public Sector Reforms',* Address to Executive Development Scheme, 8th March, Canberra.

Dawkins, J. (1984b) 'Reforming Australian Government Financial Administration', Address to National Press Club, 28th March, Canberra.

Dawkins, J. (1984c) 'New Developments in Public Sector Management', Address to ANU 6th Annual Conference on Public Sector Management, 5th April, Canberra.

Dawkins, J. (1984d) 'The Public Sector, The Economy and Economic Performance', Speech to CEDA, 24th May.

Dawkins, J. (1993) *Budget Speech 1993–94.* AGPS. Canberra.

Defence [Department of] (2000) 'Defence Portfolio: Budget Related Paper Nos. 1.4A and 1.4C' *Portfolio Budget Statements 2000–01*. AGPS. Canberra.

DEIR (Department of Employment and Industrial Relations) (1984) *Resources Management Strategic Plan 1984–85*. AGPS. Canberra.

Diagnostic Study of FMIP, see PSB & DoF (1984)

DoF (Department of Finance) (1979) *Annual Report 1978–79*. AGPS. Canberra.

DoF (1980a) *Annual Report 1979–80*. AGPS. Canberra.

DoF (1980b) *Controlling Public Expenditure*. DoF. Canberra.

DoF (1982a) *Budgeting and Expenditure Control*. DoF. Canberra.

DoF (1982b) *The Role of the Department of Finance in Providing Advice and Skilled Knowledge in Matters of Finance to Other Departments*. Paper to Reid Review (RCA). 20 October. RCA Files 82/042. Canberra.

DoF (1983) Minute 22.08.1983. DoF. Canberra.

DoF (1984a) *Annual Report 1983–84*. AGPS. Canberra.

DoF (1984b) Draft Paper, 'Preparation of Expediture Proposals', December. DoF. Canberra.

DoF (1984c) *Program Budgeting Specification and Guidelines*. October. DoF. Canberra.

DoF (1984d) Minute on Treasury Response to FMIP A.Harris to V.Fitzgerald 06.03.1984. DoF. Canberra.

DoF (1984e) Minute 31.10.1984. DoF. Canberra.

DoF (1984f) Minute 16.11.1984. DoF. Canberra.

DoF (1985) Program Budgeting Exploratory Study (1984–85 Budget), T. Harris. DoF. Canberra.

DoF (1986a) *Annual Report 1985–86*. AGPS. Canberra.

DoF (1986b) *Managing for Results*. SES Training Program 15. DoF. Canberra.

DoF (1986c) *Report on the Forward Estimates on Budget Outlays*. DoF. Canberra.

DoF (1987a) *Report on the Forward Estimates on Budget Outlays*. DoF. Canberra.

DoF (1987b) *FMIP and Program Budgeting: A study of implementation in selected agencies*. August. AGPS. Canberra.

DoF (1988) *Management Incentives in the Budgetary Process*. August. DoF. Canberra.

DoF (1989) 'Running Costs and the Efficiency Dividend: Principles and Practices' May 91/2242. DoF. Canberra.

DoF (1990a) *Submission by the Department of Finance to the Joint Committee of Public Accounts* - Inquiry into the Department of Finance, (Submission No 21). DoF. Canberra.

DoF (1990b) Minute 24.01.1990. DoF. Canberra.

DoF (1992a) *Commonwealth Financial Management Handbook*. AGPS. Canberra.

DoF (1992b) *Keeping the Score: An evaluation of estimates processes and practices within the Commonwealth Department of Finance*. DoF. Canberra.

DoF (1993) *Resource Aggreements. An update and extension of the 1991 MAB-MIAC 'Resource Agreements' booklet*. DoF Resourse Management Improvement Branch. August. Canberra.

DoF (1994a) *Annual Report 1993–94*. AGPS. Canberra.

DoF (1994b) *The Use of Evaluation in the 1994–95 Budget*. DoF. Canberra.

DoF (1994c) *Australian Government Financial Administration: Major Features of the Running Costs Arrangements*. DoF. Canberra.

DoF (1994d) *Running Costs Arrangements Handbook*. DoF. Canberra.

DoF (1994e) *Reasons Why Evaluation Should be Done and Why Finance Should Be Involved*. DoF. Canberra.

DoF (1994f) *Management Improvement Now: Progress and Future Directions in Australian Public Service Resource Management*. Updated July. DoF Management Improvement Branch. Canberra.

DoF (1995a) *Annual Report 1994–95*. AGPS. Canberra.

DoF (1995b) 'Clarifying the Exchange: A Review of Purchaser Provider Arrangements', *Resource Management Improvement Branch: Discussion Paper No.2*, November. DoF. Canberra.

DoF (1995c) *Running Costs Arrangements Handbook*. July. AGPS. Canberra.

DoF (1996a) *Commonwealth Government Resourcing Framework*. (Mary Venner), Expenditure Policy Branch. April. DoF. Canberra.

DoF (1996b) *Future of Finance: Where are we up to?* DoF. 12 September. Canberra.

DoFA (Department of Finance and Administration) (1997) *Carryovers for Annual Appropriations (excluding Running Costs and Statutory Authorities)*. Estimates Memorandum 1997/46. DoFA. Canberra.

DoFA (1998) *Decentralisation of the Construction of Estimates: Development of a Communication Strategy*. Estimates Memorandum 1998/3. DoFA. Canberra.

DoFA (2000) *Budget Reallocation: the Australian Perspective*. Paper to OECD. May.

DoF/PSB (Department of Finance and Public Service Board) (1987) *Evaluating Government Programs: Financial Management Improvement Program*. AGPS. Canberra.

Early, L. (1998) 'The Changing Role of the Public Service' *Canberra Bulletin of Public Administration*, May No.88:60–62.

ESU (Efficiency Scrutiny Unit) (1987) *Report by Efficiency Scrutiny Unit on Proposed Successor Arrangements to the Public Sector Board*. July. PM&C. Canberra.

Evans, H. (ed) (1999) *Odgers' Australian Senate Practice*, 9th Ed. Department of the Senate. Canberra.

Federal Parliamentary Australian Labor Party (1982) *Report of Task Force on Government Administration*. ALP. Canberra.

FMIP-IADC (Interdepartmental Advisory Development Committee for the FMIP) (1983) *18th meeting of the FMIP-IADC*.

FMIP Steering Committee (1988) Minutes 5.9.1988. FMIP Steering Committee. Canberra.

Fraser, M. (1976) Parliamentary Debates (Hansard), House of Representatives, 18 November, p.2898. AGPS. Canberra.

Fraser, M. (1982) Statement by the Prime Minister, Review of Commonwealth Administration, 23 September, Media Release, Canberra.

GAO (General Accounting Office [USA]) (2000) *Accrual Budgeting: Experiences of other nations and implications for the United States*. Report to the Hon. Ben Cardin House of Representatives, February. GAO Washington, DC.

Guilfoyle, M (1982) Program Appropriations Tabled. Paper No. 49: Senate, 11th November 1982.

House of Representatives (1999) 'The Budget and Financial Legislation' *House of Representatives Fact Sheet No. 10*, May. Parliament of Australia. http://www.aph.gov.au/house/info/factsht/fs10.htm

House of Representatives (2000) *House of Representatives Practice*. www.aph.gov.au/house/pubs/horpract/chap.1e.htm

HRSCE (House of Representatives Standing Committee on Expenditure) (1979) *Parliament and Public Expenditure*. AGPS. Canberra.

HRSCFPA (House of Representatives Standing Committee on Finance and Public Administration) (1990) *Not Dollars Alone: Review of the FMIP*. AGPS. Canberra.

HRSCBFPA (House of Representatives Standing Committee on Banking, Finance and Public Administration) (1994) *Stand and Deliver*. AGPS. Canberra.

HRSCBFPA (1995) *Keeping the Customer Satisfied*. AGPS. Canberra.

Howard, J. (1995) *Fair Australia*, Speech delivered to ACOSS, 13 October.

Howard, J. (1996) *Policy Launch Statement*, 1996 Election. 18 February. Liberal Party of Australia.

IAC (Industries Assistance Commission) (1992) *Annual Report 1991–1992*. Annual Report Series. AGPS. Canberra.

IADC (Interdepartmental Advisory and Development Committee) (1988) Minutes. 8 August.

IDC Taskforce Report on Forward Estimates (February 1977) PM&C, Treasury, DoF/ PSB. Canberra.

JCPA (Joint Committee of Public Accounts) (1989) *The Auditor-General: Ally of the People*—Report No.296, AGPS, Canberra.

JCPAA (Joint Committee of Public Accounts and Audit) (2000) *Review of the Financial Management and Accountability Act 1997 and the Commonwealth Authorities and Companies Act 1997*—Report No.374, CanPrint, Canberra.

Kasper, W. (1975) 'Formation and Co-ordination of Economic Policy: Possible Models For Australia,' *RCAGA Discussion Paper 2*. AGPS. Canberra.

Keating, M. (1984) DEIR Resources Management Strategies Plan 1984–85. DEIR. Canberra.

Keating, M. (1988) August Briefing Paper. DoF. Canberra.

Lynch, P. (1976) 'Questions Without Notice: Division of Treasury Department', *Parliamentary Debates: House of Representatives Hansard*, 7 December, pp. 3369.

MAB-MIAC (Management Advisory Board and Management Improvement Advisory Council) (1991) *Budget Flexibility: Carryover Provisions between Financial Periods*, No3 June 1991. AGPS. Canberra.

Mackay, K. (1996) 'The Institutional Framework for Evaluation in the Australian Government' Paper delivered to World Bank Seminar *Australia's Program and Policy Evaluation Framework: Institutionalising the Process.* 30 April. Washington DC.

Managing for Results, see DoF (1986b)

Meeting Our Commitments, see Treasurer (1996d)

Minister for Finance (1984) 'FMIP Diagnostic Study Report,' Press Release, Canberra, 6th February.

Minister for Finance (1985) Press Release. November.

Monaghan, J. (1984) 'Corporate Planning and its Application in the Public Sector' Paper Presented to APS Senior Executive Conference:*Management Issues Common to Operational and Service-Oriented Departments*. 26–27 July. Canberra.

MoF (Ministry of Finance of Canada) (1999) 'Federal Government—Public Accounts Tables 1 to 13, Fiscal Reference Tables—September 1999, Public Works and Services, Ottawa: 1–23.

NCA (National Commission of Audit) (1996) *Report of the National Commission of Audit.* AGPS. Canberra, June.

Not Dollars Alone, see HRSCFPA (1990)

Not Rhetoric Alone, see Task Force on Management Improvement (1992a)

Odgers, J. (1967) *Australian Senate Practice.* 3rd Ed. Commonwealth Government Printer. Canberra.

Odgers, J. (1991) *Australian Senate Practice.* 6th Ed. Commonwealth Government Printer. Canberra.

OECD (Organisation for Economic Cooperation and Development) (1987) *The Control and Management of Government Expenditure.* OECD. Paris.

OECD (1995) *Budgeting for Results.* OECD. Paris.

OECD (1997) *Modern Budgeting.* OECD. Paris.

PSB (Public Service Board) (1983) 'Announcement of FMIP,' Bulletin Number 45, Canberra, July.

PSB/DoF (Public Service Board and Department of Finance) (1984a) *Financial Management Improvement Program: Diagnostic Study.* February. AGPS. Canberra.

PSB/DoF (1984b) *FMIP Implementation.* July. AGPS. Canberra.

RCA (Review of Commonwealth Administration) (1983) *Report of Review Committee*, AGPS, Canberra.

RCAGA (1974) Attachment B, 4. *Treasury Submission to RCAGA*. November 1974.

RCAGA (1975) Appendix 1:C *Programme Budgeting in the Australian Federal Government* (J.Cutt)

RCAGA (1976) Report of Royal Commission - Parliamentary Paper No 185/1976, (Coombs Report) AGPS, Canberra.

RCAGA (1977) Letters Patent of RCAGA. AGPS. Canberra.

RCF (Review of Commonwealth Functions) (1981) Ministerial Statement by the Prime Minister Malcolm Fraser. (No 96/1981). Hansard. AGPS. Canberra.

Reid Report, see RCA (Review of Commonwealth Administration)

Schick, A. (1984) Seminar to the Department of Finance (notes & summary by J.Carroll & P. Thomas) DoF. Canberra, 4th May.

Sedgwick, S. (1996) 'Priorities for Change in the Public Sector—an APS Perspective', Speech delivered to *Signposting the Future'* RIPAA (Qld) Conference. 29 October. Brisbane.

Senate (1998) 'The Senate and Legislation' *Senate Brief No 8*, September. Parliament of Australia. http://www.aph.gov.au/senate/pubs/briefs/brief8.htm

Stand and Deliver see HRSCBFPA (1994)

Stone, J. (1984) Letter from Stone to Chairman of PSB 'Financial Management Improvement Program—Diagnostic Study'. 28.2.84.

TFEP (Task Force on Economic Policy) (1975) 'The Processes of Economic Policy-making in Australia', *Report to RCAGA*. AGPS. Canberra.

Task Force on Management Improvement (1992a) *Not Rhetoric Alone: the New Public Management in Australia*, [unpublished draft version of *The Australian Public Service Reformed*]. DoF. Canberra.

Task Force on Management Improvement (1992b) *The Australian Public Service Reformed: an evaluation of a decade of Management Reform*. AGPS. Canberra.

Treasurer (1985) *May Economic Statement: Government Expenditure Savings*. Parliamentary Papers: House of Representatives Hansard pp.2313–2322, AGPS. Canberra.

Treasurer (1993) Press Release. 1 September. Treasury. Canberra.

Treasurer (1996a) 'The Commonwealth Budget Position' Press Release. 12 March. Treasury. Canberra.

Treasurer (1996b) Press Release 21 June. Treasury. Canberra.

Treasurer (1996c) Press Release 15 July. Treasury. Canberra.

Treasurer (1996d) *Meeting Our Commitments*. Statement by Treasurer to the House: 15 December. Canberra.

Treasurer and Minister for Finance (1996) 'Report of the National Commission of Audit' *Press Release No33*; 24 June. Treasury and DoFA. Canberra.

Treasury (1969) 'Program Budgeting' (Accounting Development Branch, Treasury Minute 68/946. December 1969. Canberra.

Treasury (1971) Circular: 'Changes in Budgetary Procedures—Forward Estimates of Commonwealth Expenditure'. 1971/8. Treasury. Canberra.

Treasury (1974) Submission to RCAGA. Treasury. Canberra.

Treasury (1984) Letter from Treasury to Public Service Board 28.02.1984.

Uhr, J. (1995) *A Policy Management Review: Finance's Role in Promoting and Using Evaluation*. DoF. Canberra.

Vertigan Report (1999) 'Review of Budget Estimates Production Arrangements' Report by Dr Michael Vertigan. 28 July. DoFA. Canberra.

Wheeler, F. (1974) Letter covering Treasury Submission to RCAGA. Treasury. Canberra.

Wheeler, F. (1976) Letter From F. Wheeler to Treasury 17.11.76.

Whitlam (1976) Parliamentary Debates (Hansard), House of Representatives, 18 November, p.2990. AGPS. Canberra.

Woodward, L. (1976) *Splitting the Department of the Treasury*. Note For File, PSB, 25 November. Canberra.

NEWSPAPERS CONSULTED

The Age
The Australian
The Australian Financial Review
The Bulletin
The Canberra Times
The Courier Mail
The National Times
The Weekend Australian

SECONDARY SOURCES

Adams, D. (1997) 'Prime Ministerial Style', in G. Singleton (ed.) *The Second Keating Government*. Centre for Research in Public Sector Management University of Canberra, & Royal Institute of Public Administration Australia. Canberra.

Aucoin, P. & D. Savoie (1994) *Innovative Budgeting and the Management of Public Spending in Anglo-American Democracies*. Prepared for the Conference 'Ten Years of Change', International Political Science Association, September 22–24.

Andrews, G., S. Helgeby & J. Wanna (1998) *The Changing Role of the Central Budget Agency*. Paper presented to 'Insight '98' Conference, 23–26 February, Hyatt Hotel, Canberra.

Banks, J. (1989) 'Agency Budgets, Cost Information and Auditing', *American Journal of Political Science*, 33, p.670–699.

Barrett, G., S. Murphy and R. Miller (1995) 'Financial Management Reform' in J. Stewart (ed.) *From Hawke to Keating*. Centre for Research in Public Sector Management University of Canberra, and the Royal Institute of Public Administration Australia.

Barrett, P. (1988) 'Emerging Management and Budgetary Issues: The view from the centre' *Canberra Bulletin of Public Administration*. No. 54 May 1988.

Barrett, P. (1992) 'Evaluation as a strategic element of reform in the Commonwealth Public Sector' in C. O'Fairchellaigh & B. Ryan (eds.), *Program Evaluation and Performance Management: An Australian Perspective*. Macmillan. Melbourne.

Barrett, P. (1999) 'Auditing in Contemporary Public Administration' *Discussion Paper No.66*, July Public Policy Program, The Australian National University. Canberra.

Beale, R. (1985) 'A Progress Report on the FMIP' Paper Presented to Australian Society of Accountants. 24 October. ANU, Canberra.

Beckett, I. (1995) 'Microeconomic Reform and the Transport and Communications Portfolio' in J. Stewart (ed.) *From Hawke to Keating*. Centre for Research in Public Sector Management University of Canberra, and the Royal Institute of Public Administration Australia.

Beeby, W. (1976) 'Treasury Functions Split in Two', *The Australian*, 19th November, p.1.

Bendor, J., S. Taylor & R. Van Gaalen (1985) 'Bureaucratic Expertise vs. Legislative Authority: A model of deception and monitoring in budgeting', *American Political Science Review*, 79, pp.1041–1060.

Blais, A. & S. Dion (eds) (1991) *The Budget-Maximizing Bureaucrat: Appraisals and evidence*. University of Pittsburgh Press. Pittsburgh.

Blewett, N. (1999) *A Cabinet Diary*. Wakefield Press. Kent Town.

Boardman, A., D. Greenberg, A. Vining & D. Weimer (1996) *Cost Benefit Analysis: Concepts and Practice*. Prentice Hall. New York.

Boston, J. (1980) 'High Level Advisory Groups: The Case of the Priorities Review Staff' in P. Weller & D. Jaensch (eds.) *Responsible Government in Australia*. Drummond. Richmond.

Brooke, V.G. (1992) *Portfolio Organisation*, MPA dissertation, University of Canberra, June.

Brown, W. (1976) 'Fraser Divides Treasury' *The Courier Mail*. 19 November.

Bruce, C., R. Kneebone & K. McKenzie (eds.) (1997) *A Government Reinvented: A study of Alberta's deficit elimination program*. Oxford University Press. Ontario.

Buchanan, J. & G. Tulloch (1962) *The Calculus of Consent*. University of Michigan Press. Ann Arbor.

Burton, T. (1993) 'Now the Budget we Had to Have' *Australian Financial Review*, Budget '93 Supplement, 18 August, p.12a.

Burton, T. (1996) 'Costello makes Credible Debut, Obvious Points', *Australian Financial Review*, 13 May, pp.4.

Burton, T. & L. Dodson (1993) 'The Budget Fall-Out: PM Rules Out Spending Cuts' *Australian Financial Review*, 19 August, p.1.

Burton, T. & S. Ellis (1996) 'Howard's Inheritance: Labor leaves $7.6bn Deficit' *Australian Financial Review*

Caiden, N. (1992) 'Budgetary Processes', *Encyclopedia of Government and Politics*, Vol. 2. Routledge. London.

Castles, F. (ed.) (1980) *The Impact of Parties: Politics and Policies in Democratic Capitalist States*. Sage Publications. London.

Castles, I. (1983) 'Managing the Public Purse'. *Address to Australian Institute of Public Administration (ACT Group)*, 23 February. Canberra.

Considine, M. & M. Painter (eds.) (1997) *Managerialism: The Great Debate*. Melbourne University Press. Melbourne.

Davidson, G. (1976) 'New Department Formed' *Canberra Times*.

Dawkins, J. (1985) 'Reforms in the Canberra System of Public Administration', *Australian Journal Of Public Administration*, Vol 44, 1, pp 59–72.

Dennett, D. (1987) The Intentional Stance, MIT Press, Cambridge Mass.

Dodson, L. (1996) 'Find $4bn Cuts, Ministers Told', *Australian Financial Review*, 13 March 1996.

Downs, A. (1957) *An Economic Theory of Democracy*. Harper & Row. New York.

Dunleavy, P. (1991) *Democracy, Bureaucracy and Public Choice*. Harvester Wheatsheaf. London.

Eavey, C. & G. Miller (1984) 'Bureaucratic Agenda Control: Imposition or Bargaining?', *American Political Science Review*, 78, pp.719–733.

Edwards, J. (1996) *Keating: The Inside Story*. Penguin. Ringwood.

Emy, H.V. (1975) The Public Service and Political Control: The Problem of Accountability in a Westminster System with Special Reference to the Concept of Ministerial Responsibility.

Forster, J. and J. Wanna (eds.) (1990) *Budgetary Management and Control*, Macmillan, Melbourne.

Forster, J. & J. Wanna (1995) *The Implementation of Devolved Resource Management in the Commonwealth Budget Sector Under the Running Costs Arrangements*. Issues Paper Prepared for House of Representatives Committee on Banking, Finance and Public Administration. June. Centre for Australian Public Sector Management, Griffith University. Brisbane.

Forster, J. (1997) 'Government Deficit and Debt: Learning from the Canadian experience' Australian Journal of Public Administration, Vol.66 No.4, pp.128–133.

Fraser, B. (1977) 'Public Service Control of Government Spending' Lecture 3, *Who Controls Public Expenditure?* Lecture Series. Victorian Division of Australian Society Accountants.

Freudenberg, G. (1977) *A Certain Grandeur: Gough Whitlam in Politics*. Macmillan. Melbourne.

Gordon, M. (1993) *A Question of Leadership: Paul Keating Political Fighter*. University of Queensland Press. St. Lucia.

Grattan, M. (1976) 'Canberra Divides Treasury', *The Age*. 19 November.

Groenewegen, P. (1973) 'The Australian Budget Process', *Public Administration*. Vol. 32 (3).

Groenewegen, P. (1990) *Public Finance in Australia: Theory and Practice*, 3rd Ed. Prentice. Sydney.

Gruen, F. (1985) *The Federal Budget: How Much Difference do Elections Make?* Discussion Paper No. 120A August, Centre for Economic Policy Research The Australian National University. Canberra.

Guthrie, J., L. Parker & D. Shand (eds.) (1990) *The Public Sector: Contemporary Readings in Accounting and Auditing*. Harcourt Brace Jovanovich. Marrackville, New South Wales.

Halligan, J., Mackintosh, I. & Watson, H. (1996) *The Australian Public Service: The View From the Top*. Coopers and Lybrand and the University of Canberra. Canberra.

Halligan, J. and Power, J. (1991) *Political Management in the 1990s*, Oxford University Press, Melbourne.

Harder P. (1997) *Realigning and Revitalising The Treasury Board Secretariat*, Canadian Government Executive, Vol 2, No 3.

Hawker, G., R.F.I. Smith & P. Weller (1979) *Politics and Policy in Australia.* University of Queensland Press. St Lucia, Queensland.

Hawker, G. (1981) *Who's Master, Who's Servant? Reforming Bureaucracy*. Allen & Unwin. Sydney.

Hayden, B. (1996) *Hayden, an Autobiography*. Angus & Robertson. Pymble, NSW.

Hazlehurst, C. and J.R. Nethercote (eds.) (1977) *Reforming Australian Government: the Coombs Report and Beyond*, RIPA and ANU Press, Canberra.

Hazlehurst, C. (1978) 'Implications: Is That the Name of the Game?' in Smith, R.F.I. and Weller P. (eds.) *Public Service Inquiries in Australia*, University of Queensland Pres, St Lucia.

Heclo, H. & A. Wildavsky (1974) *The Private Government of Public Money: Community and Policy Inside British Politics*. Macmillan. London.

Holmes, M. (1991) 'Lessons for Central Agencies' in J. Uhr (ed.) *Program Evaluation*. Federalism Research Centre, The Australian National University. Canberra.

Hood, C. and M. Wright (1981) *Big Government in Hard Times*. Robertson. Oxford.

Hood, C. & O. James (1996) 'Reconfiguring the UK Executive: From Public Bureaucracy State to Re-Regulated Public Service?', paper delivered at the 1996 annual meeting of the American Political Science Association, San Francisco, August 29-September 1.

Horn, M. (1995) *The Political Economy of Public Administration: Institutional Choice in the Public Sector*. Cambridge University Press. Cambridge.

Hyman, D. (1990) *Public Finance: A Contemporary Application of Theory to Policy*, 3rd Ed. Dryden Economic Press. Fort Worth.

Juddery, B. (1976) 'Wider Advice Unlikely: Balances Rejected' *Canberra Times*. 19 November.

Keating, M. (1990a) 'The Role of the Department of Finance in Aiding the Australian Public Service to Reach its Objectives,' paper presented to ANU, Feb. 1990.

Keating, M. (1990b) 'The Process of Commonwealth Budgetary Control' in J.Forster &J.Wanna (eds) *Budgetary Management and Control*. Macmillan. Melbourne.

Keating, M. and Holmes, M. (1990) 'Australia's Budgetary and Financial Management Reforms', *Governance*, Vol 3 (2), pp. 168–185.

Kelleher, S. (1987) 'Scrutinising a Scrutiny: Reflections on the Efficiency Scrutiny Unit Report on the Public Service Board' *Canberra Bulletin of Public Administration*, No.52 October, pp.72–76.

Kelleher, S. (1998) 'A Look at the View from the Department of Finance and Administration' *CBPA*. No.89, August 1998, 4–7.

Kelly, J. (2000) *Managing the Politics of Budget Committees in Australia and Canada—Three Areas of Expenditure Management: 1975 –1999*. PhD Dissertation, Griffith University, Brisbane.

Kelly, J. and J. Wanna (1999) 'Once More into Surplus: Reforming Expenditure Management in Australia and Canada' *International Public Management Journal*. 2(1): 127–146.

Kelly, J. and J. Wanna (2000a) 'Are Wildavsky's Guardians and Spenders still Relevant? New Public Management and the Politics of Government Budgeting'. Presented to the *Third Bi-annual Research Conference of the International Public Management Network*. Macquarie University, February. Sydney.

Kelly, J. and J. Wanna (2000b) 'Twin Reforms: Australia's Introduction of an Accrual-Based 'Output-Price' Budgeting System', revised paper presented to APPAM Research Conference 1999, Washington DC.

Kelly, P. (1976) *The Unmaking of Gough*. Angus & Robertson. Sydney.

Kelly, P. (1978a) 'Our Leading Public Servant,' *The National Times*, 22 October–28 October, pp.8–11.

Kelly, P. (1978b) 'The Men Who Run Australia: Fraser's Brawls with the Treasury,' *The National Times*, 29 October–4 November, pp.18–24.

Kelly, P. (1984) *The Hawke Ascendancy: A Definitive Account of its Origins and Climax, 1975–1983*. Angus & Robertson. Sydney.

Kelly, P. (1995) *November 1975: The Inside Story of Australia's Greatest Political Crisis*. Allen & Unwin. St. Leonards.

Kerr, J. (1978) *Matters of Judgement: An Autobiography*. Macmillan. South Melbourne.

Machiavelli, N. [1911] *The Prince*. translated by W. Marriott. Everyman Edition. London.

March, J. & J. Olsen (1989) *Rediscovering Institutions: The Organisational Basis of Politics*. Free Press. New York.

McGuiness, P. (1976) 'Splitting the Treasury Should Work But it Probably Won't' *National Times*. 22–27 November.

Miller, G. & T. Moe (1983) 'Bureaucrats, Legislators and the Size of Government', *American Political Review*, Vol.77, pp.297–322.

McLaren, J (ed.) (1972) *Towards a New Australia*. Cheshire. Melbourne.

Mikesell, J. (1998) *Fiscal Administration: Analysis and Applications for the Public Sector*, 5th Ed. Harcourt Brace. Fortworth, Texas.

Mills, S. (1993) *The New Machine Men: Polls and Persuasion in Australian Politics*. Penguin Books. Ringwood, Vic.

Milne, G. (1996) 'Budget Trap for Howard' *The Australian*, 22 April, p.11.

Mintzberg, H. (1994) *The Rise and Fall of Strategic Planning*. Free Press and Prentice Hall. New York.

Mishan, E. (1964) *Welfare Economics: Ten Introductory Essays*, 2nd Ed. Random House. New York.

Mishan, E. (1973) *Economics for Social Decisions: Elements of Cost-Benefit Analysis*. Praeger. New York.

Mitchell, A. (1996) Comment. *The Australian Financial Review*, 13 March, p.1.

Moore, D. (1996) 'Budget Cuts Within Our Grasp' *Australian Financial Review*. p.19.

Musgrave, R. (1957) *The Theory of Public Finance*. Mc Graw Hill. New York.

Niskanen, W. (1971) *Bureaucracy and Representative Government*. Aldine. Chicago.

Niskanen, W. (1975) 'Bureaucrats and Politicians', *Journal of Law and Economics*, 18, pp.617–644.

Oakes, L. (1976) *Crash Through or Crash: The Unmaking of a Prime Minister*. Drummond. Richmond.

Peacock, A. & J. Wiseman (1967) *The Growth of Public Expenditure in the UK*, 2nd Ed. Allen & Unwin. London.

Pimlott, B. (1993) *Harold Wilson*. Harper Collins. London.

Posner, P., & B. Gordon. (1999) 'Can a Nation Save? Experiences of Countries with Budget Surpluses' Presented at *APPAM Annual Research Conference*, 4–6 November.

Pradham S. and Campos E. (1996) 'Budget Institutions and Expenditure Outcomes: Binding Governments to Fiscal Performance', *World Bank Policy Research Working Paper No. 1646*.

Premchand, A. (1993a) *Public Expenditure Management*. IMF. Washington DC.

Premchand A. (1993b) 'A Cross-National Analysis of Financial Management Practices' in T. Lynch and L. Martin (eds) *Handbook of Comparative Public Budgeting and Financial Management*. Marcel Dekker. New York.

Pugh, L. (1984) 'Program Budgeting Reforms in South Australia', *Australian Journal of Public Administration*; 43.

Quiggin, J. (1996) 'The "Black Hole": Myth or Reality?', *Public Finance Choices: Alternatives to the Coalition Attack on the Public Sector*, PSRC Collected Papers No.3, pp 1–24.

Rosen, H. (1999) *Public Finance*, 5th Ed. McGraw Hill. Boston.

Rothman, G. & B. Thornton (1990) 'Management of Budgetary Expenditures: the Commonwealth Running Costs System', in J. Forster & J. Wanna (eds). *Budgetary Management and Control*. Macmillan. Melbourne.

Reid, A (1976) *The Whitlam Venture*. Hill of Content. Melbourne.

Rubin, I. (ed.) (1988) *New Directions in Budget Theory*. Suny Press. Albany.

Rubin, I. (1990) *The Politics of Public Budgeting: Getting and Spending, Borrowing and Balancing*. Chaltham House. Chaltham.

Ryan, B. (1992) 'Evaluation in the Commonwealth Government: A Critical Appraisal' in C. O'Fairchellaigh & B. Ryan (eds.), *Program Evaluation and Performance Management: An Australian Perspective*. Macmillan. Melbourne.

Samuelson, P. (1954) 'The Pure Theory of Public Expenditure', *Review of Economics and Statistics*. 36, pp.387–89.

Savoie, D. (1990) *The Politics of Public Spending in Canada*. University of Toronto Press. Toronto.

Schaffer, B. and G. Hawker (1978) 'The Rise and Fall of R.C.A.G.A.' in Smith, R.F.I. and Weller P. (eds.) *Public Service Inquiries in Australia*, University of Queensland Pres, St Lucia.

Self, P. (1975) *Econocrats and the Policy Making Process: The Politics and Philosophy of Cost Benefit Analysis*. Macmillan. Melbourne.

Self, P. (1978) 'The Coombs Commission: An overview', in R.F.I. Smith & P. Weller (eds) *Public Service Inquiries in Australia*. University of Queensland Press. St Lucia. Pp.310–333.

Shand, D. (1987) 'The New Managerialism in Government' Notes for Address to RAIPA (WA Branch). 24 September. Perth.

Shand, D. (1988) 'FMIP—Where to From Here?' Address to Financial Management and Reform Seminar Brisbane. October.

Shand, D. (1996) 'Are we Reinventing Government?', in P. Weller and G. Davis (eds) *New Ideas, Better Government*, Allen & Unwin, Sydney.

Shead, B. (2000) *The Changing Role of Central Budget Agencies in the Context of Accrual Output Budgeting*. Masters Dissertation. Griffith University. Brisbane.

Schick, A (1990) *The Capacity to Budget*. The Urban Institute Press. Washington DC.

Schick, A. (1996) *The Spirit of Reform: Managing the New Zealand State Sector in a Time of Change*. August. Report to the State Services Commission and the Treasury, New Zealand.

Schick A. (1997) *The Changing Role of the Central Budget Office*. OECD. Paris.

Short, J. (1996) 'The Deepest Cut of All' *Weekend Australian*, 1–2 June, pp.27.

Stretton, H. & L. Orchard (1994) *Public Goods, Public Enterprise, Public Choice: Theoretical Foundations of the Contemporary Attack on Government*. St. Martins Press. New York.

Sturgess, G. (1996) 'Virtual Government: What Will Remain Inside the Public Sector', *Australian Journal of Public Administration*. 55(3) September.

Taylor, C. (ed.) (1983) *Why Governments Grow: Measuring Public Sector Size*. Sage Publications. Beverly Hills.

Taylor, J. (1990) 'Audit Control and Management of Budgetary Processes: The New Role of the Auditor-General', in J. Forster & J. Wanna (eds). *Budgetary Management and Control*. Macmillan. Melbourne.

Terry, G.J. and P.Weller (1975) 'Treasury Control of Federal Government Expenditure in Australia', *Report to RCAGA*, (mimeo) Canberra.

Thain, C. & M. Wright (1995) *The Treasury and Whitehall: The Planning and Control of Public Expenditure, 1976–1993*. Clarendon Press. Oxford.

Thompson, F. (ed.) (1997) Symposium: 'Reforming the Federal Budgetary Process: A Symposium Commemorating the 75th Anniversary of the Executive Budget', *Policy Sciences*, Vol 29, No3. 1996/1997. [R. Meyers 'Is there a key to the normative budgeting block?'; E. Patashnik 'The contractual nature of budgeting: A transaction cost perspective on the design of budgeting institutions'; B. Pitsvada 'A call for budget reform'; L. Jones 'Wildavsky on budget reform'; and J. McCaffery 'On budget reform'.]

Tiebout, C. (1956) 'A Pure Theory of Local Expenditure', *Journal of Political Economics*, 64, pp. 416–424.

Tulloch, G. (1970) *Private Wants, Public Means: An Economic Analysis of the Desireable Scope of Government*. Basic Books. New York.

Uhr, J. (ed.) (1991) *Program Evaluation*. Federalism Research Centre, The Australian National University. Canberra.

Uhr, J. (1996) 'Testing the Policy Capacities of Budgetary Agencies: Lessons from Finance' *Australian Journal of Public Administration*. 55(4): 124–134.

Walsh, C. (1990) 'Recent Trends in Introducing Devolutionary Attempts in Budgeting' in J.Forster & J.Wanna (eds) *Budgetary Management and Control*. Macmillan. Melbourne.

Walsh, C. (1991) 'The Politics and Economics of Budgetary Reform' in J. Uhr (ed.) *Program Evaluation*. Federalism Research Centre, The Australian National University. Canberra.

Walsh, C. (1995) 'Creating a Competitive Culture in the Public Service: The role of audits and other reviews' *Australian Journal of Public Administration*. 54(3).

Walsh, P. (1990) 'Labor's Scrapper from the Wheat Belt', in G.Henderson (ed.) *Australian Answers*. Random House. Sydney.

Walsh, P. (1995) *Confessions of a Failed Finance Minister*. Random House. Sydney.

Wanna, J., Kelly, J., & Forster, J. (1996) 'The Rise and Rise of the Department of Finance', Canberra Bulletin of Public Administration. No 82 December, pp.53–62.

Weller, P. & J. Cutt (1976) *Treasury Control in Australia: A Study in Bureaucratic Politics*. Ian Novak. Sydney.

Weller, P. (1977) 'Splitting the Treasury: Old Habits and New Structures', *Australian Quarterly*, Vol 49, 1, pp29–39.

Weller, P. (1989) *Malcolm Fraser PM*, Penguin. Melbourne.

Weller, P. (1999) *Dodging Raindrops—John Button: A Labor life*. Allen & Unwin. St. Leonards.

Weller, P. & B. Stevens. (1998) 'Evaluating Policy Advice: The Australian Experience' *Public Administration*. Vol.76, No.3.

Weller, P. & L. Young (2000) 'Political Parties and the Party System: Challenges for Effective Governing' in M. Keating, J. Wanna, & P.Weller (eds.) *Institutions on the Edge*. Allen & Unwin. St. Leonards.

Whitlam, E.G (1979a) *The Truth of the Matter*. Penguin. Middlesex.

Whitlam, E.G. (1979b) 'The Connor Legacy', 1st R.F.X. Connor Memorial Lecture, *University of Wolongong Historical Society (Special Issue)*, Vol.3 No.1, November.

Whitlam, G. (1985) *The Whitlam Government: 1972–1975*. Viking. Ringwood, Victoria.

Whitwell, G. (1986) *The Treasury Line*. Allen & Unwin, Sydney.

Wildavsky, A. (1964) *The Politics of the Budgetary Process*. Little & Brown. Boston.

Wildavsky, A. (1975) *Budgeting: Comparative Theory of Budgetary Processes*. Little & Brown. Boston.

Wildavsky, A. (1978) 'A Budget for All Seasons? Why the Traditional Budget Lasts', *Public Administration Review*, Vol. 38(4). pp.501–509.

Wildavsky, A. (1985) 'The Logic of Public Sector Growth', in J. Lane (ed.) *State and Market*. Sage Publications. Beverly Hills.

Wildavsky, A. (1992) 'Political Implications of Budget Reform: A Retrospective', *Public Administration Review*, Vol. 52(6) November/December.

Wilson, J. (ed.) (1998) *Financial Management for the Public Services*. Open University Press. Buckingham.

Wiltshire, K. (1982) 'The Role of the Budget in Government', in D.Shand (ed.) *Making Government Budgets Work: Canberra and the States*, Proceedings of the Autumn Seminar of the Australian Institute of Public Administration (ACT Group). 29 March 1982.

Wood, A. (1995) 'Bodgie Figures, Sharp Politics Bear Fingerprints of PM in Poll Mode' *The Australian*, 10 May, P.1.

Young, L. (1997) *Minor Parties . . . Major Players? The Senate, the Minor Parties and the 1993 Budget*. Department of the Parliamentary Library. AGPS. Canberra.

Zifcak, S. (1994) *New Managerialism: Administrative Reform in Whitehall and Canberra*. Open University Press. Buckingham.

Index

For Product Safety Concerns and Information please contact our EU representative GPSR@taylorandfrancis.com
Taylor & Francis Verlag GmbH, Kaufingerstraße 24, 80331 München, Germany

www.ingramcontent.com/pod-product-compliance
Lightning Source LLC
Chambersburg PA
CBHW060137280326
41932CB00012B/1548
* 9 7 8 1 8 6 4 4 8 7 1 3 8 *